W9-BGB-741

DATE DUE

Five Centuries of Women Singers

**Recent Titles in
the Music Reference Collection**

Five Centuries of Women Singers

Isabelle Emerson

Music Reference Collection, Number 88

Westport, Connecticut
London

Library of Congress Cataloging-in-Publication Data is available at www.loc.gov

British Library Cataloguing in Publication Data is available.

ISBN: 0-313-30810-1
ISSN: 0736-7740

First published in 2005

Praeger Publishers, 88 Post Road West, Westport, CT 06881
An imprint of Greenwood Publishing Group, Inc.
www.praeger.com

Printed in the United States of America

The paper used in this book complies with the
Permanent Paper Standard issued by the National
Information Standards Organization (Z39.48-1984).

10   9   8   7   6   5   4   3   2

For
Consuelo and Benjamin
Lars, Linnea, and Dash
George

Contents

Preface

"Women singers" conjures up immediately an image of opera divas. And certainly opera has proved to be a central arena for women to display their vocal powers. But the thought that this is the only arena is far from the truth. Indeed, the first professional female singers in modern history seem to be the well-educated women of the upper middle class or minor nobility who appeared in the late years of the sixteenth century at the courts of Ferrara, Mantua, Florence, hired to sing in the *concerti delle donne*—the consorts of ladies. They sang madrigals, pantomimes, intermedi, *balli*—all genres that merged into opera before the end of the century. When opera did appear, the next generation of ladies often took on dominant roles in the new art form, although they were soon competing for opportunities, money, and attention with the castrati who from the earliest days of opera sang the heroic male roles. (In Rome, thanks to the ban on women in stage productions imposed in 1585 by Pope Sixtus V, castrati often sang the female roles as well.) Faustina Bordoni and Francesca Cuzzoni were probably the first women to achieve the star status and concomitant financial rewards enjoyed by the castrati virtuosos of the seventeenth and eighteenth centuries. Undeniably, opera was for several centuries the most important genre for women singers who were not permitted to sing in church until late in the eighteenth century. Opera was, in fact, the only truly *public* musical genre until the second half of that century. Both women and men sang in private concerts at court or in the homes of the wealthy; typically they sang arias or scenas from operas. The increasing importance of the concert in the late eighteenth century gave rise to new repertoire, the "concert aria," composed for example by Mozart for Nancy Storace and for Josepha Duschek, and eventually in the nineteenth century the art song, especially the lied, for the increasingly more intimate ambiance of the recital. Singers excluded from the opera stage by the nature of their voice, their personality, or operatic politics could work in this new chamber setting, which often became the locus of avant-garde productions as such singers as Jane Bathori found greater satisfaction in singing new music than in repeating operatic roles night after night.

In this book I explore the careers of singers from the late sixteenth century to the middle of the twentieth. The stories of these singers tell much about contemporary musical life, about musical and dramatic ideals of the time, and about performance practice. They often reveal also how women were dealt with in the business of music and have much to tell about the ingenuity and persistence that were crucial ingredients of a successful career. Although such singers as Jenny Lind, Nellie Melba, Marian Anderson remain well-known today, a number of others—Marie LeRochois, Francesca Cuzzoni, Gertrud Mara, Lillian Nordica, for example—have almost disappeared from memory. While I hope to bring to the forgotten singers a fair measure of their due, I hope also to bring attention to new aspects of the careers of the still famous. I hope further that the material presented here (some of it for the first time in English) will inspire new research not only on these women but on other forgotten singers of the past—Caterina Gabrielli, Luisa Todi, Elisabeth Billington, Marietta Alboni, Minnie Hauk, Elena Gerhardt, Marcella Sembrich— all of whom played significant roles in the history of music for the voice. Their stories are significant, moreover, not just for the information they carry about musical practices but for the deeper insight into social and cultural structures of past times.

Although in first planning this book I envisioned a study of fifty women, including singers of pop, jazz, and classical music, it soon became clear that such a volume would be little more than a biographical dictionary. Therefore I limited the number to twenty classical musicians and set the following criteria: Each singer must have excelled in a specific area, have succeeded in achieving specific goals, her work must be significant for the art of singing, and the means by which the singer was able to achieve her goals must represent a model for later generations. Selection of individual singers became increasingly difficult with each century: Laura Peverara, Victoria Archilei, Virgini Ramponi, Adriana Basile stood out vividly against the context of their time, as did Francesca Caccini, Barbara Strozzi, Francesca Cuzzoni, and Faustina Bordoni. Nancy Storace, the first musically trained star of English musical theatre and Mozart's Susanna, was a sure choice. In the nineteenth century, selection became much more difficult. How to choose between Maria Malibran and Giuditta Pasta, or, later, among Amelita Galli-Curci, Nellie Melba, Adelina Patti, Pauline Viardot? How to choose among the striking Americans who invaded Europe in the last quarter of the nineteenth century—Emma Eames, Minnie Hauk, Clara Louise Kellogg, Lillian Nordica, all delightfully colorful and extraordinary women? Finally, I settled on women, whose stories revealed different approaches, different methodologies, different paths in their careers, and each of whom demonstrated a highly individualistic achievement. Nellie Melba was the first Australian to conquer Europe; Lillian Nordica was the first American—not the first American woman, but the first *American*—to create a role at the Wagner shrine of Bayreuth; Jenny Lind was among the first to utilize—or submit to—mass marketing techniques; Marian Anderson faced hurdles not encountered by any others, and her course with its ultimate triumphs could not be excluded.

I thought it important to include women whose careers were revelatory of musical life in various countries. Thus the life of Anna Renzi, one of the first real operatic virtuosi, has much to tell us about musical practices and customs in mid-seventeenth-century Venice; the career of Marie LeRochois speaks to the life of a French singer during the latter part of the seventeenth century in Paris, even though very little is known of her other than that she was Lully's choice for leading roles in his operas. (Both Renzi and LeRochois could profit from further research, but the trails are faint and hard to follow.)

Chapters vary in length, depending as is the case with Renzi and LeRochois on the amount of information available, but depending also on the nature of the singer's career. Nellie Melba's life, for example, soon fell into a fairly regular pattern of performances with pretty general agreement about the special qualities of her voice and presentation. Nothing, not even the outrageous scandal associated with her liaison with Duc Louis-Philippe, interrupted her career. Lillian Nordica, on the other hand, traveled down some bypaths, such as her involvement with the suffragist movement and her frustrated effort to establish an American Bayreuth; her career was brought to a halt by her disastrous first marriage, and when freed of that husband she had to build her career anew. Moreover her career was exceedingly varied in nature—from singing with Gilmore's Brass Band, to creating the role of Elsa at Bayreuth, to singing conventional operatic roles in Berlin, London, St. Petersburg, New York, to touring all over the United States in her special railroad car, the Brünnhilde. Length reflects not necessarily the importance I assign the singer but has very often to do with the nature of the singer's life and career and its significance for the musical life of the time.

The quantity and type of information available about these singers vary immensely. Many books, for example, have been written about Jenny Lind and about Marian Anderson; these range from books for children to works of a serious scholarly nature. The researcher will also find a number of novelistic works in which the authors manage to reconstruct conversations; even the most helpful sources occasionally indulge in this practice. Geoffrey Brace tells us, for example, what Nancy and Stephen Storace "would have" said to Joseph Haydn when they met in London, and Nicole Barry reports that Pauline Viardot was visited shortly before her death by the long defunct Turgenev who announced that her hour had come. Few of the early singers have benefitted from individual studies, so information must be sought in encyclopedias (*New Grove* and *Grove Music Online* are invaluable) and general studies, such as Anthony Newcomb's outstanding book, *The Madrigal at Ferrara,* or Iain Fenlon's excellent *Music and Patronage in Sixteenth-Century Mantua.* Carolyn Raney's pioneering work on Francesca Caccini led the way for studies in English on not only Caccini, but Barbara Strozzi, Faustina Bordoni, Nancy Storace, et al. Remarkably little has appeared in English about

Gertrud Mara or Wilhelmine Schröder-Devrient, although these women dominated the opera world of their times. The student of their work must rely heavily on German materials and search through various memoirs such as those by George Hogarth or the Earl of Mount Edgcumbe. Similarly a great deal of information about Pauline Viardot is available in French, but very little in English. The only study in English of Giuditta Pasta, one of the first and probably one of the greatest singer-actresses of the nineteenth century, is the dissertation by Kenneth Stern, who also wrote two brief articles. Lillian Nordica has also been virtually ignored; the biography of her by Ira Glacken remains a unicum. The studies by Stern and Glacken are repositories of vast amounts of primary source materials, such as reviews, letters, etc., and are therefore extremely helpful for anyone working with these singers.

I believe firmly that persons should be referred to by the names they used themselves. Therefore Pauline Garcia Viardot appears as Viardot, Mme Viardot, or Pauline Viardot, not as Pauline Viardot-Garcia as is usual today. Although Franz Liszt referred to the singer as Pauline Viardot-Garcia in his essay of 1859, as did La Mara (Marie Lipsius) whose 1882 essay heavily draws upon Liszt's account, I have found no other contemporary source that does so. With respect to the very delicate issue of racial definition, I follow Allan Keiler's lead in using "black" instead of "Negro" (which Anderson herself used) or "African-American," reasoning that Keiler who worked very closely with Anderson and with her nephew James DePreist would have used the appropriate term.

First-hand descriptions of the singer's *sound* are presented first, followed by a brief biography and a summation of the artist's significance. Each chapter includes a bibliography of works specifically about the singer and of general reference works that are particularly informative. Reference notes follow the final chapter; a general bibliography includes all general reference works and a few of the specialized studies if these pertain to other singers as well. All translations from German, French, and Italian for which the original text is given are mine, except where otherwise noted (as for example in Chapter 15, Jane Bathori, in which I rely mainly on translations given by Linda Cuneo-Laurent). I tried to limit reference works to those readily accessible in English, and where possible I give sources of good English translations, for example, the two editions of *Source Readings in Music History,* or Piero Weiss's recent *Opera: A History in Documents.* Similarly I refer the reader where possible to an easily available musical score or anthology, such as the *Norton Anthology of Western Music.*

Acknowledgements

I would like to express my thanks to the many librarians who assisted me in the Music Division of the New York Public Library, the British Library, the Bibliothèque Nationale in Paris, the Music Division of the Library of Congress. I owe special thanks to Susan Palmer of Sir John Soane's Museum in London and to Caitlin St. John of the Music Library at the University of California, Riverside, for their help in securing access to materials, and to Cheryl Taranto of the Music Library at the University of Nevada, Las Vegas, who not only searched and found many a source but also took the time to read the entire manuscript. My very special thanks to scholars Judith Tick who as the result of a casual airplane encounter shared with me her vast knowledge about women musicians and Carol Kimball who generously provided me with invaluable materials about Jane Bathori.

My thanks also to the University of Nevada, Las Vegas, which granted me a sabbatical leave during which the first research for this book was undertaken, to Elizabeth Potenza, editorial assistant at Praeger Publishers, and to Nicole Azze, senior project manager at Greenwood Publishing Group.

Finally I must express my gratitude to friends Faye Ferguson, Kathryn Shanks Libin and Laurence Libin, Jane Perry-Camp and Harold Schiffman, Jane Stevens, Julienne Misrahi Barnet, Alessandra Comini, Carole Fabricant, Sheila and Peter Garratt, Cecilia von Girsewald, Jan Leventer, Elizabeth Lord, Cornelia Schaafsma, Christena Schlundt, Parwin Bakhtary, Sandy Fleck, Candace Kirnon, Marcia Wallace, all of whom cheered me on in my efforts to complete the work; to George Stelluto for introducing me to James DePreist who graciously spent an hour with me answering questions about his aunt Marian Anderson; to Enrico Elisi who helped me with the translation of sixteenth-century Italian madrigals and to Morena Hill who helped me to understand and to translate the flowery Italian descriptions of Giuditta Pasta's singing; to Ralph Buechler who turned my translations of Goethe's poems into poetic English and helped with the conversion to passable English of the convoluted, flowery prose of Franz Liszt, Ludwig Rellstab, and Richard Wagner; to Robert Mader who twice rescued the text of this book from near-fatal computer crashes; to Rachel Julian-Jones for her superb formatting of the book and to Consuelo Emerson for her patient help in making the many corrections and adjustments; to Shawna Smith for translating the entire manuscript from Pagemaker format back to Word; to George Miel who read the entire manuscript more than once, fine-tuned my French translations, and accompanied me on several research forays; to my mother Marjorie Weston Emerson who nurtured in me a love of opera which, in Muncie, Indiana, we experienced almost exclusively through the Saturday broadcasts of New York's Metropolitan Opera. My deep thanks for their support go to James Chrisman and Vicki Scharnhorst. Lastly I offer my heartfelt thanks to my daughter Consuelo, son Benjamin, and brother Michael, who never let me give up on this project.

Chapter 1

Ladies of Italy

Laura Peverara (c. 1545 – 4 January 1601)
Vittoria Concarini Archilei (1550 – c. 1642)
Virginia Andrea Ramponi Andreini (1583 – c. 1630)
Adriana Basile (c. 1580 – c. 1642)

In a perverse sort of way, the emergence of women as professional musicians is deeply indebted to the third marriage of an aging, possibly sterile duke with a fifteen-year-old girl who delighted in music and dance. In February 1579 Duke Alfonso d'Este of Ferrara celebrated his marriage to Margherita Gonzaga, daughter of the duke of Mantua. Immediately after this marriage and perhaps as a consequence of it, Alfonso set about putting in place at his court a new group of musicians—a consort of lady singers, a *concerto delle donne*. He and his bride spent many hours enjoying the work of these musicians. Such a consort was not new at the Ferrarese court, but, as Anthony Newcomb[1] has eloquently demonstrated, this new *concerto* was radically different from the older ones, which had consisted primarily of talented, well-trained amateurs of noble status. The singers of this new consort were brought into court life solely because of their abilities as musicians, they were expected to perform as salaried employees, and they were paid very well for their work. They were treated with respect and were regarded as members of the court; they were not, however, in most cases even minor nobility but were talented, well-educated young women from wealthy families. All of these factors created a crucial separation between amateur and professional, between audience and performer. In earlier days, courtiers had been expected to sing and dance with just the appropriate degree of facility consistent with the ideal of the noble gentleman or gentlewoman[2] but not by any means to display a professional level of ability. Moreover they had alternated in turn as listener and performer. The musicians of the new *concerti* owed their identity and their status exclusively to their well-defined and unchanging roles as performers.

That both Alfonso and Margherita were extremely proud of their new *concerto delle donne* has been amply documented and described. They must also have been immensely gratified by the immediate and widespread imitation of their new courtly passion. For passion it was—Alfonso dedicated often as much as four hours of his day to passive enjoyment of the music, but Margherita frequently devoted even more of her time as she took an active part with her *donne* in the preparation and performance of both music and dance. Most passions abate over time; this one, however, continued to dominate the life of the Ferrara court, even as the notion spread to other courts—notably Mantua under the auspices of Margherita's brother the young duke, Vincenzo Gonzaga, and Florence at the court of the Medici family. Newcomb has pointed out that while the new *concerto delle donne* was an anomaly in 1580, by 1590 it was such a "courtly cliché" that every prince's court in northern Italy had to have at least one.[3]

Vincenzo Giustiniani, an Italian music theorist and patron of the arts, described the scene in detail in his *Discorso sopra la musica* (1628):

[E]very composer, in order that his compositions should satisfy the general taste, took care to advance in the style of composition for several voices, particularly Giaches Wert in Mantua and Luzzasco in Ferrara. They were the superintendents of all music for those Dukes, who took the greatest delight in the art, especially in having many noble ladies and gentlemen learn to sing and play superbly, so that they spent entire days in some rooms designed especially for this purpose, and beautifully decorated with paintings. The ladies of Mantua and Ferrara were highly competent, and vied with each other not only in regard to the timbre and training of their voices but also in the design of exquisite passages [*passaggi*] delivered at opportune points, but not in excess. (Giovanni Luca of Rome, who also served at Ferrara, usually erred in this respect.) Furthermore, they moderated or increased their voices, loud or soft, heavy or light, according to the demands of the piece they were singing; now slow, breaking off sometimes with a gentle sigh, now singing long passages legato or detached, now groups, now leaps, now with long trills, now with short, or again with sweet running passages sung softly, to which one sometimes heard an echo answer unexpectedly. They accompanied the music and the sentiment with appropriate facial expressions, glances and gestures, with no awkward movements of the mouth or hands or body which might not express the feeling of the song. They made the words clear in such a way that one could hear even the last syllable of every word, which was never interrupted or suppressed by passages and other embellishments. They used many other particular devices which will be known to persons more experienced than I.[4]

It is quite clear from Giustiniani's description that these ladies had achieved a very high technical level with respect not only to their singing but to the entire performance—stance, attitude, motion. Furthermore they consciously exploited emotional and dramatic possibilities by increasing or decreasing the sound, by changing the timbre, or especially by using different articulations and pacing, as well as adding passages that may or may not have been improvised by the ensemble.[5]

It speaks well for the general level of education of women—at least in upper middle-class Italian society—that there was no shortage of gifted and appropriately trained women to supply the increasing demand for female virtuosi. The most important requirement of course was the quality of voice. Occasionally a singer would be hired on the strength of that ability and then given the necessary musical education, which usually included both vocal and instrumental training. Livia d'Arco was one such: hired by the Ferrara court in 1579, she first appeared occasionally in 1582, and then as her abilities increased became a regular member of the *concerto delle donne* until at least 1598.[6]

The lives of the four women who appear in this chapter represent ways in which women first worked as professional musicians. Each came from a different level of society and achieved success by a different path. Laura Peverara (also known as Peperara or Pepperara), the dominant member of the Ferrara *concerto delle donne,* was born into a well-to-do middle-class family and educated accordingly. She spent most of her life in Ferrara, she was widely admired as a solo singer but was best-known as member of the vocal ensemble, and she was the dedicatee of three anthologies of music. Vittoria Archilei came from Rome where she may have studied with Emilio de' Cavalieri (c.1550–1602) known as composer, organist, singing teacher, dancer, choreographer, diplomat; Archilei also studied with Antonio Archilei who became her husband. In high demand as a soloist in both Rome and Florence, she may well have frequented the meetings of the Florentine Camerata, the supposed birthplace of Baroque opera. Giustiniani claims that she "almost originated the true method of singing for females."[7] Virginia Ramponi Andreini, Monteverdi's Arianna, learned her art in the *commedia* and, as a member of two theatrical troupes, *I Gelosi* and *Comici fedeli,* travelled rather widely—to the court of Maria de' Medici in France, to Prague, to Vienna. The last of the four, Adriana Basile, was a solo singer and instrumentalist who emerged from murky origins to enjoy a brilliant career during which she worked with the most prominent composers of her time. Her stature was such that she was able to dictate the conditions of her employment at the Mantuan court—the manner of invitation, position at the court, etc.; her demands manifest the extent of her fame and reveal also her concern for her reputation as a professional musician.

Laura Peverara (c. 1545–1601)

What was her voice like? Contemporary descriptions tell us that Peverara sang excellently and played an accompanimental instrument, probably the harp. In a letter to Grand Duke Francesco de' Medici the composer Alessandro Striggio (1573?-1630) who was visiting the Ferrara court of Duke Alfonso and Margherita in the summer of 1584, described the *concerto delle donne* in which Peverara sang:

Those ladies sing excellently; both when singing in their *concerto* [from memory] and when singing at sight from part books they are secure. The Duke favored me continually by showing me written out all the pieces that they sing by memory, with all the diminutions [*tirate e passaggi*] that they do.[8]

Duke Alfonso's continued interest in the work of the *concerto* and the abilities of the singers are confirmed by the Florentine singer-composer Giulio Caccini (1551–1618) visiting the court in late 1592:

Since he enjoyed my manner of singing, today he begged me (this was the word he used) to favor him both by teaching his three ladies something with these *accenti* and *passaggi* of ours and by writing a few diminutions on a favorite bass of his . . . Thus for three hours I taught some *Arie* to these ladies in the presence of His Highness.[9]

The Florentine diplomatic resident at the Ferrara court described in March 1580 the manner—probably rather typical—of Peverara's recruitment:

When His Excellency [Duke Alfonso] was at Mantua he saw a young lady who was rather beautiful and, in addition, had the virtue of singing and playing excellently. He thereupon conceived the desire of having her at Ferrara and, upon his return here, he had the Duchess send to obtain her as one of her ladies in waiting, which was done by special messenger.[10]

The Duke's instant decision was rewarded handsomely: in Peverara he found a strong leader for his new *concerto* both in terms of her voice and her musicianship. She was joined by Anna Guarini (daughter of the poet Giovanni Battista) and, briefly, by a fine but aging bass Giulio Cesare Brancaccio (who preferred the role of amateur courtier to the role of professional court musician and soon departed, not quite of his own volition).[11] This first *concerto* of two ladies was augmented in the spring or summer of 1582 by Livia d'Arco and for a time (1583–1589) by Tarquinia Molza. Descriptions speak of both the beauty of the ladies' performances and the amazingly high degree of their musicianship. They were much occupied with singing at sight from madrigal books: a visitor to the court wrote in 1582 that "the Duke passed a good deal of time listening to those ladies sing from ordinary music books. Even in that kind of singing the ladies are beautiful to hear, because they sing the low parts [le parti grosse] an octave higher."[12] We have seen already that Striggio was impressed by the ladies' abilities; his reaction is colorfully described by a 1584 letter of another visitor to the court:

Striggio and another singer are here, and some stupendous singing and playing is going on. They are astounded by the singing of these ladies and by their knowledge, for the ladies sing without rehearsal every motet and every composition that they give them, however difficult these pieces may be.[13]

That the ladies' simultaneous virtuosic passages were at least occasionally improvised is indicated by Guarini's poem, "Mentre vaga angioletta," set by

Monteverdi in the *Canti amorosi*. The poem refers to the "sound of her sweet song," the singing voice which

> forms and feigns
> in an unusual manner,
> garrulous and masterful harmony,
> acutely sounding temper, supple voice.
> And it turns and pushes forward
> with interrupted accents and with twisting turns,
> here it slows, there it is fast,
> sometimes murmuring
> in low and mobile sound, and alternating
> runs and rests and placid breaths;
> now it stays in place, now it soars,
> now it presses forward, now it breaks, now it is restrained,
> now it flashes and vibrates,
> now it wanders around,
> sometimes in a trembling manner, rambling,
> sometimes firm and resounding.[14]

Whether describing specific qualities of one singer's performance or general performance style of the time, the poem offers a telling description of the compositional style of the music they sang; and its lively evocation of the singer's manner provides important information about contemporary performance practice. Especially pertinent are the many indications of spontaneity in the performance— "broken accents," "now it hesitates, now flows rapidly," "soars and balances," "presses forward, breaks, and is restrained," "now it meanders, sometimes with tremulous, wandering modes, sometimes firm and resounding"—all of which reflect the immediacy of the musical response to the word. Music written for the Ferrarese and Mantuan courts further defines the abilities of the *concerto delle donne*. Newcomb points to Giaches Wert's Seventh Book of Madrigals (April 1581), to Luca Marenzio's First Book à 6 (also April 1581), and to Monteverdi's Book V (published in 1605, but containing material such as the famous "Cruda Amarilli" which had been in circulation for a good while). The music in these collections exhibits new use of dissonance, cross-relations, florid writing for all parts, shifting textures, long lines, short lines—features that were catalogued in the preface of Monteverdi's Book V as characteristic of the new music of the seventeenth century, the style defined by Monteverdi as *seconda prattica*.[15] The collections *Il lauro secco* (1582) and *Il lauro verde* (1583) are resonant monuments to the *concerto delle donne* but particularly to Peverara for whom both were compiled by the poet Torquato Tasso (1544–1595) and his friends in Ferrara. Tasso had first known— and loved—Peverara in Mantua, in 1563–1564.[16] He was now a member of the Ferrarese court, although suffering from a degree of mental illness that necessitated his imprisonment, at times very strict and at times as lenient as a sort of house-arrest permitting him some supervised freedom of movement. The first collection, *Il lauro secco,* contained madrigals by the best-known composers of northern Italy—Wert, Luzzasco Luzzaschi, Marenzio, Andrea Gabrieli, Annibale Stabile—and introduced work by Lelio Bertani, Ruggiero Giovanelli, Giovanni de' Bardi, and Girolamo di Virchi. The second collection, *Il lauro verde,* is even more significant both musically and sociologically, for it was compiled in 1583 to honor Peverara's marriage to Count Annibale Turco, an event that was celebrated by the Ferrara court in a degree that conveys the remarkable esteem enjoyed by Peverara. The Florentine ambassador Urbani reported on the extravagant festivities:

[T]he wedding of Laura Peverara will be celebrated with a tournament, for which the program was published yesterday. One can see from this program . . . the honors and favors that are done to this lady. To compose this program and the words to a grand ballet that will be performed in the evening by the Duchess and eleven other ladies, Cavalier Guarini was recalled from Venice.[17]

*   *   *   *   *

Aside from her participation in activities at the Ferrara court, not a great deal is known about Laura Peverara. She was born in Mantua c. 1545 or 1553,[18] the daughter of a wealthy Mantuan merchant, and we must assume on the strength of her later abilities that she enjoyed the education of a Renaissance lady, as spelled out by Baldassare Castiglione in *Il cortegiano*: "I wish this lady to have knowledge of letters, of music, of painting, and know how to dance and how to be festive."[19]

It was in Mantua, 1563–1564, that Peverara enjoyed the attentions and the poetry of Torquato Tasso who in 1565 entered the employ of Cardinal Luigi d'Este (a frequent visitor to Ferrara although his official residence was in Rome). She seems to have been in attendance on Margherita Gonzaga at the Mantuan court and was called to the Ferrarese court in the spring of 1580 shortly after the marriage of Margherita to Duke Alfonso d'Este. By this time, Tasso had entered the service of Alfonso, so he too was a member of the Ferrara court, though sporadically due to his bouts with mental illness. The first of his tributes to Peverara, *Il lauro secco,* was printed in 1582; Newcomb proposes that this may have been a farewell to the poet's love for the singer, since she was enjoying the attentions of Count Annibale Turco whom she married in 1583, at which time Tasso and his friends offered the second volume of madrigals, *Il lauro verde.* The generous dowry, 10,000 scudi, given Peverara by Duke Alfonso on the occasion of her marriage is indicative of her standing at the Ferrara court; her new husband and her mother each received the same amount. It is worthy of note also that Peverara's husband, Count Annibale Turco, was now to be accepted as a "gentleman of the court" and would receive the same provisions made for the three other barons. The newlyweds were to live in the palace apartments previously occupied by Alfonso's sister, the late Leonora d'Este, and would have as well all the rooms below that had been reserved for Count Ottavio Landi.[20] Finally, her annual salary of 300 scudi compares very favorably with the salary of court composer Luzzascho Luzzaschi, particularly when we remember that Peverara's husband and her mother each received an additional 300 scudi.

Peverara was at the outset and throughout most of her career the dominant singer in the *concerto delle donne*. She was joined often by extremely gifted musicians: the well-trained and well-educated Anna Guarini (?-c. 1598), for example, daughter of the famed madrigal poet and Ferrara court secretary Giovanni Battista Guarini and Teddea Bendidio Guarini from an old well-to-do Ferraran family; Livia d'Arco (c. 1561–1611), also from Mantua; Tarquinia Molza (Modena, 1542-Rome, 1617), a well-known poetess and singer.[21] Of these women, d'Arco, daughter of an impoverished Mantuan minor noble, was the only one who had not been educated for a life at court; hired for the sheer beauty of her voice, she studied with the composer Luzzaschi for nearly two years before she was permitted to join the *concerto delle donne*. Peverara's father, a wealthy Mantuan merchant, had given her the education required for a lady at court; Guarini's father and mother had as a matter of course provided the education appropriate to life at court, which included training in music. Tarquinia Molza, niece of the poet Francesco Maria Molza, may in fact have surpassed Peverara in vocal beauty and prowess; in addition she was a highly skilled viola player. Like Guarini and Peverara, she had enjoyed the education specified by Castiglione. The training in music would have brought them all to the level of madrigal singing and accompanying themselves when necessary on lute, viol, or harp.

In spite of her outstanding abilities, Molza was banished from the court in 1589 when her love affair with Giaches Wert, composer at the Mantuan court, was discovered. The dismissal of Molza for her amorous peccadilloes confirms the high standard of moral behavior expected of the ladies of the *concerto* and the respect in which they were held—and their status as members of the court. Such flagrant misbehavior was not tolerated; Alfonso's sister Lucrezia was not banished from court when it was discovered that she had taken a lover, but her unfortunate paramour was promptly murdered. In any event, the departure of Molza left Peverara as undisputed leader of the *concerto delle donne,* a status that she enjoyed till the dissolution of the *concerto,* which coincided with Duke Alfonso's death in November 1597 and the end of the d'Este reign.[22] Peverara died in Ferrara on 4 or 5 January 1601 and was buried in the Jesuit church in that city.[23]

*   *   *   *   *

The greatest significance of Peverara's work derives from her work with the composers who wrote for her and for her specific abilities. Writing for this consort of women with such high levels of vocal technique and their ability not only to sing together but to improvise simultaneously must have been exhilarating for composers accustomed to writing to the rather lower levels of Castiglione's noble amateurs. Examination of the music of Luzzaschi, Wert, or Monteverdi defines the virtuosity of these singers. Significant too is the astonishment of some auditors at the ladies' extraordinary ability to read music *prima vista*; clearly this skill then (as now) was much admired, sought after, and not so frequently found.

From a sociological point of view, it seems little short of astounding that women would emerge as professional musicians in a world dominated in every way by men. It is important to remember that these women were not just singers but were also trained on instruments—harp and viols, for example—and were trained as professional performers.

The *concerto delle donne* represents a significant move from the Renaissance ideal of skilled amateur performance to the establishment of a professional performing group. Newcomb emphasizes the importance and the swiftness of this shift in status: Peverara, Guarini, d'Arco, and Molza were officially ladies-in-waiting to the duchess, but it is clear that they were regarded as employees of the court, hired for their vocal prowess and expected to perform when so requested.[24] The separation of amateur and professional was now clearly defined; practitioners of the art of music were divided into the ones who listened and the ones who performed, the ones who played at will and the ones who played when commanded, the ones who were not paid and the ones who were. Finally, the proliferation of *concerti delle donne* throughout northern Italy manifests a desire for this music—music that technically exceeded the skills of trained amateurs but music that nonetheless was foreshadowed by the virtuosic vocal writing in the madrigals of the late Renaissance coupled with the delight of amateurs in singing and listening. In all probability the immensely popular sport of madrigal singing laid a fertile ground for the appreciation of the art of these trained singers. And of course, once established as a focus of admiration, the notion of the *concerto delle donne* spread from court to court, as each lord competed for superiority. The careers of Laura Peverara and her colleagues in the *concerti delle donne* serve as case histories documenting the process of success in this early opening to women of the world of professional music.

Vittoria Concarini Archilei (1550–c. 1642) "La Romanina"

Vittoria Archilei enjoyed great fame during her lifetime. Unlike Peverara, Vittoria Archilei was not associated mainly with a vocal ensemble but was known for her solo singing. Descriptions refer to extraordinary sweetness and tenderness but also to extraordinary virtuosity. Jacopo Peri, in the preface to his *L'Euridice,* touted as the "first" opera, referred to Archilei as "the Euterpe of our age" and continues with a revealing and specific detailing of her vocal technique, style, and musicianship:

This lady, who has always made my compositions seem worthy of her singing, adorns them not only with those groups and those long windings of the voice, simple and double, which the liveliness of her talent can invent at any moment (more to comply with the usage of our times than because she considers the beauty and force of our singing to lie in them), but also with those elegances and graces that cannot be written or, if written, cannot be learned from writing.[25]

In the preface to *his* music drama *L'Euridice* (1600), Giulio Caccini claimed that she was a long-time proponent of his new style and referred to her "excellence" as a singer ("cantatrice").[26] Composer Sigismondo d'India in the preface to *Il primo libro di musiche da cantar solo* of 1609 wrote that she was "above any other," she was "most intelligent," and her voice was amazingly sweet and tender[27]; Vincenzo Giustiniani stated quite simply that she "almost originated the true method of singing for females."[28]

In addition to verbal descriptions, the music composed for her affords revealing testimony. One of the most significant such documents is found in *La pellegrina,* a spectacle arranged as part of the 1589 celebration in Florence of the marriage of Ferdinando de' Medici, Grand Duke of Tuscany, and Christine de Lorraine. Not only did Archilei sing in several ensemble numbers, but it was she, representing Harmony, who appeared at the very beginning descending on a cloud machine, singing the opening number "Dalle più alte sfere." This music, replete with ornamentation and extensive passage work, attests eloquently to her amazing virtuosity, particularly when we consider that while singing she also accompanied herself on the leuto grosso (plus two other chitarroni, one played by her husband Antonio).

Around 1600 Archilei seems to have experienced difficulties with her voice, whether from illness or from overwork and perhaps too extreme demands on her vocal powers. She was not included in the 1600 celebrations of the wedding of Henry IV of France and Maria de' Medici, and apparently not involved in the performances at that time of Peri's opera *L'Euridice* and its successor by Caccini. On the other hand, her non-participation could have been the consequence of court politics. Tim Carter has pointed out that Archilei's association with Cavalieri could have harmed her own career, as Cavalieri was not popular at the Florence court. Ottavio Rinuccino, poet and librettist (for Peri's *Dafne* and for Monteverdi's *Arianna* and *Ballo delle ingrate)* created a sonnet seemingly addressed to Giulio Caccini, in celebration—or perhaps in defense?—of Archilei's singing. It begins "Where Vittoria loosens to the sweet accents | her noble voice, and strikes golden strings | to the varied sound of the mellow notes, | Giulio, rivers and torrents halt their foot."[29] Was Rinuccini reminding Caccini, who not unnaturally favored the highly gifted women in his own family—his first wife Lucia, the second Margherita (probably a pupil of Vittoria and Antonio Archilei), Francesca (see below Chapter II), and Settimia—of the profound musicianship of Archilei?

*   *   *   *   *

Archilei was a protege of Emilio de' Cavalieri, composer and instrumentalist in the service of Cardinal Ferdinando de' Medici in Rome. Little is known about her early years, which were apparently spent in Rome. In September 1578 she married Antonio Archilei, who had probably been her teacher; it may also have been a marriage of convenience—the convenience serving the Cardinal's musical establishment. Upon the death in 1587 of his brother, Grand Duke Francesco, Cardinal Ferdinando abandoned his scarlet robes and became Grand Duke Ferdinando of Tuscany. He was not long in requesting that Cavalieri join him in Florence. Cavalieri may have brought along his protege plus her husband Antonio (singer, lutenist, possibly composer), or she and her husband may have been lured to Florence independently of Cavalieri. Preparations began immediately for the enormous spectacle with *intermedi* and *concerti* that was to celebrate the wedding of Grand Duke Ferdinand with Christine of Lorraine. Many reports affirm the grandeur of these festivities, which included a number of events, chief among them Girolamo Bargagli's *La pellegrina,* given with six *intermedi* in the first-floor theatre of the Uffizi. Devised by Count Giovanni de' Bardi, the *intermedi* were directed by Cavalieri, with sets created by Bernardo Buontalenti. Cristofano Malvezzi and Marenzio composed most of the music, which included also, however, items by Antonio Archilei, Bardi, and Jacopo Peri, and even an aria "Io che dal cader" by Giulio Caccini. Many musicians, local and imported, took part in the performance. Peri himself sang, Caccini's wife Lucia and her sister Margherita (possibly a pupil of the Archilei couple) also performed,[30] but the star and recipient of the highest praise was Vittoria Archilei. Her representation of Harmony (Armonia Doria) opened the first *intermedio,* and she also sang in the terzetti of the final item. A contemporary report described "una donna" seated on a cloud, singing "molto soavemente" (very agreeably); she "sang solo very, very excellently" (eccellentissamente). Another commentator, apparently not so moved by Archilei's performance wrote only of "una donna da angiola vestita" (a lady dressed as an angel).[31]

Newcomb believes that Archilei was a member of the Florentine *concerto delle donne,* citing a document that refers to Archilei's performance during the wedding festivities in April 1584 for Vincenzo Gonzaga and Eleonora de' Medici, but that she continued to live in Rome, commuting to Florence when necessary and that although she sang frequently in Florence during the 1580s and 1590s, she also was actively in service to the Orsini family in Rome (whom Luca Marenzio probably served during the 1590s).[32] Clearly she spent a good deal of time in Florence after Ferdinando became the Grand Duke of Tuscany at which time Cavalieri settled in Florence. "La Romanina" could of course refer either to her coming from Rome or her continued dwelling in Rome. Certainly she continued to be professionally active in Rome as well as Florence. Around 1600 she may have been ill, to the point of losing her voice; she recovered, for in October 1608 she took part in the celebrations of the wedding of Prince Cosimo de' Medici and Maria Magdalena of Austria. She had at least five children: sons Ottavio (continually in trouble, even arrested in 1608) and Ferdinando (who became a priest) and three daughters: Emilia (died August 1597), Maria who became a nun, and Cleria who entered the service of the court. Antonio Archilei died in 1612. Vittoria was still performing as late as 1611, but little is known about her activities after that. In 1614 Giambattista Marino published his sonnet on her death: "In morte di Vittoria cantatrice famosa," but letters from her dated 1619 are extant, and she continued to receive a monthly payment from the Medici court until the early 1640s.[33]

*   *   *   *   *

Archilei was closely associated with the musical scene in Rome but, more significantly, she had close ties with musical activity in Florence, which as the home of the *Camerata* was an important center of avant-garde musical activity in the late sixteenth century. The *Camerata* was comprised of Vincenzo Galilei, Giulio Caccini, Jacopo Peri, and a number of other musicians, scholars, and noblemen, who gathered regularly at the home of Count Giovanni de' Bardi to discuss aesthetic issues of the day.[34] Their meetings frequently included musical performances; there is some thought that certain women composers/performers took part (see below, page 26). We can assess Archilei's significance by the frequent references of composers to her intelligence, virtuosity, and general ability. She was clearly in high demand both in Rome and in Florence, and she was equally clearly a prominent advocate for the new music of the day. The references by Caccini and Peri to her performances of their music dramas attest to both her fame and to her involvement with the avant-garde. The frequent references to her skill at improvisatory passage work demonstrate the high regard paid to this style of performance; she was undoubtedly able to improvise embellishments in the course of performance, but this praise would seem to refer also to her ability to maintain the improvisatory quality that was sought in much of the most advanced music of the time. Giustiniani's statement that she "almost originated the true method of singing for females," in addition to reiterating praise for her voice and recognizing her fame, indicates a belief that the singing of females was different from that of males not only in sound but also in technique and method. It is highly probable that she was involved in teaching; Carter believes for example that Giulio Caccini's second wife, Margherita, was a pupil of Vittoria and Antonio Archilei and suggests that she came with them from Rome to Florence.

Wherever and however long she lived, Archilei enjoyed a long career and a reputation as one of Italy's finest singers. In addition to her participation in the Medici wedding festivities of 1584 and 1589 and her performances of Cavalieri's works, she performed and inspired the music of the avant-garde composers of her time—Caccini, Peri, Monteverdi, the Spanish composer Sebastian Raval, and Luca

Marenzio whose appreciation is expressed in his madrigal "Cedan l'antiche tue chiare vittorie" in *Il secondo libro de madrigali a sei voci* of 1584.[35]

Virginia Andrea Ramponi Andreini (1583–c. 1630)

> Thus perhaps with her sweet song
> The lovely Adriana is wont to melt harsh sentiments,
> While with her voice and with her look
> She takes two paths to pierce men's breasts;
> Thus, Mantua, did you hear Florinda,
> There in the theatres beneath your royal roofs,
> Expounding Ariadne's harsh martyrdoms
> And drawing from a thousand hearts a thousand sighs.
>
> *Adone*[36]

Thus wrote the poet Giambattista Marino about the performance of Virginia Ramponi Andreini, known as La Florinda, in Claudio Monteverdi's second opera, *L'Arianna* (first performed in 1608 at the Mantuan court). The comparison with Adriana is telling, for Adriana Basile was the most famed singer of the time; the beauties of her voice and of her singing were praised without exception by audiences and composers alike. The court reporter Federico Follino, described the effect of the most famous (and only extant) number from the *dramma per musica*: "The lament that Ariadne . . . sang on the rock . . . was performed with so much feeling and in such a pathetic manner that not a single listener remained unmoved, nor did a single lady fail to shed some small tear at her plaint."[37] Andreini's success is all the more remarkable, because she was a late substitute for the brilliant young singer Caterina Martinelli for whom Monteverdi had composed the role and who died tragically of smallpox in early March 1608, some two months before the scheduled first performance.

Unfortunately we can learn little about her voice from her role in this opera, since the only surviving number is the famous lament (and it survived only in the madrigal setting created by Monteverdi probably in response to demand, Book VI, 1614). The lament, while extraordinarily expressive, depends for its effect on harmonic and dramatic intensity rather than on virtuosity. Colin Timms attributes the very lack of virtuosity in the lament (and in the women's parts in *Ballo delle ingrate* in which Andreini also sang) to the fact that it was composed for an actress, i.e., not a singer,[38] but this premises that it had indeed been composed for Ramponi and not for the deceased Caterina Martinelli. Still, if we consider the fact that hers was the title role, it is reasonable to assume that it must have been a significant part both in terms of length and vocal demands. Moreover she performed in a large theatre in the Gonzaga palace in Mantua for an audience of between four thousand (one eye-witness) and six thousand (the court historian, Federigo Follino),[39] which indicates that her ability to project vocally and emotionally must have been remarkable. It has been suggested that it was precisely her strength as actress coupled with lesser ability as singer that contributed to the development of the "genuine dramatic manner"[40] that became one of the most powerful ingredients of the new monodic style, the *seconda prattica*. It is surely safe to assume that Andreini must have enjoyed a certain amount of training as a singer, which coupled with her abilities as actress made her a formidable performer.

*   *   *   *   *

Little is known about Virginia Andrea Ramponi Andreini before her marriage in 1601. Her husband, Giovanni Battista Andreini (c. 1579–1654), was the son of Isabella and Francesco Andreini. Francesco was the director of the most famous *commedia* troupe of the time, *I Gelosi;* Isabella was the *prima donna innamorata* of the troupe but did far more than perform: in addition to being recognized as a musician with an excellent voice (*"soavissimo tocco nella musica"*) and a fine actress, she was widely known as a poet (her *Rime* and her pastoral *Mirtillo* were published)[41], and she worked with both her husband and the author Flaminio Scala to produce the scenarios in the repertoire of the troupe. In *La pazzia* (which she is credited with having authored), she played all the major parts (*maschere*) both male and female of the *commedia*: *pantalone, graziano, zanni,* Pedrolino, Franceschina, etc.[42]

This was the milieu into which Virginia Ramponi married in 1601. Her husband under the name Lelio had been a member of *I Gelosi* since 1594.[43] By the time the troupe disbanded in 1604 (coinciding with the death of his mother Isabella), he had formed his own group, *Comici fedeli,* in which Virginia, known as "La Florinda" from her memorable performance in her husband's eponymous tragedy,[44] performed as *prima donna*. Undoubtedly Giovanni Battista would have sought and found a wife whose abilities would enable her to take on this function, and it is surely safe to assume that to supplement her native ability and earlier training, Virginia would have had in her mother-in-law at least a model if not a teacher. The *Comici fedeli* seem to have enjoyed success similar to that of *I Gelosi* and in late 1613 were invited by Maria de' Medici to France, where they remained until July 1614. This marked the beginning of a series of visits to foreign countries. They returned to France for lengthy visits between January 1621 and June 1625; in 1627 they performed in Prague and in 1628 in Vienna. Virginia died either during this visit to Vienna or during the plague of 1630. Her husband soon after married Virginia Rotari, an actress in the company, whom he had been in love with for years[45]—a sort of reverse *Pagliacci* scenario?

*   *   *   *   *

The career of Virginia Ramponi Andreini is closely tied to the development of seventeenth-century music drama. Clearly her abilities as actress were valued not only by audiences but by such composers as Monteverdi, Peri, Caccini. Her success points up the importance placed on dramatic expression in early music drama. Colin Timms's point about the significance of composing for an adequate but non-virtuoso performer is surely well-taken and should be considered in tandem with the importance of dramatic representation for the new *stile rappresentativo.* Newcomb stresses in his essay, "Courtesans, Muses, or Musicians?" the respect that was accorded by colleagues and employers to Isabella Andreini on the basis of her achievements; he also points out that the ability of her daughter-in-law Virginia to learn the role of Arianna in two months demonstrates the high quality of musical training and ability of members of the *commedia* troupes. The links between the work of these troupes and the developing *dramma in musica* are further revealed by several of her husband's stage works—for example, *La ferinda* (Paris, 1622), which includes much sung music and is entirely in verse, and which he himself described as a "commedietta musicale." *La centaura* of the same year combines comedy, pastoral, and tragedy, and includes sung solo sections as well as choruses.[46] Both these works were performed before the death of Virginia Andreini and therefore would presumably have exploited her abilities.

Andreini's training and career reflect the connections between the *commedia dell'arte* and early opera. The training of actresses, like that of the "well-educated" gentlewoman, emphasized the ability to sing and play music, as well as to dance and know something of letters and the visual arts (see Castiglione's requirements, above, page 6). In the main the difference between the education of the noblewoman and that of the professional musician lay in expectations of competence and of readiness to perform at command. The fact that courtesans, too, were expected to be highly skilled in all these areas plus the art of conversation may explain the extreme care displayed by so many women musicians for their reputations. They were wary lest they be treated or viewed as women of easy virtue. Not only were women moving into a world dominated by men but they had to fear confusion with women of a different and much older profession.

Adriana Basile (c. 1580–c. 1642)

When the poet Marino turned to verse to praise Virginia Ramponi Andreini's performance in *L'Arianna,* he referred to Adriana Basile to evoke an image of the highest quality, referring to both her voice and her beauty: "with her voice and with her look/She takes two paths to pierce men's breasts."[47] Basile, probably the best known singer of her time,[48] was famous throughout Italy.

Her voice was a contralto, and it was extraordinary. But she was also highly skilled in performing on various instruments—*lira,* harp, Spanish guitar.[49] Monteverdi wrote in 1610 that he had heard Signora Hippolita [Ippolita Marotta] in Rome "sing very well" and in Florence had heard the daughter of Signor Giulio

Romano [i.e., Giulio Caccini's daughter Francesca] who also "sang quite well and played the theorbo-lute and the harpsichord," but he preferred Signora Adriana whom he had heard "sing, play, and speak extremely well. Even when she is silent and tunes up, she has qualities to be admired and worthily praised."[50]

Monteverdi was not alone in singing her praises. A letter to him from Abbot Angelo Grillo refers to "a perfect singer with a heavenly voice, such as the Signora Adriana" and continues "When Signora Adriana unites her voice with the instrument, and gives the strings life and speech with her direction, she wins our hearts with her sweet enchantment; we are carried to Heaven although our bodies remain on earth."[51] Monteverdi described music making in Mantua:

Every Friday evening we make music in the Hall of Mirrors. Signora Adriana comes to sing in ensemble music and invests it with such power and striking beauty as to delight the senses and to turn the room almost into a new theatre . . . On another such splendid occasion I shall make the household musicians play the chitarroni to the accompaniment of the wooden organ—a delightful sound. Signora Adriana and Don Giovanni Battista will sing the very beautiful madrigal *Ah, che morir mi sento* to these instruments, the other madrigal to the organ alone.[52]

The French bass viol player and writer André Maugars (c. 1580-c. 1645) tells us that the "*Bella Adriana* of Mantua . . . was a real miracle in her day." He describes a visit to Basile's daughter, Leonora Baroni ("the most perfect person for singing well"), during which Baroni sang and played with her mother (Adriana) and her sister. Baroni played the theorbo, her mother the lyre, and her sister the harp: "This concert, composed of three beautiful voices and three different instruments, so affected my senses and so ravished my spirit that I forgot my mortal condition and thought I was among the angels enjoying the delights of the blessed."[53]

Although Basile seems not to have visited other countries, her fame spread early and wide throughout Italy. The manner in which she was hired by the Mantuan court speaks both to her reputation as a singer and to her status in society. The Duke of Mantua, Vincenzo Gonzaga, who may have heard her as early as 1603 in Naples, was determined to have her as a star in his court's array. Basile's terms were not easy: she required a letter of invitation from the Duchess, Eleonora Gonzaga, and a formal request to the Neapolitan Viceroy and Vicereine that she be permitted to join the Mantuan court. After some three months of occasionally testy correspondence, her terms were met. In May 1610 with husband Muzio Baroni (a Calabrian nobleman) and son Camillo, she departed her native Naples for the swamps of Mantua and the court where Monteverdi was still rather unhappily in service and where his first two operas, *L'Orfeo* and *L'Arianna,* had made him (and in retrospect, the Mantuan court) famous. Her journey from Naples to Mantua was interrupted in Rome where she entranced Duke Vincenzo's son, Cardinal Ferdinando Gonzaga, and in Florence where she equally impressed the Medici court. In June 1610 she sang for the first time at the Mantuan court, beginning a relationship that was appreciated by employee and employer alike. Monteverdi declared her to be without doubt the greatest singer he knew, the Gonzagas were gratified by her prowess and her fame, and she in turn was satisfied enough with her position at the Mantuan court to name her first daughter born in December 1611 Leonora after the duchess, Eleonora, who had just died.

Though commentators are unanimous in their praise of Basile, they are singularly unspecific in describing her work. She is named "Bella Adriana" referring to both her beauty and her voice; Maugars calls her "a real miracle in her day" who performed an even greater miracle by giving the world her daughter Leonora Baroni the "most perfect person for singing well." She was praised for her impeccable style and her interpretations, especially of the new monodic style. This music—especially the madrigals of Monteverdi—provides the most telling documentation of her vocal technique, her sound, and the expressive qualities of her singing. That she frequently accompanied the Gonzagas to other courts—to Florence and Rome in 1618, to Venice in 1623—speaks for recognition of her stature as well as for the high respect in which she was held at the Gonzaga court. A collection of poems, *Il teatro delle glorie* (Venice, 1623), was published in her honor.

*   *   *   *   *

Born in Posillipo near Naples, Basile was recognized early as a remarkable singer. She married a minor nobleman, Muzio Baroni, with whom she had several children: Camillo, Leonora, Caterina, and apparently another son. Vincenzo Gonzaga may have heard her in Naples in 1603; in 1608 he began the lengthy process of luring her to the Mantuan court, and in 1610 she moved with her family to Mantua. Basile remained in the service of the Mantuan court until 1624 when she was given permission to go to Naples; she never returned to Mantua. It seems that she was considering offers from Prince Wladislaw Sigismund of Poland and from the Viceroy of Naples, the Duke of Alba; by the time she decided against accepting their offers the Gonzagas refused to take her back. In 1633 she established herself in Rome where she created a salon featuring musical entertainments by herself and her daughters Leonora and Caterina. When her voice faded in later years, she turned to the guitar, on which her playing received acclaim equal to that given her singing. She died in Rome around 1640.

*   *   *   *   *

Aside from her obvious success as musician, Basile's achievements should be considered from a social and a cultural point of view. The negotiations with the Gonzagas demonstrate her concern that she be accorded due respect as a musician and also as a gentlewoman of virtue; their accession to her requirements is good measure of her success in maintaining her status. As the daughter and student of Basile, Leonora Baroni provides testimony with respect to her mother's views on the training of a musician. This training would seem to emphasize both instrumental performance and theoretical education, for Baroni like her mother was a skilled instrumentalist—on the theorbo and lute in particular; she probably also composed music, and she spoke several languages and wrote verse. She performed with her mother from an early age at home and abroad and thus gained not only a wide knowledge of repertoire but also ease of manners and of performance. After the family settled in Rome in 1633, she was a vital member of her mother's salon entertainments and was soon acclaimed as the finest Italian chamber singer of the time. *Applausi poetici alle glorie della Signora Leonora Baroni* (Rome, 1639), a collection of poems by such poets as Fulvio Testi and Francesco Bracciolini, attests to the general admiration for her. Milton heard her and expressed his homage in three Latin epigrams, *Ad Leonoram Romae canentem.* At the invitation of Queen Regent of France Anne of Austria, Baroni with her husband (Giulio Cesare Castellani, d. 1662), accepted a very good situation at the French court; they remained there however little more than a year (1644–45) after which she returned to Rome where her salon with its musical activities was much frequented by the aristocratic society of Rome.

Adriana Basile is generally believed to have come from a poor or modest family. She forged a career by intelligent and canny use of her extraordinary voice coupled obviously with strong self-discipline and good fortune in finding helpful patrons early in her career. Leonora Baroni had from birth the advantage of living in a culturally rich environment, but judging by her musical and literary achievements it would seem that she too had the strong self-discipline which enabled her to make optimum use of her remarkable voice and intelligence. Her sense of her own worth surely equalled that of her mother, as demonstrated by both singers in their negotiations with patrons and also by the care taken by both to maintain reputations of impeccable virtue. Interestingly, both Basile and Baroni were known by their own names as was Laura Peverara—this may reflect the fact that all three created their careers before and independently of taking husbands. Moreover their husbands were not, as far as is known, musicians. Andreini and Archilei married men in their professions and class, and their marriages included an element of apprentice-type training—Andreini, in the troupe of her mother-in-law Isabella Andreini, and Archilei as a probable student of Antonio Archilei. Peverara came from an upper middle class family while Basile's murky origins surely indicate a lower class, poor background (Baroni of course enjoyed the setting created by her mother's success), but both married into minor nobility, and in both cases the husbands (and Basile's son as well) were treated very generously by their wives' patrons—receiving titles of nobility and gifts of land, etc. It is interesting to note that the professional respect accorded Peverara as a matter of course was granted to Basile and Baroni only after negotiation. Did they have to demand such respect? Peverara's official title was "lady in waiting" at the court, while Basile was contracted specifically to serve as a musician.

Timeline

Laura Peverara

c. 1545?	Laura Peverara born, Mantua
1563–1564	Torquato Tasso in Mantua knew, loved Peverara
1579	Duke Alfonso d'Este, Ferrara, married Margherita Gonzaga, daughter of duke of Mantua
1580, spring	Peverara employed at Ferrara court, beginnings of *concerto delle donne*
1582	Livia d'Arco hired by Ferrara court for *concerto*
1583–1589	Tarquinia Molza with *concerto* at Ferrara court
1582	*Il lauro secco,* Tasso's collection in homage to Peverara
1583	*Il lauro verde,* Tasso's second collection for Peverara Peverara married Count Annibale Turco
c. 1597	End of *concerto delle donne* and d'Este reign in Ferrara
1601, 4/5 Jan	Peverara died, Ferrara

Vittoria Concarini Archilei

1550	Vittoria Concarini born
1578, 20 Sep	Married Antonio Archilei
1584	Marriage of Vincenzo Gonzaga and Eleonora de' Medici, great festivities
1585, Dec	Son Ottavio born; later three daughters, one son
1587	Cardinal Ferdinando became Grand Duke Ferdinando of Tuscany; moved from Rome to Florence, probably taking with him Cavalieri, Vittoria and Antonio Archilei
1589	Marriage of Ferdinando de' Medici and Christine de Lorraine in Florence; Archilei prominent in spectacular musical celebrations, *La pellegrina*
1580s–1590s	Active in Florence (Medici court; Florence *concerto delle donne?*), also in Rome (Orsini family)
1593–94	Vittorio and Antonio in Rome; contact with Sebastian Raval in Spain
1600, Oct	Wedding of Henry IV of France and Maria de' Medici, Archilei not involved, also not in Peri's *L'Euridice* (Oct) or Caccini's (Dec)
1600–02	Out of favor? Illness? Troubles (expressed in letter to Grand Duchess Cristina, Jan 1602)
1608, Oct	Archilei involved in celebrations for wedding of Prince Cosimo de' Medici and Maria Magdalena of Austria
1611, Feb	Participated in *mascherata* at Florence court (composed some of music)
c. 1610–1642	Archilei in Medici account books, receiving regular payments

1612, Nov	Antonio Archilei died
1614	Sonnet by Marino, "La morte di Vittoria cantatrice famosa," refers to Archilei's death?
1619	Letter from Archilei
1642	Last entry for Archilei in Medici account books

Virginia Andrea Ramponi Andreini

1583	Virginia Andrea Ramponi born
1601	Married Giovanni Battista Andreini, son of Isabella and Francesco Andreini, directors of *I Gelosi* (*commedia* troupe)
1604	Isabella Andreini died; *I Gelosi* disbanded ; new troupe, *Comici fedeli,* of Vittoria and Giovanni Battista Andreini; Vittoria known as La Florinda
1608	Arianna in Monteverdi's opera, *L'Arianna* (replaced Caterina Martinelli)
1613–1614	Invited by Maria de' Medici to France
1621, 1625	Return visits to France
1627	Prague performances
1628	Vienna performances
c. 1630	Virginia Andreini died (Giovanni Battista married his long-time lover, Virginia Rotari)

Adriana Basile

c. 1580	Adriana Basile born, Posillipo, near Naples
	Singer, household of Luigi Carafa, Duke of Traetto?
c. 1600?	Married Muzio Baroni
c. 1588–1610	Active in Naples
1610	Basile to Mantuan court (Gonzaga family); sang there first in Jun
1611, Dec	Daughter, Leonora Baroni, born; other children Camillo, Caterina
1618–1620	With Gonzagas to Florence, Rome, Naples, Modena
1621	Sang in Guarini's *Licori, ovvero L'incanto d'amore,* Mantua
1623	With Gonzagas to Venice, May; December, singing in Rome ("Lamento d'Arianna"); *Il teatro delle glorie,* collection of poems in her honor, published Venice
1624	Basile given leave to visit Naples; never returned to Mantua
1624–1633	Mainly in Naples; visits to Florence, Genoa
1633	Rome, salon with daughters Leonora and Caterina Baroni; supported by Cardinal Antonio Barberini
1642	Return to Naples; still there in Aug 1642

Bibliography

Works about Peverara
Anthony Newcomb's "Courtesans, Muses, or Musicians?" and *The Madrigal at Ferrara, 1579–1597* (see below, General Reference Works) are the most useful major sources. Entries in *New Grove* and *Grove Music Online* are brief, with short bibliographies of mostly Italian works.

Works about Archilei
The two essays by Tim Carter are the most helpful for information about Archilei. Archilei and her husband have entries in Warren Kirkendale's work on the court musicians of Florence. Other useful studies are Newcomb's "Courtesans, Muses, or Musicians?" and Cusick's "Of Women, Music, and Power." The entries in *New Grove* and *Grove Music Online* are informative. The bibliographies include a few works in English.

Carter, Tim. "Finding a Voice: Vittoria Archilei and the Florentine 'New Music.'" In *Feminism and Renaissance Studies,* edited by L. Hutson, 450– 67. Oxford: Oxford University Press, 1999.
   This excellent essay by Carter assesses Archilei's singing and her significance for the music of her time, while reviewing also the difficulties she underwent as a "musical chattel" of both her employers and her husband.
_____. "A Florentine Wedding of 1608." *Acta musicologica* 55 (1983): 89–107.

Works about Andreini
Anthony Newcomb's "Courtesans, Muses, or Musicians?" and *The Madrigal* are again very helpful, though Andreini is given scant attention in the latter. In "Courtesans" he discusses the career of Virginia's mother-in-law Isabella Andreini in some detail. The entry in *New Grove* for Virginia, which is under Ramponi, may be quoted in its entirety: "Italian musician, wife of Giovanni Battista Andreini." The entry by Colin Timms for G. B. Andreini provides information about Virginia Andreini only insofar as her career was connected with her husband. It includes information about his parents Isabella and Francesco, and about works by Giovanni Battista which would have involved his wife. The bibliography consists almost entirely of Italian materials; there are only two French sources and one English (Nino Pirrotta, "*Commedia dell'Arte* and Opera," *Musical Quarterly* 41 (1955): 317). Virginia Andreini receives most attention in connection with her performance in *L'Arianna,* and in this respect biographies of Monteverdi (by Denis Arnold, Paolo Fabbri, Henry Prunières, and Leo Schrade) are helpful.

Works about Basile
Since Basile worked in Mantua with Monteverdi, the composer's letters and biographies of him are useful. The entries in *New Grove* by Argia Bertini for "Basile: (3) Andreana [Andriana, Adriana] Basile" and "Baroni: (2) Leonora [Eleanora, Lionora] Baroni" and *Grove Music Online* by Susan Parisi are also helpful, summing up information about the Basile and Baroni families, and including brief bibliographies.

General Reference Works
Information about all of these early professional singers must be collected from a variety of sources. The most useful are listed below.

Bianconi, Lorenzo. *Music in the Seventeenth Century.* Translated by David Bryant. Cambridge: Cambridge University Press, 1987. (Originally published in Italian as *Il seicento*, Turin: Edizioni di Torino, 1982.)
Excellent general history of seventeenth-century music, especially Italian, but including France and England, and providing several important primary documents, e.g., descriptions of a musical banquet in Florence in 1608, a court ballet in Turin in 1620, etc.
Bowers, Jane, and Judith Tick, eds. *Women Making Music: The Western Art Tradition, 1150–1950.* Urbana and Chicago: University of Illinois Press, 1987.
Carter, Tim. *Music in Late Renaissance & Early Baroque Italy.* London: Batsford, 1992.
Cusick, Suzanne. "Of Women, Music, and Power: A Model from Seicento Florence." In *Musicology and Difference: Gender and Sexuality in Musical Scholarship,* edited by Ruth A. Solie. Berkeley, Los Angeles, and London: University of California Press, 1993.
Einstein, Alfred. "Abbot Angelo Grillo's Letters as Source Material for Music History." In *Essays on Music.* New York: W. W. Norton & Company, Inc., 1962.
_____. *The Italian Madrigal.* 3 vols. Translated by Alexander H. Krappe, Roger H. Sessions, and Oliver Strunk. Princeton: Princeton University Press, 1949.
Fabbri, Paolo. *Monteverdi.* Translated by Tim Carter. Cambridge: Cambridge University Press, 1994. (Originally published in Italian as *Monteverdi*, Turin: E.D.T. Edizioni di Torino, 1985.)
Much good information and quoting of primary sources concerning performances of *L'Arianna*, etc. Fabbri also refers to a manuscript in Milan, Biblioteca Nazionale Braidense, Fondo Morbio, that contains verses in praise of Virginia Andreini titled "Pe'l suo meraviglioso modo di cantare e di suonare."
Fenlon, Iain. *Music and Patronage in Sixteenth-Century Mantua.* 2 vols. Cambridge: Cambridge University Press, 1980.
First-rate study of the Mantuan court and its music in the sixteenth century. It deals extensively with spectacle and large undertakings (e.g., Chapter 3, "Guglielmo Gonzaga and the Santa Barbara Project"). Especially useful for

information about women singers in Chapter 4, "Vincenzo Gonzaga and the New Arts of Spectacle" (119–62). Volume 2 provides musical examples. Excellent, extensive bibliography.

Giustiniani, Vincenzo. *Discorso sopra la musica,* 1628. Translated by Carol MacClintock. Musicological Studies and Documents. No city: American Institute of Musicology, 1962.

MacClintock, Carol, comp., transl., ed. *Readings in the History of Music in Performance.* Bloomington and London: Indiana University Press, 1979.

Includes Baldassare Castiglione, excerpt from *The Book of the Courtier* (22–27), and Vincenzo Giustiniani, excerpt from *Discorso sopra la musica,* (27–29). The excerpts are very short but included in a readily accessible reference work.

Monteverdi, Claudio. *The Letters of Claudio Monteverdi.* Revised edition, translated and introduced by Denis Stevens. Oxford: Clarendon Press, 1995.

Newcomb, Anthony. "Courtesans, Muses, or Musicians." In *Women Making Music: The Western Art Tradition, 1150–1950,* edited by Jane Bowers and Judith Tick. Urbana and Chicago: University of Illinois Press, 1986.

Thoughtful essay on female musicians of the late sixteenth century. More recent than *The Madrigal at Ferrara* and therefore provides more information. Excellent in every respect, this essay is particularly helpful with details about the connections—familial, political, artistic—among the courts of Ferrara, Florence, Mantua, Rome.

_____. *The Madrigal at Ferrara, 1579–1597.* 2 vols. Princeton: Princeton University Press, 1980.

Excellent, thorough study of the Ferrara court, its music, its musical personnel, and the historical context. Probably the single greatest source of information about Peverara. Music (vol. 2) includes works from anthologies dedicated to Peverara. *The Madrigal at Ferrara* provides much more coverage both geographically and musically than the title implies; see especially Chapter V: "Imitations of the Ferrarese *'Concerto delle Donne*' 1584–1589." (The entry in *New Grove* also by Newcomb does not provide additional information.)

Pirrotta, Nino. "*Commedia dell' Arte* and Opera." *Musical Quarterly* 41 (1955): 305–24.

Rosand, Ellen. *Opera in Seventeenth Century Venice: The Creation of a Genre.* Berkeley: University of California Press, 1991.

Excellent, thorough, fascinating study of Venice and opera. The four singers discussed in this chapter seldom sang in Venice, so references to them are sparse but are useful.

Rosselli, John. "From Princely Service to the Open Market: Singers of Italian Opera and their Patrons, 1600–1850." *Cambridge Opera Journal* 1 (1989): 1–32.

Chapter 2

Francesca Caccini
("La Cecchina")
(18 September 1587 – c. 1645)

Unlike most of her female contemporaries, Francesca Caccini's fame during her lifetime rested on her prowess as a composer as well as on her ability as a performer. And, also unlike most of her contemporaries, evidence of her composing activities has survived not just in descriptions but in manuscript. Although most scholars believe today that such musicians as Laura Peverara and Adriana Basile composed some of the music they performed, rarely can music be definitively attributed to these or other women of their time. Caccini, on the other hand, is given credit for a good deal of the music performed at the Medici court in Florence; moreover she published in 1618 *Il primo libro delle musiche à una e due voci* and was commissioned by the court to compose a large-scale work for the visit in 1625 of the future King Wladislaw IV of Poland. This work, *La liberazione di Ruggiero dall'isola d'Alcina,* an opera (which she called a *balletto*), was published in 1625; in 1628 a performance in Warsaw made it the first Italian opera to be performed outside of Italy. These two publications establish Caccini as a member of the monody school alongside such Florentine composers as her father Giulio (composer of the first opera to be published, *Euridice,* 1600), Jacopo Peri, Vincenzo Galilei, Giovanni Battista Gagliano, et al.[1]

*   *   *   *   *

Contemporary accounts of La Cecchina's performing are enthusiastic but frustratingly vague. Monteverdi wrote for example in 1610: "at Florence [I heard] Signor Giulio Romano's daughter sing very well and play the lute, the guitar and the harpsichord";[2] Pietro della Valle (1568–1652) in 1640: "Signora Francesca Caccini . . . has been greatly admired for many years in Florence, where I heard her in my youth, both for her musical abilities in singing, and in composing and for her poetry not only in Latin but also in Tuscan."[3] In 1604–1605, Giulio Caccini traveled with his family to the French court of Maria de' Medici (who had married Henri IV, king of France); he wrote Grand Duke Ferdinando in Florence that the French court wished to keep Francesca because the king said that La Cecchina "sang better than anyone in France, and that there was no *consorto* to equal the Caccinis."[4] We know that La Cecchina was so highly valued by her patrons the Medicis that when in 1608 the Mantuan court requested a loan of singers to perform in Monteverdi's new *Arianna,* they had to do without her.[5] And we know also that in 1617 Francesca and her husband Giovanni Battista Signorini, a Florentine singer, made a highly successful tour of Italy that included Genoa, Lucca, Milan, Parma, and Savona. The poet Gabriello Chiabrera heard her in Genoa and reported that "Here she was heard as a marvel, without any dissension; and in just a few days her fame has spread far."[6]

She traveled to Rome during the winter of 1623–1624 with Carlo de' Medici where she engaged in an improvising contest with Adriana Basile. The poet Giambattista Marino reported that Basile had a better voice and was more agile in passagework, but Caccini was the more profound musician[7] (which agrees quite nicely with Monteverdi's earlier assessment of Basile, see Chapter 1, page 14). These encomia are certainly gratifying, but not very helpful with respect to the quality of her voice and her technical abilities. In fact, the best source of information about Caccini the singer is her own music.

We do not know if she sang in performances of *La liberazione,* although as the most famed and probably most skilled singer at the Medici court she might well have sung Alcina—a role that is virtuosic and demands an extremely sure sense of intonation. *Il primo libro* on the other hand undoubtedly represents her own repertoire: the collection consists of nineteen sacred solos, thirteen secular solos, and four duets for soprano and bass. In addition to displaying her compositional style, the music reveals much about her voice and manner of singing: trills, syncopations, rapid scale passages, incisive rhythmic patterns and changes (e.g., striking shifts from eighth and quarter notes to outbursts of sixteenths), and harmonic surprises that demand a keen ear for intonation.[8]

Reception of Caccini the composer has ranged from what Doris Silbert called the "exaggerated gallantry" of A. W. Ambros to the "ill-tempered censure" of Hugo Goldschmidt, while discussions of her personality traits vary from seeing them as the source of "rather malicious gossip" (Alessandro Ademollo) to "signs of genius" (Oscar Chilesotti).[9] Silbert herself sees la Cecchina as "no trail blazer," but rather a composer who reveals in her vocally "well contrived . . . often graceful and beautiful melodic line" the experienced singer,[10] who had profited well from her father's teaching without however outdoing him, and who was "sensible enough to stay within the limits of her talent and to use the best models of her time."[11] Carolyn Raney on the other hand, credits Caccini with creating in the works of *Il primo libro* a "strong and active bass line . . . a particular individuality . . . in the use of the diminished seventh chord" and vocal lines of "lyric beauty and great variety . . . so skillfully written that each one could be used as a *vocalise* in the modern sense" and that are at the same time "extremely expressive."[12] More recently Karin Pendle has written of the "spectacular, musically varied treatment" of the Ruggiero-Alcina story; she cites Susan Cusick's appraisal of *Il liberazione* as "the first opera to reveal a feminist sensibility" in that Alcina is presented as a "suffering woman rather than an evil sorceress," an approach that she suggests may be indebted to Archduchess Christina de' Medici's suggestion that it serve as a contribution to the gender role debates that were popular at the time.[13] We might also make the connection between Alcina at the head of her court and the Archduchess who with her daughter-in-law Maria Maddalena, widow of Grand Duke Cosimo II, shared the role of Regents during the minority of the heir Ferdinand II, and who was perhaps seen as something of an evil sorceress herself. A recording of the entire opera has recently been released (by Nannerl Records).[14]

Caccini's writing shows great delight in word-painting. Raney, who transcribed the music in her dissertation considers a moving bassline, and "arching melodic lines with double peaks"[15] to be important traits of her compositional style. Contrary to the usual practice of the time she wrote out much of her ornamentation; this may well be attributable to her intent to publish the collection and her consequent desire to make it accessible to amateur as well as professional singers. Caccini's talent for varying melody is demonstrated vividly in "Dov' io credea le mie speranze vere." This aria consists formally of four variations over a repeated bassline (the bass is the one known as "Romanesca"); the elegantly simple melody is transformed by rhythmic and melodic manipulation while staying within the harmonic constraints of the bassline and cadencing each time on the same pitch.[16]

Without undertaking a comprehensive comparison of Caccini's extant music and the music of her contemporaries—Giulio Caccini, Monteverdi, Cavalieri, Luzzaschi—it is impossible to determine whether she was an extremely gifted composer skilled in the style of her time, as is well demonstrated by the extant music, or a ground-breaking innovator. On the basis of her career—publication of *Il primo libro* and *La liberazione,* her high salary at the Medici court, the fact for example that she, with Giovanni Battista Gagliano, composed music for the 1622 performance in Florence of a *sacra rappresentazione* by Jacopo Cicognini, *Il martirio di sant'Agata*[17]—we can conclude that in addition to being known as one of the finest singers of her day, she was a well-respected, successful composer.

*   *   *   *   *

Like Leonora Baroni, Francesca Caccini enjoyed the benefits of growing up in a musical environment. Her father, Giulio Caccini (c.1645–1618), called Giulio Romano (i.e., Giulio of Rome) was famed as singer (tenor), composer, and teacher. His participation in the meetings of the Florentine Camerata has been described by Bardi in the well-known letter to Giovanni Battista Doni;[18] he propagated a new style of song, the *stile recitativo,* for which he became famous throughout Italy. He and Jacopo Peri vied with each other as composers of opera; both created dramatic settings of *Euridice*—Peri in October1600, Caccini in December1600.[19] Caccini is best remembered however for his 1601 collection of solo songs with basso continuo, *Le nuove musiche,* and its preface in which he defined the new style of singing. As a member of the Florentine Camerata from the mid 1570s to the 1580s, he was in contact with avant-garde intellectual and artistic ideas, and with such leaders of the group as the Count Giovanni de' Bardi, Vincenzo Gallileo, and a number of other composers, scholars, philosophers, and patrons of the arts. He is first documented as singing at the Medici court in 1579; he was employed at the Ferrara residence of Ippolito Aldobrandini (later Pope Clement VIII), spent a brief time in Rome in 1592 as secretary to Count Bardi but soon returned to Florence and the Medici court where by 1600 he had been appointed musical director, succeeding Emilio de' Cavalieri (c. 1550–1602). His children, Francesca, Settimia, and Pompeo, benefitted not only from his teaching but from the rich cultural environment in which they grew up. Francesca wrote poetry and was praised for her ability to write in both Latin and Tuscan. At 13 she sang (probably in Peri's *Euridice*) during the festivities for the marriage of Maria de' Medici and Henri IV, King of France; four years later she went with her family to the French court where she was acclaimed by Henri IV as a better singer than anyone in France. When she reached the age of twenty in September 1607 she was officially employed by the Medici court. She remained there until at least 1627, performing as singer and instrumentalist (lute, guitar, harpsichord) and composing music for various court occasions. In addition she sang the Office for Holy Week services and she gave instruction in music to the princesses, ladies-in-waiting, and other female court personnel, as well as various other pupils; performances by her "little girls" are mentioned in reports of activities at the Medici court.[20] Although only *La liberazione* and *Il primo libro* have survived, she is known to have composed a number of other works, small and large. Emil Vogel suggested in 1889 that Francesca and Settimia Caccini as well as Victoria Archilei were members of the Florentine *Accademia degl' Elevati* founded by Gagliano, a suggestion with which Edmond Strainchamps concurred in 1976.[21] Her fame reached well beyond the borders of Italy, and she was certainly so well-known as to be seen as a model for comparison and emulation.

Caccini married Signorini in 1607, the year she was officially employed by the Medici court. Their single daughter Margherita became a singer also and entered a convent. Shortly after Signorini's death in 1626, Caccini married a wealthy Lucchese aristocrat, Tomaso Raffaelli, and left Florence. She may at that time have joined the musical establishment of a Lucchese banker, Vincenzo Buonvisi; she possibly composed *intermedi* for Raffaelli's *Accademia degli Oscuri*. The marriage was short-lived: Raffaelli died in 1630, leaving Caccini wealthy and with a son, Tomaso, born in 1628. After three years of quarantine in Lucca, Caccini returned to Florence and service at the Medici court where she remained until 1641. In February 1645 her son became the ward of his uncle Girolamo Raffaelli, due to the remarriage or possibly the death of his mother.[22]

*　　*　　*　　*　　*

La Cecchina was born into the optimum environment for a musically gifted child, male or female. Her talents were great and discovered early; that her father recognized her abilities is attested by his educating her not just as a singer (as was the case with her sister Settimia) but as a musician, i.e., she received instruction in theory and composition (Silbert believes that she was not instructed in counterpoint,[23] but Raney states that "Francesca was cited by contemporaries for her training in counterpoint"[24]). Recent researches have shown that it was not so unusual for singers such as Peverara or Basile to have created a certain amount of the music they performed and that many more sixteenth- and seventeenth-century women than previously thought did indeed compose music, but the frequency with which Francesca supplied compositions for court occasions is still remarkable, as are the facts that she was given credit for having composed the music, that she worked with well-known poets, particularly Michelangelo Buonarroti the Younger with whom she created numerous dramatic pieces or *feste* and whose poetry she often set, and that her *Primo libro* as well as her opera were published. Most remarkable is of course that she was actually commissioned to create a major work, the opera *La liberazione di Ruggiero,* for such an important occasion as a royal visit. References to a number of other compositions now lost are tantalizing, especially the commission by the Polish Prince Wladislaw of two operas, *Rinaldo inamorato* (at one time in the possession of Giuseppe Baini) and a work about St. Sigismondo. She is thought also to have composed several *intermedi* during her residence in Lucca.

Although her career and its successes seem to have been fairly equally balanced between performance and composition, we may still wonder how she would have fared if she had been a less remarkable singer. Was her position at court the result of her vocal prowess? If she had been only a composer would she have received similar benefits? Or might she have been recognized and praised as a composer but not accorded a position at court? As was indeed the case with a remarkable musician of the next generation, Barbara Strozzi, born in 1619 in Venice.

Timeline

1587, 18 Sep	Francesca Caccini born Florence, daughter of Giulio Caccini
1600	Sang (in Peri's *Euridice*?) in wedding festivities for Maria de' Medici and Henri IV, King of France
1604	With family to French court
1607	Employed as singer, instrumentalist, composer by Medici court; remained in employ until at least 1627
15 Nov	Married Giovanni Battista Signorini
1617	Tour of Italy (Genoa, Lucca, Milan, Parma, Savona) with husband
1618	Published *Il primo libro delle musiche à una e due voci.*
1622	With Gagliano composed music for *sacra rappresentazione* by Cicognini
1622, 9 Feb	Daughter Margherita born
1625	Composed and published opera *La liberazione di Ruggiero dall'isola d'Alcina*
1626, Dec	Signorini died
1627, 4 Oct	Married Tomaso Raffaelli; employed by Lucchese banker V. Buonvisi
1628	*La liberazione* performed in Warsaw
1628, fall	Son Tomaso born
1630	Raffaelli died
1633	Return to Florence and service with Medici court
1641, 8 May	Left employ of Medicis
1645, Feb	Tomaso to guardianship of uncle, Girolamo Raffaelli, as result of death? remarriage? of Caccini

Bibliography

Francesca Caccini was one of the first women musicians to find a twentieth-century champion. Carolyn Raney's 1971 dissertation was a trail blazer in that it provided a thorough study of a remarkable woman musician and established credibility for future such studies. A number of articles in English have appeared since then; perhaps even more significant, the roles of women in music-making (whether performing or composing) are recognized and discussed in general works about music.

Works about Caccini
Harbach, Barbara. Review of Francesca Caccini, *La liberazione di Ruggiero dall' isola d'Alcina.* Nannerl Records, NR-ARS 003. *Women of Note Quarterly* 6/2 (May 1998): 15–17.
 An informative review of the first recording of the first opera by a woman composer.
Pannella, L. "Caccini, Francesca." *Dizionario biografico degli italiani*, 1984.
 This biography amply repays the effort to work through the Italian.
Pendle, Karin. "Lost Voices." *Opera News* (1992): 18–19, 44.
 Survey of operas by women composers, beginning with Caccini and concluding with twentieth-century women such as Thea Musgrave and Judith Weir.
Raney, Carolyn. "Francesca Caccini, Musician to the Medici, and her *Primo Libro (1618)*." Ph.D. diss., New York University, 1971.
 This dissertation provides a thorough and impressive study of Caccini's life and career, and establishes firmly the value of investigations of the work of women musicians in this period.
_____. "Francesca Caccini's 'Primo Libro.'" *Music and Letters* 48 (1967): 350–57.
_____. "Caccini, Francesca." *New Grove*.
 Raney's entry provides a list of the published and unpublished music which includes compositions that appear in various anthologies.
Silbert, Doris. "Francesca Caccini, Called La Cecchina." *Musical Quarterly* 32 (1946): 50–62.

General Reference Works
Bianconi, Lorenzo. *Music in the Seventeenth Century.* Translated by David Bryant. Cambridge: Cambridge University Press, 1987. (Originally published as *Il seicento*, Turin: Edizioni di Torino, 1982.)
Bowers, Jane, and Judith Tick, eds. *Women Making Music: The Western Art Tradition, 1150–1950.* Urbana and Chicago: University of Illinois Press, 1987.
Fabbri, Paolo. *Monteverdi.* Translated by Tim Carter. Cambridge: Cambridge University Press, 1994. (Originally published in Italian as *Monteverdi*, Turin: E.D.T. Edizioni di Torino, 1985.)

Hammond, Frederick. "Musicians at the Medici Court in the Mid-Seventeenth Century," *Analecta Musicologica* No. 14 (1974): 151–69.
 Useful for lists of musicians at the courts of the Grand Dukes of Tuscany from 1590 to 1669.
Kirkendale, Warren. *The Court Musicians in Florence during the Principate of the Medici, with a Reconstruction of the Artistic Establishment.* Florence: Olschki, 1993.
Marshall, Kimberly, ed. *Rediscovering the Muses: Women's Musical Traditions.* Boston: Northeastern University Press, 1993. See especially the essay by Suzanne Cusick, "'Thinking from Women's Lives': Francesca Caccini after 1627."
Solie, Ruth A., ed. *Musicology and Difference: Gender and Sexuality in Musical Scholarship.* Berkeley, Los Angeles, and London: University of California Press, 1993. See especially the essay by Suzanne Cusick, "Of Women, Music, and Power: A Model from Seicento Florence."
Strainchamps, Edmond. "New Light on the *Accademia degli Elevati* of Florence." *Musical Quarterly* 62 (1976): 507–35.
Vogel, Emil. "Marco da Gagliano: Zur Geschichte des florentiner Musiklebens von 1570–1650." *Vierteljahrsschrift für Musikwissenschft* 5 (1889): 396–442.

Chapter 3

Barbara Strozzi
(August 1619 – 11 November 1677)

"Virtuosissima cantatrice"—so she was named in the dedications to her of two volumes of songs by Nicolò Fontei, *Bizzarie poetiche* (1635 and 1636); "inventress of that elegant species of vocal composition, the Cantata"—wrote Sir John Hawkins in his *General History of the Science and Practice of Music* (1776).[1] These two epitaphs evoke the two dominant aspects of her life. Unusually for her time, she was known more for her compositions than for her singing, probably because her singing was confined to the private arena of the salon or the *accademia*. Her eight volumes of compositions, on the other hand, were published; all but one have survived.

*   *   *   *   *

Barbara Strozzi apparently sang almost exclusively in the home of her adopted father, Giulio Strozzi, and in the gatherings of the *Accademia degli Unisoni*, which he founded in 1637 and which also met in his home. Fontei's dedication describes her as singing in a "bold and graceful manner" but gives her otherwise what Ellen Rosand (author of the first real study of her life and music) calls "typically rhetorical appreciation."[2] When she sang during the meetings of the *Unisoni* her voice was compared to that of Amphion or Orpheus and to the "sound of the harmonies of the spheres";[3] similar clichés are used to laud her in the biography of Giulio Strozzi that appeared (1647) in the *Glorie degli Incogniti.*[4] But praises of Barbara Strozzi's singing are truly tepid when compared with those accorded opera singer Anna Renzi by Giulio Strozzi himself (see below, pages 44–45), and may well indicate that Barbara was not in fact a remarkable singer. In spite of the fact that she was frequently in the company of opera librettists and composers and studied composition with the prominent Venetian opera composer Francesco Cavalli, she apparently never appeared in an opera.

If she herself had not been determined to see her works published, her compositions would surely have simply disappeared. It is nonetheless remarkable that of the eight volumes published in her lifetime all but volume 4 have survived; this is perhaps an indication of their value to her contemporaries.[5]

As in the case of Francesca Caccini, the only real evidence about Strozzi's singing appears in her own compositions. Examination of "Appena il sol" from Op. 7 (excerpted in Rosand's article) is revealing. The voice moves primarily in the range from f' to f''. Although rapid passagework is present, the composer—the singer— seems truly to prefer long, legato sustained lines.[6] The relation between voice and bass line is particularly interesting: sometimes the bass moves in parallel motion with the voice, sometimes it moves at its own pace but in a way that strengthens the emotional power of the voice, sometimes it moves contrapuntally in tandem with the voice. Strozzi's writing in general is declamatory and forms a sharp contrast with the virtuosity of Francesca Caccini's music. She does not give us the rapid scale passages or trills that were so prominent in Caccini's writing, but deftly exploits the expressive power of harmonic surprise and tension. It is clear that for Strozzi, word painting is an important element in the compositional procedure. It seems safe to conclude that these characteristics of Strozzi's compositional style were significant features of her vocal style as well, and that of particular importance for her both as composer and as singer was affective declamation emphasizing the text and its content.

*   *   *   *   *

Barbara Strozzi was born in August 1619 to Isabella Griega (called "la Greghetta"), a servant in Giulio Strozzi's household. Known in 1628 as Barbara Valle, by 1638 she was using the name of Strozzi. Her childhood was probably spent in the home of Giulio Strozzi, who in his last will (made in 1650) names her his "figliuola elettiva" (which as Rosand points out could mean "adopted" or could indicate that she was illegitimate).[7] Like Francesca Caccini, Barbara Strozzi enjoyed the benefits of a culturally, especially musically, rich environment. Her father, a poet and very much a part of the Venetian intellectual world, created opera librettos for some of the greatest composers of the time including Claudio Monteverdi, Francesco Manelli, Tarquinio Merula, Francesco Cavalli. His critical appraisal of the opera singer Anna Renzi (*Le glorie della Signora Anna Renzi romana,* Venice, 1644) demonstrates his theatrical and musical acumen.[8] Before founding the *Accademia degli Unisoni,* Giulio Strozzi had established similar academies—the *Ordinati* in Rome and the *Dubbiosi* in Venice; he was also a member of the very large *Accademia degli Incogniti.* The membership of the *Incogniti* included poets, historians, philosophers, clerics, most of the opera librettists in Venice; the organization published romances, poetry, letters, essays, and opera librettos. Rosand suggests that the *Unisoni* may have been a "musical sub-group" of the *Incogniti* who seem not to have practiced music during their meetings.[9] Barbara was thus in the center of the intellectual and artistic world of Venice. Moreover, she was provided with the training that would enable her to take part in this world not only as a performing musician but as a composer.[10] She proudly acknowledged in the preface to her Opus 2 (1651) that she had studied composition with Francesco Cavalli, the foremost opera composer of the time.

By 1634 at the latest Barbara was singing for Giulio's friends and colleagues at private gatherings in the Strozzi home. When Strozzi founded the *Accademia degli Unisoni,* in 1637, she became their "mistress of ceremonies" presiding over and performing at the meetings.[11] So far as is known, she did not perform in public, though there is evidence that she sang in other private settings in addition to her father's home and the meetings of the *Unisoni.*

Her first volume of compositions, the only one to include much music for vocal ensembles, was printed in 1644; further volumes were printed in 1651, 1654, 1655, 1657, 1659, and 1664. Two collections published in 1656 present her work alongside compositions by Cavalli, Giovanni Rovetta, Pietro Antonio Ziani, Horatio Tarditi, and Maurizio Cazzati: Bartolomeo Marcesso's collection of motets *Sacra corona, motetti a due, e tre voci di diversi eccelentissimi autori moderni* includes her motet "Quis dabit mihi," and Francesco Tonalli's collection of *Arie a voce sola di diversi auttori* includes two arias "Rissolvetevi pensieri" and "Chi brama in amore."[12]

The dedications of Strozzi's volumes may well reflect, as Rosand suggests, her efforts to find a position. They surely manifest as well Strozzi's determination to win for herself a measure of recognition as a composer. Op. 2 is dedicated to Ferdinand III of Austria and Eleanora of Mantua; Op. 5 to Anna of Austria, Archduchess of Innsbruck; Op. 6 to Francesco Carafa, Prince of Belvedere and Marquis of Anzi; Op. 7 to Nicolò Sagredo, Cavalier and Procurator of San Marco, Ambassador Extraordinary to Pope Alexander VII, and future Doge of Venice; and Op. 8 is dedicated to Sophia, Duchess of Braunschweig and Lüneburg. In the dedication of Op. 7 she refers to Sagredo as her "guardian deity" and cites his support of her own "modest life." Although the dedications may have brought some small financial rewards, so far as is known they were of no avail with respect to finding a position.[13]

In the late 1990s Beth Glixon turned up evidence about Strozzi's life which casts a very different light on the life and career of this enterprising musician.[14] Glixon's work reveals that Strozzi had four children, three of whom were fathered almost certainly by Giovanni Paolo Vidman, a friend of her father's who was some fourteen years older than she and was married with children. Three of Strozzi's children entered religious institutions: Isabella, born c. 1642, entered the Convent San Sepolcro in July 1656, but died the following January before taking her vows; Laura, born c. 1644, also entered San Sepolcro in July of 1656, took vows and the name of Sister Lodovica in 1659, and made her final vows in March 1661; the youngest child, Massimo, whose father *may* have been Vidman, but this has not yet been documented, entered the monastery of Santo Steffano of Belluno, taking vows and the name Giovanni Paolo, i.e., Vidman's name which certainly implies a filial relationship. The first-born child, Giulio Pietro, remained in the secular world but seems to have been slow or unable to establish himself in any money-earning situation.

In addition to her newly discovered function as mother, Strozzi was also a capable businesswoman. Glixon's archival searches turned up a request that her father be authorized to collect interest on government investments in 1640 when she was twenty-one. Again in 1642 and 1649 she requested that he handle the interest and capital for her investments; after his death in 1652, she authorized Antonio Peruzzi to collect the interest for her that year and again in 1657 and 1661. Peruzzi was replaced by Emilio Piatti in 1663. (Like Giulio Strozzi, both Peruzzi and Piatti were Florentines.) In 1642, 1653, 1656, and 1659 she made significant loans of 2,000, 200 (increased to 400), 150, and 250 ducats at business-like rates of interest; the first loan was to Vidman, the father of her children, while the others were to acquaintances. It is not clear where she acquired the initial capital, but it is abundantly clear that she dealt efficiently and profitably with the business of investments, whether in governmental or private enterprises.

Vidman died in 1648; the loan made by Strozzi was repaid at that time with interest of a bit over 1,145 ducats. At that time both her father and mother were still living. In a petition to the Doge in December 1651, she requested exemption from the very high war tax on the grounds that she was a single woman with four children and an aged mother (no mention of her father though he was apparently living in the same house with her where he died the following year) with only the interest from her government investments and holdings (which amounted to 2,400 ducats). Her children were born in 1641, 1642, 1644 (the year in which she published her first book of compositions), and before 1651 (when she applied to the Doge). It was not until after the death of Vidman and probably after the birth of her fourth child) that she began again to publish her music, and then the collections appeared in rapid succession: 1651, 1654, 1655, 1657, and 1659. The final volume, Opus 8, appeared in 1664. By that time she was alone except for her oldest son, Giulio Pietro; mother, father, lover were dead, daughter Isabella had died in the convent before taking her vows, Laura and the younger son Massimo were both fully committed to monastic life. Little information has so far come to light concerning Strozzi's activities after that final publication in 1664. On 18 July 1672 Martino Vidman drew up his last will and testament, which included annuities of 25 ducats per year for Strozzi's daughter Laura, now Sister Lodovica, and 30 ducats per year for her son, Giulio Pietro (or the sum of 1,000 ducats if he found a suitable situation to purchase). Massimo Strozzi is not mentioned. On 20 July 1672, Sister Lodovica Strozzi appears on the convent roll books as Lodovica Vidman. In May 1677 Barbara Strozzi traveled to Padua (about 50 kilometers from Venice), where on the 11th of November, she died.

*   *   *   *   *

Until Glixon's archival searches turned up the evidence of loans and business investments, Strozzi had appeared as a poor struggling composer, unable to earn a living as a professional singer (which would surely have meant on the opera stage) or as a composer. This new evidence complements the portrait of a highly gifted musician—a fine singer but who sang only in private settings, an excellent composer who published her own works but whose works were also included with those of well-known composers of the day in two prestigious publications—who was associated throughout her life with the intellectual elite of Venice and with various members of the nobility. She was also gifted with a genuine business acumen, which stood her in good stead if she was as seems the case the sole support of four children and her parents. Her education was undoubtedly thorough and made her into a woman skilled in the arts of music, poetry, and of conversation. Aside from the long-term relationship with Vidman, she seems to have led a stable, decorous life, caring for parents, children, and pursuing her musical career.

Venice was at that time the liveliest center of operatic activity in Europe, and Cavalli, Barbara Strozzi's teacher, was the leading opera composer of the time. Her father had been associated as poet and librettist with the foremost opera composers of the day, in particular with both Monteverdi and Cavalli; he had also been associated with opera theatres and productions, and his writing about Anna Renzi demonstrates his intimate knowledge of the technical and dramatic requirements for an opera singer. Why did Barbara Strozzi not take advantage of these connections and work in the world of opera? It would seem almost without question that she had neither the vocal nor the dramatic power to perform music drama, perhaps especially in the competitive commercial atmosphere that prevailed in Venice increasingly after the opening of the first public opera theatre in 1637. Why not, then, exploit her connections with the world of the stage to compose her own operas? Francesca Caccini had after all seen her opera, *La liberazione di Ruggiero dall'isola d'Alcina,* performed in Florence in 1625 and in Warsaw in 1628. But these performances were in the protected world of the court. In light of the commercial ambiance in Venice, would any sane opera producer take a chance and commission an opera from an unknown, female composer who had to date composed works for soprano and continuo or small ensembles? Commissions were awarded to composers with established reputations.

One further element comes into play when we consider the career of Barbara Strozzi: the association of music and sexual freedom.[15] The meetings of the *Unisoni* were derided in an anonymous manuscript of eight satires that circulated in Venice around 1637–1638. Slurs against Strozzi's virtue are prominent, for example: "nice to give away the flower after having dispensed of the fruit," and she is described as being chaste "since as a woman with a liberal upbringing she could pass the time with some lover, yet she nevertheless concentrates all her affection on a castrato."[16] Unlike other parts of Italy, where music-making was held to be an element of the education of a cultured, upper-class woman, music and other arts as well as a generally knowledgeable view of the world were associated with the courtesans who dominated daily life in Venice. Venice was famous for the lively charms of its many courtesans. Their attractions were not limited to sexual pleasures but often included the ability to speak foreign languages, to perform music, or to engage in lively conversation[17]—skills included among those listed by Castiglione as vital for the well-educated young gentleman or woman and that were prominent among the gifts of Barbara Strozzi. Carolyn Raney reports that Strozzi "was clearly the leading singer [at the *Academia degli Unisoni*]—and apparently a seductive attraction in other respects . . . Her deportment at the academy brought her some notoriety,"[18] and Rosand admits that she "may, indeed, have been a courtesan, highly skilled in the art of love as well as music."[19] In 1981 Ellen and David Rosand made a convincing argument for the identification of Bernardo Strozzi's *Female Musician with Viola da Gamba* as Barbara Strozzi. They point out also that various attributes—the pair of musical instruments, music for a duet (thus indicating the subject was waiting for a partner), and certainly not least the voluptuous bared breast—in the painting indicate that Strozzi was indeed a courtesan.[20] Comparison with the familiar portrait of Anna Renzi in her prim striped dress with high neck, elegant broad collar, and prim, controlling cuffs reaching halfway to her elbows, which was first printed in Giulio Strozzi's *Le glorie della signora Anna Renzi romana* of 1644 makes abundantly clear the distinction between proper young lady musician, star of the opera, and pensive but welcoming young Barbara Strozzi.[21]

The question arises again: Why did Barbara Strozzi not sing opera? Why did Strozzi fail to find a position where she could exercise her gifts, as Francesca Caccini had in fact done a generation earlier? Some explanation may lie in the different societal attitudes of northern Italy which was dominated by a court ambiance as opposed to the much more commercial world of Venice. A significant factor also, however, must be their respective performing abilities. While Barbara Strozzi's singing was probably adequate (as evidenced by praise couched in conventional but by no means enthusiastic terms), Caccini was by all accounts a stunning performer—"the best in France" as Henri IV had remarked. Her compositional gifts were a welcome byproduct, but she was taken on at the Medici court as a virtuoso singer, a jewel in the crown of the Medici's musical establishment. Caccini's opera, moreover, was not composed for a commercial opera house that had to please its public or lose money but for a court occasion, and was in the event so well-received that the Polish prince had it performed in Warsaw three years later. Whereas Strozzi published at least seven, perhaps eight, collections of her music, Caccini seems to have published only two—*Il primo libro delle musiche à una e due voci* (Florence, 1618) and her opera *La liberazione di Ruggiero da l'isola d'Alcina* (Florence, 1625). We should note also that these two women who had enjoyed many similar advantages were regarded quite differently: whereas Francesca Caccini was consistently respected personally and professionally, Barbara Strozzi suffered insidious slurs attacking her behavior. Significantly, however, these slurs appeared in 1637 and 1638, i.e., before the birth (1641) of her son, and presumably before she had entered upon a stable relationship with a single lover.

Was she indeed a courtesan? Perhaps she had been educated with this goal in mind: courtesans played a significant and well-paid role in Venetian life. At the end of the sixteenth-century, an enterprising citizen collected names and addresses into a book, documenting the presence of 11,654 courtesans in a city with a population that fluctuated between 100,000 and 150,000.[22] If this had been her intended career, she seems to have departed from that track and settled into a modestly respectable life of caring for children, composing and publishing her music, and handling financial matters with a capable hand—or being led to do so, perhaps by Vidman? Did Vidman supply the capital to initiate her financial dealings? Did the Vidman family assist her and her children after his death? We know that Vidman's widow paid the convent dowries for Isabella and Laura Strozzi—was there continued similar support, or was this an instruction left in a secret codicil by Vidman himself? Questions about Strozzi continue to multiply. We can be grateful to the two scholars, Ellen Rosand and Beth Glixon, who have brought to light so much information about her life and career. Although Glixon's work has markedly altered the portrait given earlier by Rosand, the image continues to be that of an enterprising, resourceful woman who exploited as well as possible the world available to her. We can be grateful also for Strozzi's fortitude and determination in seeing so much of her music into print, eight volumes of arias, madrigals, and cantatas. In fact she published more cantatas than any other seventeenth-century composer, male or female, and, as we have seen, her works appeared alongside those of the best-known composers of her day.

Timeline

1619, Aug	Barbara Strozzi (or Valle?) born, Venice, to Isabella Griega and Giulio Strozzi (unmarried)
1634	Barbara singing at private gatherings in home of G. Strozzi
1637	G. Strozzi founded *Le Veglie de' Signori Unisoni,* musical academy, met in his home
1638	Using name of Strozzi, as the "figliuola elettiva" of G. Strozzi
1640	Authorized father to collect interest from her government investments; again in Nov 1642, again in 1649
c. 1640?	Before 1644, portrait of Barbara? painted by Bernardo Strozzi
c. 1641	Son Giulio Pietro born
1642, Nov	Lent 2,000 ducats to Giovanni Paolo Vidman (friend of G. Strozzi, dedicatee of his libretto *La finta pazza,* probably B. Strozzi's lover, father of at least three of her children)
c. 1642	Daughter Isabella born
1644	*Il primo de' madrigali . . . a due, tre, quattro e cinque voci* (Venice)
c. 1644	Daughter Laura born
1648	G. P. Vidman died; Strozzi's loan repaid with interest amounting to slightly more than 1,145 ducats (9.5 per cent)
Before 1651	Son Massimo born
1651	Op. 2: *Cantate, ariette e duetti* (Venice)
1651, Dec	Letter to Doge, requesting exemption from war tax; refers to four children and aged mother; refers to interest from government mint, government holdings of c. 2,400 ducats, no property
1652, 31 Mar	Giulio Strozzi died
1652	Authorized Antonio Peruzzi to collect her interest from investments; again in 1657 and 1661
1653, Feb	Lent 200 ducats at 6 per cent (= 12 ducats/year) to Sforza Bissari
1654	Op. 3: *Cantate ariete a una, due e tre voci* (Venice)
1654	Loan to Bissari increased to 400 ducats, interest of 24 ducats/year Loan repaid in installments: 1670, 1674, 1677; total interest, c. 507 ducats
1655	Op. 5: *Sacri musicali affetti* (Venice)
1656	Compositions included in Marcesso's collection of motets and Tonalli's anthology of arias
1656	Lent 150 ducats at 5.5 per cent to Ostilio Bissari
1656, Jul	Daughters Isabella and Laura into convent, spiritual dowry paid by Camilla Grotta, widow of G. P. Vidman (their probable father)
1657	Op. 6: *Ariette a voce sola* (Venice)
1657, 1 Jan	Daughter Isabella died in convent
1659	Op. 7: *Diporti di Euterpe overo cantate & ariette a voce sola* (Venice)

1659, 12 Aug	Daughter Laura took nun's habit and name of Sister Lodovica
1659, Nov	Lent 250 ducats at c. 5 per cent interest to Chiara Priuli, widowed mother of Pietro Delfin, poet of texts in Strozzi's Op. 7
1661, 30 Mar	Daughter Laura (Sister Lodovica Strozzi) took final vows
1662	Son Massimo took vows as monk in Servite order, monastery of Santo Steffano in Belluno; took name of Giovanni Paolo, name of his father?
1663	Authorized Emilio Piatti to collect her interest from investments
1664	Op. 8: *Arie* (Venice)
1672	Martino Vidman's last will and testament, 18 Jul, annuities to Sister Lodovica and Giulio Pietro
	Sister Lodovica's name appears, 20 Jul, on convent list as Lodovica Vidman
1677, 11 Nov	Barbara Strozzi died, Padua

Bibliography

Comprehensive treatment of Barbara Strozzi including information about the context in which she lived and worked is provided in an article by Ellen Rosand, "Barbara Strozzi, *virtuosissima cantatrice*: The Composer's Voice," *Journal of the American Musicological Society* 31 (1978): 241–81. The entry in *New Grove* by Carolyn Raney is quite short and casts what may be unfair aspersions on Strozzi's deportment, an issue that is dealt with in a more even-handed fashion by Rosand, whose 1986 essay, "The Voice of Barbara Strozzi" (in *Women Making Music*) focuses on the qualities of Strozzi's voice. Two articles in 1997 and 1999 by Beth Glixon provide important new evidence about Strozzi's life. Three important primary sources in Italian listed in the *New Grove* entry—*Veglie de'Signori Unisoni* (Venice, 1638), *Satire, e altre raccolte per l'Accademia degli Unisoni in casa di Giulio Strozzi,* and *Le glorie degli Incogniti* (Venice, 1647)—are unfortunately not available in print.

The entry for Barbara Strozzi in *Grove Music Online* by Rosand and Glixon takes into account the new findings about Strozzi's life. Information about Strozzi's publications is provided by Rosand's 1978 essay; the entry in *Grove Music Online* lists anthologies in which her work can be found. A useful contemporary source for information about the social and cultural life of Venice in the seventeenth century is John Evelyn's diary.

Works about Strozzi

Glixon, Beth. "New Light on the Life and Career of Barbara Strozzi." *Musical Quarterly* 81 (1997): 311–35.

_____. "More on the Life and Death of Barbara Strozzi." *Musical Quarterly* 83 (1999): 134–41.

The two articles by Beth Glixon are based on archival research in Venice and give a radically revised picture of Strozzi's life.

Rosand, Ellen. "Barbara Strozzi, *virtuosissima cantatrice*: The Composer's Voice." *Journal of the American Musicological Society* 31 (1978): 241–81.

_____. "The Voice of Barbara Strozzi." In *Women Making Music: The Western Art Tradition, 1150–1950.* Edited by Jane Bowers and Judith Tick. Urbana and Chicago: University of Illinois Press, 1986.

Rosand was the first to present a study of Strozzi's life, her career, and her compositional style. Although Glixon's work has necessarily changed our view of Strozzi, it does not disagree with Rosand's analysis of the singer and composer.

Rosand, Ellen, and David Rosand. "Barbara di Santa Sofia and Il Prete Genovese: On the Identity of a Portrait by Bernardo Strozzi." *Art Bulletin* 63 (1981): 249–58.

This very interesting essay builds on Rosand's earlier work with Strozzi and convincingly identifies the portrait by Bernardo Strozzi as a portrait of Barbara Strozzi.

General Reference Works

Evelyn, John. *The Diary of John Evelyn.* Edited from the original mss. by William
Bray. 2 vols. New York and London: M. Walter Dunne, Publisher, 1901.
Evelyn's account of his travels through Europe is very informative about the
political, social, and cultural scene. See especially I, 193–207 and 213–14.

Hawkins, Sir John. *A General History of the Science and Practice of Music,* 1776.
Reprint of 1853 edition, New York: Dover Publications, Inc., 1963.
Hawkins's *History* and that of Charles Burney also published in 1776 are the
earliest histories of music in English. Both works include many references to
contemporary composers and performers.

Marshall, Kimberly, ed. *Rediscovering the Muses: Women's Musical Traditions.*
Boston: Northeastern University Press, 1993. See especially the essay by Suzanne
Cusick, "'Thinking from Women's Lives': Francesca Caccini after 1627."

Rosand, Ellen. *Opera in Seventeenth Venice: The Creation of a Genre.* Berkeley:
University of California Press, 1991.

Solie, Ruth A., ed. *Musicology and Difference: Gender and Sexuality in Musical
Scholarship.* Berkeley, Los Angeles and London: University of California Press,
1993. See especially the essay by Suzanne Cusick, "Of Women, Music, and
Power: A Model from Seicento Florence."

Chapter 4

Anna Renzi
(c. 1620 – 1660 or later)

Then, afflicted, you intoned
Your melodious complaints
With your voice divine,
O spurned queen,
And continuing your lament
You forced Love
To burst into tears and sigh.
Well do I know that,
Had the grief been true,
And the dolorous tale,
Hearing your mournful voice,
Your sweet words, your endearing expressions,
Just as they filled our breasts
With pity, ah, well do I know that
Nero would have been rendered humble
and compassionate.

Le glorie della Signora Anna Renzi romana[1]

This description of Anna Renzi's portrayal of Ottavia, the rejected wife, in Monteverdi's *L'Incoronazione di Poppea,* vividly evokes the power of her performance. Often called the first prima donna or diva of opera, Renzi (or Rentia or Renzini) played a significant role in creating the image of the theatrical performer musician.

* * * * *

She first appeared in Venice, at the Teatro Novissimo, in early 1641, in *La finta pazza* by Francesco Sacrati (1605–1650) with libretto by Giulio Strozzi. Venetian audiences were immediately taken by the intensity with which she could express the emotions of her character and communicate them in her singing. Strozzi described precisely and vividly just what was needed in dramatic representation and how Renzi fulfilled these requirements:

The action that gives soul, spirit, and existence to things must be governed by the movements of the body, by gestures, by the face and by the voice, now raising it, now lowering it, becoming enraged and immediately becoming calm again; at times speaking hurriedly, at others slowly, moving the body now in one, now in another direction, drawing in the arms, and extending them, laughing and crying, now with little, now with much agitation of the hands. Our Signora Anna is endowed with such lifelike expression that her responses and speeches seem not memorized but born at the very moment. In sum, she transforms herself completely into the person she represents, and seems now a Thalia full of comic gaiety, now a Melpomene rich in tragic majesty.[2]

The source of the above description is a volume, *Le glorie della signora Anna Renzi,* published in 1644 by the *Accademia degli Incogniti* (see above, pages 31–32), which strongly supported the Teatro Novissimo and functioned sometimes almost as a modern press agent in its advocacy for its chosen causes and personages. Such encomia often celebrated the abilities and virtues of their subjects—similar volumes appeared, for example, in praise of Isabelle Trevisan (Bologna, 1648) or Leonora Baroni (Rome, 1639)—but the descriptions are usually extremely general and vague ("divinamente," celestamente," "soavissimamente"). *Le Glorie . . . Renzi* is refreshingly specific; this very virtue serves further to increase its credibility. Taken in conjunction, moreover, with the poetic account of Renzi's lament quoted at the head of this chapter, it rings true. Strozzi, an experienced librettist and the adopted father of composer-singer Barbara Strozzi (see Chapter III), would have had first-hand knowledge of vocal technique, and thus his analysis of her vocal ability bears special weight:

She has a fluent tongue, smooth pronunciation, not affected, not rapid, a full sonorous voice, not harsh, not hoarse, nor one that offends you with excessive subtlety; which arises from the temperament of the chest and throat, for which good voice much warmth is needed to expand the passages, and enough humidity to soften it and make it tender . . . She has felicitous passages, a lively trill, both double and *rinforzato,* and it has befallen her to have to bear the full weight of an opera no fewer than twenty-six times, repeating it virtually every evening, without losing even a single caret of her theatrical and most perfect voice.[3]

He sets out as well the intellectual requirements for the ideal singing actress:

[F]or the formation of a sublime spirit these things are needed, namely, great intellect, much imagination, and a good memory, as if these three things were not contradictory and did not stand in natural opposition when found in the same subject: all gifts of generous nature, who only rarely knows how to unite these three qualities, as if in a republic, no one holding the majority.[4]

Finally he tells how Renzi prepares her interpretations:

She silently observes the actions of others, and when she is called upon to represent them, helped by her sanguine temperament and bile, which fires her (without which men cannot undertake great things), shows the spirit and valor learned by studying and observing. Whence the heavens were propitious in providing her with such an admirable and singular intelligence.[5]

Renzi took Venice by storm: as Diadamia in *La finta pazza* her performance of the mad scene contributed powerfully to the opera's popularity (it was played twelve times in seventeen days and became immensely popular outside Venice as well; in performances by travelling opera companies, it even reached Paris). Even more important, however, for operatic history, this opera and Renzi's performance established the mad scene as a set piece in opera. The "mad scene" was not a part of general theatrical convention that simply migrated to opera but was a genuinely new convention—one that by the volatile combination of drama and music met immediate acclaim.[6] The 1641 premiere of *Finta pazza* marked the beginning of a trend for inclusion of mad scenes wherever possible. What after all could more ideally provide opportunity for the diva to display simultaneously her histrionic and vocal abilities while also intensely involving the audience? A predecessor of the scene appears in *La finta pazza Licori,* music by Monteverdi, libretto—his first, 1627—by Strozzi, but this work was never produced and was probably not completed.[7] Strozzi's authorship of both librettos suggests that even if he did not create the convention he certainly exploited its possibilities.

Renzi's importance is underscored by the large number of composers who created roles for her; these included her teacher Filiberto Laurenzi, as well as Pietro Andrea Ziani, Giovanni Battista Fusconi, and Monteverdi, all of whom knew her voice and composed specifically for it. The surviving music for four of her roles—Deidamia (Sacrati's *La finta pazza*), Ottavia (Monteverdi's *L'incoronazione di Poppea*), Aretusa (Laurenzi's *La finta savia*), and Damira (Ziani's *Le fortune di Rodope e Damira*) reveals demands for vocal dexterity and flexibility but not for an unusually virtuosic technique[8] (the day of the superstar was soon to come). Renzi's style was one of dramatic intensity, just as described so eloquently by Strozzi in *Le glorie.*

That indefatigable British traveller, John Evelyn, was not overly impressed by Renzi's singing, but his *Diary* sheds interesting light on the social intercourse enjoyed by opera singers and members of the audience. He attended the Teatro Novissimo during Ascension week 1645 where he saw *Ercole in Lidia* with "famous voices, Anna Rencia, a Roman, and reputed the best treble of women; but there was an eunuch who, in my opinion, surpassed her."[9] He heard her again during Carnival week of 1646 and this time invited her to a fish dinner: "Accompanied with an eunuch whom she brought with her, she entertained us with rare music, both of them singing to a harpsichord."[10]

*   *   *   *   *

From the fact that Anna Renzi was referred to consistently as "romana" we may deduce that she came from Rome and may well have been born there. The first mention of her is a report of her singing in operas at the house of the French ambassador in Rome, where she had studied with Laurenzi. Strozzi tells us that she was brought to Venice by Francesco Sacrati specifically to sing Deidamia in his *Finta pazza* the first opera produced in the aptly named new Teatro Novissimo. She was the reigning star at the Novissimo from its first days in 1640 and created a number of roles there. During the season of 1642–1643 she sang Ottavia in Monteverdi's *L'Incoronazione di Poppea* at the Teatro SS Giovanni e Paolo; it was at this theatre that Evelyn heard her in 1645 in *Ercole in Lidia*. Account books for the Teatro S Apollinare show that she sang in the 1654 production of the very successful *Eupatra* (Ziani with librettist Giovanni Faustini).[11] She probably also sang in Genoa in 1653, the same year that she began a continuing relationship with the court in Innsbruck which she visited from October 1653 to August 1654 and from August to December 1655. During both visits she sang in operas by Antonio Cesti (1623–1669); on the second occasion she sang Dorisbe in his *Argia* for a visit by Queen Christina of Sweden. Her last Venetian appearance, so far as is known, was at the S Apollinare in *Le fortune di Rodope e Damira* during the season of 1656–1657.[12]

In June 1645 a wedding contract was drawn up (and registered in Venice) for Renzi and Ruberto (Roberto?) Sabbatini from Rome, who was apparently in the service of the King of Poland. The contract specified financial arrangements and details; there is no evidence, however, that the marriage ever took place, and no one has so far managed to identify Signor Sabbatini.[13] Certainly Renzi continued to perform for the next decade and was successful enough that she could afford to be generous in lending money to colleagues, apparently free of interest. It may be Renzi's death that is referred to in a letter to a Venetian impresario (Marco Faustini) in November 1658, but another possible reference to her in 1660 (by the Venetian agent of the Austrian Archduke) places her at the Innsbruck court in January of that year.[14] The final certain reference to her appears in documents relating to a loan she made in 1656 to Giovanni Battista Riva; the loan was repaid, two and one half years after promised, on 22 January 1660, to Renzi—or to her proxy.[15]

*   *   *   *   *

Anna Renzi truly deserves the title diva, though she seems never to have displayed the sort of temperament understood today by that term. In fact Giulio Strozzi's description of her personal character indicates precisely the opposite: "Signora Anna, of melancholy temperament by nature, is a woman of few words, but those are appropriate, sensible, and worthy for her beautiful sayings."[16]

We have seen that earlier singers such as Laura Peverara or Virginia Ramponi Andreini or Francesca Caccini were connected with a court (Peverara, Caccini) or a troupe (Andreini). Renzi is the first, or at least one of the first, not to be associated with a single patron but rather to lead the life of a modern opera singer in that she contracted to appear in specific operas (many of which were composed for her) in diverse theatres and locations. She apparently never married in spite of the contract with Ruberto Sabbatini, but no mention appears of misconduct or inappropriate behavior (and this is the same city and period during which Barbara Strozzi was rather cruelly attacked; see above, pages 35–36). So although it may be that a link existed between music and sexuality[17]—perhaps especially in Venice—it does not seem always to have come into play.

Anna Renzi created in her career the prototype of the opera prima donna: roles were created for her by the most eminent composers of her time, she was the first to create a type (the madwoman, feigned or real) that was unique to opera,[18] and she was without question a model of an acting singer—as opposed to the singing actor exemplified by Virginia Ramponi Andreini—and an acting singer who was extraordinarily effective dramatically in her portrayal of emotions and of characters. Andreini was widely and frequently praised for her performance as Ariadne in Monteverdi's second opera, *Arianna*; significantly she was especially noted for her singing of the lament, a number that requires great dramatic intensity but is not vocally demanding. Anna Renzi was perhaps the first to combine a finished and from all accounts an excellent if not particularly virtuosic vocal technique with the ability to act.

Timeline

c. 1620	Anna Renzi born, probably in Rome
1640	Sang at French Embassy, Rome (Lucinda, Laurenzi's *Il favorito del principe*)
1641	Sensational debut as Deidamia, Sacrati's *La finta pazza,* Venice
1641–1649	Continued to sing in Venice
1645	Signed agreement to marry Ruberto Sabbatini; no evidence that she did
1649	With G. B. Balbi put on opera *Deidamia* in Florence
1653	In Genoa, probably
1653–1655	Stays of several months at Innsbruck court
1655–1657	Last known performances, Teatro S Apollinare, Venice
1659	Left Venice
1660, Jan	At Innsbruck court?
22 Jan	Loan to G. B. Riva repaid
	No further information

Bibliography

Very little has been written specifically about Anna Renzi. Claudio Sartori's 1968 article is still among the most useful, but such works as Ellen Rosand's *Opera in Seventeenth-Century Venice* are very helpful. Beth L. Glixon and Jonathan E. Glixon contributed useful new information in the 1990s.

Works about Renzi

Glixon, Beth L. "Private Lives of Public Women: Prima Donnas in Mid-Seventeenth-Century Venice." *Music and Letters* 76 (1995): 509–31.
This article gives the most up-to-date information about Renzi's career available other than in *Grove Music Online.*

Glixon, Beth L., and Jonathan E. Glixon. "Marco Faustini and Venetian Opera Production in the 1650s: Recent Archival Discoveries." *Journal of Musicology* 10 (1992): 48–73.

Sartori, Claudio. "La prima diva della lirica italiana: Anna Renzi." *Nuova rivista musicale italiana* 2 (1968): 430–52.
An excellent readily available source of information about Renzi. Even though it is in Italian, the essay amply repays the effort to work through it.

Walker, Thomas. "Renzi [Rentia, Renzini], Anna," *New Grove.*
Brief summary of Renzi's life and work; especially useful for information about her career outside Venice.

Walker, Thomas, and Beth L. Glixon, "Renzi [Rentia, Renzini], Anna," *Grove Music Online.* Updates entry in *New Grove.*

General Reference Works

Evelyn, John. *The Diary of John Evelyn.* Edited from the original mss. by William Bray. 2 vols. New York and London: M. Walter Dunne, Publisher, 1901.

Rosand, Ellen. "Barbara Strozzi: *virtuosissima cantatrice*: The Composer's Voice." *Journal of the American Musicological Society* 31 (1978): 241–81.
Although this essay deals specifically with the career of Strozzi, it includes much useful data about the musical world of Venice in the seventeenth century.

_____. *Opera in Seventeenth-Century Venice: The Creation of a Genre.* Berkeley: University of California Press, 1991.
Provides helpful information about Renzi and her work in Venice together with a brief biographical summary. Excellent bibliography and musical examples.

Tomlinson, Gary. "Twice Bitten, Thrice Shy: Monteverdi's 'finta' *Finta pazza.*" *Journal of the American Musicological Society* 36 (1983): 303–11.

Chapter 5

Marie Le Rochois
(c. 1658 – 9 October 1728)

[T]he greatest performer and the most perfect model for declamation who had appeared on stage . . . Even though she was fairly short, very dark, and looked very ordinary outside of the theater, with eyes close together which were, however, large, full of fire, and capable of expressing all the passions, she effaced all the most beautiful and more attractive actresses when she was on stage . . . She understood marvelously well that which is called the *ritournelle,* which is played while the actress enters and presents herself to the audience, as in pantomime; in the silence, all the feelings and passions should be painted on the performer's face and be seen in her movements, something that great actors and actresses have not often understood. When she would become passionate and sing, one would notice only her on the stage.

Evrard Titon du Tillet, *Le Parnasse françois*[1]

*　*　*　*　*

Titon's impassioned description of Le Rochois on stage fails to say anything specific about the quality of her voice, but instead focuses on elements of great concern to French audiences, who typically despised the lack of realism displayed by Italian opera productions especially as exemplified by the castrato who played the lover in a tessitura as high or higher than his female paramour. It also implies that, at least from the French point of view, many excellent singers scarcely knew what to do with themselves on stage, particularly when waiting for the instruments to end their introductions. Since French opera typically included lengthy instrumental *ritournelles* (preludes, interludes, postludes) and relied heavily on spoken dialogue, stage presence and acting were of prime importance. But Marie Le Rochois was in fact much more than an actress. Titon tells us that she came to Paris to enter the Opéra, and "Lully admitted her for the beauty of her voice."[2] From the few extant descriptions of her performances she brought to the stage not only real and moving acting but also a voice ideally suited to the music drama of her time—which meant the various genres of music drama composed by Jean-Baptiste Lully (1632–1687).

Lully, who started life as Giambattista Lulli, son of a Florentine miller, Laurent di Lulli, came to Paris in 1646 at the age of 14 to serve as a *garçon de chambre* and teach Italian to the king's mistress, Mlle de Montpensier. By virtue of his ability as a violinist and especially because of his prowess as a dancer he very soon had worked his way into the graces of the dance-loving king of France, Louis XIV. In 1653 he was made *Compositeur de la musique instrumentale de la chambre,* in 1661 he was appointed *Surintendant de la musique de la chambre,* and in July 1662 he became *Maître de la musique de la Famille Royale.* A week later he completed his transformation into a Frenchman and further established himself in the French musical scene by marrying the daughter (Madeleine) of Michel Lambert (1610–1696). Lambert, a composer, singer, and singing teacher, had also served Mlle de Montpensier but as a member of her "six violons"; in 1661 he was appointed *Maître de musique de la chambre du Roi.* Through his relationship with the king and by devilishly clever manipulation, Lully by 1672 had obtained the "privilège" of control of the Académies d'Opéra (under the new name of Académie Royale de Musique), and very shortly thereafter by means of various patents and royal orders had gained complete and absolute power over French stage music: no work that was entirely sung could be performed without the express written permission of Lully. Numbers of instruments to be employed, numbers of singers, etc., were all under the control of Lully, and that control was strict and broad: Le Cerf de la Viéville recalled with nostalgia the days under Lully when "the female singers did not have colds for six months of the year, and the male performers were not drunk four days a week."[3]

In Marie Le Rochois Lully had found his ideal singer. During the course of her career she created major roles in a number of his stage works: *Proserpine* (1680), *Persée* (1682), *Armadis* (1684), *Roland* (1685), *Armide* (1686), and *Acis et Galatée* (1686). According to Titon, Lully even "often attributed to her the success of his operas."[4] But it was her performance as Armide in particular that brought her accolades of praise. Le Cerf de la Viéville reported a "shiver" of delight,[5] and Titon singled out what he called "the greatest and most powerful role in all our operas" for particular attention:

And in what rapture we were in the fifth scene of the second act of the same opera, to see the dagger in her hand, ready to pierce the breast of Renaud, as he slept on his bed of grass. Fury animated her face, love seized her heart. Now one, now the other agitated her in turn; pity and tenderness succeeded them in the end, and love finished the victor. What beautiful and true bearing! What movements and different expressions in her eyes and on her face during this monologue of twenty-nine lines . . . One may say that this is the greatest piece in all our opera and the most difficult to deliver well, and it was one in which Mademoiselle Rochois shone the most.

Le Parnasse françois[6]

Once again this quite detailed description omits any mention of her vocal abilities, but the music itself[7] both confirms the attributes so warmly praised and reveals details about her singing. The scene begins with an impressive twenty-bar prelude scored for strings in the rich five-part texture typical of French music and replete with the dramatic dotted rhythms established by Lully as characteristic of the French overture genre.

When Armide (le Rochois) begins singing, the instrumental texture is reduced to continuo accompaniment for the voice. The melody moves by triad or by step within the range of a tenth basically from E above middle C to the G a tenth higher, while the meter changes frequently from common time to triple, as required by the cadence of the text and the emotion of the protagonist. Armide's anguished deliberation over the sleeping body of Renaud enables the actress to reveal the full gamut of her expressive powers. She can move freely with respect to meter and rhythm and yet the voice is comfortably supported by the instruments. The music, from an Italian point of view, is neither recitative—the accompaniment is too full and too rhythmic and the melody has too much shape—nor aria—the accompaniment is purely homophonic with irregular rhythms and the meter constantly changes. But for the French such a passage, as Titon indicates, represents the apex of music-drama. The battle of love and hate that rages in Armide's heart is followed by a twenty-bar ritournelle—during which the singer would have to hold her audience somehow (but we know that Le Rochois excelled at this)—after which she sings a simple dance-type air, in regular triple meter, telling of her surrender to the force of love. Italians would have welcomed the eminently singable tune but wondered at the lack of florid embellishment of the melody which is a straight-forward syllabic setting of the text.

Such music with its rich instrumental writing, the impassioned quasi-recitative monologue, and the simple air embodied the essence of French music drama. But a few voices found it musically unsatisfying—"Our recitative sings too much; our airs not enough" sighed Charles-Henri de Blainville in 1754[8]—and foreign visitors then and later did not know what to make of it. The flutist Johann Joachim Quantz visiting Paris in 1726–27 (i.e., forty years after the 1686 *Armide*) complained: "Their recitatives sing too much and their arias, too little, so that it is not always possible to divine in their operas whether a recitative or an arioso is being heard."[9] The librettist and playwright Carlo Goldoni wrote similarly about his first visit, in 1787, to the Académie Royale:

I waited for the aria . . . The dancers appeared: I thought the act was over, not an aria. I spoke of this to my neighbour who scoffed at me and assured me that there had been six arias in the different scenes which I had just heard. How could this be? I am not deaf; the voice was always accompanied by instruments . . . but I assumed it was all recitative.[10]

James Anthony in his seminal work, *French Baroque Music,* has pointed out that the French air bore no relationship to Italian aria but rather originated in the *airs de cour* of ballets; therefore very often the most melodic passages were actually dance songs (like the one given above). In addition, the dialogue air was much more common than the solo monologue air (which was reserved for moments of great passion, such as the above example from *Armide*); the idea of such exchange between singers in an aria would in itself mislead the innocent Italian visitor who expected arias to be solo numbers with no impolite interruptions.[11]

The dominance by Le Rochois of the French opera stage is stressed though somewhat negatively by Raguenet in his treatise on French and Italian music, *Paralèle des Italiens et des Français* (1702): "If a principal actress, such as La Rochoix [*sic*], should step aside, all France can't afford another to supply her place."[12] It was his English translator who sounded the single sour note with reference to the voice of Le Rochois: "I saw that woman at Paris: she was a good figure enough and had a tolerable voice, but then she was a wretched actress and sang insufferably out of tune."[13] This remark, added to the 1709 English translation, reveals probably as much about the translator's tastes and views on French opera as about her voice. It undoubtedly reflects the preference articulated in Raguenet's essay for Italian opera over French. We can only wonder if it was the sound of sung French with its closed nasality that inspired his "insufferably out of tune." He also would have not heard her since 1698 at the most recent. Comments by the composer André Destouches (1672–1749) about the singing in her last years of Le Rochois's pupil Marie Antier may contribute some understanding of this difference in taste: after complaining that the aging singer's lack of intonation interferes with his pleasure in her "most beautiful voice, of noble quality and fantastic flexibility," he states that "her tendency to sing light music has somewhat diminished the beauty of her trills and takes away that intensity of tone so necessary when expressing terror."[14] That intensity of tone so valued by the French may be precisely what would prove anathema to English and Italian listeners.

Even though Titon fails to tell us much about Le Rochois's actual voice, we have a few statements as to its beauty, the fact that when she sang it was as though she were alone on the stage, and finally the musical testimony of *Armide.* If French opera had other ideals than did Italian, critics were no less demanding—they only required different attributes, and for them sheer beauty of voice could not compensate for indifferent dramatic ability.

*   *   *   *   *

Little is known about Le Rochois's life before 1678. Titon, who gives us the most information about her, names her Marie Rochois, but she is known in later sources as Marie Le Rochois; she occasionally appears as Marthe Le Rochois.[15] She was born of a good family in Caen but was forced to earn a living and therefore sought to enter the Paris Opéra. She may have been among the pupils of Lully's father-in-law Lambert, in which case it was probably through him that she came to the attention of Lully. Le Rochois sang at the Académie Royale as the *première actrice* from 1678 until 1698, but according to Titon it was as Arethuse in Lully's *Proserpine* (1680) that she was first noted. In addition to the roles she created for Lully during his lifetime, she sang in a number of later revivals— Medea in *Thesée* (1688), Cybele in *Atys* (1689), and Hermione in *Cadmus et Hermione* (1690) after his death in 1687 (of gangrene from a wound supposedly caused by striking his foot with his time-keeping stick). She also then created roles in operas by other composers: Thétis in *Thétis et Pélée* (1689) and Lavinia in *Enée et Lavinie* (1690) by Lully's former assistant Pascal Collasse (1649–1749), Dido in *Didon* (1693) and Venus in *Vénus et Adonis* (1697) by Henry Desmarets (1661– 1741), Medea in *Médée* (1693) by Marc-Antoine Charpentier (1643–1704), Ariadne in *Ariane et Bacchus* (1696) by Marin Marais (1656–1728), and Roxane in *L'Europe galante* (1697) by André Campra (1660–1744). Her last role before she retired in 1698 was Isis (shared with a Mlle Desmatins) in *Issy* (1697), a *pastourale-héroïque* by André Cardinal Destouches (1672–1749).

Le Rochois's career lasted until 1698, with a brief hiatus from 1694 to 1696 caused by her mistaken fear that she was losing her voice. In 1698 she retired, and with a pension of 1500 *livres* from the Opéra and a second smaller one from the Duke of Sully she was able to divide her time between a small country estate in Certrouville-sur-Seine and a small apartment in the rue St. Honoré where she maintained a salon frequented by musicians, members of the theatrical professions, and according to Titon "other individuals of spirit and talent" who enjoyed her "amiable society, her knowledge and her good taste." She died in Paris on 9 October 1728.

*   *   *   *   *

Marie Le Rochois's work with Lully, the dominant French composer of the time— virtually the creator of French opera—placed her in a uniquely important position as not only the originator but also the custodian of performance traditions established by composers and singers during the first years of French opera. Her reported generosity in teaching dramatic and vocal techniques ensured the continuance of these traditions on the French operatic stage and was a significant legacy for the next generation.[16]

In retirement, her home became a lively center for music and theatre as well as a locus of her teaching. She is described as being of "strong moral character and untouched by professional jealousy";[17] her career unlike that of her student Marie Antier seems to have been free of questions about her moral behavior. Antier in spite of great success on stage—more than twenty Lully revivals, numerous new roles, *première actrice* in 1720 of the Académie Royale and *musicienne de la chambre du roi* in 1721—foolishly permitted herself the luxury of an affair with Le Riche de La Pouplinière in 1727 and was as a result sequestered in the Convent of Chaillot, though she apparently continued to appear at the Opéra.[18] Le Rochois seems also to have had the wisdom to retire from the stage before there could be any question of faulty intonation (Galliard to the contrary) or other deficiencies associated with aging.

She gladly took on pupils, among the most important of whom were Marie Antier and Françoise Journet, and in this way assured the continuity of the traditions she had done so much to establish in the performance of French opera, traditions that emphasized the dramatic as well as the musical facets of roles. Her success is attested by descriptions of the work of her most important student, Marie Antier (1687–1747), who enjoyed in her turn a thirty-year career during which she sang major roles and continued the Lullian tradition that she had absorbed from her teacher. Fétis's summary, for example, of *Antier's* work: "She was, they say, an excellent actress, and they praise the style in which she played the roles of magicians in the operas of Lully,"[19] testifies to the effectiveness of Le Rochois's teaching and to the power of her legacy with respect to the Lullian tradition. Her effectiveness as a transmitter of the traditions of the earliest French opera is to be coupled with recognition of her achievement as interpreter and creator of Lullian music drama and of the role she thus played in the success of Lully's works—a role, if we may believe Titon du Tillet, that was generously and uncharacteristically admitted by the composer himself.

Timeline

c. 1658	Marie Le Rochois born, Caen, France
1678	Le Rochois in Paris
1678–1698	*Première actrice,* Académie Royale
1680–1686	Created major roles in Lully's operas
1687	Lully died
1688–1698	Sang Lully revivals; major roles in operas by Collasse, Desmarets, Marais, Campra, Destouches
1694–1696	Retired temporarily from stage, due to fear of loss of voice
1698	Retired; divided time between Certrouville-sur-Seine and Paris
1728, 9 Oct	Died in Paris, buried in St. Eustache

Bibliography

Information in English about Marie Le Rochois is scanty, and is essentially limited to the brief entries (both by James R. Anthony) in *New Grove Opera* and *Grove Music Online* and to information gleaned in passing from biographies of Lully and from Anthony's excellent book, *French Baroque Music from Beaujoyeulx to Rameau.* The section by Julie Anne Sadie on France in *Companion to Baroque Music* is quite helpful both in general and with respect to specific musicians of the period.

Works about Le Rochois

All discussions of Le Rochois draw heavily on the excerpts provided in *Source Readings in Music History,* both 1st (Oliver Strunk, ed.) and rev. (Leo Treitler, ed.) editions, from two primary French sources, both difficult to find:

Le Cerf de la Viéville, Jean Laurent, Seigneur de Freneuse. *Comparaison de la musique italienne, et de la musique françoise.* 1705. Reprint, Geneva: Minkoff, 1972.

Titon du Tillet, Evrard. *Le Parnasse françois suivi des remarques sur la poësie et la musique.* 1732–43. Reprint, Geneva: Slatkine reprints, 1971.

General Reference Works

Anthony, James R. *French Baroque Music from Beaujoyeulx to Rameau.* Revised edition. New York: W. W. Norton & Company, 1978.

Fétis, François-Joseph. *Biographies universelle des musiciens et bibliographie de la musique.* 8 vols. Paris: Firmin Didot Frères, 1864.

Raguenet, François. *Paralèle des italiens et des françois, en ce qui regarde la musique et les opéra.* 1702. Reprint (facsimile), Geneva, 1976.

Reilly, Edward R. "Quantz on National Styles in Music," *Musical Quarterly* 49 (1963): 163–87.

Sadie, Julie Anne, comp. and ed. *Companion to Baroque Music.* London: J. M. Dent & Sons Ltd., 1990.

Strunk, Oliver, ed. *Source Readings in Music History.* New York: W. W. Norton & Company, Inc., 1950.

Treitler, Leo, ed. *Source Readings in Music History.* Rev. ed. New York, London: W. W. Norton & Company, 1998.

Chapter 6

Francesca Cuzzoni
(2 April 1696 – 19 June 1778)
Faustina Bordoni
(30 March 1700 – 4 November 1781)

Francesca Cuzzoni and Faustina Bordoni are almost invariably referred to as a pair—a coupling that derives from the rivalry that culminated in their infamous on-stage battle during the 6 June 1727 performance in London of *Astianatte* by Giovanni Bononcini (1670–1747)—a battle delightfully satirized in *The Beggar's Opera* of 1728. Cuzzoni had been a star of George Frederic Handel's Royal Academy opera company since January 1723 and she remained with the company singing leading roles in every opera until it closed in June 1728. Bordoni joined the company in June 1726[1] and also remained until June 1728 (it was her illness in June that brought the company's season to a close). The rivalry made of course good press (its intensity owed in fact a great deal to precisely that press coverage), it undoubtedly sold tickets, it was nourished by the fanatical support of each singer's fans, and it was surely exaggerated since the two divas appeared together quite peaceably in other settings. Moreover the two had worked together before: Bordoni's stage debut was in Venice as Ginevra in Pollarolo's *Ariodante* in 1716; she repeated this role in 1718 with Cuzzoni as Dalinda. Cuzzoni had come to Venice in 1717, having made her stage debut in 1714 in Parma. They appeared together in other operas in Venice, including Gasparini's *Il lamano* and Orlandini's *Nerone* in which Bordoni sang Ottavia to Cuzzoni's Poppaea. Indeed, rivalry aside, the two artists must have complemented each other remarkably well as singers. Contemporary descriptions emphasize not only contrasts of vocal type but also of role and speak of the affective nature of Cuzzoni's pathetic heroines as opposed to the active, passionate characters portrayed by Bordoni in Handel's productions. Interestingly, their roles in Pollarolo's *Ariodante* are rather the reverse: Faustina's talent for dramatic, especially pathetic expression is exploited, particularly in the 1718 production for which Pollarolo added two *recitativi accompagnati*, while Cuzzoni's role has been characterized as "frivolous but good-hearted" with arias that require "graceful singing" and feature "dancelike movement and rhythmic lilt."[2] Similarly in *Nerone* Bordoni portrayed the abandoned wife Ottavia while Cuzzoni played the triumphant seductress Poppea.

The two singers, so well-paired on stage, enjoyed, however, radically different careers. Bordoni continued to flourish after the demise in 1728 of the Royal Academy opera and, after a long and successful career, lived out her days comfortably in Venice with her husband Johann Adolf Hasse (1699–1783) and their daughters. Cuzzoni's career, however, began soon to falter; she parted from her husband Pietro Giuseppe Sandoni, and, after a period of giving poorly received concerts to pay off her debts, is thought to have ended her days in Bologna supporting herself by making buttons.

Francesca Cuzzoni (1696-1778)

In assessing the voices of both Cuzzoni and Bordoni, we are extremely fortunate in having reports not only from the historians Charles Burney and Sir John Hawkins, but from the professional singers/teachers Pier Francesco Tosi (c. 1646–1732) who lived in London from 1693 until near the end of his life and Giambattista Mancini (1714 or 1716–1800), singing master to the Imperial Court in Vienna from 1757.

Tosi in his *Opinioni de' cantori antichi e moderni o sieno osservazioni sopra il canto figurato* (Bologna, 1723) speaks of Cuzzoni's "*Pathetick*," her "delightful soothing *Cantabile* . . . joined with the Sweetness of a fine Voice, a perfect Intonation, Strictness of Time."[3] The old singer, clearly favoring the styles of his youth, names both Cuzzoni and Bordoni as preservers of the tradition, "who with equal Force, in a different Stile, help to keep up the tottering Profession from immediately falling into Ruin."[4]

Mancini is far more specific in his *Pensieri e riflessioni pratiche sopra il canto figurato* (Vienna, 1774):

[Cuzzoni] was gifted with a voice angelic in its clarity and sweetness, and because of the excellence of her style. She sang with a smooth legato; she acquired such a perfect portamento of the voice, united to an equality of the registers, that she not only carried away those who heard her, but also captured their esteem and veneration in the same moment . . . she possessed sufficient agility; the art of leading the voice, of sustaining it, clarifying it, and drawing it back, all with such attention to perfection . . . If she sang a cantabile aria, she did not fail in fitting places to vitalize the singing with rubato, mixing proportionately with mordents, gruppetti, volatinas and perfect trills [this was amended in the edition of 1777 as follows:

pauses and passages executed in varied styles, now legato, now vibrant with trills and mordents; now staccato, now held back, now filled with redoubled volatinas; now with a few leaps tied from the low to the high; and finally by perfect execution she gave perfect attention to everything she undertook; all was done with surprising finish]; all of this together produced admiration and delight. Her voice was so given to exact execution that she never found any obstacle which she did not easily overcome; she used the highest notes with unequalled precision. She was the mistress of perfect intonation; she had the gift of a creative mind, and accurate discernment in making choices; by reason of these her singing was sublime and rare.

Pensieri[5]

In his roster of singers, Mancini places her after Vittoria Tesi (known as Tramontini) and Bordoni.

Charles Burney in his *History of Music* paraphrases Mancini's descriptions of Cuzzoni and refers us in a footnote to "an excellent professor and judge, who not only conversed with her contemporaries in Italy, but frequently heard her himself, before her decline. See *Pensieri e riflessioni pratiche, sopra il canto figurato, di Giambatista Mancini. Maestro di Canto della Corte Imperiale, e Academico Filarmonico.* In Vienna, 1774."[6]

Her appearance seems unfortunately to have detracted from her stage presence. Horace Walpole tells us that "she was short and squat, with a doughy cross face, but fine expression; was not a good actress; dressed ill; and was silly and fantastical."[7] Johann Joachim Quantz (1697–1783) confirmed this judgement, though in somewhat gentler terms, after hearing her in Handel's *Admeto* in 1727:

Cuzzoni had a very agreeable and clear soprano voice, a pure intonation and beautiful *trillo*. Her range extended from middle 'c' to the 'c' above the staff. Her ornamentation did not seem to be artificial due to her nice, pleasant, and light style of delivery, and with its tenderness she won the hearts of her listeners. The *passagien* in the allegros were not done with the greatest facility, but she sang them very fully and pleasantly. Her acting was somewhat cold, and her figure was not too favorable for the theatre.[8]

In other words, her effect on audiences was the result exclusively of her voice, and judging from the exuberance of audience reactions the voice must have been extraordinary. Contemporary descriptions refer to the moving quality of her performances, which frequently left her listeners weeping. Although Quantz found problems in her "passagien," he nevertheless described her singing as "innocent and affecting," and wrote that her graces "took possession of the soul of every auditor, by her tender and touching expression."[9] Quantz specifies Cuzzoni's range as c' to the c''' above the staff, but most accounts give her a b or b-flat above the staff. Steven Larue in his excellent study of Handel's singers and operas for the Royal Academy proposes that in writing for Cuzzoni Handel was writing to the effectiveness of her *sound,* and therefore he gave her long sustained, legato passages often with intense suspensions and dissonances, whereas in writing for Bordoni he unleashed the considerable powers of her virtuosity.[10]

The music composed for Cuzzoni by Handel exploits this capacity of her voice to move the listener as do the fates of the characters she portrayed. Between 1722 and 1726 (when Faustina Bordoni joined the company) she sang the leading roles in the operas produced by the Royal Academy; during this period she created Teofane (*Ottone*, 1723), Emilia (*Flavio*, 1723), Cleopatra (*Giulio Cesare*, 1724), Asteria (*Tamerlano*, 1724), Rodelinda (*Rodelinda*, 1725), and Berenice (*Scipione*, 1726). Already in these parts a certain character was gradually defined for her: most of her heroines are helplessly trapped by fate; her music and her role emphasize the expression of pathos very much in keeping with her natural abilities.[11] In the operas composed after Bordoni joined the company in 1726, Cuzzoni's roles became ever more consistent in their pathetic character and the number of laments she sang in the expression of her sorrows. Larue has pointed up the telling contrast of the passive, despairing Cuzzoni roles with the optimistic, active characters portrayed by Bordoni, a contrast that extended even to the nature of their disguises: Cuzzoni was invariably hidden beneath the costume of a shepherdess, whereas Bordoni was transformed into a man (it is difficult not to see a certain gender stereotyping here; on the other hand such costumes would have ideally suited the rather dumpy figure of Cuzzoni and the taller, leaner shape of Bordoni). Since Quantz's description of Cuzzoni's art would have been drawn from a performance in which she appeared with Bordoni, the pathetic nature of her work would undoubtedly have been emphasized more than it would have before 1726. Although from the early days of opera and art song most composers wrote to the abilities of their singers, Handel here adds the new dimension of writing for the character type of his performer, influenced surely by the dramatic differences in style, vocal agility, and pure sound of Cuzzoni and Bordoni.

*   *   *   *   *

Born in Parma on 2 April 1696 to Angelo and Marini Castelli Cuzzoni, Francesca Cuzzoni studied with Francesco Lanji and made her first known appearance in 1714 in an anonymous opera, *La virtu coronata, o il Fernando*. During the season of 1716–1717, she sang in Bologna in operas by Bassani, Buini, Gasparini, and Orlandini; the following season she was serving as "virtuosa di camera" to Grand Princess Violante of Tuscany and singing at Florence, Siena, Mantua, and Genoa, in operas by Orlandini, Pollarolo, and Vivaldi (*Scanderbeg*). In 1718 she made her debut in Venice as Dalinda in Pollarolo's *Ariodante* with Faustina Bordoni as Ginevra. This was the first of several performances with her future rival during the next few years in Venice, which included a production of Orlandini's *Nerone* with Cuzzoni as Poppea and Bordoni as Octavia.

Pietro Giuseppe Sandoni (1685–1748), a composer and harpsichordist living in London, whose improvisations were compared not unfavorably with Handel's, was sent by Handel to fetch Cuzzoni then performing in Venice to be the prima donna of the Royal Academy opera.[12] She arrived in London at the end of 1722, having married Sandoni on the way, and made a debut at the King's Theatre on 12 January 1723 as Teofane in Handel's *Ottone*. Handel and Cuzzoni seem immediately to have had an extremely volatile relationship. Handel's early biographer John Mainwaring (c.1724–11827) gives us the following colorful account of composer and prima donna:

Having one day some words with Cuzzoni on her refusing to sing *Falsa imagine* in OTTONE; Oh! Madame, (said he) je scais bien que Vous êtes une veritable Diablesse: mais je Vous ferai scavoir, moi, que je suis Beelzebub le *Chef* des Diables. [I know quite well that you are a veritable devil, but I will let you discover that I, I am Beelzebub, the chief of devils.]With this he took her up by the waist, and, if she made any more words, swore that he would fling her out of the window. [13]

Cuzzoni's discontent stemmed from the fact that the role had not been composed for her, and that "Falsa imagine" did not include musical material that would display the potential of her voice; in eighteenth-century musical practice these constituted perfectly good grounds to refuse to sing the number. However accurate the anecdote may be, Cuzzoni did sing the aria to sensational response, and thereby established herself as the queen of the Pathetic and of the London scene, unrivalled until the arrival in 1726 of Faustina Bordoni.

After the sad end of Handel's reign at the Royal Academy, both Cuzzoni and Bordoni left London. Cuzzoni returned a few times but never with the same success she had enjoyed during the years with Handel. Over the next twenty years Cuzzoni sang widely throughout western Europe. Immediately following her work with Handel she was invited by Count Kinsky (the Austrian imperial ambassador in London) to sing in Vienna; she was not hired by the opera due to her demand for a salary of 24,000 florins (exorbitant, but not unreasonably high, since in London she had received 2,000 pounds each season plus extra income from benefits and private concerts). During the next decade she was a prominent star throughout Italy—Bologna, Naples, Venice, Florence, Genoa, Turin, singing in operas by Hasse (Bordoni's husband), Porpora, Handel, Veracini, Leo, Caldara, and Sandoni (her husband). She returned to London with Sandoni in April 1734 to sing in the Opera of the Nobility (the rival of Handel's present company, the Second Royal Academy); she continued to sing there through the season of 1737 but never as successfully as in the years with Handel.

In 1740 she joined Angelo Mingotti's opera company in Hamburg; in 1742 now separated from Sandoni she was singing in Amsterdam with Giovanni Verocai (a Kapellmeister from Wolfenbüttel), but her career was beginning to falter. By 1749 aging had affected her voice, and she had accumulated debts. Hawkins in his *History* (published in 1776) tells us she was imprisoned for debt in Holland; her jailer permitted her to sing occasionally in the theatre, and thus she was able to pay off her debts. At some point in 1750 she performed in Paris before the French queen; that same year she visited London but was received poorly. Burney heard her concert there on 23 May 1750:

[I] found her voice reduced to a mere thread; indeed her throat was so nearly ossified by age, that all the soft and mellifluous qualities, which had before rendered it so enchanting, were nearly annihilated, in her public performance; though I have been assured by a very good judge, who frequently accompanied her in private, that in a room fine remains of her former grace and sweetness in singing Handel's most celebrated songs . . . were still discoverable.[14]

She appeared in London again in 1751, and seems shortly thereafter (around 1752) to have retired to Bologna, where, says Hawkins, she died, "having experienced the miseries of extreme poverty"[15] on 19 June 1778.

What went wrong? In her prime—from 1722 until around 1740—Cuzzoni was one of the great artists of her day and one of the highest-paid. Yet by 1749 she seems to have been in trouble, with debts, an aging voice, cool reception, and presumably without the protection of husband or other assistance. In 1750 she would have been fifty-four—fairly old still to be singing. Was she profligate with her high earnings? She was notorious from early days for her extravagance. Did her husband profit by her fame and then abandon her? (If so, no censure has adhered to him.) Interestingly, in 1740 he was working in Amsterdam as a keyboard player and composer, while she was in Hamburg. He returned in 1745 to his native Bologna, where in 1748 he died; she retired to the same city around 1752. If the dissolution of their marital status was by mutual consent, it left her nonetheless alone and in need of protection that was apparently not available. The worst of her troubles, however, seem to have come after his death—the imprisonment in 1749 for debts, and the sad failing of her voice. Charles Burney made a distinct effort to visit Bordoni and her husband Hasse in Vienna, but although he was in Bologna in 1770 and visited both Padre Martini and the renowned castrato Farinelli (who according to Burney's *History*[16] had frequently sung with Cuzzoni in Venice during the carnival seasons of 1729 and 1730), he makes no mention of Cuzzoni who must have been living there by that time.

*   *   *   *   *

If Anna Renzi was one of the first prima donnas, that is, a starring leading lady for whom roles were created, Cuzzoni and Bordoni were the first female high sopranos to enjoy the leading roles and adulation given to such male castrato sopranos as Farinelli or Senesino.[17] Stephen Larue has made a convincing case for the importance of their roles in Handel's development as an opera composer.[18] Unlike Margherita Durastanti (*fl*. 1700–1734), Cuzzoni's predecessor at the Royal Academy opera, a good musician who seemed to have been equally comfortable in diverse roles (female and male!) and types of music but seems not to have been spectacular in any particular area, Cuzzoni immediately established her own special character with respect to both role and musical style. Her identity as a singer of the pathetic, a singer with the power to move solely by the intensity of her vocal sound, was impressively strengthened by Handel in the roles he created for her at the Royal Academy, particularly after Faustina Bordoni joined the company. Castrati singers, associated with opera from its very beginnings, dominated the operatic stage from 1650 to 1750, singing the heroic male roles and even, in the Papal states where women were banned from the stage, the female leads. They were widely and enthusiastically admired (except in France) and paid accordingly. Women singers had not, however, enjoyed such recognition. Now, like the great castrati of her day, Cuzzoni was sought after throughout Europe and was paid immensely high sums to perform. The excitement generated by her performances was after all not new; what was new was its creation by a female soprano instead of by a castrato.

Cuzzoni was also among the first as was Bordoni to travel internationally, to appear as a star without a home base; she was hired by the season or by the opera as an independent musician. Hers is a cautionary tale as well: as a star commanding high fees (£2,000 in 1726 would equate to about $400,000 in 2004), she would have earned an immense fortune and could have lived in comfort in her old age. But somehow the money disappeared, and by the time she was fifty she was beset by debts. Hawkins tells us that she was of a "turbulent and obstinate temper"; Burney refers to many stories of her "extravagance and caprice" and concludes that she outlived not only her "talents and powers of pleasing" but also her ability to earn a "subsistence."[19]

Faustina Bordoni (1700–1781)

For Bordoni also, Giambattista Mancini's *Pensieri e riflessioni* provides the most detailed and most precise assessment of her singing.

This singer . . . developed a rare method, consisting of a distinct and purified vocal agility, which she used with incomparable facility . . . Her style of agility was so pleasing because it sounded to the very end, and in a way so new, and above all so difficult, in sustaining a passage with notes in sextolets, or even in triplets, and performing with such exact proportion, without ever slowing down in ascending or descending, giving to each its proportionate coloration, as is exactly necessary for the setting forth of each passage. The perfect and happy execution of this agility is extraordinary . . . Our Faustina Hasse sang with this rare method, so she could not be imitated. Besides this natural excellence of agility she had another kind of agility, accompanying with everything a fast and very solid trill and mordent. She had a perfect intonation, a secure knowledge of spinning forth the tone and sustaining the voice. The refined art of conserving and refreshing the breath, and the excellence of a finished taste. All of these were sublime gifts in her, perfectly mastered, and maintained through assiduous study, by which she attained a facile execution of great perfection, united to the just precepts of the art.

Pensieri[20]

Mancini's report is as interesting for what it tells us about contemporary practice as for what it says about Bordoni. Clearly the precision with which she sang rapid passages and her adherence to tempo, i.e., "without ever slowing down in ascending or descending," were new for the time, were "extraordinary." Her "rare method . . . of vocal agility" which pleased because it "sounded to the very end" would seem to imply that she was singing virtuoso passages in a more sustained manner, i.e., *legato* rather than *staccato,* and that this too was rare in contemporary practice. Other descriptions emphasize her virtuosic agility and her trill as well as her perfect intonation, but only Mancini stresses her capacity for "spinning forth the tone and sustaining" and associates it all with her "art of conserving and refreshing the breath."

Burney in his *History* quoted the following description by the German flutist Johann Jacob Quantz, who heard her with Cuzzoni, during his visit to London in 1727:

Faustina had a *mezzo-soprano* voice, that was less clear than penetrating. Her compass was only from B flat to G in alt; but after this time, she extended its limits downwards. She possessed what the Italians call *un cantar granito*: her execution was articulate and brilliant. She had a fluent tongue for pronouncing words rapidly and distinctly, and a flexible throat for divisions, with so beautiful and quick a shake that she could put it in motion upon short notice, just when she would. The passages might be smooth, or by leaps, or consisting of iterations of the same tone, their execution was equally easy to her as to any instrument whatever. She was doubtless the first who introduced, with success, a swift repetition of the same tone. She sung *adagios* with great passion and expression, but was not equally successful, if such deep sorrow were to be impressed on the hearer, as might require dragging, sliding, or notes of syncopation, and *tempo rubato*.[21]

Quantz's appraisal of Bordoni's communication of deep sorrow reminds us that this was precisely the area of Cuzzoni's greatest gift and confirms the sense that these two singers complemented each other so wonderfully. His reference to her "articulate and brilliant" execution, the "beautiful and quick" trill that could be introduced at any instant, and above all his comparison of her passage work with that produced by an instrument reinforce the vocalist Mancini's assessment from the view of an instrumentalist. Quantz continues:

She had a very happy memory in arbitrary changes and embellishments, and a clear and quick judgment in giving to words their full power and expression. In her action she was very happy; and as she perfectly possessed that flexibility of muscles and features, which constitutes face-playing, she succeeded equally well in furious, amorous, and tender parts: in short, she was born for singing and acting.[22]

The remainder of Quantz's description confirms contemporary reports that Bordoni was indeed a finished singer and a good actress. It is also important to remember that he was experiencing Bordoni's work in tandem with that of Cuzzoni; it is precisely the area in which Cuzzoni excelled that he faults, however gently, Bordoni. Moreover Quantz was describing a performance of Handel's *Admetus*, which had been composed specifically for the two women and therefore emphasized their respective strengths.[23] Charles Burney also gives us two amusing comments about performances of the same opera: while Cuzzoni was singing her aria "Sen vola," which ends the first act, a man in the gallery cried out: "D—n her! she has got a nest of nightingales in her belly";[24] in a libretto in Burney's possession, the original owner, Lady Cowper, had written next to Bordoni's name, "she is the d—l of a singer."[25]

Remarks about Bordoni's technical prowess are frequently coupled with references to her good taste. Here a report by a German traveller, Johann Christoph Nemeitz, is of interest:

I heard at the theatre of San [Giovanni] Grisostomo in Venice among others the celebrated Faustina, who always sang the first part of an aria exactly as the composer had written it but at the da capo repeat introduced all kinds of *doublements* and *maniere* without taking the smallest liberties with the rhythm of the accompaniment; so that a composer sometimes finds his arias, in the mouths of their singers, far more beautiful and pleasing than in his own original conception.

Nachlese besonderer Nachrichten von Italien, Leipzig, 1726 [26]

Clearly her ability to sing passage work, even presumably of the most virtuosic nature, and yet adhere to the established tempo or rhythm was somewhat remarkable.

An aria with the notation "Del S. Giuseppe Vignati di Milano—Cantata in detta Citta da Faustina—con li suoi modi scritti come la cantava" was discovered by George Buelow in an early eighteenth-century manuscript (M1500 S28 G5) owned by the Library of Congress in Washington, D.C.[27] The scribe (who Buelow suggests might have been the harpsichordist) has written below the vocal line Bordoni's fully embellished version of the opening section of the aria. The embellished aria accords nicely with the above descriptions of Bordoni's vocal style: frequent, spontaneous trills, frequent repeated pitches often coupled with triplets. Buelow considers Bordoni's embellishments in general "simpler than might have been anticipated," and he was struck by the "self-imposed goal of moderation and simplicity," even in the final cadence which as he says is "certainly without the kind of vocal brilliance usually and perhaps incorrectly associated with all Italian virtuoso singing."[28] He concludes that this aria may well represent an approach different from that of the castrato, which has been generally thought of as the prevailing if not the only manner of singing. It may be a question of different physical abilities—castrato versus female physique—but it may also be a question of taste. This exciting discovery documents Bordoni's artistry in a way that cannot be matched by verbal descriptions.

*   *'   *   *   *

Bordoni was born in Venice on 30 March 1697. Her remarkable gift was apparent very early, and she was taken under the protection of the famed musician brothers Alessandro and Benedetto Marcello (Benedetto authored the satirical *Il teatro alla moda,* Venice, c. 1720). She studied singing with Michelangelo Gasparini (possibly a brother of the composer Francesco Gasparini with whom Benedetto Marcello had studied). Her debut took place in Venice in 1716, in Carlo Francesco Pollarolo's *Ariodante,* an opera in which she would appear with Cuzzoni in 1718 again in Venice. Differences in the music for the 1716 and 1718 productions provide evidence that during the intervening two years Faustina made marked advances in her technique and her dramatic power, and even expanded the range of her voice.[29] She sang mainly in Italy—Venice, Reggio, Modena, Bologna, Naples, Florence, Parma—until 1725, with occasional appearances in Munich during the 1720s; she had great success in Vienna during the season of 1725–1726 where she sang in operas by Caldara, Fux, and others. In the spring of 1726 she joined Handel's Royal Academy opera company and continued there until the summer of 1728. Her London debut was as Roxana in Handel's *Alessandro,* with Cuzzoni and the castrato Francesco Bernardi known as Senesino singing the other main roles. The rivalry that fomented between Bordoni and Cuzzoni erupted into the infamous nasty on-stage fight on 6 June 1727 during a performance in the presence of the Princess of Wales of Bononcini's *Astianatte.* In spite of this—because of this?— both combatants were hired again for the season of 1727–1728, which sadly, however, proved to be the last for this phase of the Royal Academy opera.

Bordoni was now an international star and in demand throughout Europe. In 1730 she married Johann Adolf Hasse and was thereafter closely associated with his operas. In 1731 both were engaged by the Saxon court in Dresden, where Hasse served until 1764 as *maestro di cappella* and Faustina until 1751 as *virtuosa da camera.* Commitment to the Dresden court interfered little with the international careers of either composer or singer; they journeyed frequently to Italy, especially Venice, and to Vienna, even taking up residence in other cities for protracted stays. They also had fairly frequent contact in Dresden with Johann Sebastian Bach (Cantor of St. Thomas's Church and Director of Church Music for the city of Leipzig, 1723–1750). Bach performed on the Silbermann organ at St. Sophia's Church in Dresden on the afternoon of 14 September 1731, as we are told "in the presence of all the Court musicians and virtuosos."[30] Bach's recital took place the day after the premiere of Hasse's opera *Cleofide* in which Faustina had made her Dresden debut and which Bach surely attended; Bach's oldest son Wilhelm Friedemann was organist at St. Sophia's Church from 1733 to 1746. In January 1742 Frederick the Great of Prussia in Dresden to discuss continuation of the "first Silesian War," heard Hasse's *Lucio Papirio* with Faustina as Papiria, and was "enchanted" by her and by the music.[31] Thereafter Hasse's operas were often performed in Berlin, and Frederick seems to have been a not infrequent visitor to the Dresden court, drawn there by the music as well as by demands of his Silesian battles. Although Faustina retired in 1751 from her position at the Dresden court, she retained the title and the salary until 1763, when Hasse's appointment at the court ended. Burney lists her still in 1756 as a singer at the Dresden court. No actual mention of her singing after 1751 was known, however, until recently when a musicologist spotted her listed as *prima buffa* for a production during Carnival 1758 of *Il filosofo di campagna* (Galuppi/Goldoni) in Faenza, Italy. Welcome though it is, this new information raises far more questions than it answers. Why would she have been singing the *buffa* not the *seria* role? Was it as a favor to the sponsoring aristocrats, the Accademia dei Remoti? Did she take it on as a lark? Or simply to show that she, the great *seria* artist of the 1730s, could do it? Was she considered incapable of singing the *seria* role (which was sung by Francesca Dondini)?[32] When Burney visited the couple in Vienna fourteen years later in 1772, Madame Bordoni-Hasse responded to his request that she sing: "Ah non posso. Ho perduto tutti le mie facoltà." (Ah, no. I've lost all my ability.)[33]

The couple, to whom daughters had been born in 1732 and 1734, lived in Vienna from 1763 until 1773; it was here that Burney visited them twice during his 1772 tour and remarked on the singing abilities of both daughters. In 1773 the family moved to Venice where Bordoni died on 4 November 1781 and Hasse on 16 December 1783.

*   *   *   *   *

Like Cuzzoni, Bordoni was among the first women to achieve international star status—on a par with the most famed castrati of her time. She is also one of the very few stars, male or female, to have been known generally by her first name alone and the only star in classical music: examples that come to mind include Cher, Madonna, Elvis, and perhaps a few others such as Ella or Woody, but none from any area of classical music let alone opera. There are for example no entries for Bordoni (or under Hasse) in the index of Burney's history of music; she appears under Faustina and this is the name by which she was referred to in reviews, commentaries, etc., during her lifetime. Sociologically, and perhaps psychologically, this indicates perhaps a degree of popularity and even familiarity not enjoyed by other artists in the discipline. Even after her marriage to Hasse, she continued to be referred to as "Signora Faustina" or "La Faustine" (by the Francophile Frederick the Great). Aside from her stardom, however, contemporary critiques indicate that she really was introducing new levels of technique and new styles of singing. The aria discovered by George Buelow yields much information about her manner of performance, as do the descriptions by such professional musicians as Mancini, Tosi, and Quantz. While Tosi stresses that "the Notes . . . be all articulate in equal Proportion, and moderately distinct, that they be not too much join'd, nor too much mark'd,"[34] Mancini is pleased by the more connected manner that he praises in Faustina's work: her "style of agility was so pleasing because it sounded to the very end, and in a way so new . . . in sustaining a passage . . . without ever slowing down." Mancini also mentions her "accompanying with everything a fast and very solid trill and mordent"[35]—is this a reference to what we would today term vibrato? Certainly of interest is the fact that she used as trills both the two-pitch oscillation and the repetition of a single pitch, which was common practice in the seventeenth century. (Although Quantz believed that Faustina was the originator of this *trillo,* it is described by Giulio Caccini in *Le nuove musiche* of 1602.)[36] Both Cuzzoni and Bordoni are credited with singing in a more sustained style than was apparently general practice of the time. Is this an early manifestation of the *galant* appreciation of the singing line? Does this explain Mancini's claim that Bordoni's style was "new"? And reinforce Buelow's thesis that Faustina's singing was different from the castrato prototype?

Clearly Cuzzoni and Bordoni made a formidable pair on stage. Their infamous on-stage battle may well have resulted from their equally intense and powerful personae, but the rivalry seems to have been more a product of journalistic activity and the passions of their admirers than of real conflict between the women themselves. Before Cuzzoni arrived on the London scene in 1722, the newspapers had prepared the public and Cuzzoni's predecessors (especially Margherita Durastanti) at the Royal Academy opera: "Mrs *Cotsona* [Cuzzoni], an extraordinary Italian Lady . . . has a much finer Voice and more accurate Judgment, than any of her Country Women who have performed on the English Stage."[37] When Bordoni's arrival was imminent in 1726, the papers were actively setting the stage for battle again; the battle is virtually announced by the *London Journal,* 4 September 1725, "Signiora *Faustina,* a famous Italian Lady, is coming over this Winter to rival Signiora Cuzzoni."[38] It was good press; who would want to miss such a competition? (And it must be admitted that Cuzzoni and Bordoni were worthy rivals, unlike Cuzzoni and the capable but not very exciting Durastanti.) From March of 1727 on, pamphlets were distributed to ignite the smoldering embers of rivalry. Quantz describes the atmosphere at a performance that spring of an opera by Bononcini: "The factions were so incensed that one whistled when the other applauded, and vice versa, so that finally the opera had to be suspended for the time being."[39] These were the tensions that finally erupted into the scandalous on-stage battle of the divas on 6 June 1727.

And yet off-stage the singers co-existed rather peacefully. Hawkins reports that the Lady of Sir Robert Walpole would invite both to dinner in his absence and "She was at first distrest to adjust the precedence between them at her table, but their concessions to each other were mutual."[40] They also appeared with the castrato Senesino in a concert at the Crown Tavern on 22 November 1727.[41] The final season, 1727–1728 of the Royal Academy opera, was a triumph with respect to quality of performance and works produced by the composer/director Handel. Sadly, this season featuring an opera company that was certainly among the best to be found, with such singers as Cuzzoni, Bordoni, and Senesino, marked the end of the Royal Academy opera. During the final season, subscriptions expired and were not renewed. The success that year of John Gay's *Beggar's Opera* with its inclusion of an on-stage hair-pulling fight between the two female leads (Polly and Lucy, i.e., Cuzzoni and Bordoni), while probably not the source of the Royal Academy's troubles, certainly did not help. Cuzzoni left for the Continent; when she returned to sing with a different company, the Opera of the Nobility, during the season of 1729–1730 she met with much less success. Bordoni departed a bit later and never returned. Although Bordoni enjoyed a long and profitable career, the peak of Cuzzoni's career may well have been the six years in London with Handel.

The lives and careers of the two international stars contrasted as powerfully as did their presence on stage. Both commenced brilliantly. But whereas Cuzzoni seems to have begun a slow deterioration immediately after the demise of Handel's Royal Academy, Bordoni's career continued for many years. Bordoni married well and perhaps wisely; her husband Johann Adam Hasse was an established, indeed beloved composer of Italian operas, and the two lived out their professional days in relative comfort at the Dresden court and then in retirement in Vienna and finally Venice. Cuzzoni, we remember, committed herself to the composer sent to fetch her from Venice; he may not have been the wastrel of common reports, but after the two separated in 1742, her career declined rapidly. While Cuzzoni's unfortunate marital career may have contributed to her unhappy end, her notorious temper and outrageous extravagance surely also played a role.

Tosi's words make a fitting close to this chapter on Cuzzoni and Bordoni, two of the first female stars of the international world of opera:

[T]wo of the fair Sex, of a Merit superior to all Praise; who with equal Force, in a different Stile, help to keep up the tottering Profession from immediately falling into Ruin. The one is inimitable for a privileg'd Gift of Singing, and for enchanting the World with a prodigious Felicity in executing, and with a singular Brillant, (I know not whether from Nature or Art) which pleases to Excess. The delightful soothing *Cantabile* of the other, joined with the Sweetness of a fine Voice, a perfect Intonation, Strictness of Time, and the rarest Productions of a Genius, are Qualifications as particular and uncommon, as they are difficult to be imitated. The *Pathetick* of the one, and the *Allegro* of the other, are the Qualities the most to be admired respectively in each of them. What a beautiful Mixture would it be, if the Excellence of these two angelick Creatures could be united in one single Person![42]

But, had they been so united, audiences would never have experienced the extraordinary pleasure of witnessing these two complementing artists—and posterity might never have seen at least two great Handel operas composed specifically for the contrasting characters of these two amazing women.

Timeline: Cuzzoni

1696, 2 Apr	Francesca Cuzzoni born, Parma, to Marini Castelli and Angelo Cuzzoni
1714	First known appearance: *La virtu coronata, o Il Fernando* (anon.)
1716–1717	Bologna, operas by Bassani, Buini, Gasparini, Orlandini
1718	Virtuosa di camera, Grand Princess Violante of Tuscany; singing at Florence, Siena, Mantua, Genoa; Venice debut, Pollarolo's *Ariodante,* with Bordoni (first of several operas with Bordoni)
1722	Pietro Giuseppe Sandoni sent from London by Handel to fetch Cuzzoni for his opera company; arrived late 1722, married to Sandoni
1723, 12 Jan	London debut, King's Theatre, Teofane in Handel's *Ottone*
1723–1728	Prima donna of Handel's Royal Academy operas
1726	Faustina Bordoni joined Royal Academy company
1727, 6 Jun	London, fight on stage by Cuzzoni and Bordoni during Bononcini's *Astianatte*
1728	*The Beggar's Opera*, huge success
1728, Jun	Bordoni's illness; close of Royal Academy season and end of company under Handel
1728–1729	Vienna, invited by Count Kinsky (imperial ambassador in London) not hired by opera, due to demand for salary of 24,000 florins (got 2,000 pounds per season in London, plus extras from benefits, private concerts, etc.)
1729	Modena, Venice
1730–1731	Bologna, Naples, Venice, operas by Hasse, Sarro
1731–1732	Venice, Florence, operas by Hasse, Sandoni (her husband)
1733, 1734	Genoa, carnival seasons, with Sandoni
1734, Apr	London, Opera of the Nobility (rival to Handel's company) operas by Porpora, Hasse, Handel, Sandoni, Veracini
1737–1738	Florence, operas by Leo, Caldara
1739	Turin, carnival season, operas by Leo, Arena, huge salary (8,000 lire); Vienna
1740	Hamburg as member of Angelo Mingotti's opera company
1742	Amsterdam with Giovanni Verocai (Kapellmeister from Wolfenbüttel); separated now from Sandoni
1749 on	Debts; voice faltering, aging; spent time in prison for debts, singing engagements to pay them off
1750	Paris, performed before the French queen
1750, 1751	London, visits, received poorly
1752?–1778	Bologna (?), eking out living by making buttons.
1778, 19 Jun	Died, Bologna

Timeline: Bordoni

1700, 30 Mar	Faustina Bordoni born, Venice; taken early under protection of Alessandra and Benedetto Marcello; studied singing with Michelangelo Gasparini
1716	Debut, Venice, in Pollarolo's *Ariodante*
1718	Sang with Cuzzoni, Venice, in *Ariodante* and several other operas
1716–1725	Sang mainly in Italy: Venice, Reggio, Modena, Bologna, Naples, Florence, Parma
1720s	Occasional appearances Munich
1725–1726	Vienna, great success, operas by Caldara, Fux, et al.
1726, spring	London, with Handel's Royal Academy opera company; debut in Handel's *Alessandro*, with Cuzzoni and Senesino
1727, 6 Jun	On-stage fight with Cuzzoni during Bononcini's *Astianatte*
1727–1728	Last season of Royal Academy opera company
1728, Jun	Bordoni ill; opera company closed
1728-c. 1750	Bordoni international star; sang in Italy, Austria, Germany
1730	Married Johann Adolf Hasse
1731	Bordoni and Hasse engaged by Saxon court, Dresden, as *virtuosa da camera* (until 1751) and *maestro di cappella* (until 1763); Bordoni retained title and salary of position until 1763; busy at Dresden court, continued to work and even take up residence in other cities, always, however, returning to Dresden
1732	Daughter born, Cristina? (known as Peppina)
1734	Second daughter born
1742	Frederick the Great of Prussia heard Bordoni singing Hasse's music at Dresden court, with result that Hasse's operas were often performed in Berlin with Bordoni
1763	Hasse-Bordoni family moved to Vienna
1773	Family settled in Venice
1781, 4 Nov	Faustina Bordoni died, Venice
1783, 16 Dec	Johann Adolf Hasse died, Venice

Bibliography

Works about Cuzzoni and Bordoni

Buelow, George J. "A Lesson in Operatic Performance Practice by Madame Faustina Bordoni." In *A Musical Offering: Essays in Honor of Martin Bernstein,* edited by Edward H. Clinkscale and Claire Brook. New York: Pendragon Press, 1977. Fascinating analysis of Bordoni's work from an aria that includes the notation of her embellished version.

Larue, C. Steven. *Handel and His Singers: The Creation of the Royal Academy Operas, 1720–1728.* Oxford: Clarendon Press, 1995. First-rate study of Handel's operas for the singers he worked with during the years of the Royal Academy, 1720–1728. Includes an in-depth, perceptive analysis of the vocal styles and techniques of Cuzzoni and Bordoni, based on the music and roles created for them by Handel. Larue's thesis is that Handel's development as a dramatic composer is directly tied to his work with these two very different *prime donne.*

Millner, Fredrick L. *The Operas of Johann Adolf Hasse.* Studies in Musicology, No. 2. Ann Arbor: UMI Research Press, 1979. Useful brief biography of Hasse and Bordoni after their marriage. Good discussion of Hasse's operas, list of his *Opere serie, Serenate,* and *Intermezzi* plus alphabetical and chronological lists of all operas attributed to him.

Niggli, A[rnold?]. "Faustina Bordoni-Hasse." In *Sammlung musikalischer Vorträge,* edited by Paul Graf Waldersee. Leipzig: Breitkopf und Härtel, 1880. Useful for some primary material (e.g., correspondence between Frederick the Great of Prussia and Count Algarotti) that is otherwise difficult to find; in German. This essay titled "Faustina Bordoni-Hasse" devotes a great deal of attention to Hasse, and is frustratingly silent about Bordoni's performances after she took up residence in Dresden; she is treated as a companion with no mention of her participation (or non-participation) in performances of Hasse's operas in Vienna, Venice, or other Italian cities in these later years.

General Reference Works

Burney, Charles. *A General History of Music: From the Earliest Ages to the Present Period (1789).* 1776. Reprint with critical and historical notes by Frank Mercer, New York: Dover Publications, Inc., 1957. Burney's descriptions of Bordoni and of Cuzzoni in her prime, i.e., during the years with Handel (1722–1728 for Cuzzoni and 1726–1728 for Bordoni) are based on the experience of Johann Joachim Quantz who did indeed hear both singing in the spring of 1727, when Burney was celebrating his first birthday. The frequent citation of the descriptions that appear in Burney's *History* are often misleadingly presented (even by respected musicologists) as stemming from Burney himself, although Burney specifies that his descriptions are based on Quantz's accounts plus the evidence of the arias composed for the two singers. Burney was, however, present in the flesh at Cuzzoni's concert in London in May 1750, when he would have been 24 years old.

Fétis, François-Joseph. *Biographie universelle des musicians et bibliographie générale de la musique.* 8 vols. Paris: Firmin Didot Frères, 1864.

Hawkins, Sir John. *A General History of the Science and Practice of Music.* 1776. Reprint, with introduction by Charles Cudworth, New York: Dover Publications, Inc., 1963.

The descriptions of Cuzzoni's and Bordoni's vocal art in Hawkins's *History* are like Burney based on the accounts of others. Like Burney, however, Hawkins (1719–1789) draws on many accounts that were contemporary with the two singers and that therefore constitute primary sources. Where Burney relies considerably on Quantz's accounts, Hawkins cites Riccoboni's accounts of theatres in Europe.

Mancini, Giambattista. *Practical Reflections on Figured Singing,* (*Pensieri e riflessioni pratiche sopra il canto figurato*), editions of 1774 and 1777 compared, translated, and edited by Edward Foreman. Masterworks on Singing, Vol. VII. Champaign, Ill.: Pro Musica Press, 1967.

Very helpful, technical descriptions of vocal practice during early and middle of eighteenth century. Mancini, born in Ascoli in 1716, died in Vienna on January 1800. He had studied with Leonardo Leo, Antonio Bernacchi, and Padre Martini, and was invited by Maria Theresia in 1757 to serve as singing master to the Imperial court in Vienna; he received the title of *Kammermusikus* in 1758. He had been active in Germany and Italy as a singer and singing teacher (for which he was better known), and would thus have had first-hand knowledge of the singing of Bordoni and Cuzzoni. In addition, he was active in Vienna during the years, 1763–1773, of Bordoni's and Hasse's residence there.

Quantz, Johann Joachim. "The Life of Herr Johann Joachim Quantz, as Sketched by Himself." In *Forgotten Musicians,* edited by Paul Nettl. New York: Greenwood Press, 1969.

This is a translation of the original printed in F. W. Marpurg, *Historisch-Kritische Beyträge zur Aufnahme der Musik,* i (Berlin: Johann Jacob Schützens, 1755; facsimile, Hildesheim: Georg Olms, 1970) from which Burney drew his information.

Sadie, Julie Anne, comp., ed. *Companion to Baroque Music.* London: J. M. Dent & Sons Ltd., 1990.

A very useful general compendium of information about performers and composers during the Baroque age. The first and most extensive section, "Places and People," is organized by country or region; a second section addresses "Forces and Forms"; and the third is devoted to issues of performance practice.

Tosi, Pietro Francesco. *Observations on the Florid Song (Opinioni de' cantori antichi e moderni o sieno osservazioni sopra il canto figurato).* Translated by Johann Ernst Galliard. 2nd ed. London: J. Wilcox, 1743.

Perhaps the most important single source of information about early eighteenth-century vocal practice. Tosi (1646–1732) was a traditionalist and thus speaks with disdain of "modern" degeneration of the art, but he also speaks with the expertise of a trained singer and a renowned performer and teacher. Though getting on in years, he heard both Cuzzoni and Bordoni during their stint with Handel, and is thus another "ear"-witness. Unlike Mancini who refers to Bordoni's style as "new," Tosi considers her with Cuzzoni to be preserving the true traditional art of singing.

Chapter 7

Gertrud Elisabeth Schmähling Mara
(23 February 1749 – 8 January 1833)

Nature favored me with everything that is necessary for a perfect singer, health, strength, a brilliant voice, a wide range, pure intonation, a flexible throat, a vivacious, passionate, feeling character.[1]

Thus Gertrud Schmähling Mara wrote in her Autobiography, which she evidently prepared during the last years of her life in Reval (now Talinn), Estonia. The Autobiography is refreshingly candid and sets forth the events of her quite adventurous life. Although it was written nearly half a century after most of the events she describes, much of what she writes is confirmed by other sources. Certainly this is true of her description of her voice: her own testimony is supported eloquently by Ernst Ludwig Gerber (1746–1819), author of the *Historisch-biographisches Lexicon der Tonkünstler* (1790–1792) and cellist in Johann Adam Hiller's Leipzig orchestra (the Grosses Concert) during the period when Gertrud Schmähling sang with Hiller:

Here [Leipzig] it was that I heard behind my continuo bass the divine singing of this praiseworthy [liebenswürdige] singer and through her found my own joy and satisfaction in my beloved art heightened on every concert day.[2]

Hiller (1728–1804) was a dynamic music director and composer in Leipzig who organized subscription concert series, directed the *Grosses Concert,* and worked energetically at training young musicians, instrumental and vocal alike (in addition to Mara, then Miss Schmähling, he nurtured the talent and career of the singer Corona Schröter). In the 1760s he edited the Leipzig *Wöchentliche Nachrichten,* an invaluable source of information about contemporary musical life, and from 1789 to c. 1800 he served as Cantor of the Leipzig Thomaskirche (the position held by J. S. Bach from 1723 to his death in 1750). Hiller was a powerful force in the musical world of his time and place and played a decisive role in the education and training of the young Gertrud Schmähling.

After two or three years in Leipzig, Gertrud decided she needed to work in Italy. She chose a somewhat circuitous route—Leipzig to Italy via Berlin, where she secured an audition for Frederick the Great in Potsdam. Frederick, the flute-playing king, an admirer of "old Bach," had shown no interest in Miss Schmähling after his ambassador reported that she "sings like a German" (canta come una tedesca). Mara's description in the Autobiography of the audition tells as much about her voice as it does about the event:

I looked through [the bravura aria "Mi parenti, il figlio indegno" from Graun's *Britannicus*], and, as was my habit, took the tempo half again as fast as my predecessor, the "Astroa" had sung. The "Astroa" was famous at that time because she was probably the first who sang difficult passage work, mainly arpeggios; she represented in other words the *non plus ultra*. Since however similar passages had already come my way and in particular I had accustomed my throat to all kinds of styles, I sang this aria . . . half again so fast; the orchestra, not accustomed to such a tempo, had real difficulty keeping up with me. This then made people think of me as a kind of witch. The King seemed to marvel at my competence. The aria was in fact a real test of difficulties, nothing but arpeggios from beginning to end; after that all composers who had to write for me put together the most unthinkable creation they could imagine. I cannot therefore comprehend why everybody has made such a miracle of Catalani's agile throat. I am entirely convinced that I did the passagework much faster than she did, and in fact with expression, shading, and light, of which she knows nothing.[3]

Her journey to Italy ended for the moment in Potsdam; Frederick engaged her immediately and she remained at the Prussian court until 1779. Her Leipzig admirer, Gerber, provided in his biographical lexicon a very specific description of what she sounded like at that time:

Her voice is sparkling, full and resonant, and with an amazing lightness is still so strong, that I heard her in Leipzig sing without exerting the least amount of forcing over choirs with timpani and trumpets, made up of close to fifty singers and players. Her astounding range extends from G with no lines to the three-line E, entirely equal and similarly powerful. Her bright sound stirs the fevers of her listeners and through the tempo, the perfection, and roundness [Runde] of her passage work all are brought to enchantment and astonishment. It is impossible for the listeners, their souls filled with wonder, to listen in silence—a general audible applause regularly interrupts her singing, and the greatest, the most demanding difficulties disappear through the agility with which she performs them. Her special style is in fact the bravura aria. But thanks to her divine talents and her profound insights, she sings rondos and adagios with the greatest charm and sensitivity, and it is remarkable that at the Concert spirituel in Paris she entirely satisified the great expectations of the French through her singing of Naumann's expressive rondo, "Tu m'intendi." She sings German, Italian,

French, and English, each with the utmost clarity and the most excellent accent.

She is not a large person, nor is she a beauty, but because of that has no unattractive character traits. Indeed her splendid heart shines from each of her features, with the result that one is absolutely taken with her at the very first sight.[4]

Mara's self-descriptions reveal a certain hubris as well as a willingness to criticize her fellow singers, but a number of other sources confirm most aspects of her appraisal and of Gerber's enthusiastic descriptions of her vocal powers. Few claimed, on the other hand, that she was much of an actress. She spent much time in London, where she enjoyed great success both on the opera stage and in concert performances. Lord Mount Edgcumbe, whose *Reminiscences* give a vivid account of London theatre and music in the late eighteenth and early nineteenth centuries, had this to say:

Mara's talents as a singer (for she was no actress, and had a bad person for the stage) were of the very first order. Her voice clear, sweet, distinct, was sufficiently powerful, though rather thin, and its agility and flexibility rendered her a most excellent bravura singer, in which style she was unrivalled; but she succeeded equally well in some of Handel's most solemn and pathetic songs, though there appeared to be a want of that feeling in herself, which, nevertheless, she could communicate to her hearers. Her performance in this opera [*Didone*, a pasticcio] was perfect, and gave entire satisfaction.[5]

"Bad person for the stage" probably refers to her lack of stature and her not particularly attractive form (since she had suffered from rickets as a child, it is entirely possible that she had some real physical misalignment). His statement that she was "no actress" may well reflect a recent English demand for genuine, or at least improved, acting in their operas. Singers frequently failed to learn their roles, relying instead on very audible prompters; deep bows acknowledged every burst of applause.[6] Obviously dramatic continuity took second place to the musical aspects of the performance. On the other hand, although inferior acting was still accepted as a frequent companion of fine singing, audiences were beginning to recognize the power of real acting combined with first-rate singing, as we see from the following remarks by an anonymous member of the audience about Mara's 1786 performance of Dido at the King's Theatre:

She . . . is in all respects a far better tragedy Queen than I had expected. For she really plays as well as sings. But I had imagin'd that she w'd merely walk on, sing her song, and then walk off without ever stretching out an arm or kicking up a heel. On the contrary, she was a very Didoish sort of body.[7]

These remarks, coupled with those of Lord Mount Edgcumbe above about the same performance, reveal probably a shift in audience expectations: Mount Edgcumbe, a seasoned and well-traveled connoisseur of opera and theatre in general, demands more in the way of dramatic ability; the words of our anonymous reporter reveal the absence of dramatic effort by most singers and testify at the same time to the fact that Mara was at least conscious of the dramatic demands of opera.

Again and again, Mara is praised for her musical virtues. George Hogarth in his 1838 *Memoirs of the Musical Drama* describes her as a great Italian singer who was not a native of Italy and tells of her "wonderful justness of intonation and facility in taking all sorts of intervals, however unusual and difficult."[8] He includes Charles Burney's description of Mara's prowess at the age of twenty-three:

She began with a very difficult *aria di bravura,* by Traetta, which I had heard before at Mingotti's. She sang it admirably, and fully answered the great ideas I had formed of her abilities, in everything but her voice, which was a little cloudy, and not quite so powerful as I expected. However, she had a slight cold and cough, and complained of indisposition: but with all this her voice was sweetly toned, and she sang perfectly well in tune. She has an excellent shake, a good expression, and a facility of executing and articulating rapid and difficult divisions, that is astonishing. Her second song was a *larghetto,* by Schwanenburg, of Brunswick, which was very pretty in itself; but she made it truly delightful by her taste and expression. She was by no means lavish of graces, but those she used were perfectly suited to the style of the music and idea of the part. After this she sang an *andante,* in the part which she had to practise for the ensuing carnival, in Graun's *Merope*; and in this she acquitted herself with great taste, expression, and propriety."[9]

Burney's assessment is especially telling, for he was a trained musician and had traveled widely through Europe gathering material for his *General History of Music.* He tells in the *History* of hearing Mara sing at Westminster Abbey for "near three thousand of the first people in the kingdom, not only with pleasure, but extacy and rapture."[10] He also reported on her London opera debut in 1786 in the pasticcio opera, *Didone abbandonata,* the same opera attended by Lord Mount Edgcumbe and our anonymous audience member quoted above. Burney, the trained musician, found Mara's performance

so superior to all other performers in the troop, that she seemed a divinity among mortals. The pleasure with which she was heard had a considerable increase from her choice of songs; which being in different styles by Sacchini ["Son regina"], Piccini ["Se il ciel mi divide"], Mortellari ["Ah, non lasciarmi, nò"], and Gazzaniga [a *Scena* in the last act], were all severally encored during the run of the opera; a circumstance, which I never remember to have happened to any other singer.[11]

Burney's remarks are particularly significant, for he was typically sparing with praise and was particular on the matter of pitch and intonation. His approval of her insertion of different arias into the evening's opera reflects the taste of the time for variety and reflects also the nature of the genre—a pasticcio opera.

Hogarth tells us that Mara had great success in several English operas including

The Beggar's Opera, in which she "exhibited the extraordinary versatility of her talents by the exquisite manner in which (notwithstanding her personal disadvantages) she performed the character of *Polly* [in *The Beggar's Opera*] . . . her performances were listened to with unbounded admiration and delight."[12] Mount Edgcumbe on the other hand did not care greatly for her Polly; he tells us that she sang at the Ancient Music and other concerts when she was not at the opera, and she also sang at Covent Garden where he thought she was "rather out of her place. She could not sing ill, but was not exactly suited for the *pretty Polly* of the Beggars' Opera . . ."[13] This is consistent with Mount Edgcumbe's reservations concerning her acting and stage work in general. It would surely have been difficult for Mara, trained to play the tragic heroines of Italian opera, to deal with a role that demands comic and satirical abilities as well as great liveliness of character and physical movement.

The twenty-four-year-old Mozart heard her in 1780 in Munich and was not impressed: "Mara has not had the good fortune to please me. She does too little to equal a Bastardina—(for this is her peculiar style)—and does too much to touch the heart like a Weber—or a sensible singer."[14] It is difficult to understand Mozart's disdain for Mara's singing, since at that time she would have been at the peak of her powers. The reference to Weber is perhaps a clue—did Mozart resent this interloper who threatened to overshadow the abilities of the young soprano Aloysia Weber, who was striving for recognition at the Munich court, and with whom Mozart was very much in love? On the other hand there is little doubt, too, that Madame Mara was of an independent, even arrogant nature—Goethe's friend Carl Friedrich Zelter, the Berlin composer, conductor, and teacher, reported a story of Mara at Oxford haughtily walking "with all the grandeur of *Rodelinda's* self, out of the orchestra, rather than stand up while 'the Hallelujah chorus' was performed."[15] But Zelter also described the extraordinary effect of her singing the aria "Mi paventi il figlio indegno!"

with a voice of tremendous power, and yet with a maternal pathos that forced bitter tears from my eyes every time I heard her. The piece is a regular *bravura* air . . . it was as if a thousand nightingales were straining their throats to warble for revenge— . . . I never beheld any thing grander than her *Queen Rodelinda.* Connoisseurs censured her for want of action in passionate parts. "What!" she used to exclaim, "am I to sing with my hands and legs? I am a singer; and what I cannot do with my voice, I will not do at all."[16]

Mount Edgcumbe echoed these sentiments. Speaking of Mara and the deservedly acclaimed English soprano Elizabeth Billington, he declared:

Both were excellent musicians, thoroughly skilled in their profession; both had voices of uncommon sweetness and agility, particularly suited to the bravura style, and executed to perfection, and with good taste, every thing they sung. But neither was an Italian, and consequently both were deficient in recitative; neither had much feeling or theatrical talent, and they were absolutely null as actresses; therefore they were more calculated to give pleasure in the concert-room than on the stage.[17]

To sum up her vocal attributes: in addition to a range of nearly two octaves (G on the staff to high E) and an extraordinarily facile throat that permitted her to sing just about anything, her pitch and intonation were as close to perfection as mortals can come. Add to that a technique derived from the Italian school and musicianship gained in a long apprenticeship, which included study of repertoire with Hiller and study of music theory with Johann Philipp Kirnberger, and it becomes clear that Mara was one of the outstanding musicians as well as singers of her day. And, as she said, it was her voice that carried the message, not her body or her actions.

*   *   *   *   *

Born 23 February 1749 in Cassel, Gertrud Elisabeth Schmähling was the daughter of a town musician and instrument maker.[18] She suffered from rickets (the "englische Krankheit") and thus did not take part in typical school or play activities with other children but spent a good deal of time in her father's workshop. Intrigued by the instruments, especially the violin, she one day attempted to play it during her father's absence. She was discovered and ordered not to touch the instruments, but temptation was too strong for her; when found at the violin again, she was assigned as punishment to learn to play it. The father's displeasure turned to joy at the talent she displayed for the instrument; she made such rapid progress that by the age of 5 or 6 she was performing in public. In 1755, Gertrud and her father left Cassel on what became a lengthy period of touring interspersed with longer stays in major cities—first the Frankfurt Fair (Messe), then down the Rhein visiting spas for her health and courts for her performances, on to Brabant, Flanders, Rotterdam, Utrecht, Amsterdam, Haarlem, and finally in 1759 London.

Their travels were not wonderfully productive financially, but the pair eked out a living. Fortunately the young Gertrud had a real gift for making friends; thus on several occasions they were assisted both financially and socially. She refers in the Autobiography to two "ladies," one in Antwerp and one in the Hague, whose Italian singing masters gave her lessons briefly in scales and solfège. She was still at this time offering concerts of her violin playing; whether she included singing in these performances is not clear, though she remembers learning a "few little Italian arias." They arrived in London in 1759 and stayed there till 1764—five years marked by struggles for recognition. Although they sought out the dominant figures on the musical scene, Johann Christian Bach (1735–1782), Carl Friedrich Abel (1723–1787), and Felice Giardini (1716–1796), and she prepared a concert with a clavier-playing daughter of Charles Burney (probably the oldest, Esther, born c. 1750), a cellist Cervetto, and another violinist identified only as Byron, success eluded them. In the Autobiography she attributes this to the fact that she was the first such prodigy to attempt a career (it should be remembered that the Mozarts were also not very successful in London during their stay from April 1764 to July of 1765). The Schmähling father and daughter visited various cities—Rochester, Canterbury, Dover, York—and spent some time in Ireland without ever enjoying real success; indeed father Schmähling was imprisoned briefly in Ireland at the behest of a landlord nervous about the bill and again for three months in London in a debtor's prison.

They gained substantially, however, with respect to Gertrud's musical development. During the first years in London, she learned to play the guitar (which she tells us was "a zither fitted with wire strings, which was at that time a fashionable instrument played by all the ladies. A German instrument maker made one which had a deeper bass than usual and was fitted with heavier strings which made it possible for me to produce a beautiful sound; my father bought it for me."[19] She studied with a Portuguese guitarist who taught her to accompany herself on this instrument, even though it was quite different from his own Spanish guitar. She also spent four weeks working with an Italian singer (her biographer Grosheim names Paradisi,[20] but the Autobiography omits a name), who apparently offered the usual but entirely unacceptable terms of apprenticeship. These terms, spelled out in the Autobiography were not unusual for the time: the child at the age of seven or so to be bound over to the teacher, who would provide about three years of instruction; as soon as the young talent was ready, the teacher would arrange engagements and dress the young artist. In return the teacher took all the earnings of the first year, one half of the second, and one quarter of the third, after which the artist, now aged about 13, would be permitted to enjoy all fruits of her or his talent. During the London stay Gertrud abandoned the violin, because "a number of English ladies found it unsuitable for a young girl."[21] She devoted herself now to singing and to the guitar, and her appearances in London and other English cities were henceforth as a singer, both with orchestra and with her guitar alone.

Father and daughter departed England in 1764 (after his release from prison which was facilitated by East Indian friends, Herr and Frau de Brun, now living in Haarlem) and returned sometime during 1765 to Frankfurt and Cassel (where, the Autobiography tells us, Gertrud's mother had died in 1764). During the winter (1765–1766) in Cassel, the young singer missed no opportunity to hear other singers, whether in concert or opera. She attributed her growth as a musician especially to her listening to other artists: "[my] style of singing changed after I had industriously and attentively visited the theatres in Cassel and Braunschweig."[22] It was at this time that Frederick II of Prussia sent his court singer Morelli to hear her; Morelli's report: "ella canta come una tedesca" (she sings like a German) ended Frederick's interest. In 1766 she was engaged as Concert-Sängerin in Leipzig, where she worked with Johann Adam Hiller (1728–1804), music director of the Grosses Concert. In addition to the performances in Leipzig, she was frequently invited to sing at various courts and in other nearby cities such as Dresden and Ludwigslust. Her schooling up till now had been quite haphazard: violin lessons, a few singing lessons from various Italian teachers, clavier and continuo playing with organists in England.

Now in her new, stable situation, she devoted herself to becoming a true artist, working at vocal technique with the aid of a singing manual, her *Singlehre,* by Pier Francesco Tosi,[23] at least four hours each day and studying arias by the best masters. She worked with two language teachers, a German writing instructor [Schreibmeister], and a dance master, and she studied clavier. In addition soon after her engagement as first Concert Singer in Leipzig, she began reading through opera scores with the music director Johann Adam Hiller. He delighted in her ability to sing *prima vista*—more evidence of her early training as a violinist—and spent many evenings with her singing through entire works. Whether he actually gave her vocal instruction is unknown (she denies this vehemently in the Autobiography), but she obviously gained from this highly trained musician not only musical skills but also a vastly expanded repertoire. Nevertheless when the widowed Kurfürstin of Saxony, Marie Antonie, invited her in 1767 to sing a role in the Dresden Opera Theatre, young Gertrud had to confess that she had never sung an opera on stage. The Kurfürstin, a gifted musician and composer, took the young singer in hand and spent hours coaching her on stage movement, manner, declamation, and especially in the art of singing recitative. Posture and gesture she had learned from her dancing master, and she had of course sung arias in concert performances, but she had never acted and had never sung recitative in a dramatic context.

After two years in Leipzig Fräulein Schmähling, decided to go to Italy and Vienna in order to experience first hand the true source of Italian singing. It would seem that she agreed with King Frederick and Morelli about her vocal deficiencies—singing like a German—since her dominant goal in Leipzig had been to acquire mastery of the Italian method as laid out by Tosi. Her projected journey to the south took her to the north through Potsdam where, through the mediation of Frederick II's court Concertmeister Franz Benda (1709–1786) and a court official General Tauenzien, she sang for Frederick (see her description above, page 78). Obviously she no longer sang "come una tedesca" for she was engaged on the spot as court Prima Donna at an annual salary of 3,000 Thaler.

Frederick's affections were divided almost equally between playing war and playing the flute. His court had from the earliest years of his reign enjoyed the presence of the most eminent German musicians of the time: Johann Joachim Quantz (1697–1773), Carl Heinrich Graun (1703/4–1759) and his older brother Johann Gottlieb (1702/3–1771), and Carl Philipp Emanuel Bach (1714–1788). Johann Friedrich Reichardt (1752–1814) was Kapellmeister to the Royal Berlin Opera, and the eminent composer/theoretician Johann Philipp Kirnberger (1721–1783) was in the employ of Frederick's sister, Anna Amalie. Her court was a center of Berlin music making and played an important role in the circulation in manuscript of the music of Johann Sebastian Bach; it was here that the young ambassador from Vienna, Gottfried van Swieten, first encountered the music of J. S. Bach, much of which he had copied and took with him when he returned to Vienna, where he delighted in having his Sunday soirée guests—Franz Josef Haydn,

Wolfgang Amadeus Mozart, Ludwig van Beethoven—perform the keyboard works for him.

The rich musical environment of Berlin must have been stimulating for the new nineteen-year-old Prima Donna. We know that she studied music theory with Kirnberger, and that she sang under Reichardt in whose operas she often appeared, usually, however, singing her own substitute arias instead of the ones he composed. Here also she met the cellist Johann Baptist Mara (1746–1808), whom she married c. 1778 in spite of the great and vehemently expressed displeasure of King Frederick.

In the Autobiography, Mara describes music at the Prussian Court:

The work was very comfortable. Carnaval lasted about six weeks; two operas were produced, each given five times. The personnel consisted of eight persons: *Porporino,* contra-alto and outstanding adagio singer, sixty years old; *Concialini,* soprano and pleasant cantabile singer, probably thirty-six . . . *Grassi,* a moderately good tenor, also three moderately good sopranos. . . . A *seconda Donna* by the name of *Casparini,* sixty years old . . . and I . . . Entry to the opera was free . . . The opera house was so large that the king would have a company from one of his regiments go in the parterre to warm up the house. The king stood with his generals right behind the orchestra and eyed [lorgnirte] us, saying Bravo often.[24]

In spite of the comforts of the Prussian court, the Maras found life there too confining, especially after their marriage. After two unsuccessful attempts to flee were foiled by an adamant and even infuriated Frederick, they finally escaped in 1779, going first to Prague and then to Vienna where Mara was promised protection by Emperor Joseph II and was received by his mother, the aged widow Maria Theresia (died 1780). Madame Mara did not neglect to visit the sixty-five-year old composer, Christoph Willibald Gluck, who sang at her request "a cantata which thanks to his passionate declamation and in spite of his rather rough voice made a powerful impression on me."[25] It was during her journey from Vienna to Paris that Mozart heard her at the Munich court of Elector Karl Theodor and was not "pleased" (see above, page 81). Mozart, in Munich for the completion and première of his opera *Idomeneo, rè di Creta,* reported that when it came time for Madame Mara to sing, her cellist husband crept through the orchestral ranks and tried to displace the usual cellist, Innocenz Danzi. The conductor, Christian Cannabich, told Danzi to keep his place so Herr Mara stood behind him holding his "big fiddle" while his wife sang. Mara herself, according to Mozart, decided not to sing the second part of her aria but neglected to inform the orchestra of this and after the ritornello of the first part just moved away "with her usual *air d'effronterie* to pay respects to their highnesses." At this point Herr Mara attacked the conductor, saying that his wife was complaining about his bad treatment and that it would be the end of Cannabich (which it of course was not). Mozart concludes his lengthy account: "If you only knew these people, you would at once see conceit, arrogance and blushing *effronterie* written on their faces."[26] Father and son Mozart both enjoyed gossip, and were often acid-tongued when describing their colleagues. Nevertheless the story is evidence of the troubling behavior exhibited by Herr Mara early in the marriage, which continued to be a problem until the couple finally separated. Grosheim also tells us that Mara was obnoxious during his wife's performances, was a drunkard, profligate with her money, and unfaithful.[27]

The next decade, 1781–1791, would see Mara's greatest successes. In 1782 she sang at the Paris Concert spirituel where she encountered rivalry with the Portuguese soprano, Luisa Todi (1753–1833), and emerged triumphant; she sang at the French courts in Paris and Versailles and was appointed by Queen Marie Antoinette a *première chanteuse de la Reine* (she had probably brought with her a letter of introduction from the Queen's mother, Empress Maria Theresia). Finally in 1784— after twenty years!—she returned to London where she now was hailed as the foremost singer of the day, both in concert and in opera. She took part in the 1784 Handel Commemoration in Westminster Abbey; she debuted at the King's Theatre in the pasticcio opera *Didone abbandonata* in 1786 (see above, pages 79–80). London remained her base until 1802, but she traveled to Italy in 1788, 1789, and made a lengthy tour in 1791 to Venice, Milan, and Genoa, where she triumphed in spite of local cabals. She describes in the Autobiography the ghastly experience in 1792 of seeing Marie Antoinette being carted through the streets of Paris. (Marie Antoinette was guillotined in 1793, shortly after the execution of Louis XVI.) It was at about this time that her husband's dissolute life became unbearable; in 1792, with the aid of English friends, she bought him off with a lifetime income[28] and never saw him again.

She carried around a portfolio of her own arias and apparently used these whenever possible. This was standard procedure for the time, though she may have exceeded normal practice in her insistence on singing from her private collection. She also seems to have been very careful to pack up her own scores and parts after a performance, thus protecting her musical property. We have observed Charles Burney's pleased response to the variety of musical styles offered in her debut on the London opera stage, but that was in a pasticcio opera (*Didone abbandonata*)—would Burney have been equally delighted if she had introduced a similar number of xenolithic arias into an opera by Handel or Piccinni?

Connoisseurs enthusiastically praised her performances of Handel in concerts. Mozart's first Basilio and Don Curzio (in *Le nozze di Figaro,* Vienna, 1786), the Irish tenor Michael Kelly, who sang with her in Westminster Abbey at the annual Handel Commemoration in 1787, reports that

what made an everlasting impression on me was, the powerful effect produced by Madame Mara, in the sublime recitative, "Sing ye to the Lord, for he hath triumphed gloriously;" [end of *Israel in Egypt*] in that

> Her voice was heard around,
> Loud as a trumpet with a silver sound.

I have often sung with her the recitative tenor part, "And Miriam the Prophetess took a timbrel in her hand"; and never heard her but with increased delight.[29]

Kelly initially got off on the wrong foot with Madame Mara by referring in her presence to Nancy Storace as "the best singer in Europe" without qualifying that he meant "in her line"; they made peace when he courteously provided a pot of porter for her dehydrated friend, the horn player Giovanni Punto (1746–1803, born with the very un-Italian name of Johann Wenzel Stich). Mara subsequently offered to perform for Kelly's benefit evening; he tells us that she "fixed on Mandane, in *Artaxerxes,* and brought the greatest receipt ever known at that house."[30]

Hogarth tells us that Mara's residence in England, 1784–1802, was a period for her of

almost unexampled splendour: in the church, the theatre, and the concert-room, her performances were listened to with unbounded admiration and delight. At the time of her departure from England in 1802, she was in the height of public favour. Her farewell concert produced above seven hundred pounds, and the audience testified their admiration and regret by repeated acclamations.[31]

At some point she had become associated with Charles Florio a flutist, and with him set off in 1802 on a tour that took them to Frankfurt, Gotha, Weimar, Leipzig, Berlin (where she sang the solo in Graun's *Tod Jesu* in the Nikolaikirche for a benefit concert for the widows of royal musicians), Vienna, St. Petersburg, and finally Moscow. Here in 1805 she bought an estate and retired. She should now have been able to enjoy the fruits of a long and successful career, fruits earned through her early performing experiences and through her assiduous study of music. Unfortunately she lost nearly everything in the Moscow fire of 1812 set by the Russians during the siege by Napoleon. Mara and Florio parted in 1815, and she settled in Reval (now Tallinn in Estonia) where she died on 8 January 1833. Sad to say, she made one final "concert" trip in 1819 (at the age of 70!) through Berlin to London where she sang at the King's Theatre but displayed now only what Hogarth described as the "wreck of her once transcendent powers."[32]

*   *   *   *   *

Gertrud Schmähling (or Schmeling) Mara was for some twenty years recognized in Germany, France, and England as the reigning soprano of opera and concert. Gerber called her the "greatest and most splendid of living singers in Germany, Italy, France, and England, i.e., in the world."[33]

Mara attributed her vocal prowess to an extraordinarily flexible throat ("Kehle"), which permitted her great facility and virtuosity. She also enjoyed a remarkably wide range. She believed, and others agreed, that her incomparable trueness of pitch owed much to her early study, indeed her early career, as a violinist. In the autobiography she stressed the importance of studying a string instrument:

I advise every person who wishes to train as a singer to see to it that he or she will learn to play the violin or the violoncello (even if only scales), because how will one otherwise comprehend what a pair of commas too high or too low is than by the movement of the finger? [34]

She elaborated on this in an interview with Richard Bacon, author of *Elements of Vocal Science*:

In a conversation that I [Bacon] lately had with Madame Mara, she assured me that, had she a daughter, she should learn the fiddle before she sang a note. "For," said Madame Mara, "how can you best convey a just notion of slight variations in the pitch of a note? By a fixed instrument? No. By the voice? No. But, by sliding the finger upon the string, you instantly make the most minute variation visibly as well as audibly perceptible."[35]

Clearly Madame Mara's early studies and performance on violin and on guitar were important for the development of an acute ear. But we must add to this her dedication to music and her perseverance in study in areas not then normally part of a singer's training. Her keyboard studies and her early study of thoroughbass (Generalbass) in England, which was then continued with Kirnberger in Berlin, gave her an understanding of more than just the vocal line. She describes herself in around 1763 as being able to read music well, "even if the method was surely not the best and her taste not the finest"; her brilliant voice, pure intonation, and again that "flexible throat" compensated for the lack of method and taste.[36] Referring to Morelli's pronouncement, "she sings like a German," she remarks "He was of course quite right, for where would I have had the opportunity to learn an Italian method (which is the only true one, which all nations, all singers, and all instrumentalists strive to imitate), where did I have the chance to get this?" [37] She *made* the chance to get this by rarely missing an opportunity to hear other singers not only during that winter in Cassel but throughout the early years of her singing career. She seems to have had a real gift for learning from observation, and her early discipline as a violinist probably stood her in good stead. Even though she had only a few actual lessons in singing, she endeavored to profit from every opportunity to improve her musicianship; she remembers in the Autobiography her determination that "persistence and industry" would have to make her into a "true artist," for she would never be satisfied to be just a singer.[38]

Like Mozart, Mara was a prodigy and was much wondered at for her abilities, first as violinist and then as singer and singer with guitar. (Nancy Storace was also touted for her ability to accompany herself on the guitar, an accomplishment that was frequently exploited in her dramatic performances; although Mara did often provide her own accompaniment in the first years of her career, there is no mention that she ever did this in an operatic performance.) The prodigy aspect of her career seems to have been much more effective in Germany than it was in England; similarly the Mozarts found little financial success in England, though the young Wolfgang was marveled at (and even examined carefully by Dr. Daines Barrington, who reported his findings to the London Royal Society in 1769).[39] The breadth of Mara's musical education recalls the training of such musicians as Laura Peverara, Francesca Caccini, Barbara Strozzi. Such an education was not routine in the late eighteenth century; Nannerl Mozart, for example, studied keyboard playing but she received no training in other skills—reading a figured bass, putting harmony to a melody, or even performance on another instrument (by contrast, her brother in addition to systematic study of all compositional skills was trained as a violinist). Mara was not only an excellent violinist in her childhood but expanded her musicianship by keyboard studies, by thoroughbass studies with various organists in England and then with Kirnberger in Berlin, by reading through scores with Hiller in Leipzig, and by the Kurfürstin Marie Antonie's coaching in dramatic music. She was blessed, as she says, with a wide range and an unusually flexible throat, but a great deal of her success stems from her dedicated study of music. She enjoyed little vocal instruction—a few lessons with Domenico Paradies in London perhaps, probably some coaching from Hiller in spite of her denials, perhaps some help from Reichardt in Berlin, and perhaps as well some tips from other singers at the Prussian court, especially Concialini and Porporino. King Frederick's lack of interest in her following Morelli's report in 1766 and his immediate engagement of her when he heard her sing in 1770 indicate that the style of her singing had changed radically. Although she had certainly enjoyed a good measure of success as a "German singer," she herself recognized the need to cultivate the method she called "die einzige wahre" (the only true one) and thus transformed her art of singing. She accomplished this in large part by her own private studies but also by her intense observations of other musicians. This ability and willingness to learn continually was noted also by Gerber, speaking of her musical development during the years (1770–1779) at the Prussian court:

Until then she had been only a great concert singer, in that she performed even those passages that give violinists trouble with an agility [Leichtigkeit] and precision that astounded everyone. But now working alongside Concialini and Porporino she formed herself into an expressive adagio singer and a great actress.[40]

In large part a self-trained musician, Gertrud Mara dominated the world of serious opera from 1780 to around 1800. She was one of the first non-Italian, and non-Italian trained, singers to establish an international (i.e., inter-European) career.

Mara's old friend and admirer Zelter persuaded Germany's greatest poet, Johann Wolfgang von Goethe, to create a poem to mark her eighty-third birthday. This was set to music by Johann Nepomuk Hummel, the court composer in Weimar, and sent to her, with the poem the student Goethe had composed many years before after hearing her sing in Leipzig at the beginning of her career:

For Demoiselle Schmeling after the
Performance of Hasse's *Santa Elena*
Leipzig 1771
Sparkling voice, fresh in spirit—
Purest gift of youth,—
With the queen, you approach
The holy sepulcher.

    There, where all was achieved,
Among the fortunate
Your commanding song
Tore me, most enchanted, asunder.

To Madame Mara
For her joyous Birthday
Weimar 1831
Rich in song was your day of honor
Filling every breast;
I also sang on path and trail,
Cheering my toil and travel.
Near the goal, I think today
Of that time, of that sweetness;
Feel with me, how I rejoice
Greeting you with blessings.[41]

Timeline

1749, 23 Feb	Gertrud Elisabeth Schmähling born, Cassel; suffered as child from "englische Krankheit" (rickets)
1755–1759	With father to Frankfurt Messe, traveled down the Rhein, spas for her health, courts to perform; to Brabant, Flanders, Holland; in Antwerp played, sang, had lessons briefly in scales and solfege with Italian singing master of an unnamed lady; Rotterdam and the Haag, another lady whose Italian singing master taught her scales, solfege, and a few "little Italian arias"; concerts in Leyden, Utrecht, Amsterdam, Haarlem where met new friends Herr and Frau de Brun (from East Indies, now established in Holland) who drew up papers to adopt her in case her father died
1759	London: struggles for recognition; contacts with J. C. Bach, Abel, Giardini; concert with Byron (violin), Cervetto (cello), Burney daughter (clavier), Gertrud violin; studied with Portuguese guitarist Roderigo (guitar, and zither?); studied briefly with Italian singer (Pietro Domenico Paradisi?) but declined to apprentice with him; toured around England: Rochester, Canterbury, Dover, eked out living
1761	Ireland: difficulties, father arrested for inn bills and fear of not paying
1763	England; concert in York, travelled city to city, singing with local organists; studied (in York?) with clavier master, learned continuo playing; by now at age 14 had brilliant voice, pure intonation, performed with orchestra and alone with her guitar
1764	Mother died; father arrested, 3 months in prison for debt; Gertrud sought help from Haarlem friends (de Bruns); tour in Holland, winter in Hague, again clavier study
1765?	Return to Frankfurt and Cassel; Frederick II of Prussia sent court singer Morelli to hear her: "Ella canta come una tedesca"; end of Frederick's interest
1765–1766	Cassel, Göttingen, Braunschweig: Gertrud often to theatre to hear singers
1766	Beginnings of success; consciously altering her German method of singing
1766?	To Leipzig, engaged as Concert-Sängerin Gertrud now c. 17; performed under J. A. Hiller, Leipzig Musikdirector; spent much time with him playing through scores of operas; studies with language teachers, German writing master, clavier and dance masters; learned arias by "the best masters," studied Tosi's *Singlehre*
1767	Called to Dresden by Kurfürstin Marie Antonie to sing in opera

	production; coached by Marie Antonie on stage manner, declamation, singing recitative
1768	Left Leipzig to go to Italy and Vienna to study Italian vocal method and technique
1768?	Potsdam, sang for King Frederick, immediately engaged as court singer; very successful and enriching decade at Potsdam/Berlin court; music theory with Kirnberger; sang, worked with Reichardt; met cellist Johann Baptist Mara (1746–1808), married him against Frederick's will
1779	Fled Prussian court with Mara; eventually given release by Frederick
1779-	Toured, Germany, Holland, Vienna, sang for widowed Empress Maria Theresia, met Gluck; Munich where Mozart heard her
1782-	Paris, Concert spirituel, sang at courts in Paris, Versailles; appointed *première chanteuse de la Reine* by Queen Marie Antoinette
1784	London, triumph, Handel commemoration in Westminster Abbey
1786	Debut King's Theatre in *Didone abbandonata*
1788	Turin, Carnival season, very successful, in spite of cabal by Italian tenor
1789	Venice, more opposition by Italian singers, but ultimate triumph
1790	London, trouble caused by husband's dissolute life
1791	Left London, for Venice, Milan, Genoa, through France to London to "order her life"
1792	Paris; London; bought off husband, never saw him again
1802	Left London, with flutist Charles Florio as travel companion; to Frankfurt, Gotha, Weimar, Leipzig
1803, spring	Berlin, concert for widows of royal musicians, sang solo in Graun's *Tod Jesu* in Nikolaikirche
1804	Vienna and St. Petersburg
1805	Moscow (population of 300,000) where settled, bought house, estate, retired; left impoverished by fire of Moscow
1815	Parted from Florio, settled in Reval (now Tallinn)
1819	Berlin, then London, sang at King's Theatre, no voice left
1821	Cassel: nostalgic visit, grand welcome, met future biographer Grosheim, fests, court visit, Mara now 72
1833, 8 Jan	Gertrud Mara died, nearly 84, in Reval

Bibliography

A major difficulty in finding information about Gertrud Mara is that most of the major resources to date are in German and remain untranslated. The two most helpful and extensive sources of information about her life are the Autobiography discovered after her death, which covers however only to 1793, and the biography published in 1823 by G. C. Grosheim. These sources are complementary if occasionally contradictory.

The chapter devoted to Mara in *Berühmte deutsche Frauen* by A. von Sternberg is marred by a romantic approach and total lack of documentation. *Die Primadonna Friedrichs des Grossen: Roman* by Oskar Anwand (Berlin: Verlag von Rich. Bong, 1930) is self-described as a novel ("Roman") and is worthless as a source of reliable information; its presence in the bibliography for the *New Grove* entry for Mara is difficult to justify. (George Sand's *Consuelo* based on the life of Pauline Viardot and Willa Cather's *The Song of the Lark* founded on the life and career of Olive Fremstadt have at least the virtue that the authors were well acquainted with their subjects, a claim that cannot be made for Anwand's 1930 work.) Valuable data may be culled from the writings of a variety of contemporary and slightly later music connoisseurs and critics such as Charles Burney (1726–1814), Lord Mount Edgcumbe (1764–1839), George Hogarth (1783–1870), and Henry Chorley (1808–1872). The letters exchanged between Leopold and Wolfgang Mozart (Wolfgang encountered Mara in 1780 at the Munich court) are informative as are the accounts in Michael Kelly's ebullient *Reminiscences* (Kelly sang with Mara in England on a number of occasions); Kelly's memories of Mara's singing are vivid, but his memory for dates and events is not always infallible, and his memory failings are compounded by the carelessness of his ghostwriter, Theodore Hook (1788–1841), a professional writer with some knowledge of music. The best edition of the *Reminiscences* is the one prepared by Roger Fiske, published in 1975.

Works about Mara

Mara, Gertrud Elisabeth Schmähling. "Eine Selbstbiographie der Sängerin Gertrud Elisabeth Mara." Published by O. von Riesemann. *Allgemeine Musikalische Zeitung* 10, Nos. 32–39 (1875): no. 32: cols. 497–501; 33: 513–17; 34: 529–35; 35: 545–50; 36: 561–65; 37: 377–82; 38: 593–97; 39: 609–13.
Although written in her old age after she had retired to Reval (now Tallinn) in Estonia, the Autobiography is an extremely useful source of information about Mara's childhood and early training and career. She remarks occasionally on her inability to remember names and she has of course her own bias concerning encounters with patrons and other performers, but the work remains valuable for her discussion of musical as well as vocal training.
Gerber, Ernst Ludwig. "Mara (Elisabeth) Gebohrne Schmehling." In *Historisch-biographisches Lexicon der Tonkünstler.* 4 vols. Leipzig: J. G. I. Breitkopf, 1790–1792.

Gerber's lengthy entry for Madame Mara is particularly valuable as the eye- and ear-witness account of her voice, style, and musicianship by a trained musician (he was cellist in Johann Adam Hiller's Leipzig orchestra; his father Heinrich Nikolaus, had studied with J. S. Bach).

Grosheim, Georg Christoph. *Das Leben der Künstlerin Mara.* Cassel: Luckhardt'schen Hofbuchhandlung, 1823.

This biography, written shortly after Mara's 1821 visit to her hometown of Cassel, was printed during the singer's lifetime. It would be surprising if Grosheim who made her acquaintance during the visit had not sent his biography to her. At any rate his account corresponds fairly well with the *Selbstbiographie* (Autobiography) and is particularly valuable for its first-hand account of her visit to Cassel.

Niggli, A[rnold?]. "Gertrud Elisabeth Mara: Eine deutsche Künstlerin des achtzehnten Jahrhunderts." In *Sammlung musikalischen Vorträge,* edited by Paul Graf Waldersee, vol. 3, 163–209. Leipzig: Breitkopf & Härtel, 1881.

Very helpful biographical and critical discussion of Mara and her career. Based on work of Riesemann (the Autobiography), Grosheim, Gerber, Rochlitz, Sternberg, et al.

Assesses material about Mara: Grosheim and Gerber are reliable sources of information; Rochlitz and Sternberg dwell on anecdotal evidence. Niggli complains that the researcher must penetrate the "schwankende Nebel pikanter Anekdoten" to find the real Mara.

Rochlitz, Friedrich "Gertrud Elisabeth Mara." In *Für Freunde der Tonkunst.* 2nd rev. edition, vol. 1, 48–114. Leipzig: Karl Knobloch, 1830.

Rochlitz gleaned information about Mara's early life in Leipzig from Johann Adam Hiller and in Berlin from Friedrich Nikolai. He himself made her acquaintance in later years. His long essay confirms most of what is found in the Autobiography, the Grosheim biography, and Gerber's entry in the *Lexicon.* It is probably Rochlitz, however, who earned Mara's wrath (expressed in the Autobiography) by stating that she owed much of her musical education to Hiller. As Niggli points out, Rochlitz is prone to the repetition of anecdotes that often descend to little more than gossip.

Sternberg, A. von. "Elisabeth Mara." In *Berühmte deutschen Frauen des 18. Jahrhunderts,* 203–90. Leipzig: F. A. Brockhaus, 1848.

Useful for inclusion of material from early sources (for example, letters to friends) but documentation is not provided, making sources difficult to evaluate. Highly romantic approach to the subject; contradictions demonstrate that Sternberg did not know Mara's Autobiography. The tone is generally very defensive. Sternberg ends his chapter on Mara with a thorough and eloquent description of her vocal powers by a contemporary "Kunstverständiger" (connoisseur of art) whose anonymity, however, detracts from the value of the quote.

General Reference Works
Burney, Charles. *A General History of Music from the Earliest Ages to the Present Period (1789)* 1776–1789. Reprint, with critical and historical notes by Frank Mercer, New York: Dover Publications, Inc., 1957.
All of Burney's writings are characterized by a sharp ear and candid expression of his views on music and musicianship. He heard Mara sing on a number of occasions, on the Continent as well as in London at the first Handel Commemoration in 1784 and in opera performances.
Chorley, Henry Fothergill. *Modern German Music.* 1854. Reprint, New York: Da Capo Press, 1973.
This book provides excellent discussions of Mara's voice, work, and reputation, but clearly Chorley does not speak from personal experience (he would have been 11 in 1819, the date of Mara's last appearance in London).
Gerber, Ernst Ludwig. *Historisch-biographisches Lexicon der Tonkünstler.* Leipzig: J. G. I. Breitkopf, 1790–1792.
Very useful lexicon in German of composers and performers.
Hogarth, George. *Memoirs of the Musical Drama.* London: Richard Bentley, 1838.
Hogarth's *Memoirs* offer detailed descriptions of Mara's work, but it is not clear here that Hogarth is speaking as an eye witness. She departed from England in 1802 when Hogarth would have been nineteen, and even his account of her ill-fated "come-back" London appearance in 1819 leaves ambiguous the question of his actual presence at the event. It is however very useful as a confirmation of earlier accounts and as a measure of how she was regarded in the 1830s when Hogarth was preparing the *Memoirs.*
Kelly, Michael. *Reminiscences of Michael Kelly, of the King's Theatre, and Theatre Royal, Drury Lane.* 1826. Edited with an introduction by Roger Fiske. London: Oxford University Press, 1975.
Kelly's colorful *Reminiscences* present much useful information; his occasional lapses are corrected in the careful explanatory notes provided by the editor.
Mount Edgcumbe, Richard. *Musical Reminiscences of the Earl of Mount Edgcumbe: Containing an Account of the Italian Opera in England from 1773 to 1834.* 4th ed., 1834. Reprint, New York: Da Capo Press, 1973.
Thorough descriptions of concert and operatic performances by a well-educated and sensitive connoisseur of theatrical and concert music, who writes with the authority of knowledge of the London scene and the personal experience of having attended the musical events he describes.

Special Works
Among the several works about the London theatre world of the late eighteenth century which have appeared during the last two decades, the following are particularly informative about Mara:

Fenner, Theodore. *Opera in London: Views of the Press, 1785–1830.* Carbondale and Edwardsville: Southern Illinois University Press, 1994.
Reviews by London papers of performances, with commentary by Fenner.

Fiske, Roger. *English Theatre Music in the Eighteenth Century.* Oxford, New York: Oxford University Press, 1986.

Milhous, Judith, Gabriella Dideriksen, and Robert D. Hume. *The Pantheon Opera and Its Aftermath: 1789–1795.* Vol. 2 of *Italian Opera in Late Eighteenth-Century London.* Oxford: Clarendon Press, 2001.

Price, Curtis, Judith Milhous, and Robert D. Hume. *The King's Theatre, Haymarket: 1778–1791.* Vol. 1 of *Italian Opera in Late Eighteenth-Century London.* Oxford: Clarendon Press, 1995.

Woodfield, Ian. *Opera and Drama in Eighteenth-Century London: The King's Theatre, Garrick and the Business of Performance.* Cambridge: Cambridge University Press, 2001.

Chapter 8

Anna Selina Storace
(27 October 1765 – 24 August 1817)

A most charming and scientific singer. Her person clumsy, her face coarse and ordinary, and yet there is so much enchanting vivacity and . . . so many nameless excellences about her that she always delights whenever she appears.[1]

The above description succinctly summarizes the virtues and faults of Anna Selina Storace, known as Nancy. All accounts agree that her vocal powers were uneven. Her success derived from her magnetic—perhaps even charismatic—stage presence, and from her extraordinary ability to sing in character, an ability that was recognized by audiences and composers alike. Reports of her performances are contradictory: many reviews mention a "roughness" in her voice or a coarseness in voice and manner, but almost all concede that she "sings very well."[2]

The music composed for her by Mozart shows that she could handle the sustained lyric line of an aria such as Susanna's "Deh vieni, non tardar" (*Le nozze di Figaro,* Act IV), but it is not particularly demanding in length or virtuosity. Moreover, this is her only aria in the entire opera, and it comes late when she would have been well warmed up. It is more to the point that she is the central figure in *Figaro,* present from the very first to the very last number, interacting with every other character in the rapid dialogue and comic exchange of the ensembles. Does this tell us that the composer did not entirely trust her with solo numbers? Or rather that he recognized and exploited her comedic talent and her gift for acting in music and wrote to these abilities? We know that Mozart delighted in his opera ensembles and demanded much from his singers in them: consider his words to the aging tenor, Anton Raaff (*Idomeneo* in the eponymous opera of 1780): "As if in a quartet the words should not be spoken much more than sung . . . as far as trios and quartets are concerned, the composer must have a free hand."[3] In Storace he would seem to have found the perfect exponent of his views. Her aria ("Deh vieni, non tardar") in

Figaro also testifies to her acting in music: we are shown her ability to sustain a lyric line while also sustaining the deception that she is singing to the Count when she knows that Figaro is listening; she is in fact singing to Figaro while gently torturing him. Unfortunately Mozart never described her portrayal of Susanna or her actual voice; we have from him only the evidence of her music in that one opera, an aria from his unfinished *Lo sposo deluso,* and the concert aria "Ch'io mi scordi di te." created for her farewell concert in Vienna. This aria, "für Mselle Storace und mich," documents Mozart's respect for Storace as a fellow artist: not only is it tailored to her voice and thus can be read as the description he never verbalized, but it includes a stunning obbligato piano solo, which he himself performed at the farewell concert in late December 1786.[4]

The virtuosity that might be expected from the diva of Vienna was noted at her London debut, 25 April 1787, in Paisiello's *Gli schiavi per amore* (which as *La gare generose* she had sung in Vienna; she played an American Negro slave):

[N]ever did a debut give such earnest of perfection. Her figure petite—yet pleasing—eyes full of fire—features finely formed—a volubility of expression admirably calculated for the recitative of *burletta* [a term for opera buffa sometimes used in English newspapers]—a sweetness and depth of tone, rarely to be met with in a female voice—a delightful shake with the most perfect knowledge of "music's art" sum up the perfections of this new operatical star.[5]

The Morning Chronicle admired her "clear and powerful voice" and her "chaste and pleasing manner," and the "animation" of her acting.[6] The report in the *Times* gives a good sense of the audience's expectations and of Storace's response:

Signora Storace—an old favourite of all the fashionable operatical circles—though new to the English stage, was so evidently overcome by that diffidence, ever the companion of real merit—that she was for some time unable to give utterance to her most exquisite powers— and the symphony was obliged to be repeated—the applause however soon had its proper effect, and she went through her part with that nicety of accent—marked propriety of emphasis—and truth of character—as agreeably to surprise those who expected only fine singing and bad English from the *Signora*—who, though brought up in Italy, is completely English.[7]

Her technical prowess was noted again in December of that year when she sang in Paisiello's *Il re Teodoro*. Especially pleasing was the substitute aria composed for her by her brother Stephen Storace:

Her obligato song, in the second act, of *Care donne che bramate* was executed in style of brilliancy and taste hitherto unparalleled; the rapidity and articulation with which she executed the different arduous and masterly divisions, forced them on the imagination. This song is a charming composition by her brother and was encored *una voce*.[8]

But that same year, 1787, she sang "I know that my Redeemer liveth" (*Messiah*) and "Let the bright seraphim (*Samson*) at the Handel Commemoration Festival in Westminster Abbey to mixed reports: one listener found that her voice "wants the energy and fullness necessary to express the feelings, particularly in so large a place," while both the music historian Charles Burney and the opera connoisseur Lord Mount Edgcumbe believed that a certain harshness of her voice was mitigated by the large space of the Abbey.[9]

All of these remarks support the conviction that she could handle quite impressively virtuosic passages as well as cantabile singing. The agility and beauty of the voice seem, however, to have begun to deteriorate fairly early: although in 1792 the critic for *The Times* exclaimed that "she ran up her divisions with as much ease as the most finished Italian singer that ever trod the stage,"[10] in 1801 when she was just 36 hoarseness was mentioned, and by 1808 the criticisms were pointed—"the imperfection of her voice" and "the cracked voice of Signora Storace [which] destroyed the sweetness of the harmony."[11] Geoffrey Brace, who has written the only full-length biography of Storace, suggests that this early demise of her voice may well be attributable to a lack of solid training in her early years (her first instruction was from her double bass playing father) and to too much public singing at a very early age (8 or 9!). When around 1774 she began studying with the castrato soprano Venanzio Rauzzini, his first action was to forbid her singing in public— but he lifted this restriction in 1776 (she was 11) to permit her appearances in his own opera *Le ali d'amore* at the King's Theatre and to sing with him the following year in some five Lenten oratorio performances at Covent Garden. When Rauzzini left London for Bath in July of 1777, Nancy sang with him a duet he composed specifically for his farewell concert.[12]

Early in her career, singing with the famous castrato Marchesi in Italy, she is reported to have imitated immediately and very accurately his fabulously virtuosic cadenza to the great delight of the audience and the indignation of the castrato. (He demanded that she be fired and she was.)

Some critics found her more vulgar than effective, though they still admitted the power of her presence: "Her person is short and lusty, her complexion very dark. If she inspired amorous sentiments it must be more by her vivacity than her appearance, as her voice, manner and tout ensemble are very coarse."[13] The vulgarity was noted also by Emperor Joseph II of Austria: he wrote of her 1783 performance in Paisiello's *Barbiere di Siviglia* that she "sang her cantabile aria very nicely and, although she tried to use Adamberger's technique at times, her innate vulgarity always prevailed."[14] Her figure was not especially attractive and indeed came in frequently for rather unflattering comments: Emperor Joseph on hearing that she was pregnant remarked: "Storace has the advantage that she is the size of a pregnant woman most of the year round, so the difference is not going to be easily noticed."[15] Count Johann Karl von Zinzendorf, that indefatigable Vienna operagoer and diarist, on the other hand, was pleased with every aspect of her appearance and performance in Sarti's *Fra i due litiganti il terzo gode* which he heard "with exquisite pleasure.

Storace sang like an angel. Her lovely eyes, her snow-white neck, her fine bosom, her fresh mouth made a charming effect."[16]

Even the unflattering descriptions of her physical appearance are matched by praise for the power of her acting, indeed of her singing acting. Emperor Joseph, writing to his ambassador in Paris, Comte de Mercy-Argenteau, expressed his recognition of her special effectiveness on stage:

The lady bearing this present letter is La Storace who has been our leading singer at the opera buffa for several years. She wishes to be presented to the Queen and asked me for a letter to this effect; but I didn't think it suitable to entrust one to her, I preferred to send you the enclosed: I beg you to pass this on to the Queen. If she wishes to listen to her sing, I think she will be pleased with her skill and technique, although she isn't as outstanding singing to the keyboard as she is on the stage, where she acquits herself much more worthily.[17]

She had a remarkable combination of vocal virtuosity combined with excellent diction, which served her well in serious opera and made her an outstanding success in the comic, as attested by the following: "Her vocal powers and good taste prove her to have very few superiors in the serious style; and in the comic she confessedly stands unrivalled";[18] she "delivered the dialogue very articulately, and the humour lost not its points: her first song showed embarrassment, but the *acting* in it was good;—her second was charmingly sung."[19] She was also not above upstaging her colleagues on occasion, according to the *Chronicle*: "The enchanting Storace was beating time with her garden clippers" during another singer's aria.[20]

Probably her happiest and most successful years in England were those spent from 1789 to 1796 at the Drury Lane Theatre, where her brother Stephen's operas were regularly produced. Here she performed regularly as part of an ensemble that included Michael Kelly (Mozart's original Basilio and Curzio), Anna Maria Crouch, and John Bannister. Crouch and Kelly typically sang the serious, high-minded roles; Storace and Bannister were the comic characters. Not only was the ensemble highly satisfactory from a musical point of view, but reports agree that both Storace and Bannister had a particular affinity for the comic and that they worked together incomparably well. John Adolphus writes in his *Memoirs of John Bannister* that:

In [*The Haunted Tower*] Bannister and Storace supported each other, and commenced a career which was long maintained to the great delight of the public . . . In Adela, Storace was Bannister in petticoats. The same *naïvete* the same bluntness of manner, the same appearance of integrity and warmth of affection, distinguished both. They shared, and they well deserved, the meed of fervid applause continued during two successive seasons.[21]

His words confirm the evidence of Storace's role as Susanna in *Figaro* that her genius lay in acting in music, particularly in comic or witty roles, and that she was extraordinarily capable of communicating the dramatic sense of the music. Count Zinzendorf had earlier noted her extraordinary ability to communicate with the audience, which he found to be on occasion even too powerful: "I thought this delicate, expressive duet ["Pace caro sposo," in Martin's *Una cosa rara*] between Mandini and Storace was quite dangerous for young ladies and gentlemen in the audience. You need some maturity to be able to see it done without being over stimulated."[22]

Zinzendorf's appraisal of her communicative powers is all the more telling when we consider that Storace was singing Italian to a German-speaking audience. Mount Edgcumbe sums up quite well the positive and negative aspects of her singing and musicianship:

[Storace] was never heard in this country till her reputation as the first buffa of her time was fully established. She had a harshness in her countenance, a clumsiness of figure, a coarseness in her voice, and a vulgarity of manner, that totally unfitted her for the serious opera, which she never attempted. But her knowledge of music was equal to any thing, and she could sing well in every style, as was proved by her performances in Westminster Abbey, where she sung with the best effect: in my opinion she rarely appeared to greater advantage, for in that space the harsh part of her voice was lost, while its power and clearness filled the whole of it . . . Her voice being of a nature soon to crack and grow husky, on finding her powers decline she left the stage some time before her death, which took place a few years ago. [23]

*   *   *   *   *

Anna Selina Storace[24] was born in London, 27 October 1765, to Stefano Storace, an Italian double bass player who had made himself a decent career as musician and musical entrepreneur in England, and Elizabeth Trusler daughter of John Trusler a pastry maker who was for some time manager of the pleasure garden, Marylebone Gardens. The child's first public performance was at the Haymarket Theatre in London, in April 1774. Her first teacher was her father; around 1774 she began vocal studies with the castrato soprano Venanzio Rauzzini (1746–1810), Mozart's original Cecilio in *Lucio Silla*. It was for Rauzzini that he composed the concert aria "Exsultate jubilate" (K. 165/158a). Having moved to England in 1774, Rauzzini sang at the King's Theatre until 1777, and then settled in Bath where he enjoyed a long-lasting career as singer and teacher. Among his pupils were Gertrud Mara, Michael Kelly, and John Braham, all of whom were significantly involved in the life of Nancy Storace. Kelly, Braham, and Storace maintained their ties with Rauzzini throughout his life; when he died Storace and Braham had a plaque in his memory placed in the Bath Abbey, "erected by his affectionate pupils Anna Selina Storace and John Braham."[25] Rauzzini is said to have forbidden Nancy to sing publicly but he withdrew that ban to permit her to appear, with Caterina Gabrielli, in the premiere of his own opera, *Le ali d'amore* on 29 February 1776.

In 1778 Storace left England with her mother (and probably her father) to join her older brother Stephen in Naples, where he was studying at the Conservatorio San Onofino. Her first Italian appearance was probably in Florence when she was fourteen in Bianchi's *Castore e Polluce*. She spent the next three years moving around Italy, singing both prima seria and prima buffa roles in opera revivals, gaining experience and reputation. In 1782 at the age of seventeen she appeared in the first opera composed for her, *Fra i due litiganti il terzo gode,* by Giuseppe Sarti (c. 1729–1802). Her fame reached Emperor Joseph II in Vienna, and at his behest in 1783 Prince Franz Orsini-Rosenberg, Director of the Imperial Opera, engaged her for Joseph's new Italian opera.

Storace's debut in Vienna at the Burgtheater in Salieri's *La scuola dei gelosi* (created for her in Venice) marked the beginning of a triumphant reign as the queen of Vienna opera. In addition to the operas then popular she sang roles created for her by Paisiello, Martín y Soler, Salieri, and in May 1786 the role for which she is best remembered today—Susanna in Mozart's *Le nozze di Figaro.* Early in her Viennese stay she married an English composer, John Abraham Fischer who was twice her age, and had a child. She is said to have cared little for the child who was immediately farmed out to a wet nurse and died in infancy. The marriage was disastrous. Rumors circulated that Fischer beat his young wife; Emperor Joseph banished him from Vienna on the grounds of his brutal treatment of Storace, but gossip had it that Joseph had his own ideas about Ms. Storace (as usual, no evidence supports the gossip).

For various reasons, Storace decided late in 1786 not to renew her contract with the Italian Opera in Vienna and set out in February 1787 for London, accompanied by her mother, her brother, her friend and sometime musical partner the tenor Michael Kelly, Thomas Attwood (a young English composer who had spent two years studying with Mozart), and her English lover, Lord Barnard (Harry Vane, Earl of Darlington and 2nd Duke of Cleveland). The entourage made its way slowly to London, via Salzburg and Paris where they spent at least a week, and arrived in England at the end of March. On 24 April 1787 Storace debuted in Paisiello's *Gli schiavi per amore* at the Italian Opera playing at King's Theatre, Haymarket. In spite of what her brother termed "great opposition from the Italians," she enjoyed success singing comic roles in the Italian opera and remained with it for the next two years. But for the 1789–1790 season she joined her brother Stephen at the Drury Lane Theatre, where he was musical director. Here she sang primarily English musical theatre, much of the repertory either composed by or assembled by Stephen, and obviously enjoyed it immensely, judging from accounts of her activities and remarks about her performances. She continued at Drury Lane, singing as did Michael Kelly, at the Italian Opera when she was needed.

Storace appeared frequently in concert settings as well, at the Handel Festival in Westminster Abbey, at various festivals in England, such as Hereford or Salisbury; she also sang at the Oxford concerts that took place during Haydn's visit. The happy years at Drury Lane came to an end in 1796 with the death of her beloved brother on 19 March—he was just shy of 34. With the aid of Michael Kelly she completed Stephen's last opera, *Mahmoud, Prince of Persia,* and performed in it at the Drury Lane on 30 April 1796. In August 1797, she departed for the Continent with a Jewish tenor nine years her junior, John Braham (1774–1856), whom she had taken under her wing. They went first to Paris where they remained for nearly a year, enjoying great success in spite of the turbulent times. In 1798 they took their leave of France and spent several years moving about from one Italian opera theatre to another—this must have reminded Signora Storace powerfully of her youthful exploits. They returned to London in 1801, set up house together in unmarried bliss (which amazingly seems to have offended no one particularly; their social circle included an array of very respectable upper middle class bourgeois citizens and minor nobility, including the prominent architect Sir John Soane[26]). For the next seven years Storace sang with and without her tenor partner in comic opera at both the Covent Garden and the Drury Lane theatres.

After the return from Europe, however, Storace's voice declined steadily, and her acting did not always compensate for the vocal problems. Reviewers still found much to praise: "this lady is equally qualified to appear in either department of sense or sound, and maintain the lead in both. She had several opportunities of displaying this versatility as Zulima [in *Chains for the Heart* at Covent Garden, 1801], and did not fail to take advantage of them" (*Post*) and "sung and acted with spirit" (*Times*). The critic for the *Monthly Mirror* liked her Floretta in the 1802 *Cabinet*: "The archness and true *Buffa* of Madame Storace are unusually effective." In 1803, the same critic wrote of the charming display of "her peculiar naïveté as a comic actress." But negative comments increased: in 1801 the critic for the *Times* noted that she was "occasionally affected with a hoarseness," and the *Chronicle* critic remarked during the same season: "She would please more, however, if she attempted to do less. There is a graceful elegance of manner which gives to gaiety its proper zest, and in this Madame Storace is not always successful. Her *naivete* is of a more humourous cast. She leaves nothing to the imagination to conceive." By 1806 she "was by no means happy in her character. Neither nature nor habits have qualified her for an Italian fine Lady; but her first song had point, and was uncommonly droll" (*Morning Chronicle*). The traits perceived as charming in the young singer were harshly criticized in the aging Storace. In 1808 she played Rozella, a "Circassian beauty," in *Kais,* and it was not a fortunate choice. DuBois (*Monthly Mirror*) described one of her songs as "to the last degree absurd. The coarseness of her look and manner, and the imperfection of her voice, makes such attempts preposterous." Most devastatingly, that same year she sang again Zulima, and Hunt wrote in the *Examiner*: "Who can refrain from disgust, when he sees an unwieldy matron attempting all the personal giddiness and tricksome levity of a skittish girl . . . [She] shakes her whole frame with huge enjoyment . . . The galleries always applaud with proportionate vehemence, for they are well pleased with their own likeness."[27] Finally, on 30 May 1808 she made her farewell to the stage in her brother's *No Song, No Supper*, sharing her farewell with that of her old friend Michael Kelly.[28]

The course of the next few years was anything but smooth. Storace had never married John Braham (because she was still married to Fischer, who died only in

1806?), although they had maintained an overt liaison—lived together in fact—for nearly twenty years. Their son, William Spencer Harris Braham, also known as William Storace Spencer or as John Spencer Braham, was born on 3 May 1802. The Storace-Braham relationship began to deteriorate around 1812. Braham seems to have behaved quite badly, dallying with and eventually eloping at the end of 1815 with Sophie Wright who with her husband had been close friends of Storace and Braham. The husband actually brought charges against Braham, claiming damages of £5,000 (he was awarded only £1,000 because Braham's lawyers asserted that Mr. Wright should have known the dangers of introducing his wife to such a person as Signora Storace!). Sophie Wright was in her turn abandoned by Braham, who married in 1816 a wealthy young woman, Frances Elizabeth Bolton (Sands). True to real life, Braham lived happily ever after with his beautiful wife and their six children; his career flourished and he continued to be known as one of the finest tenors in Europe. The breakup of the Storace-Braham relationship was difficult, marked by battles over furniture, musical scores, silverware, etc., in addition to the trial forced by Mr. Wright.[29] The newspapers were not slow to relish the scandal; it is pleasing to report that they tended to favor Signora Storace. Sir John Soane, a prominent architect in London, who had been a close friend of the Storace-Braham couple, showed now his true mettle: he served as go-between for Storace and Braham and remained her faithful friend to her very last day. A number of letters in the Soane Museum in London between Soane, Storace, her young son Spencer, and Braham provide moving testimony to Soane's loyalty as well as to the heartbreak of Storace, the pain of her son, and the rather unadmirable behavior of Braham.[30]

In July 1817 Storace suffered a stroke. She continued to schedule social events, but the following month she had a second stroke. On 24 August 1817 she died in her home at Herne Hill.

During the retirement phase of her life, Storace was known as a vivacious hostess, visited by people from many different fields; Soane was only one of a number of prominent professional people who frequented her gatherings. Herne Hill, bought with Braham but eventually ceded to her, was a gathering place for the bright, interesting people of her age. An obituary notice in the *Gentleman's Magazine* evokes a dramatically attractive personality:

Of her professional talents as a singer and an actress it is sufficient to say that they were the delight and admiration of the public: and certainly she was altogether unrivalled in her particular line. She was not handsome, not feminine in her person, but one of the most accomplished and agreeable women of her age, fascinating everyone by her habitual good humour, her lively and intelligent conversation, and her open and ingenuous character . . . her house at Herne Hill was a seat of hospitality to numerous respectable friends.[31]

*   *   *   *   *

We remember Nancy Storace primarily for her creation of Susanna in *Le nozze di Figaro,* and we tend to interpret this as Mozart's recognition of her unusual ability to interact on stage. But it is perhaps even more significant that this is the only Mozart opera in which one character is so pivotal, so involved with other characters, that she appears only once, at the end of the opera, in a true solo aria ("Deh vieni"). Don Alfonso in *Così fan tutte* is also pivotal but not to anywhere near the extent or complexity of Susanna. Mozart, with his own deep appreciation and love for theatre of all kinds, must have reveled in the unique talents of Storace.

For a singer to act while singing serious opera was a novelty for English audiences. The frequent remarks about Storace's acting attest her talent as a singing actress but also underline the unusualness of her stage manner. Indeed, transplant of Storace's style of action and interaction with her fellows on stage to the opera seria theatre must have shocked London, accustomed to having its singers either engage in rowdy behavior (à la *Beggar's Opera*) at the Drury Lane or work within strict traditions of formality that prescribed the manner of entrances and exits and polite behavior on stage. Roger Fiske suggests that soloists at Covent Garden actually moved forward to the footlights and away from their dramatic partners, in order to address their arias directly to the audience.[32] He stresses also the novelty introduced to Italian opera in London by Storace and Kelly of having singers continue to act while singing ensembles instead of standing in line facing the audience[33]—staging that might have been beneficial from a purely musical point of view, but certainly strains even further the premise necessary for most opera of suspending disbelief. James Boaden, author of biographies of the actors John Philip Kemble and Mrs. Jordan, described the effect of Nancy Storace's and Michael Kelly's stagework:

The foreign habits of these accomplished singers enabled them to sing steadily while moving about the stage (a difficulty of no mean rank) and infused a life, and a bustle into our opera, which before had hardly trusted itself with action.[34]

Storace's incorporation into serious opera of her comic opera manners and actions did not necessarily please many devotees of opera seria who regarded her performance occasionally even as a travesty that offended their respect for the art they held in such high esteem. Nevertheless a number of writers speak of her influence in raising the levels of English musical theatre. Sutherland Edwards writing in 1862 referred to the "new heights" to which she had raised English opera, presumably meaning opera in general.[35]

Reviews of music and of performances attest also to the powerful influence of Nancy and Stephen Storace and of Michael Kelly in raising levels of musical performance and of the music itself in the arena of comic opera. While Kelly and Nancy Storace introduced their new acting style into serious opera, at Covent Garden, all three brought their high level of musical training to the world of musical theatre with astonishing and well-received results. Adolphus referring here to the production of *The Haunted Tower* at the Drury Lane, sums her legacy to English musical theatre:

[They] gave to the town a better style of music than had of late been attempted; and presented to them, in Signora Storace, a new performer, whose qualifications, both as singer and comedian, elevated her to the highest favour. Although she came from the Opera-house, where, for some seasons, she had been first comic singer, and her name was sounded according to the Italian pronunciation, she was an Englishwoman; and the audience was not doomed, as had been the case with Miss Prudom and Signora Sestina, to hear the King's English mercilessly hacked, and to draw an obscure meaning from under an oppressive mass of mispronunciation.[36]

In sum, Nancy Storace was an excellent musician, who from all accounts lived almost exclusively for her art. Frequent remarks appear about her loyalty, her fine musicianship, her extensive knowledge of musical techniques, her lack of a diva mentality. James Boaden in his *Memoirs of John Philip Kemble* in 1825 described her behavior and character:

Storace was certainly one of the most effective burletta singers in the world. She took business as a pleasure, and seemed always happy when employed. In the discharge of her public duty, she was highly exemplary; laughed at colds and nervous complaints; used her shoes in the dry, and her pattens in the wet, to convey her to and from the theatre, and had not a grain of affectation about her.[37]

The obituary notice from *Gentleman's Magazine* (see above, page 104) speaks of an accomplished, agreeable woman, not handsome, not feminine, always in good humor, an open, ingenuous character who captivated by all these traits and by her lively and intelligent conversation. Reviews and other descriptions of her performances indicate that these characteristics formed a part of her stage persona and were communicated vividly to her audience; surely it was these characteristics also that secured for her the respect of London society in the face of irregularities in her private life. The greatest composers of the day wrote for her—Mozart, Haydn, Paisiello, Piccinni, Salieri, Sarti. She sang the 1784 revival of Haydn's *Il ritorno di Tobia* in Vienna and must have pleased the composer, for in a 1790 letter to the London music publisher John Bland, Haydn refers to a new cantata "for the voice of my dear Storace, whom I kiss many times."[38]

Among the best summaries of Storace's work and achievements is that provided by Lord Mount Edgcumbe (see above, page 101), who heard her a number of times and could assess objectively and articulately the quality of her art and the extent of her contribution to the English musical stage:

In her own particular line on the stage she was unrivalled, being an excellent actress, as well as a masterly singer . . . after quitting the opera (to which she was frequently recalled in times of distress, when the performers engaged proved bad, as was too often the case), she engaged at Drury Lane, where the English opera was raised to an excellence not known before, by her singing, with that of Mrs. Crouch, Mrs. Bland, Kelly, and Bannister, and under the direction of her brother Stephen Storace.[39]

She delighted in interplay with other performers and she had a solid technical understanding of music—it is well to remember that she played the keyboard (perhaps also the harp) and the guitar; she actually played her own guitar accompaniments on stage. She understood basic harmony and counterpoint (with Michael Kelly she completed her brother's last opera after his untimely death), and she could read music at sight, an uncommon ability for singers. She possessed an innate comic sense and the ability to communicate through gesture, timing, dramatic movement, and musical nuance the message of the music. This is what Mozart and other composers took delight in writing for. And, after all the words, the most vivid testimony of her musical and dramatic abilities remains the music of Susanna composed for her by Mozart.

Timeline

1765, 27 Oct	Anna Selina (Nancy) Storace born London, daughter of Stefano Storace, Italian double bass player, and Elizabeth Trusler
1774, Apr	First London concert, Haymarket Theatre, Apr
1776, 29 Feb	Sang with Caterina Gabrielli premiere of Rauzzini's *Le ali d'amore*
	Studied with Rauzzini and Sacchini
1778	To Italy with mother (and father?) to join brother Stephen, Naples
1779	Florence, sang Phoebe and Ebe, Bianchi's *Castore e Polluce*
1780–1781	Sang comic opera roles, prima seria and prima buffa
1782	Milan, Turin, Parma, Rome, Venice; Milan, Sarti, *Fra I due litiganti il terzo gode,* composed for her
1783	Venice, Teatro S. Samuele (Michael Kelly also); engaged by Durazzo for newly organized Italian opera in Vienna, debuted at Burgtheater as Countess, Salieri's *La scuola dei gelosi* (created for her in Venice)
1783	Married composer J.A. Fisher, soon parted (abused her?)
1783–1784	7 productions; partner Francesco Benucci
1786–1787	Relationship with Lord Barnard
1783–1787	Vienna, roles created for her by Paisiello, Martín, Mozart
1787, Feb	Departed Vienna for London, with mother, brother, Attwood, Kelly, Barnard; visited Leopold Mozart, Salzburg
1787, 24 Apr	Paisiello's *Gli schiavi per amore* at King's Theatre, Haymarket
1787–1789	Italian opera at King's Theatre
1789–1796	Joined brother Stephen Storace at Drury Lane for 1789–90 season, mainly at Drury Lane till 1796; important roles in Stephen's operas
1791	Handel Festival, Westminster Abbey
1792	Hereford Festival, Salisbury Festival, Oxford concerts during Haydn's visit (sang "Bess of Bedlam," Handel's "Let the Bright Seraphim," air from *No Song, No Supper*, Haydn cantata)
1790s	Close relationship with Prince of Wales who with Duke of Bedford, Marquis of Salisbury tried to hire her for their secret court theatre at the Pantheon concert hall in Oxford St.
1793	Season of Italian opera at King's Theatre
1796, 19 Mar	Stephen Storace died
1796, 30 Apr	*Mahmoud* 30 Apr 1796, finished by Nancy Storace and Michael Kelly; first performance with tenor John Braham at Drury Lane
1797	With John Braham to Continent for tour; Paris; Italy, quite successful.
1801	Returned to England, sang alternately at Covent Garden (Italian opera) and Drury Lane (comic opera)

1802, 3 May	Son born to Storace and Braham
1808	Farewell performance (also Kelly's) at Drury Lane, Stephen Storace's *No Song, No Supper*
1812–1815	Troubles with Braham, ending in his elopement with Sophie Wright, eventual marriage with Frances Bolton
1817, 24 Aug	Nancy Storace died, Herne Hill

Bibliography

Works about Storace
Storace-Soane-Braham Letters, Sir John Soane Museum, London.
These uncatalogued letters deal primarily with the ending of the Braham-Storace relationship; they reveal a strong, honest, and deeply hurt Storace and document Soane's stalwart loyal friendship.

Brace, Geoffrey. *Anna . . . Susanna: Anna Storace, Mozart's First Susanna: Her Life, Times, and Family.* London: Thames Publishing, 1991.
The most comprehensive biography of Storace. Does not cite sources carefully (i.e., arranges notes by chapters without always giving specific note numbers in the text), and frequently indulges in imaginative recreations of probable events, such as the reunion in London of Storace siblings with Joseph Haydn—"would have shown," "would have inquired after," etc. Nevertheless has an excellent bibliography (up to 1990) useful appendices (for example, Storace's diary of engagements for 1794), and makes good use of the letters between Storace and Sir John Soane (in the Soane Museum in London).

Geiringer, Karl, and Irene Geiringer. "Stephen and Nancy Storace in Vienna." In *Essays on the Music of J. S. Bach and Other Divers Subjects: A Tribute to Gerhard Herz,* ed. Robert Lamar Weaver. Louisville and New York: Pendragon Press, 1981.

Lewy Gidwitz, Patricia. "Vocal Profiles of Four Mozart Sopranos." Ph.D. diss., University of California, Berkeley, 1991.

Matthews, Betty. "The Childhood of Nancy Storace." *Musical Times* 110 (1969): 733–35.

_____. "Nancy Storace and the Royal Society of Musicians." *Musical Times* 128 (1987): 325–27.

Sands, Mollie. "Mozart's First Susanna." *The Monthly Musical Record* (1944): 178–84.
Mollie Sands and Betty Matthews were among the first to study Storace's career.

General Works
Adolphus, John. *Memoirs of John Bannister, Comedian.* 2 vols. London: Richard Bentley, 1839.
These *Memoirs* of Storace's frequent partner, John Bannister, provide contemporary views of her own work as well as of their work together.

Bingley, William. *Musical Biography: Memoirs of the Lives and Writings of the Most Eminent Musical Composers and Writers Who Have Flourished in the Different Countries of Europe during the Last Three Centuries.* 1834. Reprint, New York: Da Capo Press, 1971.

Burney, Charles. *A General History of Music from the Earliest Ages to the Present Period (1789).* 1776. Reprint with critical and historical notes by Frank Mercer, New York: Dover Publications, Inc., 1957.

Fenner, Theodore. *Opera in London: Views of the Press, 1785–1830*. Carbondale, IL: Southern Illinois University Press, 1994.

Fiske, Roger. *English Theatre Music in the Eighteenth Century.* New York: Oxford University Press, 1986.

Girdham, Jane. *English Opera in Late Eighteenth-Century London: Stephen Storace at Drury Lane.* Oxford: Clarendon Press, 1997.

> Deals peripherally with Nancy Storace, but gives a very good and well documented account of Stephen Storace's work and of English opera in general in London.

Highfill, Philip Jr., Kalman A. Burnim, and Edward a. Langhans. *A Biographical Dictionary of Actors, Actresses, Musicians, Dancers, Managers, and Other Stage Personnel in London 1660–1800.* Carbondale, Ill.: Southern Illinois University Press, 1973.

Hogarth, George. *Memoirs of the Musical Drama.* 2 vols. London: Richard Bentley, 1838.

> Hogarth, author, publisher, passionate theatre-goer, also father of Catherine Hogarth (married to Charles Dickens), presents a compilation of contemporary accounts of performers, works, and productions.

Kelly, Michael. *Reminiscences of Michael Kelly, of the King's Theatre, and Theatre Royal, Drury Lane.* 1826. Edited with an introduction by Roger Fiske. London: Oxford University Press, 1975.

> Kelly's accounts are lively and colorful but not always entirely accurate. The *Reminiscences* represent nonetheless the most direct source for information about both Storaces, especially Nancy with whom he frequently sang in both Italian and English opera. It must be used with caution but remains invaluable as an eyewitness account of performances and theatre life in Vienna and London. Roger Fiske's edition provides an admirable sifting of fact from the hazes of memory. See also: S. M. Ellis, *The Life of Michael Kelly, Musician, Actor, and Bon Viveur, 1762–1826* (London: Victor Gollancz Ltd., 1930) which attempts to introduce reality into Kelly's accounts of events.

McVeigh, Simon. *Concert Life in London from Mozart to Haydn.* Cambridge: Cambridge University Press, 1993.

Milhous, Judith, Gabriella Dideriksen, and Robert D. Hume. *The Pantheon Opera and Its Aftermath: 1789–1795.* Vol. 2 of *Italian Opera in Late Eighteenth-Century London.* Oxford: Clarendon Press, 2001.

> Thorough, well-documented comprehensive work. Invaluable source for general and more specialized information about performers and theatres during this period.

Mount Edgcumbe, Richard. *Musical Reminiscences of the Earl of Mount Edgcumbe: Containing an Account of the Italian Opera in England from 1773 to 1834.* 1834. Reprint, New York: Da Capo Press, 1973.

Mozart, Wolfgang Amadeus. *Mozart: Briefe und Aufzeichnungen, Gesamtausgabe.* Collected and annotated by Wilhelm A. Bauer and Otto Erich Deutsch. 6 vols.

Kassel: Bärenreiter, 1962–1975.

_____. *The Letters of Mozart and His Family*. Chronologically arranged, edited, and translated by Emily Anderson. 3rd ed. New York and London: W. W. Norton & Company, 1966.

Miss Anderson's generally accurate translations of Mozart's letters make them easily accessible to non-German readers. Anderson was the first to produce an unexpurgated edition of the letters.

_____. *Mozart's Letters, Mozart's Life: Selected Letters*. Translated by Robert Spaethling. New York: W. W. Norton, 2000.

Spaethling's lively translations are vivid and very true to Mozart's language.

Petty, Frederick. *Italian Opera in London: 1760–1800*. Ann Arbor: UMI Research Press, 1972.

Price, Curtis, Judith Milhous, and Robert D. Hume. *The King's Theatre, Haymarket: 1778–1791*. Vol. 1 of *Italian Opera in Late Eighteenth-Century London*. Oxford: Clarendon Press, 1995.

Thorough, well-documented comprehensive work. Invaluable source for general and more specialized information about performers and theatres during this period.

Zinzendorf, Count. *Diary: Tagebuch des Grafen Johann Karl Chr. H. Zinzendorf*. Manuscript in French, in Kabinettsarchiv, Haus-, Hof-, und Staatsarchiv, Vienna. One of the best sources of information about musical and theatre life in Vienna during the late eighteenth century. An ardent devotee of opera and theatre, Zinzendorf confided to his *Diary* candidly and knowledgeably his views on performances and performers. Translations of his comments appear in standard biographies of Mozart, Haydn, books about Vienna, etc.

Chapter 9

Giuditta Pasta
(26 October 1797 – 1 April 1865)

Pasta's voice was entirely uneven over its range, with distinct registers, each marked by a very different timbre. Her lower tones were marked by a veiled quality; her highest notes were occasionally harsh. Pitch and intonation problems, frequent even in her peak years, grew worse as she aged. Yet she was acclaimed as one of the great operatic singers of the nineteenth century. Nearly all who heard her agreed that the timbral variations, the veiled husky quality, even the harshness contributed to her extraordinary dramatic expressiveness, the unique power of her operatic performance. Critics despaired of reporting accurately the qualities of her singing and mourned that future generations could have no idea of the depths of her operatic portrayals. The novelist and frequent music critic Stendahl (Henri Beyle) was so enamoured of her work that he devoted a chapter of his Rossini biography to describing her voice and style.[1]

* * * * *

Stendahl, in spite of often flowery non-musical language, gives an extremely detailed description of Pasta's voice. Many of his points simply affirm those made by other reviewers, but in some cases he is able to describe very specifically the traits that made Pasta's operatic singing unique.

First, the purely technical: Stendahl tells us of "the superb assurance of Madame Pasta's *portamento,* the infinite skill and subtlety of her glides, the unparalleled artistry with which she can inflect, sustain and smoothly control an extended vocal phrase."[2] She can "achieve perfect resonance on a note as low as bottom *A,* and can rise as high as *C#,* or even to a slightly sharpened *D*; and she possesses the rare ability to be able to sing contralto as easily as she can sing soprano." While he believes that her real range is that of the mezzo-soprano, he describes notes outside this ambitus as having "the ability to produce a kind of resonant and magnetic vibration, which, through some still unexplained combination of physical phenomena, exercises an instantaneous and hypnotic effect upon the soul of the spectator."[3] He praises the

amazing facility with which she alternates head-notes with chest-notes; she possesses to a superlative degree the art of producing an immense variety of charming and thrilling effects from the use of *both* voices. To heighten the tonal colouring of a melodic phrase, or to pass in a flash from one *ambiance* to another infinitely removed from it, she is accustomed to use a *falsetto* technique covering notes right down to the middle of her normal range . . . [she will] alternate *falsetto* notes with ordinary chest-notes . . . [she] finds as little difficulty in securing a smooth transition between the two voices when she is employing notes in the *middle* of her normal chest-range, as she does when she is using the highest notes . . . [Her] head-notes are almost diametrically opposed to the characteristics of her chest-notes; her *falsetto* is brilliant, rapid, pure, fluent and enchantingly light. As she approaches the lower part of this *falsetto* register, she can *smorzare il canto* (diminish her tone) to a point where . . . the existence of sound becomes uncertain.[4]

Stendahl then labors to define the exact effect of Pasta's operatic singing. An essential element, he believes, is a "palette of breath-taking colour" that enables her to achieve

the over-mastering force of natural expression which we have learnt to associate with her— a miracle of emotional revelation, which is always true to nature and, although tempered by the intrinsic laws of *ideal Beauty,* always alive with that unmistakable, burning energy, that extraordinary dynamism which can electrify an entire theatre.[5]

He particularly praises what many twentieth-century critics and singing teachers would find a fault: the fact that Pasta's voice had at least three very distinct parts: "[It] is *not all moulded from the same metallo* . . . (*i.e.,* it possesses more than one *timbre*); and this fundamental variety of tone produced by a single voice affords one of the richest veins of musical expression which the artistry of a great *cantatrice* is able to exploit."[6] This is, he continues, an important factor in her dramatic expressivity:

No voice whose *timbre* is completely incapable of variation can ever produce that kind of *opaque,* or as it were, *suffocated* tone, which is at once so moving and so natural in the portrayal of certain instants of violent emotion or passionate anguish.

Madame Pasta may indeed sing the same *note* in two different scenes; but, if the spiritual context is different, it will not be the same *sound.*[7]

He confirms other writers' praise of the relative simplicity of her ornamentation, finds it impossible to name a single of her usual ornaments which is "not a monument of classical grace and style, or which is unfit to stand as a model of unrivalled perfection. Extremely restrained in her use of *fioriture,* she resorts to them *only* when they have a direct contribution to make to the dramatic expressiveness of the music." In sum, he considers her *fioriture* to be additional evidence of her "perfect intelligence, moderation and good taste."[8]

Pasta's was a voice that thrilled, delighted, and mystified her audiences. The weaknesses were noted early, but a survey of critiques from throughout her career demonstrates that while the same problems recurred—intonation, harshness, huskiness—they interfered scarcely at all with the power of her performance.

Pasta's first appearance on the international stage—Paris, Théâtre Italien, 19 June 1816, as Rosina in *Il Principe di Taranto* (by Ferdinando Paër, 1771–1839)— was not impressive. The reviewer said little other than that her low range was more agreeable than her high, but he was among the first to note the veiled quality of her voice that remained a constant trait throughout her career.[9] By the end of the summer her work was found to have some "moments de force."[10] Was she gaining in stage presence and confidence, or had she found a role that suited her better? The English, on the other hand, who heard her a few months later (January 1817) were quite enthusiastic, referring to a "most flexible and pleasing voice" and finding that her "execution is brilliant, but not to the exclusion of feeling . . . taste, elegance, and expression."[11] Leigh Hunt wrote of "a natural eloquence about her singing," called her voice "good" and referred to her "handsome face and very handsome legs."[12] (The English seem to have been unusually taken with her shape; references to her form, and especially to her legs—she did several "pants" roles—are frequent.) But even the adoring English noted problems with pitch in her February performance of Cherubino (*Le nozze di Figaro*).

The following fall (1817) she was in Venice where she sang Adelaide in Giovanni Pacini's *Adelaide e Comingio* at the Teatro San Benedetto. Here the critics wrote of her "agile homogeneous and extended voice" as well as "an extremely animated expression of the voice and the actions and an uncommon skill in her art; whereby all these gifts truly hers are not lacking the necessary development which places her in the first category of the most distinguished virtuose."[13] Later, on 19 October in Padua, she sang Rossini's *La Cenerentola* (her first work by Rossini), and her voice was described as "that true eloquence of song that penetrates to the very core of the heart"; her "appropriate and expressive gestures" were noted as well.[14] In Brescia during the summer of 1819, where she sang Antonio in *La morte di Cleopatra*: "Her voice is agile, extended, and perfected; her sweet sound, her restrained ornamentation . . . This young virtuosa is much applauded, and justly, not out of kindness."[15] This summer in Brescia was particularly important for her artistic growth: she worked with the famed contralto Giuseppina Grassini and surely gained technically with respect to both her voice and her stagecraft. She sang Pavesi's *Arminio, o sia L'Eroe Germano* in Venice during the carnival season of 1820–1821, and the critic wrote of the "great grace and precision of her voice, which can be felt but is not easy to describe."[16] Thus, early in her career listeners found a quality in her voice which was extremely difficult to describe, but which was a vital factor in its expressivity.

Pasta returned to Paris in the summer of 1821. Her voice and style were now set, and the critics were ecstatic: of her *Otello* (5 June, Théâtre Italien): "Mme Pasta combines all her exterior charms with a beautiful voice and truly dramatic expression" and "her soprano voice conquers the highest notes with the greatest facility."[17] Having now decided that this was indeed an important voice, a number of reviewers set out to analyze its strengths and weaknesses:

Courrier des spectacles: [V]ery beautiful in the low and medium range, tends to pull back a bit in the high range. Such a voice, difficult by its very nature to control, does not lend itself ordinarily to melodic ornamentation; all the same, Mme Pasta, without being prodigal with her embellishments—which is not a fault—lets us hear perfect execution and irreproachable taste. She sang the entire role with soul.[18]

Le Drapeau blanc: The voice of Mme Pasta, full, even, and well-timbred, in her middle and high range, appeared a bit veiled in the low tones, her sounds in this range of her voice recall often those of Mme Grassini, who had the same failing, well-redeemed by the affecting expression sometimes given to the tone of the singer.[19]

Particularly significant is the reference to Mme Grassini, for Pasta had spent the summers of 1819 and 1820 singing secondary roles in the Brescia company with Grassini. Although this veiled quality had been noted earlier by a Paris reviewer in 1816, i.e., *before* Pasta sang with Grassini, it may well be that Pasta learned to *exploit* the dramatic possibilities of this quality as a result of her work with Grassini. Critics now found that her strengths considerably outweighed her deficiencies— the veiled quality complained of earlier was now seen as contributing to her expressivity, her declamation was near perfect—indeed the deficiencies were no longer liabilities but actually served her expressive force.

Journal des Débats: The voice of this singer is strong and extensive; but the low tones are veiled and correspond not at all to the brightness of the high range.

La Quotidienne: It is impossible better to articulate the recitative and to give more of soul and expression to melody; an instrument still a bit rebellious, which she must have taken great pains to form, sometimes fails to respond to her efforts, but it requires an exacting ear to notice it; one is generally struck only by its strength and its range.

Journal des Débats: [She has] risen victorious to complete approbation. She surpassed what was expected from her soul and her talent; she was sublime. We applauded her with passion . . . her voice, a bit veiled, is eminently dramatic, her manner noble and pure, her warmth transports [us].[20]

Thus the French critics, virtually unanimous about the extraordinary expressive qualities of the voice.

The English on the other hand were now of a different mind. The harshness seen by the French as a dramatic asset was not attractive to the English, who found her wanting in fullness of her tones and perhaps in power as well as "execution." Reviews from her London season of 24 April to 7 August 1824 reveal interesting differences in aesthetic desires of French vs. English critics, particularly with respect to the quality of the sound.

The Times (review of her performance in Rossini's *Otello*, 24 April): Her powers of voice are very considerable; but her tones are deficient in that full and rich melody, which . . . comes home to the bosom, and captivates the feelings. Some of her notes are, indeed, sharp, almost to harshness. Her style of singing is chaste and expressive.

The Examiner: Her first notes were rather harsh and hard, and it was not until the ear became familiarized to them that we felt confident of her success . . .—At times her voice is rather crude, but it still possesses a fullness and body that are very peculiar and very delightful. Execution she possesses little of, but she substitutes graces of a very elegant character, and fully compensates, by her pathos, for the deficiency.

The Morning Chronicle: Madame PASTA'S voice is, in technical language, termed a mezzo-soprano, by which is meant a low female voice: its compass is extensive, and though not strong, has power enough . . . Her tones are rich and sweet, and though devoid of that clearness and vibration which the real soprano—Madame [Giuseppina] RONZI [DE BEGNIS], for instance—possesses, yet they are well suited to her style of singing . . . Her intonation is unimpeachable; we did not discover that one false note escaped from her during the whole evening; her style is pure, it is totally divested of all the spurious finery, the gew-gaw, that has been too prevalent lately. She adds little to what "is set down" for her . . . As an actress, Madame PASTA is not less worthy of distinction; her expression and gesture are in excellent keeping with her singing; all three are the offspring of a deep feeling and a correct judgment.[21]

This same reviewer remarked on her small stature (although admitting that her proportions were good) and on the fact that her first appearance was in male costume in which "her form [was] greatly admired."

But in London again, the following summer (10 May-7 June 1825), Pasta had regained the full approval of the critics:

Morning Herald: [I]n power of voice, execution, and expression, she is, if possible, greater. Nothing could exceed [the aria's] exquisite pathos but the delicacy of its execution. Her cadences are unrivalled: in feeling and expression she has no competitor on the stage . . . Her whole recitative last night was given with unusual power. Her voice appears to have gained greater depth and strength; there was a mellow richness in her tones we never heard before. Some of her lower notes were unequalled . . . Her voice is the very soul of music.

The Examiner: In person she is improved, but in voice infinitely more so,—the lower tones have no longer that thick husky accompaniment, which went far to destroy them, and the upper ones have more volume, without that harshness that was too often evident when she exerted her powers. In graceful ornament . . . originality seems to be her study, and her genius leads her to the invention of graces of the most extraordinary beauty, not depending on rapidity of utterance, but upon a quiet placid sentiment and an exquisite sweetness that has no parallel.

Quarterly Musical Magazine and Review: [I]t seems that the Italians have adopted a novel manner of forming the low notes of a contralto—at least I do not recollect to have heard such as are produced by Mad[ame] Pasta before.[22]

The reviewer explained in a footnote that her lower notes were "what the French call *sons voilées,* that is they are not clear, but come forth husky." He continued that this resulted from using too much force but could be "overcome by industrious practice. Madame Pasta's low tones were this season much less husky than before."[23] Clearly Pasta had developed technically. Again reviewers commended her restrained ornamentation. The remarks about her veiled tones may well indicate a more judicious, controlled use of the very special effect created by the husky sound.

When she returned to London for the summer season of 1826, she sang Rossini's *Zelmira,* which included an aria specifically composed for her voice, "Da te spero, o ciel clemente," with great success. The reviewer for *The Atlas* raved:

It is the peculiarity of this incomparable performer, that she executes the most difficult passages with an ease which leaves general hearers in utter ignorance that anything extraordinary has been accomplished. Most of our singers take half-a-dozen ways to prepare us for their exploits—before they take their grand bound, they draw their breaths hard, distort their faces to engage attention, and take a good run to the goal; then, generally, after all this fuss, tumble down in the middle of the difficulty. PASTA clears it like a greyhound. In the *scena* to which we have alluded, she goes over the chromatic scale with an exactness that is wonderful, and an ease that makes it seem the most simple, feasible thing imaginable.[24]

This is a long way from the *Examiner* critique of 1824: "Execution she possesses little of . . ." (see above, page 117).

In summary: Pasta used her voice with a well-calculated eye and ear to its dramatic effectiveness, exploiting not only the sheer beauty of the sound and her formidable technique, but also the expressive powers of the voice's idiosyncrasies—its distinctly differentiated registers, the different timbres of register and color, and of course the veiled tone spoken of so often. She was sparing in her use of ornamentation, and, though problems of intonation persisted throughout her career, by the mid

1820s she had brought her vocal technique to an extremely high level.

Pasta the actress is scarcely separable from Pasta the singer, since she combined the two aspects of her art so successfully. On the other hand her acting was constantly singled out for comment, and thus it is informative to look at it apart from her singing.

By 1822 she had found herself as *attrice cantante*. On 23 April she sang the first Paris performance of Rossini's *Tancredi* at the Théâtre Italien (she was twenty-four and it was her forty-first role) to enormous acclaim. It was not her singing alone but the manner in which singing, movement, gesture, and acting were united in the creation of Tancredi that brought the critics to their knees:

> It was expected that the role of Tancrède would be sung by Mme Pasta in a superlative manner; but no one would have believed that a young and pretty woman would portray the chevalier Syracusain with this imposing nobility, with a charm so moving and so true; her presence, her sustainment, her declamation breathe the motto Voltaire gave to his protagonists: *l'Amour et l'Honneur!* she sings the work in Italian and acts the work in French.[25]

Of particular significance is the last sentence—"sings in Italian and acts in French ("elle chante la pièce italienne, et joue la pièce française"). Pasta seems here to have brought about a marriage of Italian and French goals not seen since Couperin's *Les goûts-réunis* in which Apollo declares: "The union of French and Italian styles must produce perfection in music."[26]

The critic for *Le Reveil* articulated this marriage in slightly different words when he wrote later that summer (14 August 1822): "Mme Pasta has introduced the customs of tragedy into the Italian *scena*: it is a veritable innovation."[27] Here is spelled out, albeit in highly nationalistic terms, what is perhaps Pasta's most important contribution to the operatic stage: she was not just singing a role, hers was not a concert in costume with some traditional gestures thrown in; she *became* her character—according to some writers, she *was* that character before she even set foot on the stage—and the music was sublimely the extension and expression of the very being of that character. She was not singing a part; what she sang was the consequence of who in the drama she was. For the French who for the most part admired Italian singing but deplored Italian acting, she would seem to have created a new art, as the reviewer stated: "une veritable innovation." Perhaps even more remarkable is that she achieved this without ever singing a role in French; Pasta sang Italian, and only Italian, wherever she was—France, England, Germany, Russia.

Her abandonment of self in the role was again praised by the same critic two weeks later: he found a striking theatrical depth in her Romeo (Zingarelli's *Giulietta e Romeo*): "Mme Pasta finds in her declamation a sadness so vivid and so profound that she creates a veritable theatrical illusion, in sharing with the spectator all the feelings that she is stirred by. It is no longer a role that she sings; one would say that she surrenders to an immediate response of her soul."[28]

French critics may have been universal in their praise of Pasta's art, but now the English refused to sing in unanimous chorus. The critic for the *Morning Herald* writing in May 1825 recognized her achievement: "There is so much of passion, power, and dramatic art in her performance, that serious opera in her hands is raised to its proper level—that of lyric tragedy," but the reviewer for the *Quarterly Musical Magazine and Review* was not in agreement. Conceding that her singing was much improved he still found her to be "greatly over-rated" as actress and singer. He praised her technique ("of the highest order,") but termed her application of it frequently inappropriate: "we think her expression often totally wrong and seldom quite right." As example he cited her entrance in *Tancredi*: "The recitative *Oh Patria* she certainly gives well, but not supremely well; the air is sacrificed to an endeavour at novelty of effect . . . [Pasta] has not that delicate apprehension of the nicer shades of the working of the passions that enables her to portray them justly and strikingly . . . she seems to us strangely to misapply her powers."[29] Are we dealing again with the difference between French and English ideals of music and drama?

In fact the English seesawed between desiring a more reserved application of her histrionic abilities and finding her acting virtually perfect as did this reviewer of her London performance in *Otello,* 24 April 1824:

Her acting admirably kept pace with her singing, and displayed to great advantage a very expressive countenance and a figure of great symmetry . . . she really gave an interest and intellectuality to [Desdemona's scene listening to the song of the Gondolier], that threw a mournfulness over the scene, and a feeling of pity rarely excited on the Opera stage.[30]

(Once again, the English could not refrain from referring to her physical shape.)

Pasta appeared occasionally in comic opera, but she never was really successful at it. As a critic had pointed out already in 1817 of her Lisetta in Paër's *Griselda,* she lacked "a little lightness and finesse. Her pretty face is better adapted to the Opera <u>Seria</u> than the Opera <u>Buffa</u>."[31] That same season she sang Mozart's Cherubino (*Le nozze di Figaro*) with what seems to have been a Romeo-influenced interpretation; critics remarked on her slow tempi in a role that required "quickness and agitation."[32] A rather endearing side note about that first London season: her final appearance was as Servilia in Mozart's *La clemenza di Tito*; she seems to have paid more attention to friends in the audience than to her stage colleagues: "she threw away all her love upon the spectators," ignoring her stage lover who tried in vain to "recall her wandering affections."[33] She was not quite twenty.

A final example from French critiques illustrates how Pasta's interpretation might be altered by her singing partner. In December 1825 she sang her seventy-fourth Desdemona in Rossini's *Otello* with Giovanni Battista Rubini singing his first Otello. The critic for *La Quotidienne* noted a new conception of Desdemona: "It is not only the singing and the acting of the same actress, improved, perfected, brought to a higher degree of expression, it is another actress and another singer superior to the former; it is, in a word, a new creation of the role of Desdemona." Stendahl wrote of the same performance in the *Journal de Paris*: "Mme Pasta acted and sang in a miraculous manner."[34]

The Italian critics were the slowest to recognize the merits of this *attrice cantante* whose art was for them a radical departure from the purity of *bel canto,* but by 1829 she had won them over. The reviewer of her Desdemona (in Rossini's *Otello*) in Verona was not only enthusiastic but obligingly specific in detailing the qualities of her voice: "As a singer Pasta has the resource of a lovable voice, extended, limpid, and strong in her beautiful high range. Her general vocal agility, her trills, her scales are amazing . . . and the embellishments, which she uses sparingly, are always varied, graceful, and judiciously integrated [into the music]."[35]

In 1831 Pasta sang the role of Norma in the eponymous opera composed by Vincenzo Bellini and his librettist Felice Romani specifically for her. While the music is a vivid and realistic portrait of her voice, music and drama together constitute a primary source documenting Pasta's extraordinary power on stage.[36] Composer and librettist exploited situations already proven successful: Norma's scene with her children, for example, is very similar to the scene of maternal love succeeded by filicide in Pasta's earlier success *Medea*, a scene that had never failed to move and astound audiences and critics. But they also wrote expertly for the vocal and histrionic gifts of a performer they knew intimately. The long dramatic recitative preceding her aria "Casta diva" with fast and frequent changes of mood speaks to her dramatic power; the long sustained lines are telling evidence of Pasta's amazing breath control and her delight in extended legato passages. She was especially famed for the beauty of her descending scales; Bellini gave her plenty, both chromatic and diatonic.

The caballetta "Ah! bello, a me ritorna" in particular documents Pasta's remarkable ability to use vocal virtuosity in the service of dramatic expression. The drama of her amazing leaps was especially admired; in the trio at the end of Act I Norma sings a coloratura passage followed by two upward leaps of an octave and a half. Vocally and dramatically, Norma is one of the most demanding roles in opera. The performer must be able to sing coloratura as well as long sustained passages, to communicate violence juxtaposed with profound tenderness, power alongside fragility. Superb vocal technique must be partnered with intense declamation. The music of *Norma*[37] documents vividly and more explicitly than words the vocal and dramatic powers of Giuditta Pasta in her prime.

*　*　*　*　*

Giuditta Negri Pasta was born 26 October 1797 in Saronno, a small town between Milan and Como. Her father Carlo Antonio Negri was a pharmacist, married to Rachele Ferranti (apparently the name, Rachele, suggested to François-Joseph Fétis, author of the *Biographie universelle des musiciens* [Brussels, 1835–1844][38] that Pasta was Jewish; no other evidence has appeared in support of this). She spent two years (1809–1811) at the Collegio Reale where she studied singing with Bartolomeo Scotti, *maestro di cappella* of the Como cathedral. In 1811 she moved with her aunt and uncle, Rosalinda and Filippo Ferranti to Milan where she studied with Giuseppe Scappa, an assistant maestro at La Scala and may have been a student at the Conservatory of Milan. On 17 January 1816 Giuditta Negri married Giuseppe Pasta, a tenor, and the two promptly began appearing together, probably for the first time in February 1816 at Milan's Teatro degli Accademici Filo-Drammatici in Scappa's *Lope de Vega*. In April they departed with Rachele Negri for Paris to sing in the Théâtre Italien. Giuseppe promptly developed throat problems which prevented his singing, a harbinger of the course of his career. Although his voice was described as "beautiful . . . when in full control of his powers,"[39] he was not quite simply cut out for a career in opera. By 1822 he had settled comfortably into the role of manager for his wife (they worked well together in this respect: he held out for the high fees she desired while she winsomely explained that her manager/husband would not permit her to sing for whatever lower fee might be offered).

Giuditta Pasta was received well, but with reservations, in this her first appearance in Paris. The veiled quality of her middle range was noted (see pages 115–16 under descriptions of her voice), and she was generally advised to keep working, as by the critic for *Annales Politiques, Morales et Littéraires*: "She is tiny, well-made, and pretty; but she needs to work . . . since she is in Paris, she is at a good school to learn ease in her movement and her gestures."[40]

A review in August of her performance as Elvira in Mozart's *Don Giovanni* does not reveal much progress: "she puts great intelligence into her manner of performing. But in the Théâtre Italien, both voice and method are required, and the voice of Mme Pasta, while pleasant enough, has neither strength nor range, and her method is nonexistent."[41] One might ask whether the role of Elvira was beyond the capabilities of the nineteen-year-old singer? By September, however, something had happened. Her last Paris role, in September 1816, was the part of Giulietta in Niccolò Zingarelli's *Giulietta e Romeo,* and in this part she literally astounded the critics: "Mme Pasta has astonished with several happy inspirations and moments of strength, to which until now her public was not accustomed."[42] Was this evidence of her determination? Did she just take the time to study the role? Or was it simply much better suited to her? Or, was the Romeo (Marianna Sessi) an electrifying force for her? (Interestingly enough, it was as Romeo that she won over the critics five years later; they praised her performance as "noble, passionate, tender, et moving.")[43] While in Paris she was contracted by William Ayrton, manager of the King's Theatre to sing the winter season in London. Here she found the real success that had eluded her in Paris. The English liked her voice, and they especially liked her shape, referring specifically to her "*very* handsome legs" (see above, page 115, review by Leigh Hunt).

She returned to Italy, pregnant, in the fall of 1817; on 27 March 1818 her only surviving daughter, Maria Clelia Luigia Teresa Pasta was born in Milan. (In 1823, after a severe bout of measles, she suffered a miscarriage.) By September Pasta was back on the opera stage. The next few years were formative ones for her; she toured all over Italy, singing in Venice, Padua, Rome, Brescia in operas by Cimarosa, Generali, Mayr, Nasolini, Nicolini, Pacini, Rossini (*La cenerentola*), Trento. She also refused several contracts that did not meet her requirements—level of fees, benefits such as housing or benefit performances, title, e.g., "assoluta." She demanded and usually got high fees even early in her career. The experience of singing in so many different houses and of singing so many different operas (by the time she was twenty-four she had performed forty-one roles) surely contributed to her ease on stage, but probably the most significant experience for her artistic development was working in the summers of 1819 and 1820 with the well-known contralto Giuseppina Grassini (1773–1850). Grassini was noted for her cantabile, for her extraordinary breath control, and for her stage deportment. She had enjoyed a long successful career, culminating in her appointment as court singer to Napoleon from 1806 to 1814. For the twenty-two-year-old Pasta, Grassini would have presented a very healthy and helpful model. In Brescia Pasta was singing the secondary roles, which placed her in an ideal position to observe every aspect of the older singer's technique and style. In Sebastiano Nasolini's *La morte di Cleopatra* (Brescia, 1819) the two had a duet which included chains of thirds and sixths and vocal fioritura sung *in alternatim*. They would necessarily have had to work together on phrasing, tempos, etc. After another year of touring Italy, during which she sang in Trieste, Padua, Turin, and Venice, and five roles were created for her (in operas by Farinelli, Orlandi, Pacini, Nicolini, and Pavesi which are heard nowhere today), she spent the summer of 1820 in Padua, singing once again in the same company with Grassini. Padua was also the home of the great castrato soprano Gaspare Pacchierrotti, now retired. There is no evidence that she met him or did not meet him, that he heard or did not hear her; Kenneth Stern, whose Ph.D. dissertation is the only source of information in English about Pasta has pointed out, however, that many of the traits associated with Pacchierrotti—his amazing trills, the variety, originality, and appropriateness of his embellishments, his delivery of recitative, and above all what the eighteenth-century English amateur Richard Mount Edgcumbe termed his "touching expression and exquisite pathos"—are the very characteristics singled out by critics to define Pasta's style.[44] Whether she studied with Grassini or with Pacchierotti, the experiences of these two summers were significant in reinforcing her strengths in singing serious roles. In addition, while working with Grassini, one of the great and respected contraltos of all (operatic) time, she could scarcely have failed to note the older singer's technique, her cantabile, coloratura, her breathing, her articulation, i.e., these two summers would have served as periods of very productive apprenticeship. Stendahl states that she never heard Pacchierotti or Marchesi, but adds that every connoisseur of his acquaintance who had heard them found that Pasta sang in that same revered old style. He continues that the "only teacher from whom she has received singing-lessons is Signora Grassini, with whom she once spent a season in Brescia." [45]

Is it a result of these summers that Milanese reviewers that fall (1820) praised

Pasta for her "voice, method, spirit, bearing, all the necessary virtues"[46] (the opera was Paër's *opera semi-seria, Sargino, ossia L'allievo dell'amore*).

On 10 March 1821, Pasta signed a contract to sing at the Paris Théâtre Italien for seven months for the amount of 14,100 francs, exactly what she had requested.[47] This was the turning point in her career. She debuted in Rossini's *Otello* on 5 June 1821 to raving reviews (see above, page 116) most of which concentrated on the unusual qualities of her voice and attempted to define its uniqueness. One critic remarked on "the difference that exists between a student and a professional."[48] Rumor had it that she had spent two years entirely in retirement working on her voice; as we have seen she had been performing widely around the Italian circuit, gaining experience and maturing as an artist.

Pasta was now, at the age of twenty-four, reaching the pinnacle of her powers. She continued at the Théâtre-Italien till November of 1821, returned in March of 1822, and performed there exclusively until April 1824. When she finally left then for London, the Parisians were desolated at their loss. A crown was tossed on stage at the end of her final performance (in Paisiello's *Nina, ossia La pazza per amore*); the French wondered (characteristically!) if the English could appreciate "their" Pasta: "Let us hope that she can find in England . . . a public that understands how to listen and hear her!"[49]

But the English could, and did. She enjoyed an immensely successful season in London at the King's Theatre, from April to 7 August 1824, during which she added to her repertoire the title role of Rossini's *Semiramide* (first performed 15 July); Rossini himself conducted the first three performances. When she returned to the Théâtre-Italien at the end of September, French audiences found her acting even improved by the English sojourn. Stendahl wrote that her Romeo seemed entirely new, "not for her singing [in which] Mme Pasta long since arrived at perfection, but for her acting."[50]

For the next seven years Pasta alternated fairly regularly between the King's Theatre and the Théâtre-Italien; her last Paris performance seems to have been at the end of October in 1831, but she continued to sing in London through the summer season of 1833. Her contract with the King's Theatre for the 1826 season in London named her *Prima donna assoluta, Musico Assoluto,* and specified that she would sing only leading female and male roles in opera seria, her fee of £2,300 would be paid in advance, she had absolute choice of roles, sang no more than six times in a thirty-day period, enjoyed the right to approve casting of operas and supervise staging, was not required to participate in any concert or benefit at the King's Theatre except her own, but she could sing in any public or private concert that did not interfere with her work at the King's Theatre, and she was also given one eight-day leave of absence.[51] Giuseppe Pasta and Manuel Garcia tried at one point in vain to take over the management of the King's Theatre. Giuseppe Pasta also went to New York to investigate the possibilities for Giuditta to sing there but after six months returned to Europe empty-handed (the Garcia family had earlier tried their fortunes in America, see Chapter 12, and Mozart's librettist, Lorenzo da Ponte (1749–1838), was in New York).

Pasta's most important professional partnership during this time was with the tenor Giovanni Battista Rubini, famous for his singing of long sustained melodic lines. (Chopin recommended that his piano pupils listen to Rubini in order to understand his melodic writing in the *Nocturnes*.) Pasta and Rubini first appeared together in November 1825 in Rossini's *Otello*; it was a partnership made in heaven. Their voices, as well as their stagecraft, meshed perfectly; they continued to delight Paris audiences through the end of the 1831 season. It was in October 1831 that Chopin, just arrived in Paris, heard them sing: "Never have I heard . . . *Otello* as with Rubini, Pasta and Lablache . . . They say that Pasta has gone off, but I never saw anything more sublime. Malibran impresses you merely by her marvelous voice, but no one *sings* like her. Miraculous! Marvellous!"[52] It's particularly interesting that according to Chopin people are saying she has "gone off," while he found her "sublime" and "miraculous."

In 1826, Pasta had returned to Italy for a season to sing at the Teatro San Carlo and Teatro del Fondo in Naples; she was not particularly well received in Naples, perhaps because her mixture of dramatic singing and beautiful sound did not accord precisely with current ideals of the pure *bel canto*. She returned quickly to London where she spent the next two years, and where she now enjoyed absolute dominance. She was hugely successful in all her roles, which included the first performance in England of Mayr's *Medea in Corinto* (1 June 1826). Pasta was in excellent form; her vocal and dramatic powers were eulogized by all who heard her. Reviewers dwelt particularly on her effectiveness in the scene from *Medea* in which she murders her children following a moving expression of maternal love. This opera she had first sung in Paris in 1823 (14 January) as a favor to her friend Manuel Garcia, and it had become one of her most important roles. (She never performed Cherubini's *Médée* because she sang only in Italian.) Castil-Blaze described for the *Journal des Débats* the moment when Medea moves from caressing the children to conceiving their murder:

This sublime transition, prepared with great art and executed with forceful emotion, a frightening realism in her speaking and gestures, struck all assembled with terror and tore from them a cry of admiration. I speak foremost of this scene, considering that it is the most remarkable of the work. Mme Pasta played the remainder of her role with depth, nobility, feeling; she surpassed herself; that is the best elegy that one can give her. We have seen in succession this actress charming in her brilliant costume as the spouse of Othello; ravishing in the armor of the chevalier; seductive in the Moabite turban. All of these riches adapted— the sorceress Medea.[53]

Pasta was now at the very peak of her powers and the height of her fame. During the period from September 1828 to October 1831 she added a number of new operas to her repertoire, including the principal roles in *La sonnambula* and *Anna*

Bolena. In addition to her regular seasons in London and Paris, she sang in Vienna, Milan, Verona, Bologna, and Mantua. The Austrians liked her as much as did the English and French: the critic for the *Allgemeine musikalische Zeitung* raved in 1829 about her "beautiful trills, with such finely shaded transitions, and unbelievable duration."[54] In April she was in Milan where her dramatic ability and singing in *Semiramide* were acclaimed: "as an actress she is a model of the art, second to no one . . . as a singer she might be surpassed in purity of sound and strength of voice—in expressivity it would be difficult to find anyone superior or even equal to her."[55] Her Tancredi was equally praised, the critic for *I Teatri* writing "surely Pasta is recognized as the supreme master of dramatic singing."[56]

She spent summer and autumn of 1830 at her new Villa Roda, where in November Gaetano Donizetti (1797–1848) joined her and composed most of his *Anna Bolena.* Sadly, the premiere in Milan's Teatro Carcano was only moderately well-received; public and critics were not impressed by either the opera or its diva, saying that "as a singer and as an actress, [her performance] left something to be desired."[57] On 6 March at the same theatre Pasta appeared as Amina in Bellini's *La sonnambula,* the first opera composed for her by Bellini; both opera and star were great successes. After a month's rest she was off to London for the summer. Her performance as Medea on 12 May ravished her audience. The critic for *The Court Journal* was very specific:

[H]er voice, splendid as it was, is improved, and has become more soft, more adoucie, more free from a sort of hoarse coating with which it was occasionally covered heretofore . . . She has the same energy, the same marvelous physical power, that rendered then, what she still is, the greatest *actress* in the world. The particular characteristic of this wonderful singer's voice is a moaning sound, which colours it throughout, deepening and intensifying its effect and beauty. Her Medea is a matchless performance. We can scarcely imagine Mrs. Siddons could have been finer. Fanny Kemble we observed in a high box, intensely studying her great prototype.[58]

She also introduced to London her new operas, *Anna Bolena* and *La sonnambula* in which her partner was Rubini. They spent September and October in Paris at the Théâtre-Italien; it was during this season that the young Chopin heard them (see above, page 125). French critics also found Pasta even more improved: her voice was "even more flexible; now she executes the descending chromatic scale and the trill with an abundance of agility."[59] The critic for *La France nouvelle* wrote:

[H]er voice, always lightly veiled, lends itself better than ever to the dramatic expression of tense situations; this is the voice of a tragedienne; she was above all admirable in the final scene; this transition from the rapture of madness, to terror, her cries of a poor woman who sees death before her, she has rendered all with a pathos and an inimitable truth.[60]

In light of these reviews, we can only wonder who told Chopin she had "gone off."

In November 1831, Pasta made her long-awaited debut at Milan's famous La Scala as Norma in Bellini's opera of the same name. Written expressly for her, it could not help but show all the powers of her voice and her unique stage persona (see above, page 121). Reviews of Pasta's singing were highly laudatory, but the opera did not please particularly. It was nevertheless performed twenty-four times that first season and gradually won more acclaim. And, although the opera was not wonderfully successful at first, its heroine was.

Pasta, it seems, could scarcely now do wrong. Even if the opera failed to please—as was the case with *Norma*—reviewers found Pasta's work to be of the highest caliber. English critics were transported by the drama of *Anna Bolena* (perhaps the subject, being close to home, was particularly affecting). The *Morning Post* raved that "the thrilling energy of her manner carries the sympathies of the auditory as irresistibly as though she were delivering the language of SHAKESPEARE," while the *Morning Herald* named Pasta "the Queen of classic tragedy."[61] The reviewer in *The Times,* like his Milanese colleagues, did not care for *Norma,* but found plenty to praise in Pasta's singing of it: "She was in grand voice, and sang with a purity of intonation, with a truth of expression, with an intensity of feeling, perfectly unrivalled"; he was also impressed by "the exquisite acting of Madame Pasta."[62]

By 1835 Pasta had been singing publicly for nearly twenty years. She began now to sing less frequently in opera and attempted during the 1837 season in London to make her way on the concert circuit. Even the kindliest of critics, however, found that her art was not suited to the concert situation. Pasta, the quintessential dramatic singer, needed the drama of opera to fulfill her gifts. The critic of the *Morning Post* noted especially the difference between hearing an aria in the dramatic context of the opera and hearing it isolated on the recital stage; he pointed out that:

Pasta is essentially a dramatic singer, and, though at all times her thrilling and mellifluous tones enchant every ear, while her pathos and energy leave their impression indelible on every heart, yet her soaring genius is as much depressed in a concert-room as her attitude is constrained by the formality of holding a sheet of music in her hands.[63]

It is interesting to note that she was not singing from memory, and that the critic believed that the need to hold and look at the sheet of music interfered with her performance.

The critic for the *Morning Herald* wrote that

acting with her is not an art, but her very nature . . . Her voice is still what it was, delicious in the sweetness of its soprano, most touching the slight huskiness of its *contr'altro,* in both having a separate and peculiar quality of which seems essentially the grand—the epic. We never heard her sing more delightfully than she did occasionally last night, or execute with a more delicate trill some of the prolonged shakes which always formed so special a feature in her style.[64]

Both critics clearly searched for positive remarks about the performance, yet both noted the same basic problem: this was a singer who depended on the drama of the situation to realize her potential, and in recital she lacked the very fabric that was vitally necessary to her art. The second critic, even while praising the continued beauty of her singing, nevertheless pointed out that the full beauty was apparent only "occasionally." Henry Chorley, writing in 1861 and thus from some distance of time, remembered that "her voice was steadily out of tune, with some exceptional moments."[65]

Perhaps the less frequent performances led to the loss of good intonation (pitch problems had always been with her, however), and the power of her voice decreased. But even though she slowed her professional activities she nevertheless continued to achieve remarkable triumphs. During the season of 1840–1841 she toured eastern Europe, singing opera excerpts in private and public concerts in Warsaw, Moscow, and St. Petersburg. On 14 May 1841 she made her last opera appearance in her old success *Anna Bolena* at the Bolshoi Kannerny Theatre in St. Petersburg. That same year she took Teresa Parodi as a student/protégé and essentially retired to Villa Roda, where in 1846 her husband died and in 1847 her mother Rachele Negri died. An ardent supporter of the movement for Italian liberation from the Austrians, Pasta spent several months in self-imposed exile in Lugano during 1847. Sadly, drawn perhaps by the need for money or simply by the desire to sing one final season, Pasta appeared in London in 1850, where she did three concerts at the old King's Theatre, now Her Majesty's Theatre. The critics were kind. They wrote mostly about her splendid past and touted her as an example of a noble style no longer being practiced:

[A] manner of phrasing and a grandeur of expression which belong to a style of singing now, unhappily, almost extinct. A method of respiration which allowed of the longest sentences being uttered without any perceptible break was also remarked with admiration, while a classical severity of taste in the choice and use of ornaments offered a not less striking example for the consideration of the present school of singers. These high qualities, which, being purely mental, defy the encroachments of time, are still observable in Madame Pasta's singing. Upon the rest it would be ungraceful to dilate . . . What she is—a relic of one of the most admirable monuments of executive art—must be contemplated with the veneration due to a fame well earned.[66]

At this first concert on 8 July she had sung notably Gluck's "Che farò"; for the second concert she sang with Teresa Parodi the duet from *Anna Bolena* and then the final mad scene. The critics were again kind, but they described what they heard:

Gradually Madame Pasta's dignified and impressive delivery of the recitative made the audience conscious of a style to which they had not been accustomed; and it was very soon apparent that much more vocal power was retained than could possibly have been expected. It is in the upper notes, of course, that the voice has suffered most, but in the middle notes there is still much tone and sweetness, while the *sfogato* lower notes are yet full of thrilling power. The style, which of course is what all reasonable people went to study, is grand beyond conception—a simplicity and force of vocalization conveying direct the impulses of the soul, and without any conventional exaggeration."[67]

This same critic wrote of the mad scene that she performed some amazing vocal feats, considering her physical condition, but it was the style that remained her great forte: "there is no artist on the stage who could mark out a more lofty and tragic conception. The emotion is conveyed by the countenance, not by merely physical demonstration of excitement, and the attitudes are grand and statuesque."[68] The hard-to-please Henry Chorley was also in the audience; eleven years later in *Thirty Years' Musical Recollections* he remembered the performance. Her voice, he wrote, "had been long ago given up by her. Its state of utter ruin on the night in question passes description." Many artists were present, hearing her for the first time, some surely with the thought that "her reputation had been exaggerated"— the great actress Rachel was in the audience and made no secret of her amusement at the spectacle, thereby drawing a great deal of attention to herself as she sat there "one might even say sarcastically enjoying the scene." Chorley's close friend, the singer Pauline Viardot was also in the audience hearing Pasta, says Chorley for the first time (although Viardot's brother Manuel Garcia was an old friend of Pasta). "Dismal as was the spectacle, broken, hoarse, and destroyed as was the voice, the great style of the singer spoke to the great singer [Viardot]." Chorley describes the duet (sung by Pasta and Parodi as Ann Boleyn and Jane Seymour) and then the final mad scene. And here

the old irresistible charm broke out; nay, even in the final song, with its roulades, and its scales of shakes ascending by a semitone, the consummate vocalist and tragedian, able to combine form with meaning—the moment of the situation with such personal and musical display as form an integral part of operatic art—was indicated: at least to the apprehension of a younger artist "You are right!" was Madame Viardot's quick and heartfelt response (her eyes full of tears) to a friend beside her; "You are right! It is like the *Cenacolo* of da Vinci at Milan—a wreck of a picture, but the picture is the greatest picture in the world!"[69]

These three concerts marked the end of Giuditta Pasta's life as a singer. For the remainder of her life, she divided her time between Milan and the Villa Trempo (a smaller villa near her former residence Villa Roda, where she had moved after the deaths of her husband and mother), with occasional visits to her daughter Clelia who had married and moved to Genoa. She is said to have grown quite heavy in her later years; Prosper Mérimée visited her at the Villa Trempo and reported that "Elle a augmenté singulièrement en largeur."[70] On 1 April 1865, at the Villa Trempo, Giuditta Pasta died rather suddenly of a viral infection. She was 68.

*   *   *   *   *

Just as Nancy Storace was the first truly successful singer of comic opera, Giuditta Pasta was the first great actor-singer of tragic opera. This sometimes interfered with her reception as a singer during a period in which *bel canto* was the ideal—her voice was characterized as harsh and raw—but as her interpretative powers matured, the qualities of her voice which had been earlier seen as problematic came to be viewed as contributing to her dramatic expressiveness. It was five years from her first unremarkable season (1816) in Paris to the success of 1821 when she was described as singing "tout son role avec âme," with "une execution parfaite et [un] goût irreprochable." This may be attributed to the above cited unusual qualities of her voice but also to her growing skill in exploiting these qualities to serve the drama. She spent those five years, too, in hard-working apprenticeship—singing all around Italy, learning through performing, and growing musically and technically into her unique voice.

Pasta went against the current, too, in her use of vocal ornaments: she seems to have very carefully prepared the ornamentation in her studio and seldom deviated from the prepared versions in performance. Furthermore, although the embellishments were typical *bel canto* style, she was careful and rather sparing in her use of them, and her *fiorituri* were in distinct contrast to the often exaggerated ornaments of the earlier *bel canto*. Critics mentioned frequently her reliance on ornamentation as a means of expression, but her splendid (though sometimes unpredictable) roulades, scales, and trills served the drama and the character; they were a means, not an end in themselves.

Recitatives took on new and extraordinary life in Pasta's rendition; they became as important for drama as the words in a Shakespeare play. Viewed earlier as necessary but frequently boring preparations for the aria, the recitative now became a vital part of the performance. In her declamation Pasta was aided by her extraordinary sense of timing and phrasing, and by an amazing ability to vary the colors of her voice, what Stendahl called the three different parts of her voice.

Her gestures and attitudes were also remarked upon as being natural expressions of text and not just traditional stage movements. She often assumed the attitudes seen in antique sculpture; she could remain almost completely still and yet impart an extraordinary emotion. Again and again, critics refer to her "majesty." Pasta in tragic opera and Nancy Storace in comic made the characters vivid, real, no longer types or caricatures. Critics found it difficult to describe her effect on stage, perhaps because her approach was so new—a great deal of talk had been made about opera singers as actors, Mara had been accused of being absolutely deadly on stage, while LeRochois had been praised for her realistic acting, but none had approached the level of presentation offered by Pasta. As the operatic manager John Ebers wrote, in 1818, Pasta was not acting, she *was* the part even before going on stage:

Nothing, indeed, can be more free from trick or affectation than Pasta's performance. There is no perceptible effort to resemble the character she plays; on the contrary, she enters the stage the character itself; transposed into the situation, excited by the hopes and the fears, breathing the life and the spirit of the being she represents.[71]

Perhaps most telling of all are the tributes paid to her art by such dramatic artists as the English Sarah Siddons (Pasta was often apostrophized as the "Siddons of the Opera") or the French François-Joseph Talma who exclaimed after attending Pasta's performances as Tancredi (Rossini) or Romeo (Zingarelli), "This is the first time I've seen tragedy acted . . . What took me a year of study she knows instinctively." Talma even visited the singer to tell her "you realize the ideal of which I have dreamed; you possess the secrets I have sought to discover during my entire theatrical career—that to touch the heart is the true aim of the tragic artist."[72]

Writers bemoaned the fact that later generations would have no conception of the greatness, the depth, of her performances. While this is surely true, we still may be grateful for the insightful critical reviews of her work which give a sense of how vital and moving her performances were and for the documentation of her art in the music written for her by such composers as Rossini, Donizetti, Bellini.

Timeline

1797, 26 Oct	Giuditta Negri born, Saronno, to Rachele Ferranti and Carlo Antonio Negri
1809	Collegio Reale, studied singing with Bartolomeo Scotti, *maestro di cappella* of Como cathedral
1811	Moved with Rosalinda and Filippo Ferranti (aunt and uncle) to Milan; studied with Giuseppe Scappa, assistant maestro at La Scala, perhaps attended Conservatory of Milan; met Giuseppe Pasta
1816, 17 Jan	Married Giuseppe Pasta
Feb	First performances with Giuseppe at Teatro degli Accademici Filo-Drammatici, as Baroness Isabella in Giuseppe Scappa's *Lope de Vega.*
11–25 Apr	Both Pastas with Rachele Negri to Paris to sing in Théâtre Italien; Giuseppe's series of throat problems prevented his singing
1817, 11 Jan	London, King's Theatre, debut as Telemacho in Cimarosa's *Penelope*
fall	Pregnant; home to Milan
1818, 27 Mar	Daughter, Maria Clelia Luigia Teresa Pasta born, Milan
Aug	Sang in Venice, Padua, Rome, Brescia, operas by Cimarosa, Generali, Mayr, Nasolini, Nicolini, Pacini, Rossini, Trento Engagements as *prima donna assoluta* in Venice, Padua, Rome
3 Sep	Venice, Pacini's *Adelaide e Comingio*
19 Oct	*La Cenerentola,* Padua, first Rossini opera for Pasta Acquired a theatrical agent, Valentino Bertoja
26 Dec	Carnival season in Rome, 26 Dec – Ash Wed. Rejected full-year contract as *prima donna buffa, e seria*, with benefit performance
1819	Offered contract with Munich court opera: 15 Oct-15 Jun 1820, sing ca. 40 times, no more than 2/week, plus good fees for concerts at court, with title *prima donna seria, buffa*; Pasta requested title of *assoluta*, benefit performance, paid housing, travel expenses, and more money; Munich court could not meet these high demands of the 22-year-old Pasta
11 July	Brescia, *La morte di Cleopatra* (Nasolini) and *Gli orazi i curiazi* (Cimarosa); in company with famed contralto Giuseppina Grassini
Dec	Continued to work in Italy: Trieste, Padua, Turin, Venice; new roles;
1820, Jun	Padua, again with Grassini
1820, Dec to	Venice; no La Scala offers, Pasta's fees too high? Five roles
1821, Mar	composed for her: Farinelli's *La Festa Patria* (Diana), Orlandi's *Fedra* (Ippolito), Pacini's *La Schiava in Bagdad* (Zora),

	Nicolini's *La Conquista di Granata* (Gonzalvo), Pavesi's *Arminio* (Arminio)
1821, 10 Mar	Signed contract to sing at Théâtre Italien, Paris: 7 months, 60 per cent of annual salary of 23,500 francs
Apr-Nov	Turning Point! Rossini's *Otello,* 5 Jun, Théâtre Italien
Nov	Turin, not particularly successful; last performances in Italy till 1829; turned down later offers from Turin, never sang there again
1822, Mar	Paris, Théâtre Italien, performed here exclusively till Apr 1824 Giuseppe now Giuditta's manager
	Operas performed: Zingarelli's *Giulietta e Romeo,* Cimarosa's *Gli Orazi e I Curiazi,* title roles in Mayr's *Medea in Corinto,* Paisiello's *Nina, Pazza per amore,* Rossini's *Elisabetta, Regina d'Inghilterra, Tancredi;* Mayr's *La rosa bianca e la rosa rossa* (Enrico), Mercadante's *Elisa e Claudio* (Elisa), Rossini's *Mose in Egitto* (Elcia)
1823, spring	Medical problems, pregnant, performed Jul and Aug; ill six weeks with serious measles, miscarriage
1824, Apr	End of Paris contract; to London
1824, Apr to 1825, Jun	Alternated between King's Theatre, London, and Théâtre Italien, Paris
1824, Jul	London, new role *Semiramide,* Rossini conducted first three performances
Sep	Return to Paris, tumultuous welcome.
1825, spring	Paris: three new roles composed for her: Rossini's *Il Viaggio à Reims)* (Corinna), Armando (Mayerbeer's *Il Crociato in Egitto*), Zelmira (Rossini's *Zelmira*)
	Giuseppe Pasta and Manuel Garcia tried unsuccessfully to take over management of King's Theatre, London; Giuseppe tempted by offers for Giuditta to sing in New York; she not interested
1825, Nov	Sang for first time with Giovanni Battista Rubini (then 31)
1826, Apr to Oct	King's Theatre, *Prima donna assoluta, Musico Assoluto;* sang only leading female and male roles in opera seria; fee £2,300, paid in advance; great success in all roles, first performance in England of Mayr's *Medea in Corinto*
1 Jun	Huge success in *Zelmira;* first talk of retirement (Pasta 29!)
Nov to 1827, Apr	Naples: Teatro San Carlo and Teatro del Fondo; Rivalry between "Fodoristi" and "Pastisti"
Apr to 1828, Aug	London; joined in 1828 season by Henriette Sontag; Pasta's benefit: sang Otello to Sontag's Desdemona (Rossini's *Otello*)
11 Aug	Milan to rest
Sep to 1831, Oct	Created principal roles in *La Sonnambula, Anna Bolena;* added other new roles; first appearances at Vienna's Kärntnertortheater, Milan's Teatro Carcano, Verona's Teatro Filarmonico, Bologna's

	Teatro Communale, Mantua's Teatro Sociale; sang new roles in London and Paris; new home, Villa Roda on Lake Como; 1829, in Vienna, Milan, Verona. Pasta at peak of her career (and of her fees)
1831, Jul	First London performances of *La sonnambula* (with Rubini) and *Anna Bolena*
Sep, Oct	Paris, *La sonnambula* and *Anna Bolena* (with Rubini)
Nov	Milan, La Scala debut, Bellini's *Norma*; 24 performances that season
1831–1835	Created title roles in Bellini's *Norma, Beatrice di Tenda*; Bianca in Donizetti's *Ugo, Conte di Parigi*; sang in Venice, London, Bologna, Milan (La Scala), Romeo in *I Capuleti e i Montecchi*, sang *Norma, Il Pirata, Anna Bolena, Medea, Tancredi, Semiramide*.
1833–1834	Carnival season Venice (La Fenice), rested spring and summer
1834, Oct	Bologna, returned to La Scala
1835, Jan-Mar	*Emma d'Antiochia* and *Norma*
1835–1850	Withdrew gradually from opera stage; always problematic intonation worsened, power of voice lessened, interpretation and expression still strong; concert performances (1837) not really successful
1840–1841	Eastern Europe: Warsaw, Moscow, St. Petersburg, opera excerpts, private and public concerts
1841, 14 May	Last opera performance, *Anna Bolena,* Bolshoi Kannerny Theatre, St. Petersburg
1844	Retired to Villa Roda, took Teresa Parodi as student/protégé
1845, 6 Sep	Bergamo, duet from *Anna Bolena* with Parodi
1846	Death of husband, Giuseppe Pasta
1847	Death of Rachele Negri, mother
	Several months exile in Lugano as result of her support of movement to liberate Italy from Austrian rule; requested by Giuseppe Mazzini to sing benefit for Italian exiles.
1850	London with Parodi, Parodi's debut at Her Majesty's Theatre (former King's Theatre); sang three concerts: 8, 11, 12 Jul 1850 (last one was a benefit for Italian refugees in London); voice gone
1850–1865	Private life; divided time between Milan and Villa Trempo (Como); daughter Clelia in Genoa, married with children
1865, 1 Apr	Died suddenly, 68, of viral infection; funeral at cathedral in Como

Bibliography

The only study of Pasta available in English is the 1983 dissertation by Kennth A. Stern, "A Documentary Study of Giuditta Pasta on the Opera Stage." Stern's two articles, cited below, are also very useful.

Works about Pasta

Stendahl [Henri Beyle]. *Life of Rossini by Stendhal.* 2 vols. New and revised edition. Translated and annotated by Richard N. Coe. Seattle: University of Washington Press, 1970.
  Stendahl devoted an entire chapter of his *Life* to Pasta's voice. Rossini worked with Pasta a number of times; she sang the first Paris staging of his *Otello* in November 1821, and he conducted the first three performances with her in *Semiramide* in London, 1824.

Stern, Kenneth A. "A Documentary Study of Giuditta Pasta on the Opera Stage." Ph.D. diss., City University of New York, 1983.
  Stern is wonderfully thorough in his coverage of newspaper reviews, memoirs, etc., including many letters from Pasta to family and friends; and the data are well-documented. The disadvantage for the English reader is that all reviews and letters are left in the original language with no translations offered. The study is objective and gives a broad view of Pasta's performing career, her reception, the quality and sound of her voice, and her unique gift for communicating the dramatic content of the music. A good bibliography of books, newspapers, and journals is provided.

_____. "The Theatre of *Bel Canto*: Giuditta Pasta Introduced a Romantic New Style of Acting to Early Nineteenth-Century Italian Opera, Taking Her Cue from Reigning Figures of the English Stage." *Opera News* 40 (1975/76, no. 16):10–16.
  Thoughtful and provocative essay about Pasta's work as an actress and its relationship to the work of her contemporaries in the purely dramatic theatre.

_____. "Pasta Diva: Bellini's First Norma, Celebrated across Europe, Settled into a Different Life at Her Villa on the Shores of Lake Como." *Opera News* 46 (1981/82, no. 12): 8–11.

General Reference Works
The following works are helpful as eye-witness accounts of Pasta and many other singers.

Chopin, Fryderyk. *Selected Correspondence of Fryderyk Chopin.* Translated and edited with additional material and a commentary by Arthur Hedley. 1963. Reprint, New York: Da Capo Press, 1979.

Chorley, Henry. *Modern German Music.* 1854. Reprint, New York: Da Capo Press, 1973.

_____. *Thirty Years' Musical Recollections.* New York: Alfred A. Knopf, 1926.

Ferris, George. *Great Singers—Faustina Bordoni to Henriette Sontag.* New York: D. Appleton and Co., 1895.

Fétis, François-Joseph. *Biographie universelle des musicians et bibliographie générale de la musique.* 8 vols. Paris: Firmin Didot Frères, 1864.

Moscheles, Ignatz. *Recent Music and Musicians.* New York: Henry Holt and Company, 1873.

Mount Edgcumbe, Richard. *Musical Reminiscences of the Earl of Mount Edgcumbe: Containing an Account of the Italian Opera in England from 1773 to 1834,* 4th ed., 1834. Reprint, New York: Da Capo Press, 1973.

Mount Edgcumbe's remarks are candid and are particularly valuable due to his wide knowledge of opera in England and on the Continent.

Chapter 10

Wilhelmine Schröder-Devrient
(6 December 1804 – 26 January 1860)

Noble eagle, seek not the distance
With the harp, fly not to the heights!
Remain with our singer,
That we may praise you together.[1]
                    Johann Wolfgang von Goethe
                    Weimar, 22 April 1830

All accounts agree that Wilhelmine Schröder-Devrient did not have a spectacularly beautiful voice. Yet she made her singing debut as Pamina in *Die Zauberflöte*, a role that demands a certain amount of virtuosity in terms of coloratura as well as sustained singing, and she managed by dint of continued study and hard work to build a vocal technique that enabled her to perform such roles as Bellini's Norma. Beethoven was present at her Leonore in the 1822 revival of *Fidelio* and seems to have been deeply moved by it. The singer tells us that the following day Beethoven came to offer his "thanks and his congratulations . . . in my joy, I would not have exchanged anything in the world for this praise from Beethoven's lips. He promised at that time to write an opera for me, but unfortunately it remained nothing but a promise."[2] She also tells us that many changes were made in her part to accommodate "the limits of my underdeveloped young voice" (she was 17), and that due to his deafness Beethoven could not hear a single note of the music. It was this Viennese performance of *Fidelio* (29 April 1823) under Carl Maria von Weber that established the beginnings of her career. She then sang the first Dresden performance of *Fidelio* in 1823 under Weber's baton. Weber is supposed to have said of her Agathe in his opera *Der Freischütz*. "She is the greatest Agathe in the world and has exceeded everything I thought I had written in this role."[3] She sang the Dresden premiere of his *Euryanthe* on 30 April 1824. She continued vocal studies for several years, and obviously improved in both vocal quality and technique. Her success in roles such as Norma, Donna Anna (Mozart's *Don Giovanni*), Amina (Bellini's *La sonnambula*), Senta (Wagner's *Der fliegende Holländer*) indicate her ability. When Maria Malibran died tragically young, Schröder-Devrient was hailed as her only possible successor. Extrapolating from the evidence of these roles, we can assess fairly well the range of her voice— middle C or D to high B, with a strong middle range—and its capacity for florid singing (as in *Norma* or *La sonnambula* in particular).

Reviews and other descriptions speak rather scantily about the voice. Henry Chorley, the English critic, tells us for example:

In truth, a singer the lady never was, though she promised to become one in the early days when she appeared as *Pamina* . . . Her voice, since I have known it, was capable of conveying poignant or tender expression, but was harsh, and torn—not so inflexible as incorrect.[4]

Lord Mount Edgcumbe heard her London debut in *Fidelio* and considered her to be "indeed a very superior performer, with a voice less sweet perhaps than powerful, capable of great exertion and strong expression."[5]

Eduard Genast, a singer-actor, who played opposite Schröder-Devrient on many occasions (though he was older than she), knew her as a young girl of sixteen or so. In his autobiography (*Aus dem Tagebuche eines alten Schauspielers*) he includes a discussion of her singing the role of Norma, a role that demands vocal agility as well as dramatic intensity:

She never could have become a brilliant coloratura singer—partly her high respect for the nobility of the art of song opposed the kind of virtuosity that always amazes the crowds, partly her throat was too weak. Whatever she needed in the way of embellished melody for a role such as Norma she learned, and executed the passages cleanly, even though she did not exactly project them like rockets into the air.[6]

He also describes eloquently her determination (for example, she worked for hours on end at mastering a good rolled "R" and a sung trill), and he remarks on her gains from hearing "the best Italian singers." He claims further that as a declamatory singer Wilhelmine in her mid-twenties already outshone many of her German and Italian contemporaries; this talent for declamation made it possible for her to perform with artistic integrity a virtuosic role such as Norma."[7]

Chorley waxed indignant on the subject of Schröder-Devrient's vocal style; he extended his rage to take in the entire nation of German singers:

But . . . the German and the Italian artist can hardly be mentioned on the same page. What Pasta *would* be, in spite of her uneven, rebellious, uncertain voice—a most magnificent singer—Madame Schröder Devrient did not care to be; though Nature, I have been assured by those who heard her sing when a girl, had blessed her with a fresh, delicious *soprano* voice. In this respect, she is but one among the hundreds who have suffered from the ignorance and folly of German connoisseurship—from the obstinacy of national antipathy, which, so soon as Germany began to imagine the possibility of possessing an opera of its own, made it penal to sing with grace, taste, and vocal self-command; because such were the characteristics of the Italian method.—Had she been trained under a wiser dispensation, Madame Schröder Devrient might have been singing by the side of Madame Sontag at this very day; and, when she retired, might have left behind her the character of a great dramatic vocalist, instead of the fame of a powerful actress who appeared in some German operas.[8]

Even Chorley, however, had to concede the very real power of Madame Schröder-Devrient. After explaining that many German singers attempted to emulate the Italians in producing roulades, shakes, etc., and when found to be incompetent fell back on the excuse "I am a German singer," he states that "Madame Schröder Devrient resolved to be *par excellence* 'the German dramatic singer,'" and to this end she incorporated into her work a vehement level of intensity and passion that often amounted to little more than dominating the stage (coincidentally drawing all attention to herself at the expense of her colleagues). From this technique, however, rose her tremendous success in *Fidelio*, an opera as he says that contains only one "acting character," who has the responsibility of giving to

the drama the importance of terror, suspense, and rapture when the spell is broken, by exhibiting the agony and the struggle of which she is the incessant victim . . . There was something subduing in the look of speechless affection with which she at last undid the chains of the beloved one, saved by her love—the mere remembrance of which makes the heart throb, and the eyes fill.[9]

As this description makes abundantly clear, it was not the voice that was remembered; it was the dramatic passion that composers, critics, and audiences found irresistible and unforgettable.

This was borne out for Chorley by her performance as Lady Macbeth in Chélard's *Macbeth*: "One could not look at her without at once recollecting the ideal which Mrs. Siddons is reported to have conceived of this 'grand, fiendish' character (to use her own epithets)," and he concluded that "the figure of Madame Schröder Devrient's *Lady Macbeth,* too, rises, as one of those visions concerning which young men are apt to rave and old men to dote . . . the stage has had few more striking personations."[10] The inveterate opera-goer, Lord Mount Edgcumbe too remarked on her portrayal as "a very fine piece of acting, particularly in the sleeping scene, to which she gave a novel though natural effect" in an opera that was otherwise unpleasing.[11]

The German composer-pianist Ignaz Moscheles experienced her Fidelio and her Norma: "Schröder-Devrient appeared again; her Fidelio was incomparable as ever, her Norma, however, not up to Pasta's mark."[12] Chorley too found that in *Norma* and Bellini's *La sonnambula* she "failed, owing to her deficiency in vocal accomplishment."[13] Their remarks are revealing: the music of *Norma* is, in spite of its dramatic intensity, Italian *bel canto* with corresponding vocal demands of technique, agility, and discipline; *Fidelio* on the other hand requires impassioned acting and the ability to suspend disbelief, and depends vocally less on the current Italian style of singing than on an ability to infuse the often instrumental style of writing with the emotional intensity of the drama. An excellent example is Leonora/ Fidelio's great recitative and aria "Abscheulicher!" in Act I. The singer must express a gamut of emotions: horrified disgust at the villain's evil, the hope of finding her beloved husband, the inspiration of true conjugal love which strengthens her resolve. Beethoven has no mercy: Leonora sings her high G-sharps on the word "Gatte" (husband) over full orchestra and sustains it over three horns before she joins them in an astounding run of an octave and a half.[14]

While illustrating well the kind of dramatic performance that so thrilled Schröder-Devrient's audiences, the music of this scene also makes abundantly clear that her vocal deficiencies were not so great as to interfere with her ability to perform such an aria. But it is doubtless these deficiencies that became ever more noticeable as she aged. Weber, delighted to find in her the ideal of his total dedication to the dramatic, recognized nonetheless the failings of the voice: he first heard her in a rather bad staging of *Freischütz* in Vienna (18 February 1821). The production elicited from him only "*Der Freischütz!* ACH GOTT!" but he noted the Agathe of Wilhelmine Schröder: "pretty; superb voice, apt acting, pure intonation, though in many ways a deficient singer."[15] Although Richard Wagner's descriptions of her performances say virtually nothing about the actual quality of her voice, he was dumbfounded by the power of her portrayal, i.e., the total portrayal, and the marriage of drama and music intrinsic to her work.

The comparisons made by both Chorley and Moscheles with Maria Malibran, who had been hailed for the dramatic intensity of her portrayals as well as the splendor of her voice, point up the passion that communicated in the singing of both artists. Giuditta Pasta, for whom *Norma* had been created, commanded a stunning technique and voice in addition to her genuine ability to get *into* the role; she was the consummate singer-actress in almost equal parts, which undoubtedly gave to her Norma the additional musical excitement that was not at Schröder-Devrient's command (though the vocal deficiencies were compensated for in some eyes by the raw passion she brought to the role). Chopin's remarks about Malibran versus Pasta are again of interest. He had heard Pasta sing Desdemona in Rossini's *Otello*: "I never saw anything more sublime. Malibran impresses you merely by her marvelous voice, but no one *sings* like [Pasta]."[16] Schröder-Devrient's appraisal of these two sopranos reveals much about her own conception of the dramatic singer: "Pasta is not at all as great as her reputation, but Malibran is a thousand times greater. This is an artist, before whom one must kneel down."[17] Might we surmise that Malibran as the superb singer was less of a competitor and more of an ideal, whereas Pasta with her dramatic intensity and her vocal problems was much closer to Schröder-Devrient's own realm? Unlike Pasta, Schröder-Devrient was able to communicate her dramatic intensity in musical genres other than opera. In February 1830 she visited Goethe in Weimar and sang for him Schubert's setting of his poem "Der Erlkönig," a setting that had hitherto evoked from Goethe no friendly response. Genast, who lived in Weimar and had arranged the meeting, describes the poet's reception of her performance:

[S]o powerfully was he gripped by the highly dramatic performance of the incomparable Wilhelmine, that he took her head in both hands and kissed her on the forehead with the words: "A thousand thanks to you for this grand artistic performance"; then he continued "I heard this composition once before and it said nothing at all to me; but so performed, the entirety takes form as a visible scene [Bild]."[18]

Julius Bab cites in his chronicle of the Devrient family the reaction by French critics (c. 1830) to Schröder-Devrient's work:

She sings not as other artists sing; she speaks not as we are accustomed to hear. Her acting is not at all in conformity with the rule of the art, *it is as though she knew not at all that she stood on a stage*. She sings with the soul far more than with the voice; her tones originate more from the heart than from the throat; she forgets the public, she forgets herself in that she disappears completely in the being that she is presenting.[19]

This is uncannily similar to the words of John Ebers, describing Pasta's work: "she enters the stage the character itself; transposed into the situation, excited by the hopes and the fears, breathing the life and the spirit of the being she represents" (see above, page 130).

The biography of Schröder-Devrient by Carl Hagemann, which appeared in 1947, is the most recent study of the singer. It often resembles an apologia for her deficiencies as a singer, claiming rather nationalistically that the art of singing should not be synonymous with Italian singing to the exclusion of German. Even he must admit, however, that she was unable to execute passages of roulades, trills, scales, and runs with the necessary agility and strength; in her chest register she lacked power, and even her friends (especially as she aged) found her high notes to be more of a scream than a musical tone. Her best range was the middle, which had a stunning sound especially in *mezza voce*. Hagemann concludes his account by remarking on her "perfect declamation even in the most difficult passages, the absolute purity of her intonation and not least the great artistry of her soulful sound."[20] Unfortunately Hagemann does not cite sources for his description, but other critiques speak to its accuracy. Moreover the description is largely corroborated by Eduard Genast who *did* know the voice in person, both as a member of the audience and as her partner on stage. We have seen above (page 138) his accounts of her determination in pursuing her goal. He tells also of her performance on 27 April 1840 (she was thirty-six) as Romeo in *Montecchi und Capuleti*: she had made wonderful strides of progress with her voice; although she strained to take on the high pitches from A on the staff up to C, she had gained musically in her attack, nuance, and control of the sound. But then he describes her recitative, which was clearly her great strength as a dramatic singer: "Her recitative, the greatest difficulty that a dramatic singer must overcome, stood now at the highest attainable level of achievement, and I have never, from the most famous Italian or German singers, heard such musical-characteristic declamation."[21]

Even in the days of greatest success, Schröder-Devrient occasionally overshot the mark in her interpretation. Chorley who had admired her Fidelio, "thought her Valentine, in *Les Huguenots*, too much of a virago [with] not a touch of the French noble's daughter in her demeanour; she was the impetuous, angry, persecuted woman, whose hour of virgin elegance and virgin reserve had long been over."[22] Hector Berlioz was in complete agreement about the portrayal of Valentine which he experienced in 1843. While he had found her "admirable" in *Fidelio* many years earlier, he now found in her performance of *Les Huguenots* in Dresden "very bad habits in her singing, and much affectation and exaggeration in her stage action." He complains about the manner, style, and quality of her singing, especially about her habit of speaking certain words for dramatic emphasis (which Berlioz terms "anti-musical declamation"), and expresses much the same displeasure as had Chorley: "Valentine the young bride of a day . . . is surely better represented by modest passion, dignified acting, and expressive singing, than by all the exaggerated volleys and detestable egoism of Madame Devrient."[23]

Unfortunately as the singer aged, she became less restrained in her emotional expression and less controlled in her vocal production. The very obsession with dramatic credibility that marked her career in early days and that made her the darling of such composers as Beethoven, Weber, and Wagner, became in later years a fault. It was exaggeration of her dramatic tools that was complained about by the Berlin critic Ludwig Rellstab, for example:

The decline of her artistic star in this late period was largely due to excess in application of a number of means intended to conceal this decline. She fell into the error of making the light too sharp, the shadows too dark; *Contrast* was employed to achieve the conquest of the audiences who formerly had been won by tender graceful melting away, lightly held reins, even there where she strove with all her might to achieve the most splendid effect.[24]

It was this same Rellstab who had marveled at her Iphigenia (in Gluck's *Iphigenie auf Tauris*):

This moment of dramatic representation could excite the feeling that a beautiful artwork of Phidias had suddenly come to life and moved before us with the nobility of Greek divine figures, in that even the deepest pain preserves an imperceptible but imperishable touch of grace, just as the highest import of divine earnestness, divine sadness, is never lost in the smile of joy.[25]

Lord Mount Edgcumbe, summed up Schröder-Devrient's abilities quite thoroughly in his description of her London debut in 1824:

Beethoven's *Fidelio* was produced for the début of Madame Schroeder Devrient. she was indeed a very superior performer, with a voice less sweet perhaps than powerful, capable of great exertion and strong expression. She was a capital actress (considered in Germany as by far the best in opera, as is her mother, Madame Schroeder, in tragedy), and one of the most striking and effective performers I ever saw. Though by no means a pretty woman, and without marked features, such as produce most effect on the stage, she had the power of great expression and change of countenance. In *Fidelio* she was throughout in male attire. I was present at her first appearance, and so charmed by her performance that I not only went to see that opera a second time, but never failed afterwards going to hear, once at least, every other that was acted during that season and the next . . . Devrient's Lady Macbeth [by Chélard] was a very fine piece of acting, particularly in the sleeping scene, to which she gave a novel though natural effect.[26]

Richard Wagner was present at a performance by Schröder-Devrient in *Fidelio* in 1829—his first experience of the opera—and it changed his life. He was sixteen years old, and he immediately sent her a letter overflowing with praise and his own emotions at the experience; years later he was deeply moved when she recited for him the words of that letter.[27] This performance was the determining event in his choice of career. The combination of the extraordinary singer-actress and the drama of *Fidelio* set his feet firmly on the path to creation of his own music dramas. In 1851, twenty-two years after that performance, he wrote to a friend:

The most distant contact with this extraordinary woman struck me like an electric shock: for a long time, in fact up until this very day, I heard and felt her, whenever the force for artistic creation possessed me.[28]

*   *   *   *   *

Wilhelmine Schröder[29] was born 6 December 1804 in Hamburg, Germany. She was the oldest of four children born to baritone Friedrich Schröder (1744–1816), the first singer to perform the role of Don Giovanni in German, and Sophie (née Burger) Schröder (1781–1868), the foremost German dramatic actress of her time. As a child Wilhelmine appeared in the ballet in both Hamburg and Vienna and in dramatic productions with her mother and younger sister. Her debut in a leading role came in 1819, not as a singer but as an actress: she appeared in Vienna as Aricida in Schiller's *Phädra* on 13 October. Later that same year she played Ophelia in Shakespeare's *Hamlet* at the Hoftheater in Vienna.

Trained in diction and movement by her mother, she was undoubtedly slated for a career as a dramatic actress, but her remarkable voice apparently motivated her to move into the world of opera (a world not dominated by her mother with whom she never got on particularly well). She studied singing with a Viennese singing master, Giuseppe (Joseph) Mozatti, and must have made pretty remarkable progress, for on 20 January 1821 she made her singing debut as Pamina in Mozart's *Die Zauberflöte* at Vienna's Kärntnertortheater. Her success was extraordinary; a member of the audience reported that: "These advantages, combined with an acting talent, such as has been demonstrated by few great singers, guaranteed a special magic and charmed the surprised audience so much that the house echoed with applause."[30]

The same season she performed Emmeline (a speaking role) in Weigl's *Schweizerfamilie,* Marie in a German version of Grétry's *Barbe bleu,* and the following season she sang Agathe in Weber's *Der Freischütz,* directed by the composer. Her greatest triumph however was on 3 November 1822 as Leonore in Beethoven's *Fidelio*; as mentioned above (page 137) the composer was deeply struck by her performance of which he clearly heard not a single note. Probably as a result of Weber's admiration of her Agathe, she was given a two-year contract in 1823 as a member of the Dresden German Opera, which he directed. The association with the Dresden Opera lasted until 1847. She studied singing here again, now with the chorus master Johannes Aloys Mieksch.

Around 1823 she married the actor Karl Devrient (1797–1872). The marriage was stormy, with both partners enjoying flings on the side, and was dissolved in 1828. Wilhelmine had apparently construed his infidelity as sufficient grounds for her own; the courts deemed otherwise and gave custody of the four children to their father. The separation from the children caused her great sorrow, which frequent, stormy, and well-publicized affairs failed to relieve. Nevertheless her career flourished: she continued to sing in Dresden, had great success in Berlin in 1828, and in 1830 made her first tour to Paris. She stopped on the way in Weimar, where for the great German poet Johann Wolfgang von Goethe she sang Schubert's "Erlkönig" so powerfully that his original disinterest in the Lied was completely reversed, and he created on the spot the brief poem of praise for her artistry quoted at the beginning of this chapter.[31] In Paris she appeared with the German company as Agathe (*Freischütz,* 6 May 1830) and Leonore (*Fidelio,* 8 May).

The 1830s were the peak years of her career. She returned in 1831 and 1832 to Paris, sang in the Italian opera with Maria Malibran in *Don Giovanni* and in Rossini's *Otello.* In 1832 she journeyed on to London where during the months of May, June, and July, she appeared in thirty performances, including *Fidelio, Don Giovanni, Macbeth* (by Chélard, who was the conductor for the season). She returned to London in 1833 and sang in *Freischütz, Zauberflöte, Euryanthe,* and Rossini's *Otello,* but her success was lessened slightly by the competition of the dancers Marie Taglioni (1804–1884) and Fanny Elssler (1810–1884). By this time her fame was such that when Malibran died suddenly in 1836, Schröder-Devrient was named as the only possible artist to take her place. Toward the end of the decade, however, her vocal powers began to degenerate. Her turbulent life style has been named as a reason, but a lack of careful consistent training in her youth surely played a role. Even her most stalwart champions realized that she had never enjoyed sound vocal training; Genast's remarks in 1840 about the difficulty with which she reached her high notes are indicative of a less than solid technique. She continued to sing with great success in Germany. It was during the late 1830s and early 1840s in fact that she sang for Wagner the roles of Adriano (*Rienzi*), Senta (*Der fliegende Holländer*), and Venus (*Tannhäuser*), and that she added to her repertoire Gluck's *Iphigenie in Aulide*.

The last years were hard. Her bad luck with men continued in 1847 with her marriage to a Saxon officer, Herr von Döring, who embezzled all the earnings from appearances she had made in St. Petersburg and Copenhagen. With the help of friends, she escaped from that marriage. Finally, after many years of painful separation from her children, she was permitted to have visits from them, but in May 1848, her only daughter Sophie died suddenly. In 1850 Schröder-Devrient married a third time; her final choice of husband was the far more appealing and very supportive Livonian Baron von Bock. The couple retired to his estate at Trikaten, and seemed set to end their lives in peaceful seclusion. Returning briefly to Dresden in 1850 or 1851, however, she was arrested for the sympathies she had displayed earlier with the 1848 revolution (it was Wagner's activities during this revolution that earned him ten years of exile), and she was banned by the Berlin court not only from returning to Saxony but also from re-entering Russia. With great difficulty her husband managed to get the sentences overturned. Her last known appearances were in Germany, probably during 1856. By 1858 she was ill, deeply depressed, and in painful "Unruhe." Her doctors regarded her case as hopeless, a feeling echoed by her in a letter of 2 April 1858. She sought refuge with her sister Auguste Schloenbach in Koburg where Auguste was engaged as an actress at the Hoftheater. When Auguste had to fulfill an engagement in Gotha, Wilhelmine was left with a young Russian relative in Koburg. Here, on 26 January 1860, she died. Her husband was apparently absent, but a son may have been with her.

Schröder-Devrient's life was in truth utterly devoted to the theatre. Writers then and now delight in stating that she carried the drama of the stage into the core of her personal life. Certainly this life was colorful: her behavior was consistently impetuous, and she was generous with favors of her person. It is a pleasure to report that the *Memoiren einer Sängerin* (Altona, 1861) were not her doing but are, in the words of the scholar John Warrack, "a pornographic fabrication."[32] She was equally generous with offerings of her art and of her pocketbook. She believed so strongly in the genius of young Richard Wagner that not only did she take on performance of many roles, but she also agreed to make him a generous loan. It was bad luck for both of them, especially for him, that before the loan was consummated she made that second disastrous marriage in which she lost all her earnings. (Given Wagner's track record at repaying debts, however, it might have been much worse for her—spiritually and financially—if she *had* been able to lend him the money.)

*   *   *   *   *

Her power in performance lay not solely in her vocal prowess but was inseparably bound up with her dramatic abilities. Her early training in ballet, her work on diction and stagecraft with her formidable mother, laid the foundations for her development as an acting singer (some preferred to call her a singing actor). Criticisms reflect the dichotomy between the singer and the actor; clearly Schröder-Devrient saw neither singing nor acting as paramount—rather her aim was to unite all the art at her disposal in the service of the drama, whether a stage play (she continued to appear in non-singing roles during much of her career) or a music drama/opera. The novelty of her approach is confirmed by the outrage expressed by Dresden critics at her lack of stage etiquette manifested by her weeping actual tears on stage.[33] It is important to note also the meticulous care with which she approached a role, from creation of the costume to formulation of the stance and gestures that defined the character. Her portrayals of male protagonists (for example, Romeo in Bellini's *I Capuleti e i Montecchi*) were marked by the utmost attention to detail and to giving realism to an entirely unbelievable situation, i.e., a woman playing a young man in love:

Nothing could betray her sex, lest the entire situation become ridiculous. She had to walk, stand, kneel like a man, she must draw the dagger and position herself for battle like a good fencer, and above all anything feminine must be banned from her costume. No tender locks, no dainty foot, no pretty waist. Putting on and off the hat or the glove is not less important.[34]

Her approach to operatic roles carried over to the singing of lieder. Robert Schumann, who dedicated to her that intense and passionate Romantic cry, "Ich grolle nicht," referred to her as "demoniacal"—a trait that would have certainly served this lied which contains such lines as "the snake who gnaws at your heart" and "I see, my love, just how wretched you are" but "ich grolle nicht"—I do not complain.[35] Schumann also claimed that Schröder-Devrient was "the only singer who could survive with [Franz] Liszt as an accompanist."[36]

Her success as a dramatic singer was directly connected to the ideals expressed by a number of nineteenth-century opera composers. Wagner is certainly the composer most often associated with the idea of *Gesamtkunstwerk*—total artwork—but he was by no means the only one. Weber in a lecture in Breslau in 1824 expressed that very ideal: "*Euryanthe* is a purely dramatic experiment, its effect dependent on the united working together of all sister arts; robbed of their assistance [it] is certain to be without effect."[37] It was Schröder-Devrient, with her insistence on music cum drama cum costume cum gesture cum setting, who sang the premiere of *Euryanthe* under Weber; it was Schröder-Devrient who was the ideal performer for the new music drama, the *Gesamtkunstwerk.*

Her influence on Romantic music was not limited to opera or music drama but extended to the singing of lieder as well. Mara half a century earlier had found it necessary to study the Italian method, as she said, "the only true method." Schröder-Devrient now retained her German approach and characteristics in her work with the greatest German composers of her time to fulfill their concept of the new art.[38]

Throughout his life Wagner retained the power of that performance of *Fidelio,* the force of Beethoven's music and the dramatic intensity of Schröder-Devrient's portrayal of the heroic Leonore. His words below echo Genast's analysis of her approach to her art, as they also sum up the significance of her work for the German music drama of the nineteenth century:

Neither in her art nor in her life had Schröder-Devrient the appearance of that virtuoso mentality that only thrives through complete individualization and in this alone is able to sparkle: she was ever entirely the dramatic actor, in the full meaning of the word, she was permeated with touching, with merging with the total, and this total was precisely in life and art our social life and our theatrical art.[39]

Wagner dedicated *Über Schauspieler und Sänger* to her memory. He paid further and more personal homage to her art by choosing her image to represent the spirit of tragedy (his second wife, Cosima Liszt Wagner, represents the spirit of music) in the portal over the entrance to Wahnfried, the Bayreuth dream house built for him by the largesse of Ludwig II of Bavaria. Her image presides today over the streams of tourists who visit the house, now a museum.

Timeline

1804, 6 Dec	Wilhelmine Schröder born Hamburg, oldest of four, to baritone Friedrich Schröder (1744–1816;1st German Don Giovanni) and actress Sophie Schröder, née Burger (1781–1868)
1816, 15 Mar	Appeared in ballet in Hamburg and Vienna
1819, 13 Oct	Debut as actress: Aricida, Schiller's *Phädra*; Ophelia; at Hoftheater, trained in movement, diction by mother Studied singing with Giuseppe Mozatti
1821, 20 Jan	Opera debut: Pamina (*Die Zauberflöte*) at Kärntnertortheater, Vienna Emmeline (Weigl, *Schweizer-familie*), Marie (Grétry, *Barbe bleu*, in German as *Raoul Blaubart*)
1822, 7 Mar	Agathe (*Freischütz*) under Weber
3 Nov	Leonore (*Fidelio*), greatest triumph and basis of her fame; also sang in Dresden
1823	Dresden, two-year contract at Hoftheater; associated with Dresden till 1847; singing lessons with chorus master Aloys Mieksch
182?	Married actor Karl Devrient (1797–1872); 4 children including actor Friedrich Devrient (1825–1871)
1828	Marriage dissolved.
1828	Berlin: great success, though refused to sing title role of *La vestale* (offended Spontini), sang it 1829 in Dresden
1830	Visit to Weimar, sang for Goethe, Goethe's poem in her praise Paris: appeared with Röckel's German company as Agathe (6 May), Leonore (8 May).
1831, 1832	Paris again, Italian opera, with Malibran in *Don Giovanni, Otello*
1832	London: King's Theatre, ten times each month during May, Jun, Jul, *Fidelio, Don Giovanni, Macbeth* (Chelard)
1833	London: *Der Freischütz, Die Zauberflöte, Euryanthe, Otello.*
1836	Malibran died; Schröder-Devrient hailed as only artist to replace her
1837	London: *Fidelio, La sonnambula, Norma;* health failing, paid nothing as company went bankrupt.
1837	Voice declining, but continued success in Germany; sang Adriano (R*ienzi*), Senta, Venus, Iphigenia (Gluck, *Iphigenie in Aulide*)
1847, 17 Dec	Riga, 17 Dec; married Saxon officer, von Döring, visits with him to St. Petersburg and Copenhagen; he embezzled her earnings; marriage dissolved
1848, May	Daughter Sophie, 21, died
1850	Married Livonian Baron von Bock, retired to his estate at Trikaten; returned to Dresden, arrested for earlier sympathy with 1848 revolution, banned by Berlin court from returning to Saxony

	and from re-entering Russia; husband managed to get sentences overturned.
1856	Last known appearances, in Germany; Bab gives 6 March 1859 in Leipzig as last appearance; ill: deep depression, painful "Unruhe," seen by doctors as hopeless
1858, 2 Apr	Wrote of being lost; went to her sister Auguste (Schloenbach) in Koburg (Auguste engaged at Koburg Hoftheater)
fall	Auguste to engagement in Gotha, Wilhelmine left in Koburg with young Russian relative
1860, 26 Jan	Wilhelmine Schröder-Devrient died in Koburg

Bibliography

Works about Schröder-Devrient

Memoiren einer Sängerin (Altona, 1861).

A colorful, lascivious purported autobiography, assessed by Warrack as a "pornographic fabrication." See entry for Schröder-Devrient in *Grove Music Online*.

Bab, Julius. *Die Devrients: Geschichte einer deutschen Theaterfamilie*. Berlin: Georg Stilke, 1932.

Since Bab is writing about the Devrient family, emphasis is on theatre aspects of Schröder-Devrient's work, but he gives a quite thorough survey of her career. Unfortunately he seldom cites sources for his information.

Genast, Eduard. *Aus dem Tagebuche eines alten Schauspielers*. Leipzig: Voigt & Günther,1862.

Genast, though much older than Schröder-Devrient, played opposite her on many occasions and thus provides an eye-witness account of her stagecraft. Since he first knew her when she was sixteen or seventeen he also presents welcome information about her development as an artist. Genast and Hagemann are both very defensive of German music and singers; both take particular umbrage with Chorley's statements about German singing.

Hagemann, Carl. *Wilhelmine Schröder-Devrient*. Berlin, 1904; 2nd ed. Wiesbaden: Verlag der Greif Walther Gericke, 1947.

Good biography and assessment of the singer's technique and style. No documentation; rather defensive of both German music and Schröder-Devrient as a German singer. No bibliography.

Warrack, John. "Schröder-Devrient [née Schröder], Wilhelmine." *Grove Music Online*.

General Works

Berlioz, Hector. *Memoirs of Hector Berlioz from 1803 to 1865 Comprising His Travels in Germany, Italy, Russia, and England,* transl. Rachel Holmes and Eleanor Holmes, annotated, translated, and revised by Ernest Newman. 1932. Reprint, New York: Dover Publications, Inc., 1966.

Chorley, Henry Fothergill. *Modern German Music*. 1854. Reprint, New York: Da Capo Press, 1973.

_____. *Thirty Years' Musical Recollections*. 1862. Edited with an introduction by Ernest Newman. New York: Vienna House, 1972.

Gutman, Robert. *Richard Wagner: The Man, His Mind, and His Music*. New York: Harcourt Brace Jovanovich, Inc., 1968.

Mount Edgcumbe, Richard. *Musical Reminiscences of the Earl of Mount Edgcumbe: Containing an Account of the Italian Opera in England from 1773 to 1834*. 4th ed., 1834. Reprint, New York: Da Capo Press, 1973.

Wagner, Richard. *Mein Leben*. 2d ed. Leipzig: Breitkopf & Härtel, 1914.

_____. "Über Schauspieler und Sänger." *Gesammelte Schriften,* ix. Leipzig, 1873; English translation, v, 1896.

Chapter 11

Jenny Lind
(6 October 1820 – 2 November 1887)

Thackeray thought her "atrociously stupid," and was relieved when she was done and he could go to his cigar; Richard Wagner remarked on her "curious pensive individuality"; Frederic Chopin spoke of "a kind of Northern Lights."[1] Her career as an opera singer was little more than a decade (1838–1849), a year of which she spent in prescribed silence and study with Manuel Garcia Jr., and yet she cut a swath broader and deeper than any female singer until Madonna. Was she the saintly singer propagated by Phineas T. Barnum who managed her first tour of America? Was she the carefully calculating canny businesswoman who took over from Barnum the management of her subsequent American tour and who as some said never committed an act of charity unseen? Certain it was that she had an uncanny ability to move her audiences; perhaps it was the remarkable purity of her voice coupled with the careful simplicity of her presentation of her self—invariably in simple, usually white, gown, little make-up, plain hair style, the embodiment of the non-threatening compliant female. And, as Cori Ellison has pointed out, she "irrevocably changed the topography of the music business."[2]

* * * * *

Her range was wide, from middle C (or some say the B below it) to G four lines above the staff. Richard Hoffman (who was connected with the American tours) wrote that her voice was "not so brilliant as it was deliciously rounded, and of an exquisite musical timbre. It possessed great volume, and what seemed an inexhaustible reserve force."[3] Henri Appy in an article for *Century Magazine* wrote "Its timbre was like a clarinet, penetrating and tearful and sweet, and it flowed out with great volume and power . . . She possessed two qualities of voice—one somber, the other of a clear, sunny ring, brilliant and sparkling. She carried her middle voice in one quality up to high B flat without a break, and sang there in the same rich tone as in her middle octaves."[4] Europe's best-known voice teacher Manuel Garcia Jr., who taught her for nearly a year (August 1841 to June 1842) described her first notes of "Come unto me" as "so full, pure, and perfect in intonation that the refrain which preceded them sounded out of tune."[5] An American listener, John Addington Symonds, was deeply moved: "At the first tones of her voice, I quivered all over. It is not her wonderful execution, her pathos, varying expression, subtle flexibility, that surprised me, but the pure timbre which so vibrated and thrilled my very soul that tears came into my eyes."[6] Her trills were acclaimed as was her *messa di voce*.[7] Another articulate admirer, J. B. Mozley, wrote that her voice was not as full as he had expected, but her power over it was amazing:

She could positively do anything with it. It was absolutely obedient; I never heard anything at all equal to its flexibility; she tossed it about as conjurors do their balls, and seemed to have twenty voices at once. She shook [i.e., trilled] with such perfection that the note seemed self-undulating . . . Then she imitated an echo, first a slow, then a quicker one, till the echo of the last note was, as in the case of the real echo, mixed with the succeeding note. Then she had astonishing powers of sustaining long slow notes, which she displayed in the song from Weber.[8]

The historian Thomas Carlyle experienced mixed reactions: he described her voice as "of extraordinary *extent* and *little* richness of tone."[9] Longfellow compared her with the morning star and referred to her "clear, liquid, heavenly sounds."[10] Queen Victoria referred to her "pure angelic voice."[11] Lind's daughter, Mrs. Maude, related that after working with Garcia the voice "developed to a brilliant and powerful soprano, of beautiful quality and varying shades, and its compass extended from the B below the line to the G in the fourth line above it . . . [the] pianissimo rendering of [her high F-sharp and A] was one of the most remarkable features of her singing. It was as rich in power as her mezzo-forte, and though falling on the ear like a whisper, reached the farthest corner of theatre or concert."[12] Mendelssohn's "Hear Ye, Israel" (*Elijah*) composed explicitly for her exploits the control and beauty of the F-sharp which he particularly admired. Her voice was not naturally flexible, the flexibility so often touted had been achieved by hard work. "Her breathing capacity was also not naturally great, but she renewed her breath so quietly and cleverly that the closest observer could not detect her doing it, and the outside world credited her with abnormal lung capacity."[13] In 1868 in a letter to a musical colleague, a Professor Bystrom, she described the problems with her voice:

[T]he difficulties with my throat were so great, the hindrances were so tremendous, necessitating such constant energy and patience . . . that only my burning love for Art in its spiritual sense could enable me to go through the dreadful slavery. My breathing was naturally very short, not a sign of *coloratur* and an impossible attack. I never heard such an attack in anybody else. For twenty-five years have I steadily worked on the chromatic scale and only five or six years ago did it come perfectly—when I no longer needed it.[14]

On the other hand, Garcia told his biographer that he "had never heard her sing even a hair's-breadth out of tune, so perfect was her natural ear."[15] She was typically acclaimed for the "naturalness" of her singing, a characteristic she herself frequently mentioned. The idea of the "nightingale," early associated with her singing (in Denmark she was first called "the Swedish nightingale") and strengthened by Hans Christian Andersen's "The Emperor's Nightingale,"[16] was cultivated by her admirers throughout her career, but does it truly jibe with the picture of the young woman working for hours, days, to accomplish a technical feat, such as the chromatic scale? And does it agree with her early recognition of the fact that her voice was being damaged by overuse and misuse, and her consequent decision to spend a year (or whatever it took) working with Garcia in Paris? Whatever it did take, however, she was in the end triumphant. Chopin heard her in May 1848: "She impresses me as a remarkable Swedish type, surrounded not by an ordinary halo, but by a kind of Northern Lights. She produces an extraordinary effect in *La somnambula*. She sings with amazing purity and certainty and her *piano* is so steady—as smooth and even as a thread of hair."[17]

The praise accorded her voice was not extended to her acting. Wagner wrote that she could not "rise to a great dramatic portrayal."[18] The roles she carried out most successfully were the ones that conformed to her own personality, such as the sweet sleepwalking victim Amina in *La sonnambula*. Her Norma, for example, was a rather gentle creature suffused with maternal love, difficult to reconcile with the traditionally murderous mother created by Giuditta Pasta (for whom the role was composed). Her cadenzas, which she created herself or improvised, were sometimes criticized as too ornate, departing from the style and interpretation of the role. But in oratorios she is said to have sung no cadenzas at all, and no other ornamentation; her singing of this music reflected her personal image in its unadorned simplicity, even severity.

*   *   *   *   *

Johanna Maria Lind,[19] known throughout her life as Jenny, was born 6 October 1820 in Stockholm. Although her parents lived together they did not marry until 1834 when Jenny was eighteen. Her childhood was spent only partly with her own parents; she lived some four years with a foster mother in the country, then later with the caretakers of the Home for Widows where her grandmother lived. It was here that she is said to have been heard singing to her cat in the window and as a result brought to the attention of the director of the Royal Theatre, Stockholm's opera house. In September 1830, the nine-year-old Jenny was taken on as a student in the opera house school, given education, professional training, and maintenance. She boarded at home with her mother at first, but this was never satisfactory, as the two did not get along; in 1836 Jenny ran away from home, eventually settling as a boarder with the matron of the opera school.

Her teacher was at first a professor identified only as Craelius, then in 1831 Isak Berg, and she seems to have made rapid progress as actress and singer. Her first stage appearance (she was ten years old) was in a spoken drama, and her acting was highly praised: "Little Jenny Lind acts excellently . . . such spirit and theatrical assurance, such utter lack of shyness in a little girl . . . if Jenny Lind continues as she has begun, she will unquestionably be a valuable asset to the Swedish stage."[20] The reviewer expresses alarm at her precocity, hoping that it will not have an "adverse influence on the moral training of the grown woman."[21] This early review is particularly interesting in view of later negative reviews of her operatic acting; did moral training overshadow a natural dramatic expressive ability? Her debut as a singer took place in 1836 to great success, and as a result she was seriously overworked during the next few years. At seventeen she was the opera's "most admired and fêted star," but she soon began experiencing serious vocal problems. She was twenty-one in July 1841 when she sought out Manuel Garcia in Paris, desperate for help.

Garcia, son of a highly successful singer Manuel Garcia, brother of the brilliant soprano Maria Malibran (who died tragically early in her career after a fall from a horse) and of the equally renowned singer, Pauline Garcia Viardot, was touted as Europe's finest vocal teacher. His judgement: "Mon enfant, vous n'avez plus de voix" was followed by the prescription that she refrain entirely from singing (and speak little) for three months. By September she had recovered sufficiently to begin work and Garcia set her to mastering the very basics of technique. "I have to begin from the beginning, sing scales up and down, slowly and carefully, work at the shake (unchristianly slowly) and try to get rid of the hoarseness if possible . . . He is very particular about the breathing."[22] Her year of patient penitence and grueling hard work paid off. On 10 October 1842 she sang again in Stockholm, as Norma; witnesses raved about her legato, her staccato, her scales, her trill ("shake"), and spoke of a new depth to her singing. Jenny Lind's international career was about to take off. Although notes in her middle range remained veiled (she herself said they had "never come quite right"[23]), her voice overall had become strong and flexible, with a good range (B below the staff to the G on the fourth line above) and with high notes that simply dazzled the listener. Her breathing was so skilled that she could hold notes for long times and then just as though it seemed she must breathe she would continue the phrase. Her *piano* so admired by Chopin was equally remarkable: described as scarcely a breath, yet full and rich, it penetrated to the farthest reaches of the hall. Though she liked to describe herself as a "natural" singer (like the nightingale she was called), she surely owed much of her control, her technique, and above all, her breathing method to Garcia. She must have not only overworked her voice in her early years but have been using it badly: when she went to Garcia she could scarcely sing and complained, significantly, of hoarseness. Only after her work with him do we find the critics praising her technique, her virtuosity, the beauty of her sound, her control in lengthy sustained passages, her coloratura, and especially that marvelous shake which varied from slow to fast, from *pianissimo* to *forte* and back again.

After two years of singing mainly in Stockholm with a few excursions around Scandinavia, Lind ventured in 1844 to Germany, singing in Berlin, Hamburg, Frankfurt, Darmstadt, and Leipzig where in December that year she met and worked with Felix Mendelssohn. Mendelssohn became a dear friend for the brief remainder of his life; his tragically early death in 1847 was a great blow. In 1846 she made her Viennese debut in *Norma,* and also took part with Mendelssohn in the Lower Rhine Music Festival, where she sang in Haydn's *Creation,* Handel's *Alexander's Feast.* She toured Germany that year, singing in Munich, Stuttgart, Karlsruhe, Nuremberg, and then returned to Vienna to sing Marie in the *Fille du regiment* with huge success.

On the 4th of May 1847 Jenny Lind made her London debut as Alice in Meyerbeer's *Robert le diable* (in Italian) at Her Majesty's Theatre. Queen Victoria, present with her consort Albert, wrote in her diary: "The great event of the evening was Jenny Lind's appearance and her *complete* triumph. She has a most exquisite, powerful, and really quite peculiar voice, so round, soft, and flexible, and her acting is charming and touching and very natural." The evening marked the beginning of "Lind fever." From this point on Jenny Lind was the rage—a rage marked by all sorts of memorabilia. Whereas Lisztomania centered on personal belongings (clothing, cigar stubs, coffee grounds, clippings of his hair), Lind fever produced thousands of such cute items as handkerchiefs, hats, purses, just about anything that could have her image imprinted on it.

At the end of the 1847 opera season, Lind toured the English provinces. It was apparently during this tour that she decided to abandon the stage. A final season, spring 1848, of opera in Stockholm and in London, was followed by a tour of Great Britain plus Dublin. Having announced her resolution to leave the stage, she nevertheless sang during the spring of 1848 six farewell performances at Her Majesty's Theatre, billed as concert presentations. The first of these, a real concert presentation of *Il flauto magico,* (Mozart's *Magic Flute*), was such a dismal failure that she relented and sang the remaining five as fully staged operas. Her final appearance on 10 May 1849 was as Alice in *Robert le diable,* the role in which she had first stunned the London public. Her career as opera singer had lasted barely a decade, including the year of silence spent with Garcia.

But she was not through with singing. Quite the contrary. In September 1850 Jenny Lind, with conductor Julius Benedict and baritone Giovanni Belletti, her old singing partner from the early days in Stockholm, began under the aegis of the flamboyant entrepreneur Phineas T. Barnum a tour of the United States which would take her all over the country, from the East Coast to New Orleans, Louisville, Cincinnati, many other large and small towns, and even included Havana, Cuba. The tour comprised a total of ninety-three concerts. She swept the country which responded in various levels of sophistication, from enthusiastic critiques by the connoisseurs of New York and Boston to rough and ready cheers of coalminers in the far reaches of the American West. Barnum practiced an only slightly muted version of his commercial practices. He was tireless in arranging events and advertising the splendor of his star: he made sure that colorful biographies of Lind preceded her entrance into every city, and his energetic persistence guaranteed that houses would almost invariably be sold out. Both Barnum and Lind made a pile of money.

Barnum's reputation to the contrary, he was an ardent adherent of temperance, and he included lectures on the topic at every possible opportunity during his Lind tour. We can imagine that this aspect of his personality undoubtedly appealed very much to the deeply religious Lind, who with her serious, almost religious approach to music had always shunned the more frivolous byproducts of her life as an opera "star." On the other hand, was she offended by the colorful advertising that was a significant feature of Barnum's managerial style?

However that may be, Lind was a spectacular success wherever Barnum took her. The first concert on 11 September 1850 was in New York City at Castle Garden. A young man from St. Louis was in the audience which he wrote consisted of

seven thousand human beings closely packed together, in one of the most magnificent rooms in the world . . . Her form is of a full medium height, very finely moulded, and possesses an exceedingly graceful carriage. She is not what some would call handsome but when she smiles, her sweet face lights up to almost positive beauty. Her complexion is beautiful, and her eyes large blue of the sweetest expression . . . She has light, wavy, auburn hair.

She began the first piece falteringly and tremblingly . . . As she proceeded in the first piece she regained herself and gave to the Casta Diva a most brilliant and startling effect . . . When something like quiet was restored, she reappeared and sang the "Trio Concertante" [Meyerbeer, *Camp of Silesia*]. Never did I ever dream that I should listen to such a miraculous execution of music. She accompanies two flutes, and as she motions her sweet little fingers, as though she was performing on a flute, you cannot distinguish the difference so greatly does her voice resemble the sweetest notes you ever heard upon that instrument.

She then sang the *Echo Song*:

In my wildest fancy, I had never imagined anything like it. It was a new revelation of the capability of the human voice, and appeared to all a miracle. The instantaneous echo of her own voice by an inhalation of the breath, to a full gush of melody poured from the lips, and this produced many times in succession . . . to give you a better idea of this echo song . . . with her voice she would give us the bellowing of the cow, the Herdsman calling his sheep, the cheerful laugh intermixed, and off yonder in the mountains we could hear the echo which was of the sweetest and wildest melody that ever was listened to by the ears of man. It was such a perfection of art, and so closely resembled nature that you could not distinguish the difference.

. . . her pronunciation of the English [in "Welcome to America," song composed for the tour] was exceedingly beautiful.[24]

New York was followed by concerts at Boston's Tremont Temple, which were equally successful and well-received by critics. The fourth concert consisted of sacred music—selections from Haydn's *Creation,* Rossini's *Stabat Mater,* and Handel's *Messiah,* including "I Know that My Redeemer Liveth," one of her favorites. A member of the audience described the effect of this number:

Nothing . . . grander and more sublime than was her rendering of the air. The dignity and the breadth which she bestowed upon her phrasing, her fine and pure conception of such ornament as she introduced, and her crisp and intelligent intonation of the words, combined—with the clearness of that sweet and thrilling voice—to render it one of the noblest readings . . . [that has] ever been given to the public. I would also call attention to the *crescendo* passage on the words, "And now has Christ arisen," as one of the most brilliant and perfect of the musical jewels with which her delivery of this air is strewn.[25]

Lind and Barnum now headed south, taking with them a core orchestra of ten: two violins, cello, double bass, two flutes, oboe, clarinet, horn, and trumpet. This group was to be augmented by local hires. They gave concerts in Providence, Philadelphia, Baltimore, Washington, Richmond, Charleston, Havana, New Orleans, Natchez, Memphis, St. Louis, Nashville, Louisville, Madison, Cincinnati, Wheeling, Pittsburgh, returning to New York City for fourteen concerts followed by a final appearance in Philadelphia. They traveled by train, by carriage, by steamship. She was greeted everywhere with storms of applause. The critics raved. The following from the Nashville *Daily American* is representative:

As a singer, indeed, she possesses a marvelously refined and delicate voice, many of the finer qualities of which she has cultivated to an extent which may be regarded as well nigh incredible and it may, in most respects, be considered as near perfection as anything human can be. The extreme burst of her voice in the upper portion of its register is far beyond the ordinary range of sopranos and she has—as we understand—by long and arduous practice— acquired the power of moulding the higher notes entirely at her will. Apparently their utterance costs her little or no effort and she is able to dwell long and with a most brilliant clearness without any visible exertion on the very highest notes within her compass. By this she is enabled to produce some of the most astonishing effects upon the listener. When after a musical play through the lower and more ordinary compass of the voice she bursts forth into tones clearer and higher than we have ever before heard from any singer, her power completely astonishes the audience.

Another of the more special beauties which particularly mark the voice of Mademoiselle Lind is the unexampled quality and delicacy of its *piano* . . . it sinks almost into a whisper, when the delicate melody is heard in every corner of the theatre. While the breath which a bare whisper would at once destroy the effect is finding its way through every portion of the house, nothing can be more thrillingly poetical . . . It can literally be compared to nothing of which we have previously any experience in the beauties and capabilities of sound. As for her trills, we confess that we should feel puzzled to suggest any capability of improvement. Nothing could well be more correct—more rapid—or more thoroughly musical. Here it is that her voice more nearly approximates to the warblings of the feathered choir. Now it increases and again it falls in volume. At one time it gushes forth, flooding the senses with its wondrous melody and at another it vibrates, so sweetly and so deliciously on the ear, that the listener cannot but acknowledge that in the mechanical portion of the art—that which is acquired by arduous and laborious study—she has no equal. Indeed, in her musical education, scarcely a point has been slurred over. The transition from the high to the low notes is rapidly effected and seems as though it cost her no effort . . . She utters an ascension or descent of successive notes as rapidly and distinctly as they could be touched by a musician on any instrument. The most irregular passages flow from her with an unrestrained and natural ease.[26]

New types of memorabilia emerged—a knitted Jenny Lind cap, cooking stoves, the Jenny Lind Portable Parlor Grate; perhaps most exotic: in New Orleans doubloons with her image on them were produced; but in Memphis the mules sported special Jenny Lind blinders. "The Jenny Lind Mania," a song with words by W. H. C. West to "a popular melody," documents the wealth of items commemorating Ms. Lind:

Of manias we've had many,
And some have raised the wind,
But the tallest far of any
Is that for Jenny Lind,
Causing quite a revolution,
To compliment her fame;
from a toothpick to an omnibus
All call-ed by her name.
Chor: O! manias we've had many, etc.

If you step into a grocer's,
(Upon my word, 'tis true!)
There is Jenny Lind lump sugar
And Jenny's cocoa too.
We shall all become great singers,
Thro' Jenny Lind pipes high;
At each snuff shop in London
Jenny Lind pipes you may buy.

My wife has a Jenny Lind bonnet
And a Jenny Lind visite;
With Jenny's portrait on it,
My handkerchief looks neat.
My wife is a slave to fashion,
Against it never sinned;
Our baby and the kitten
Are called after Jenny Lind.

Yes, all is Jenny Lind, now—
In every shop she's found;
Jenny Lind you there get retail,
By the yard, quart, pint or pound.
We've Jenny Lind shirt collars,
And round my neck; O fie!
I've fastened lovely Jenny Lind,
A charming Opera tie.

The final verses, however, display a rare note of commercial realism:

John Bull on foreign music
We see most dearly dotes,
While with cash he fills her pockets,
Jenny crams his with notes.
A charming Swedish Nightingale
They call you, Jenny, too;
Do not think that I'm a Chaffinch,
When a Goldfinch* I call you.

O! Jenny, when you leave us,
what shall we ever do,
To catch another Nightingale
To sing as sweet as you?
You are but a bird of passage,
You'll leave us with the rest,
But you, I think, may plume yourself,
You've 'feathered well your nest.'

*Now a "Goldsmith" (Goldschmidt)[27]

The original contract with Barnum specified that Lind would receive $1,000 per night for up to 150 concerts. Shortly after her arrival in New York he proposed changing the contract, saying that he was convinced they would be far more successful than even he had thought, and he wanted her to share in the additional profits. The new contract insured her fee of $1,000 but after Barnum took $5,500 per night for expenses and his services, they would evenly divide the balance. When they parted amicably in May 1851, Jenny had sung a total of ninety-five concerts. The total receipts amounted to $712,161. Her share of the profits was $176,675, after payment of $32,000 in forfeits since she did not sing the agreed-upon 100 concerts. In addition to these ninety-five concerts, she sang a number of concerts to benefit various charities, and she gave to charity $10,000 of her receipts from the first concerts in New York.[28]

Lind made now a second tour of America on her own; although it was predictably not as financially successful, it nevertheless secured her financial security for life. In February 1852, very quietly, she married Otto Goldschmidt, a pianist nine years younger than she, a pupil of Mendelssohn, who had been serving as her accompanist for some time. After a number of quite successful "farewell" concerts, they returned to England at the end of May 1852. They lived in Dresden from 1852 to 1855 and settled in England in 1858. Lind continued to sing concerts and oratorios in Germany and England, often with Goldschmidt as pianist or conductor, but essentially she retreated into a contented life as mother and wife. In 1883, the year of her last public performance, she accepted the position of professor of singing at the new Royal College of Music and taught there until the fall of 1886. One of her students, a young black woman Amanda Ira Aldrich would later befriend Marian Anderson in London. She spent the winter of 1886 as usual in Cannes; here it was discovered that she had internal cancer. During the spring spent in Cannes with Otto and with occasional visits from her children, she seemed to improve a bit. They returned to England on 21 May, and it soon became clear that the doctors could do nothing other than relieve her pain. She died on 2 November 1887 at Wynds Point in Herefordshire, the home she had shared with Goldschmidt since 1858.

*   *   *   *   *

Jenny Lind's early years provide a cautionary tale for young singers. Singing too much too soon and singing without a solid technique brought her voice to the verge of total destruction. Her solution—to seek out Europe's most acclaimed vocal teacher, Manuel Garcia Jr.—and her recovery brought about by his help and her determination exemplify the importance of method and discipline. Garcia, who interestingly did *not* regard her as his most promising student, never forgot that determination: "Jenny Lind would have cut her throat sooner than have given me reason to say, 'We corrected that mistake last time.'"[29] She would spend hours working on a detail until it was conquered. In a letter from Paris written shortly after she had begun to work with Garcia she described her routine: "I have to begin again, from the beginning . . . "[30] (see above, page 154). Years later, in 1865, she wrote that she had "acquired [her art] by incredible work, and in spite of astonishing difficulties; it is from Garcia alone that I learned some few important things."[31] She does not acknowledge any other teachers, although she studied briefly with Craelius at the Royal Opera School in Stockholm, and then with his pupil, Court Singer Isak Berg.

She herself taught only briefly from 1883 to 1886 as First Professor of Singing at the new Royal College of Music, in London. Her students remember her as strict, not "motherly" said Amanda Aldrich; Liza Lehmann reported that she was "always wonderfully kind to my humble self, but sometimes she treated certain of her pupils with almost cruel harshness and sarcasm. No doubt her musical nerves were strained almost to breaking-point . . . but, curiously enough, I believe she *loved* teaching." Charles Stanford remembered her examining her pupils: without music and without a piano she would sing torturous passages, which they had then to repeat by ear.[32] Her own testimony about teaching, in the letter to Professor Bystrom, stresses the importance of nature and character, but she also states that the "old Italian method is the only right and most natural one." This would confirm the idea that her method was based on her work with Garcia, although she told Professor Bystrom that "Garcia could only teach me a few things. He did not understand my individuality . . . What I most wanted to know was two or three things and with those he did help me. The rest I knew myself, and the birds and our Lord as the maestro did the rest . . . To be able to sing, the whole character must be trained . . . A singing teacher's calling is difficult and important. Difficult because almost every voice has to be treated individually and the whole character *widened out* . . . incautious studying *ruins* the health, for the whole body sings—yes, even the legs!"[33]

It is difficult to understand why Jenny Lind left the opera stage after what may be the shortest career on record—scarcely a decade, including the year spent working with Garcia. It might be—in fact usually has been—attributed to her religious convictions, always strong but increasingly dominant in her later years. On the other hand, she was at one time engaged to a very pious young man who made it clear that as his wife she would no longer appear on stage. Her letters about him and his puritanical relatives make it clear that she saw the world of opera as her own world and one that was not at odds with her deeply felt piety. His insistence that she renounce the stage seems to have contributed to her ending the relationship. More significant for her decision may be the intense physical suffering she underwent before almost every performance. She had dreadful stage fright, to the point where she frequently refused to go on, but then did and was invariably extremely successful. But performances were often followed and sometimes preceded by breakdowns with fearful migraines, and instead of abating, this became more severe as she grew older.

Probably Jenny Lind's most extraordinary achievement was that astonishing American tour under the management of the flamboyant showman Phineas T. Barnum. She was not the first European singer to venture on tours in the New World—for example, Manuel Garcia Sr. had brought his entire family including son Manuel and daughters Maria and Pauline in the 1820s. They enjoyed little success though they energetically presented themselves in New York and various other locations winding up in Mexico, where they were waylaid by bandits and lost their pitifully small earnings. Lind was outrageously successful, and she laid out new paths in her willingness to work with an entrepreneur such as Barnum, to cooperate at least to a certain extent with his flamboyant marketing. Each appearance in a new city was carefully prepared by all kinds of advance advertising, including biographical information about Lind that frequently verged on fiction, as for example, the rumor that her hair was carefully arranged to hide the fact that she had no ears. Her share of profits from the tour, which extended from September 1850 to June 1851 and included ninety-five concerts, was around $175,000 (which would be least ten times more or $1,750,000 in 2004 dollars). Did Lind know who and what Barnum was? She had indeed investigated, seeking out in particular Mr. Joshua Bates of Baring Brothers who knew Barnum and his work and who assured her of his credibility and presumably his honesty. In the event, Lind had no reason at all to complain; Barnum was not only honest but even generous in his dealings with her. In all probability she learned something from him about the art of marketing, just as he undoubtedly learned a great deal about just how far he could push the limits of truth in advertising when dealing with musical artists. Her independent tour, which followed immediately the Barnum tour, was by no means as successful. This was surely due in part to her more low-key marketing—she must have realized just how much Barnum had done to prepare all those concerts—but also due to the fact that she was no longer the complete novelty she had been the preceding year.

Jenny Lind presented by P. T. Barnum swept the eastern part of the United States in 1850–1851. By the 1880s small companies of singers plus instrumentalists were touring all around the country, presenting concerts of a variety of music or performing operas in such places as Chicago, St. Louis, Kansas City, Cheyenne, Denver, Salt Lake City, San Francisco, not forgetting the smaller towns in between such as Reno or Virginia City, Nevada. It was a far cry from the feeble efforts of

Manuel Garcia in 1825–1829. Lind and Barnum had opened up the American market for further forays by Europeans even as he, mostly with her cooperation, established a new approach to the marketing of classical music.

The Barnum-Lind company consisted of tenor Giovanni Belletti, conductor Jules Benedict, and ten instrumentalists. A typical concert would begin with an overture, continue with an aria sung by Belletti, then one by Lind, insert an instrumental number (violin fantasy for example, or on her own tour a piano solo by Goldschmidt), and end the first half with some real show piece for Lind—a favorite was a Meyerbeer trio for voice and two flutes, which showed off Lind's high notes and her ability to match pitch and virtuosity with the flutes. The second half would feature again an overture followed by solos by Belletti and Lind, but now of a more popular nature, including such numbers as Taubert's "Bird Song," "Home, Sweet Home," and a folk song, or an especially beloved number, "The Herdsman's Song" by Lind's first teacher. The programs were designed cleverly to show off the abilities of the two singers but also to appeal to the tastes and levels of the audiences. It is worthwhile to note that while folk songs such as "Comin' through the Rye" were aimed at pleasing the audiences, the programs also included serious gems of the classical repertoire, for example "Come unto Me" from Handel's *Messiah,* the overture to *Der Freischütz* (Weber), and arias from operas by Bellini, Donizetti, Meyerbeer, Verdi. In many cases the company was performing for audiences who had never heard of such music—in Madison, Indiana, for example, the company performed in a pork butcher's shed for an audience many of whom had never before attended a concert; in Pittsburgh they sang on a Friday evening to a crowd that consisted in large part of industrial workers who had just received their paychecks but had already spent of portion of them in the saloons and were therefore in a fairly rowdy condition. The mayhem inside the hall was exacerbated by the noise from outside made by people who had not been able to buy tickets; at one point Lind's "Echo Song" was accompanied by the sound of smashing glass, as rocks were thrown from outside.

But Barnum was also capitalizing on Lind's already established fame. Lind fever was no myth. The eager creation and consumption of Lind souvenirs such as caps or handkerchiefs, pens, etc., which had swept England in particular were paralleled, even exceeded, by American fervor. Small and large items, ranging from tea kettles, sausages, bonnets, opera glasses to cooking and parlor stoves, all bore the name of Jenny Lind. What was it about this woman that excited such maniacal enthusiasm? Niccolò Paganini and even more impressively Franz Liszt had found themselves lionized by adoring men as well as women. Both these virtuosi, however, cultivated this attitude by their life styles and their demonic stage presence. Lind, on the contrary, dressed simply, with no makeup; she almost sneaked on stage. Was it precisely her humble, non-threatening, pure image that drove her audiences to frantic reception of her performance? And that made them desperate to own something that related to her? Interestingly, Franz Liszt's worshippers sought something directly connected with his person—hair clippings, discarded cigars, dregs from his coffee cup—while Lind's admirers collected commercial products (but when she accidentally dropped a shawl from a balcony while greeting a crowd, the shawl was torn into pieces by her admirers, each eager for a scrap). Liszt was jealous enough of his own status as hero that he refused in 1847 to appear with her at the Rhein Music Festival.

Lind mania was a real phenomenon for its time; among women performers only Madonna has ever approached reception of such intensity. She undoubtedly gained from her work with Barnum an appreciation of the efficacy of his advertising techniques; as Cori Ellison pointed out, she did indeed (with Barnum's assistance) alter forever "the topography of the music business."[34] Lind mania, marketing techniques, questions about her sincerity aside, in the end, however, it must be recognized that it was her voice and her control of it that wildly intoxicated her audiences. Her range was extremely wide, and even if as so many reports say the notes in the middle range were veiled—never "came right" as she herself said—the timbre and control of the very high notes were the delight of composers and never failed to affect listeners, whatever the context—opera or concert, secular or sacred. She excited wonder and awe in her audiences by her amazing abilities, but she also brought to her audiences an idea of artistry and introduced many, especially during her American tours, to different genres and levels of music.

Timeline

1820, 6 Oct	Jenny [Johanna Maria] Lind, born Stockholm
1830	Pupil Royal Opera School, Stockholm; studied with Craelius, Berg
Nov	First stage appearance
1838	Formal debut, Agathe (*Der Freischütz*); also that season Pamina (*Die Zauberflöte*), Euryanthe
1838–1841	*La vestale, Robert le diable* (1839), *Don Giovanni* (Donna Anna), *Lucia di Lammermoor* (1840), *Norma* (19 May 1841)
1841	Fatigue, especially noted in middle register
Aug	To Paris, to Manuel Garcia, rest (absolute silence?); Garcia's pupil, 10 months
1842, 10 Oct	*Norma,* Royal Theatre Stockholm, great improvement in voice, technique; new roles Valentine (*Les Huguenots*), Ninetta (*La gazza ladra*), Countess (*Nozze di Figaro*), Amina (*La somnambula,*
1844	*Il turco in Italia, Armide* (Gluck), *Anna Bolena*
1844 fall	Berlin, Vielka (*Ein Feldlager in Schlesien*) written for her by Meyerbeer but first sung by her in Apr in Hamburg,
9 Jun	Stockholm to sing Marie (*La fille du regiment*), then Frankfurt, Darmstadt, Copenhagen; Berlin (5 months);
4 Dec	Sang in Leipzig Gewandhaus concert under Mendelssohn
1846, 22 Apr	Viennese debut in *Norma*; Lower Rhine Music Festival with Mendelssohn; Haydn's *Creation,* Handel's *Alexander's Feast.* Toured Germany: Munich, Stuttgart, Karlsruhe, Nuremberg.
1847, Jan	Vienna, Marie (*Fille du regiment*), huge success.
1847, 4 May	London debut, Her Majesty's, Victoria and Albert present, sang Alice (*Robert le diable,* in Italian)
	Lind fever! *La somnambula* (13 May), *Fille du regiment* (27 Jun) both very successful, *Norma* not popular
	Created Amalia in Verdi's *I masnadieri* (22 Jul), sang Susanna (*Le nozze di Figaro*), 17 Aug; after opera season toured provinces: Birmingham, Manchester, Liverpool, Edinburgh, Glasgow, Norwich, Bristol, Bath, Exeter
1847	End opera career? Decision to give up theatre; sang in Stockholm in winter
1848, 12 Apr	Last opera performance in Stockholm, as Norma
1848	Second season in London at Her Majesty's, then tour of Great Britain, plus Dublin
15 Dec	Sang Mendelssohn's *Elijah*, Exeter Hall, London
1849, spring	Six farewell performances at Her Majesty's;
10 May	Final performance in opera: Alice (*Robert le diable*)

1850	United States with conductor Julius Benedict and baritone Giovanni Belletti (old singing partner from early days in Stockholm) to tour for Phineas T. Barnum.
11 Sep	New York, first concert; May 1851, Philadelphia, last (93rd) concert; American tour included Boston, Baltimore, Washington, Richmond, Charleston, Havana, New Orleans, Louisville, Cincinnati, et al. Benedict back to England; Otto Goldschmidt took over as accompanist.
1852, Feb	Married Goldschmidt.
1852	Return to Europe; residence mainly in Germany; continued to sing concerts and oratorios, Germany and England
1858	Settled in England
1883	Last public performance; professor of singing at new Royal College of Music, London
1887, 2 Nov	Jenny Lind Goldschmidt died, Wynds Point, Herefordshire

Bibliography

Works about Lind

Lind, Jenny. Letter to Professor [Oscar?] Bystrom, Stockholm, 2 June 1868. "Jenny Lind's Singing Method." Translated by V. M. Holmstrom. *Musical Quarterly* 3 (1917): 548–51.

Letter discovered around 1913, in which Lind explains how her voice was trained and discusses her methods and views on teaching and singing.

Bulman, Joan. *Jenny Lind: A Biography.* London: James Barrie, 1956.

General biography, includes quotations from letters, critiques, etc., but has absolutely no documentation. Meager bibliography.

Caswell, Austin. "Jenny Lind's Tour of America: A Discourse of Gender and Class." *Festa musicologica: Essays in Honor of George J. Buelow.* Edited by Thomas J. Mathiesen and Benito V. Rivera. Stuyvesant, N.Y.: Pendragon Press, 1995.

Excellent, thought-provoking study of Lind and contemporary American society, and significance of her tour.

Holland, Henry Scott, and W. S. Rockstro. *Memoir of Madame Jenny Lind-Goldschmidt.* London: John Murray, 1891.

Prepared with help of Lind's husband Otto Goldschmidt (died 1907); very useful but ends with beginning of American tour.

Maude, Mrs. Raymond [Jenny]. *The Life of Jenny Lind: Briefly Told by Her Daughter.* London: Cassell and Company, Ltd., 1926.

Gentle but very useful account by her daughter of life and personality of Jenny Lind.

Wagenknecht, Edward. *Jenny Lind.* Boston and New York: Houghton Mifflin Company, 1931.

Useful for many quotations from people who heard, knew, worked with Lind. Very defensive. Any disparaging remark is explained away.

Ware, W. Porter, and Thaddeus C. Lockard, Jr. *P. T. Barnum Presents Jenny Lind: The American Tour of the Swedish Nightingale.* Baton Rouge and London: Louisiana State University Press, 1980.

Exhaustive study of Lind's tour, well-documented, sympathetic but objective presentation of material about both Barnum and Lind. Particularly valuable for its citing of material from a number of primary sources that are extremely difficult to procure.

General Reference Works

Chopin, Fryderyk. *Selected Correspondence of Fryderyk Chopin.* Translated and edited with commentary by Arthur Hedley. 1963. Reprint, New York: Da Capo Press, 1979.

Chorley, Henry Fothergill. *Modern German Music.* 1854. Reprint, New York: Da Capo Press, 1973.

_____. *Thirty Years' Musical Recollections.* 1862. Edited with an introduction by Ernest Newman. New York: Vienna House, 1972.

Gutman, Robert. *Richard Wagner: The Man, His Mind, and His Music.* New York: Harcourt Brace Jovanovich, Inc., 1968.

Hogarth, George. *Memoirs of the Musical Drama.* London: Richard Bentley, 1838.

Lahee, Henry C. *Famous Singers of Today and Yesterday.* Boston: L. C. Page Co., 1898.

Lumley, Benjamin. *Reminiscences of the Opera.* London: Hurst and Blackett, Publishers, 1864.

Director for twenty years of Her Majesty's Theatre, Lumley brings great expertise and practical knowledge to his accounts of the mid-nineteenth-century London operatic world.

Moscheles, Ignaz. *Recent Music and Musicians: As Described in the Diaries and Correspondence of Ignatz Moscheles.* Edited by his wife, adapted from the original German by A. D. Coleridge. 1873. Reprint, New York: Da Capo Press, 1970, 241.

Pleasants, Henry. *The Great Singers from the Dawn of Opera to Our Own Time.* New York: Simon and Schuster: 1966.

Chapter 12

Pauline Garcia Viardot
(18 July 1821 – 18 May 1910)

In November 1862 a weeping Charles Dickens was spotted by Louis Viardot in the lobby of the Théâtre Lyrique after the performance of Gluck's *Orphée*. Viardot took the author and his companions, composer Arthur Sullivan and critic Henry Chorley, backstage to the source of Dickens's emotional state, Viardot's wife, Pauline Viardot née Garcia, who had just sung the title role. "Nothing could have happened better as a genuine homage to her performance," wrote Dickens "for I was disfigured with crying" after what he considered to be a "most extraordinary performance—pathetic in the highest degree, and full of quite sublime acting."[1]

*   *   *   *   *

Pauline Viardot's Orphée was in many ways the acme of her career; it came also near the end of it. This revival, carefully prepared and conducted by Hector Berlioz, enjoyed some 150 performances between 1859 and 1862; and on 24 April 1863, Viardot sang *Orphée* for her farewell performance at the Théâtre Lyrique. Her career had lasted a quarter of a century, but many reports indicate that her career had in fact outlasted her voice. That she could continue at all seems to have been due to her consummate skill and talent as a dramatic actress and her awe-inspiring presence. Although at the beginning of her career the voice had been praised as equalling that of her recently deceased sister Maria Garcia Malibran in its quality and range, critics also noted quite early a harshness and even expressed fears of its rapid demise. Viardot herself in later years warned her students: "I wished to sing everything and I have ruined my voice."[2]

Viardot's older sister, Maria Malibran, had experienced a meteoric rise to international fame after her Paris debut in 1828; she died tragically in 1836 as the result of a fall from a horse. Her voice was of extraordinary range: she was considered a mezzo-soprano, but through the training of her father Manuel Garcia Sr. her range had been extended into the upper soprano register as well as into the contralto. Like Viardot, Malibran displayed vocal problems. Chorley described Malibran's voice as one that was preferred by connoisseurs even though imperfect and claimed that her range had exceeded the usual mezzo-soprano range at both extremes, into the high soprano and the contralto register as well.[3] Viardot exploited this same range of over three octaves and this same technique—they had, after all, studied with the same teacher, their father. When Pauline began singing publicly in 1837, after Malibran's death, the amazing likeness of her sound to that of her sister was noted at once. The French poet Alfred de Musset wrote of a young English girl who upon hearing Pauline sing in another room believed she was in the presence of Malibran's ghost and fainted. Musset continued:

I, too, rather had the impression that I was seeing a ghost . . . from the very first notes it is impossible for anyone who loved her sister not to be moved. The likeness . . . more in the voice than in the features, is so striking that it would appear to be supernatural . . . It is the same timbre, clear, resonant, audacious, that Spanish coup de gosier which has something at the same time so harsh and so sweet about it . . . similar to the taste of a wild fruit . . . if Pauline Garcia has her sister's voice, she also has her soul; and, without the slightest imitation, it is the same genius . . . She abandons herself to inspiration with that easy simplicity which gives everything an air of grandeur . . . She sings as she breathes . . . before expressing something, she feels it. She does not listen to her voice, but to her heart.[4]

These remarks would be repeated throughout Viardot's career. The French novelist George Sand wrote of her singing: "This voice goes from the heart to the heart . . . [she] enters into the mind of composers; she is alone with them in her thoughts."[5] Igor Turgenev said simply: "She was an intelligent singer," and the German music critic Ludwig Rellstab who heard her in Berlin in 1838 found her voice not especially beautiful "but in it one senses a soul, a mind, or, if you like, what one might term the physiognomy of the voice, and it is this individual expression which moves the writer of this article to such an extent."[6]

If most of these descriptions center on the emotional content and reaction, it is nonetheless clear that already in the early years Viardot possessed not only extraordinary musicianship but a sound vocal technique. The roles of those early years document her virtuosic capacities—Rossini's Desdemona, Cenerentola, Rosina, for example. Her transcriptions of six Chopin mazurkas reveal in some detail the kind of ornamentation that suited her: rapid chromatic descents through an octave or two, written both in time and as a series of free embellishments; and arpeggios and trills, again both metrical and quasi-improvisational.[7]

Chopin, who complained that Liszt never played his music as it was written, apparently approved of Viardot's transcriptions, which were probably created during the period when the Viardots were frequent visitors to George Sand's country home, Nohant. He reported in a letter about his London concert in 1848: "Mme Viardot has been so gracious as to sing my mazurkas at the concert in the theatre—without my asking her to do so." Not only did she sing them as a guest soloist on his concert but she performed them on her own concerts. Chopin remarks with some asperity that Viardot no longer lists the works as "Mazurkas of Chopin" but rather as "Mazurkas arranged by Mme Viardot."[8]

Although the quality of the voice declined, she retained her solid technical foundation. Henry Chorley described her singing of Orphée in Berlioz's 1859 revival of Gluck's opera:

The torrents of *roulades,* the chains of notes, unmeaning in themselves, were flung out with such exactness, limitless volubility and majesty, so as to convert what is essentially a commonplace piece of parade, into one of those displays of passionate enthusiasm, to which nothing less florid could give scope.—As according relief and contrast, they are not merely pardonable—they are defensible; and thus, only to be despised by the indolence of the day, which, in obedience to false taste and narrow pedantry, has allowed one essential branch of art to fall into disuse.[9]

We should bear in mind that Chorley was Viardot's very close friend and early supporter, and in this particular case may have been responding to the criticism of Berlioz who had voiced his disapproval of some ornamentations she had added to the original text. Nonetheless, Chorley was an expert and principled music critic, and his testimony should be valued.

Aside from her virtuosity and her range (healthy though it probably was not), Viardot's work was remarkable for its quality of communication—precisely the aspect singled out by George Sand. Pasta too had this extraordinary power, but in a quite different way. Pasta simply *was* the character she portrayed; all indications are that her performances were the result of intense study of the music and profound identification with her character. She seems to have worked in an instinctive manner. Viardot's portrayal developed from her intimate involvement with the role, the music, the composer, and necessarily resulted from her intellectual approach which she was then able to transcend in her portrayal of the character. One element of that approach—apparently unique for the time—was a thorough study of the literary and historical background of the libretto and a zeal for historical accuracy that extended to the designing of her own costumes. One writer has described her as an "acting singer who foreshadowed Callas."[10] Although Berlioz complained about her ornamenting the sacred text of Gluck, he was nonetheless astounded by her opening night performance: "Her gifts are so complete, so varied, they touch art at so many points, they combine so much learning with such seductive spontaneity, that they evoke both astonishment and emotion at the same time; they are striking and moving; they impose respect and they convince."[11]

Though the references to harshness and cracking appear early in Viardot's career, it would be a mistake to overemphasize the limitations of her voice. She undoubtedly exceeded her natural, comfortable range, and by sheer will power forced her voice to work in both higher and lower ranges (as had also her sister, which would lead to the conclusion that they were adhering to their father's training). But there also seems to have been a unique quality in the voice—a quality that never disappeared judging from the descriptions in the late 1860s and even 1870s. Her friend Chorley wrote for example: "A more perfect and honeyed voice might have recalled the woman too often . . . Her musical handling of so peculiar an instrument will take its place in the highest annals of art."[12] Berlioz, who was never one to flatter or overlook failings or to let friendship get in the way of accurate assessment wrote about the revival of *Alceste* in 1861 that Viardot "struggling against the rebellion of her voice, as does Gluck against the monotony of the libretto, like him retained the upper hand . . . *Alceste* is a fresh triumph for Madame Viardot, and the one which was, for her, the most difficult to achieve."[13] The bass-baritone Charles Santley, a pupil of Manuel Garcia Sr., heard the young Viardot frequently in concerts and in performances of oratorios: "No woman in my day has ever approached Madame Viardot as a dramatic singer . . . She was perfect, as far as it is possible to attain perfection, both as singer and actress . . . She is a wonderful woman, more wonderful even than her wonderful brother. What a genius!"[14]

*   *   *   *   *

In view of her family circumstances, it is difficult to imagine any career other than as a singer for Pauline Garcia Viardot:[15] her mother Joaquina Sitches (1780–1854) sang opera in Seville before she married Manuel Garcia (1775–1832), singer, composer, teacher, entrepreneur. Rossini remarked to Manuel Garcia Jr., "If your father had had as much sense of tact as he had musical sense, he would have been the foremost musician of the age."[16] Her sister, Maria Malibran, enjoyed a flamboyant, meteoric career from her Paris debut in 1828[17] until her untimely death in 1836, and her tenor brother Manuel Jr., inventor of the laryngoscope, became one of the most sought-after voice teachers in Europe. Nevertheless it looked at first as though Pauline would be a pianist, which would seem after all perfectly logical—what could be more practical than to have a soprano, a tenor, and their accompanist, all in the same family? The possibility of such an ensemble was early quashed by Maria's escape (1826) into independence by making a disastrous (but short-lived) marriage with Eugène Malibran, and was then of course permanently ended by her tragic death in 1836. Pauline enjoyed, however, several years of piano study, with Charles(?) Meysenberg[18] and then with Franz Liszt. Her musical education was in fact quite thorough; she studied piano and possibly organ with Marcos Vega (cathedral organist in Mexico City), and she also studied counterpoint and composition with Anton Reicha (then at the Paris Conservatory). But perhaps her most valuable training came in actual practice as pianist (from the age of eight!) for her father's lessons—valuable especially since from her post at the piano she must have absorbed a great deal of vocal instruction as well as having gained practical experience as an accompanist in a not particularly gentle school.

Manuel Garcia, though usually patient and kindly with Pauline, was known for his tyrannical behavior with his older daughter Maria (1808–1836) and with his son Manuel Jr. (1805–1906).

In 1825 the Garcia family plus three other singers sailed for New York City, where they planned to establish Italian opera. Soon after their arrival on 7 November, they received a visit from Mozart's librettist Lorenzo da Ponte now living in New York eking out a living from his various abilities which included teaching Italian at Columbia University. The Garcia company performed in New York's Park Theatre with moderate success a repertoire that included Rossini's *Il barbiere di Siviglia, Tancredi, Otello, Il turco in Italia,* and *La Cenerentola,* as well as Mozart's *Don Giovanni,* plus two operas by Manuel Garcia, *L'amante astuto* and *La figlia dell'aria.* Unfortunately they were early deserted by Maria. She escaped her dominating father for an elderly and seemingly wealthy French businessman Eugène Malibran; he soon went bankrupt, and Maria returned alone to France where she made her spectacularly successful Paris debut and launched her brief career. Recognizing that New York audiences were not adequate to support his operatic enterprise, Garcia took his troupe minus Maria to Mexico City in hopes of financial gain. False hopes, though the seven-year-old Pauline was able to study piano with Vega in Mexico City. On their way to the coast to sail for Europe, they were robbed by bandits of whatever profits they had. The memory of that stayed with Pauline throughout her life. She described once to a friend the scene she half-saw, half-heard, as she lay hidden nearby in the forest:

From time to time a shot was heard, preceded, accompanied and followed by fearful shouts and curses—the blows of the hammers breaking open the cases and luggage, the groans of the women who had followed Mamma's example, and were lying down near us instead of going "into the forest," the laughter of the robbers, the tramping of the horses and, as a pedal-note to all this discord, the howling of the wind which was blowing through the gorge surrounded by mountains in which we were—all this was terribly beautiful, and although it made my teeth chatter, I liked it.[19]

The Garcia family arrived in Paris around March 1829 minus one singer and with even less money than when they had left. No longer in demand as a singer, Garcia resumed his teaching with great success, but unfortunately for all concerned died only three years later in 1832. Pauline and her mother joined Maria Malibran and her companion the Belgian violinist Charles-Auguste de Bériot in Brussels;[20] around 1835 Pauline began performing as pianist for Maria and Charles. She was by now having lessons with Franz Liszt, and like almost every other female in Europe was half in love with him: "He was so handsome, so inspired, so attractive," she recalled many years later.[21] But all this ended with the death of Malibran in 1836, shortly after she and Bériot had finally been able to marry. Madame Garcia now decided that Pauline would be a singer, not a pianist. Was she meant to replace the lost Malibran? Was it that for Madame Garcia any career other than as a singer was out of the question? Whatever her motivation, and difficult though it was for Pauline, the daughter had to accept the decision. In 1837 Pauline Garcia made her first public appearance as a singer with Bériot in Brussels, and in 1838 she made a quite successful tour of Germany, during the course of which she sang in Berlin where she was heard and acclaimed by Ludwig Rellstab (see above, page 170). Her reception in Paris was not as promising. Although her first public concert (15 December 1838) was reviewed enthusiastically by Berlioz and particularly by Alfred de Musset, she made little headway against the dominance of the French operatic stage by Giulia Grisi (1811–1869) at the Théâtre Italien and by Rosine Stoltz (1815–1903; also known as Heloise Stoltz) at the Opéra.

Pauline Garcia's career in fact got off to a slow start. After a season of Italian opera in London, which was also dominated by Grisi and her companion, tenor Giovanni Mario (1810–1883), she debuted at the Paris Opéra as Desdemona in Rossini's *Otello.* In spite of good notices no further engagements were forthcoming, presumably due to the control of the Paris scene by Grisi and Stoltz, but perhaps also due in part to intrigue against George Sand and her circle, of which Pauline was now an intimate member. This group included Frederic Chopin, the painters Eugène Delacroix and Ary Scheffer, and the Polish expatriate poet Adam Mickiewicz, all of whom remained lifelong friends of Pauline. It also included the new director of the Théâtre Italien, Louis Viardot, twenty-one years older than Pauline, whom she married in 1840.

The next two decades were for her an extraordinary combination of family responsibilities and work as a performing artist. Her first child, Louise Pauline Marie, was born in December 1841; during 1842 she performed a few concerts in Paris (including one with Chopin on 21 February) and in Spain where she sang her first Norma, in Madrid. She had almost no engagements in Paris, but, apparently at the urging of George Sand, she sought—and found—success outside Paris, away from the musical and political intrigues that hindered her progress. She sang in Madrid, London, Vienna, St. Petersburg, Prague, Berlin, consistently finding success, sometimes immediate, sometimes after a few appearances. In Berlin she came in contact with Giacomo Meyerbeer, newly appointed General Music Director in Berlin; he became an ardent supporter and played an important role in her ultimate success in Paris. Her biggest breakthrough came in 1843 when she joined a company established by the tenor Giovanni Battista Rubini to perform Italian opera in St. Petersburg at the Bolshoi Theatre. The Bolshoi, built in 1818, had been renovated in 1836 and now with nearly 3,000 seats was one of the largest theatres in Europe. The audiences of St. Petersburg, starved for opera, responded enthusiastically during this first season. Rubini's company was engaged for two more seasons, although neither the second (1844–1845) with seventy-six performances nor the third (1845–1846) repeated the overwhelming success of the first.

For Viardot the triumphs in St. Petersburg must have been a salve after the hostile reception she had met in Paris. She was not only gratified by the appreciation of Russian audiences but discovered in herself a deep sympathy with Russian music and literature. She learned the language well enough to communicate satisfactorily, and she made it a point to sing Russian songs in Russian at any opportunity. Thus, for example, as Rosina in Rossini's *Il barbiere di Siviglia* she sang a Russian melody in the singing lesson scene. She read widely in Russian literature, especially the work of Alexander Pushkin, and she came in contact with a number of writers. The most significant of these was Ivan Turgenev, who fell deeply in love with her and in one way or another was associated with her until his death in 1883. The Russian experience—her success as a singer and her encounters with Russian literary figures—deeply affected her development as an artist. Not only did she zealously bring music of Russian composers—Glinka, Dargomyzhski, Borodin, Tchaikovski, and others—to the west, but she herself composed and published two sets of lieder using the poetry of Turgenev of course, but also of Pushkin, Fet, and Lermontov.[22]

But the third Russian season ended early for Viardot when she was struck down by whooping cough (following daughter Louise's bout) and finally had to leave St. Petersburg for a milder climate. After a summer spent recuperating (perhaps also doing some soul-searching with respect to Turgenev and his declaration of love), she was engaged for the 1846–1847 season in Berlin. Here she sang in German *Fidelio* (Beethoven), *Iphigenie* (Gluck), and Meyerbeer's *La Juive* and *Robert le diable*. On one occasion she even sing the roles of both Alice and Isabelle in *Robert,* the singer of Isabelle having fallen ill. Audiences were enthusiastic, but more important for her, Meyerbeer was immensely impressed by her performance and became one of her most ardent supporters. Tours of Germany and Austria were followed by the summer season of 1848 at Covent Garden in London, where she triumphed as Valentin in the premiere of Meyerbeer's *Les Huguenots.*

In spite of such powerful allies as Berlioz, Chopin, and Rossini, Viardot still had found little success in Paris. In 1848, thanks to new directors at the Paris Opéra and probably to Meyerbeer's insistence, she was engaged to sing Fidès in the premiere of *Le Prophète* at the Opéra. Now at last, she found the triumph she had worked so hard to achieve. Arriving home after the first performance, exhausted but elated she scribbled a note to George Sand: "Victoire! VICTOIRE! et bonsoir." She was not alone in proclaiming victory. Although the opera itself met very mixed reactions—Chopin was scandalized, Delacroix pronounced it "the annihilation of art," Berlioz termed it "frankly detestable" (franchement détestables)[23]—Viardot was acclaimed unanimously as admirable. Meyerbeer wrote his mother that "as singer and as actress [she] achieved a height of tragedy that I have never seen in the theatre."[24] Berlioz published his views in the *Journal des Débats* a few days later:

Madame Viardot's success was immense. No one (in France) believed her to be so eminently gifted in the dramatic talent she displayed in the role of Fidès. All her stances, her gestures, her physiognomy, even her costumes have been prepared with profound art. The perfection of her melody, the capacity of her vocal technique, her musical confidence, these are known

. . . She is one of the greatest artists who can be cited in the history of music, past and present. This is art, pure and complete.[25]

Other critics agreed. *L'Illustration* declared that she was "Malibran and Mlle Rachel united," and the *Gazette de France* wrote that her performance was the "epitome of truth, expression, grace, and feeling."[26] One critic demanded, obviously in response to some remarks about Viardot's physiognomy:

Who ever would ask if Mme Viardot was pretty, or even if she had a voice? There is in her singing so much expression. drama, passion, fury, that when one listens to her without seeing her, one is entranced, transported, with no thought of discussing the quality or the extent of her voice.[27]

Viardot had indeed conquered. The next decade was one of energetic concertizing and operatic singing, including seasons in London, again in Russia, and tours of the Continent. Sadly, however, by 1859 when she was only thirty-eight it was clear that her voice was beginning to deteriorate. In spite of this she sang that year the title role in Berlioz's monumental re-creation of Gluck's revered masterpiece *Orphée*. This, which was expected to be a *succes d'estime,* met an ecstatic reception, powerfully moving its audiences and leaving many of them—not just Dickens— in tears. Even Berlioz who had expressed concerns about her voice was astounded by the power of her performance. After this extraordinary success, Viardot was invited almost as a matter of course to sing the title role in the Opéra's new production of Gluck's *Alceste* in 1861. Berlioz would have at first nothing to do with the production, saying he could not countenance the transpositions necessary to suit the role to Viardot's voice; nevertheless he did supervise some rehearsals and advised Viardot on her interpretation. Again in spite of vocal problems she achieved an extraordinary performance in this her final role for Paris. Even Berlioz found her performance superb, writing that this was "a fresh triumph for Madame Viardot, and the one which was, for her, the most difficult to achieve."[28]

In 1863 Viardot retired from the stage. She continued, however, to perform in concerts and private performances—for example in March of 1870 she sang the first performance, in Jena, of Johannes Brahms's *Alto Rhapsody.* The greatest change in her life was now the move she made with her family to Baden-Baden where they in essence created their own musical world—with such visitors as Clara Schumann, Franz Liszt, Berlioz, and of course Turgenev (who built his own house in Baden-Baden very near the Viardot family). Here Pauline taught, performed privately and at local events, and wrote music. The operettas she composed to texts by Turgenev—*Trop de femmes, L'Ogre, Le dernier sorcier*—were quite successful; the last-named with some additions and orchestrated by Liszt and Edward Lassen (now court musician to the Grand Duke of Weimar, a position once held by Liszt) enjoyed two performances in the court theatre at Weimar in 1869.[29] This very pleasant life was ended by the Franco-Prussian war in 1870; the

Viardots retreated with little money to London where Pauline supported the family by singing in the English provinces and by teaching (Manuel Garcia Jr. had long been established in London). On their return to France in 1871, the Viardot menage, which now openly included Turgenev, divided their lives between Paris during the winter and a country home, *Les Frênes* (Turgenev built his own small *dacha* on the grounds) in Bougival during the summer. Although the Viardot establishment in Bougival attracted a number of visitors, it was in Paris that Viardot found the lively intellectual life that was essential for her. Her circle of friends, in addition to the old Sand group, included writers, politicians, artists, old and young, from all around Europe. Long after she had retired from public appearances, she held regular semi-private and private evenings at which she performed new music including her own. Moreover, she was known as an excellent though very strict teacher and had a large studio of young singers, many of whom turned often to the omnipresent Turgenev for comfort after their encounters with the stern and intimidating Madame Viardot.

On 5 May of 1883 Louis Viardot died; on 3 September of the same year Turgenev died. Pauline, having nursed each in turn, lived for another two decades. She gave up the home in Bougival and remained in Paris, teaching (until 1901), much visited (by Tchaikovsky for example, in 1886), and very active in the musical life of the city. In 1901 she was awarded the Légion d'honneur. She died in Paris on 18 May 1910.

*   *   *   *   *   *

Although her voice had an unforgettable timbre, the Spanish *coup de gossier* referred to by Musset, the unique aspects of her singing were rooted in her intelligence and her carefully researched and prepared characterizations. The voice, damaged as she admitted by her forcing it in extremes of range and by her singing unsuitable roles, began to deteriorate fairly early in her career (Gounod complained about it already in 1850 when she was 29; even her staunch supporter Henry Chorley never denied her vocal problems), and she retired from the public stage when she was just 42. Possibly the vocal training that she absorbed from those days of accompanying her father's students—we must remember his tyrannical teaching of Manuel Jr. and Maria—was coupled with her own determination so that she strained her voice, her will exceeding her ability (it is worthy of note that Maria also extended her range probably unhealthily in both directions). Chorley, in his memoirs (*Thirty Years' Musical Recollections,* 1862) referred to this and to the rebellious qualities of her voice also noted by Berlioz who wrote that

nature had given her a rebel to subdue, not a vassal to command, in her voice. From the first she chose to possess certain upper notes which must needs be fabricated, and which never could be produced without the appearance of effort. By this despotic exercise of will it is possible that her real voice—a limited mezzo-soprano—may have been weakened.[30]

Chorley also remarked in the same passage on her "art which has never . . . been exceeded in amount," a claim that stood without contradiction throughout her career.

Surely the profound musicianship that was the hallmark of her work derived at least in part from her early studies of piano. When she left the opera stage, a number of friends questioned why she did not continue her musical career as a pianist, comparing her abilities to those of such performers as Clara Schumann; her response was that she quite simply no longer thought of herself as a pianist. Her ability to play *prima vista* and to learn music rapidly permitted her to cover an immense quantity of repertoire. Several well-documented reports detail amazing feats of quick study of roles, as for example the Berlin performance of Meyerbeer's *Robert le diable* in which, a singer having fallen ill, Pauline sang that part as well as her own. Her talent for languages was an advantage in learning operas of different national schools, but it surely contributed also to the strength of her dramatic performance and played a significant role in her intellectual life. In addition to the major figures of Parisian circles—Rossini, Berlioz, Delacroix, Scheffer, Sand, Chopin—her friends included Nicholas and Anton Rubinstein (Anton married her pupil, Vera Tschekouanoff), Dickens, George Eliot, Clara Schumann, Liszt, Julius Rietz, i.e., people from all of Europe. She was the model for Sand's Consuelo in the eponymous novel of 1842; she was also undoubtedly the model for George Eliot's Armgart.[31] Although she did a great deal of teaching she was not particularly influential (although her brother Manuel certainly was); one wonders if she came to doubt the efficacy of her father's method since her own voice began so early to deteriorate. Or did she ascribe that failure to her own ambitious determination to sing everything? Her influence lay in her extraordinary creation of roles, her enthusiastic support and performance of new music, and in her participation in the intellectual world of the nineteenth century. She was recognized as completely disciplined and entirely devoted to her art, and is indeed portrayed precisely thus by Sand and Eliot, both of whom knew her well. This was a singer who knew exactly what she was doing—who though undoubtedly possessing a formidable musical instinct never relied on that but created her roles through painstaking research and thought. And in this she laid the groundwork for the modern dramatic singer, the Maria Callas, the Teresa Stratas, the Phyllis Curtin of the twentieth century.

A significant aspect of Viardot's career was her knowledge and performance of contemporary music. She actively encouraged young composers, for example, Charles Gounod (who enjoyed her patronage for several years but sad to say returned it with spiteful comments), Gabriel Fauré, Camille Saint-Saëns. Nowhere does her intellectual stature show more strikingly than in her approach to new music, particularly that of the Russian school: during her first season in St. Petersburg (1843) she began to sing in public Russian songs in Russian. At least once she sang a Russian song as Rosina's lesson aria in *Il barbiere di Siviglia*. She learned the language well enough to enjoy lively conversations and to assist Turgenev with translations, and she included Russian songs on her concerts in western Europe.

Tchaikovsky visited her in 1886 apparently out of a sense of duty and found himself entranced: "She is such a wonderful, interesting woman, that I am completely captivated by her."[32] He stayed for three hours caught up in talk with her (she had acquired the score of his opera *Eugen Onegin* several months before its premiere, 1879, in Moscow); she showed him the autograph score of Mozart's *Don Giovanni,* which she had purchased in 1855 from the heirs of the German publisher André.[33] Tschaikovsky was fascinated by her and overwhelmed by Mozart's score. He wrote to Nadezhda von Meck: "I cannot express the feeling which overwhelmed me as I examined that musical sacred relic! It was just as if I had shaken hands with Mozart himself and chatted with him."[34]

Saint-Saëns remained a friend to the end. He often performed as her accompanist in the home music-making; *Samson et Dalila,* begun in 1868 with Viardot in mind as Dalila was dedicated to her. The opera was performed for the first time in Weimar in 1877, thanks to Liszt who was by then living his *vie trifourquée* in Weimar, Budapest, and Rome. Viardot was no longer singing publicly by then, but she had sung the role at a private performance in 1874 of the first two acts, with student singers and Saint-Saëns at the piano. An anonymous audience member left a telling description of her effect as a performer, more than a decade after her retirement from the stage: "Madame Viardot's voice was then already impaired, especially its middle register; but its upper and lower notes were wonderfully preserved, and her performance made one forget both her age, which was unsuitable for Dalila, and the defects of her voice, and everything else."[35] Such was the power of her musical and dramatic creation.

Pauline Garcia Viardot represents in many ways the consummate nineteenth-century artist: gifted singer, pianist, composer, involved in many different genres of music, profoundly interested in all aspects of cultural and intellectual life not excluding politics, containing within herself very different nationalities: of Spanish ancestry, she grew up and lived most of her life in France, and she was closely attuned to the language and literature of both Germany and Russia. Like Pasta, Viardot was totally given to her art but on a much broader stage and with far greater influence from other arts. Liszt's assessment in an 1859 essay in the *Neue Zeitschrift für Musik* is particularly significant for comprehending the stature of this remarkable woman. He praises her pianism, her compositions (no thought of "female" quality here), her interpretations; he stresses that her virtuosity serves only to express the idea, thought, character of a work or a role,[36] and he predicts that

she will ever be one of the first in that outstanding group—Pasta, Malibran, Schröder-Devrient, Ristori, Rachel, Seebach, et al.—and through the manifold gifts with which she unites Italian, French, and German art, through outstanding spiritual understanding, through the splendid disposition of her personality, through the nobility of her character, through her honorable behavior in her private life, she will enjoy an extraordinarily special position.[37]

Liszt's essay includes reviews of her performances in Weimar of *Norma* and *Il barbiere di Siviglia*. For the singing lesson in Act II Viardot apparently accompanied herself at the piano as she sang one of her own arrangements of a Chopin mazurka—thus presenting simultaneously Pauline Viardot singer, pianist, and composer. Liszt's description is a fitting summation of her artistry:

[I]n the art of song she outdoes herself in the second act, when she reveals the unimaginable richness of her coloratura and her soulful expression in the Spanish songs and in Chopin's famous mazurka. How she then draws with the gold pencil of her voice the boldest rainbows in the air and then with the swiftness of a swallow soars from the depths into the heights, and rests on the trill as on a branch, and shakes off its drops of dew in pearly, saucy cadenzas. Then she delighted the audience with the gifts of her piano playing, as in her preluding or fantasizing she seized upon charming inspirations.[38]

Timeline

1821, 18 July	Pauline Garcia born Paris to Manuel Garcia (1777–1832) and Joaquina Sitches
1823–1825	London seasons, 1825 debut of Maria Garcia as Rosina
1825, 25 Nov	Garcias, 3 children (Pauline, older sister Maria (1807–1836), brother Manuel Jr. (1805–1906) plus 3 singers, departed Europe for New York City to establish Italian opera; visited there by Lorenzo da Ponte
1826	Maria married Engène Malibran; Garcia troupe (minus Maria) to Mexico; Pauline studied piano with Marcos Vega, organist at Mexico City cathedral
1828	Return to Europe, Paris; Maria famous; Garcia established teaching studio
c. 1829	Pauline pianist for father's lessons; important for her as pianist and singer
1832	Manual Garcia Sr. died; Pauline with mother to Brussels to live with Malibran and companion Bériot
1832–1836	Piano studies with Meysenberg, then with Liszt
1836	Malibran's death; Pauline forced to give up piano for voice
1837, 13 Dec	First public appearance, with Bériot, (violin), charity concert, Brussels
1838	German tour; Rellstab (Berlin) deeply moved by Pauline's voice
1838, 15 Dec	First concert Paris, Théâtre de la Renaissance, reviews by Musset and Berlioz
1839, spring	London debut as Desdemona (Rossini's *Otello*); season of Italian opera, Her Majesty's Theatre
1839, 8 Oct	Paris debut, Théâtre de l'Odéon, Desdemona
1840, 18 Apr	Married Louis Viardot, director Théâtre Italien
1840–	Paris opera scene dominated by Grisi and Stolz
	Viardot circle of friends included Sand, Delacroix, Chopin, Scheffer, many political exiles (e.g. Mickiewicz); Schumann's *Liederkreis* (poems by Heine) dedicated to her
1841, Feb	London, private performance of Rossini *Stabat Mater*
1841, 14 Dec	Birth of first child, Louise Pauline Marie Viardot
1842	Concerts, including one with Chopin, 21 Feb, Salle Pleyel
1842, May	Spain, difficulties but success; first Norma (Madrid)
1842	*Consuelo*, Sand's novel about Pauline Viardot, published serially (sequel: *La Comtesse de Rudolstadt*)
1842–1843	Contract with Théâtre Italien; problems with Grisi; successful concerts
1843	Published collection of 8 compositions; Vienna, 19 Apr, Rosina, triumph; successful German tour; Prague also success; Berlin,

contact with Meyerbeer (new General Music Director); renewed acquaintance with Fanny Mendelssohn Hensel; St. Petersburg with Rubini's Italian opera company, Bolshoi theatre (built 1818, renovated 1836, almost 3000 seats, among largest theatres in Europe); Russian literary scene: Gogol, Goncharov, Dostoevsky, Turgenev (25), Tolstoy (15); Pushkin and Lermontov recently died; composer Glinka (39); great success in Russia; learned Russian, sang Russian songs occasionally (e.g., as Rosina's lesson piece in *Il barbiere di Siviglia*), sang for students at University; began life-long relationship with Turgenev

1844	Purchased estate Courtavenel, Seine et Marne, near Rozay-en-Brie; second Russian season, 76 performances
1845	Turgenev to France, Paris, Courtavenel
1845–1846	Third Russian season, less success; ill (whooping cough), left for milder climate; spent summer recovering
1846–1847	Berlin season, great success; sang in German *Fidelio, Iphigenie, La Juive, Robert le diable*
1847, Feb	Turgenev also to Berlin; Viardot circle: Francois Ponsard, Renan, Corot, Doré, Scheffer, Rossini, Franck; Pauline touring regularly
1848 summer	Covent Garden, with Grisi, Persiani, Mario; Her Majesty's with Lind; sang *La Sonnambula, I Capuleti, Don Giovanni*, all moderate successes; premiere of *Les Huguenots*, sang Valentin, triumph!
1848–1849	Paris Opéra, Fidès in *Le prophète* (Meyerbeer), first Paris victory
1849, 20 Oct	Chopin's funeral, sang alto solos in Mozart Requiem (requested by Chopin)
1849	Worked with Gounod, *Sapho* composed for her
1850	Turgenev to Russia (until 1856)
17 Jun	Paris premiere *Sapho* (Gounod), mixed success; London premiere, disaster, music called weak, Pauline's performance praised; Gounod to friend: Pauline "already nearing her end [as singer], and singing out of tune all the time"
1852, 2 Apr	Birth of second child, Claudie
1853 Jan	Russia; great success in *Il barbiere* and *La Cenerentola* (Turgenev banished to estate, sneaked into St. Petersburg to meet Pauline)
1853	Birth of third child, Marianne
	Continued to promote Russian music, sang in Russian
1855	Charles Dickens in Paris, introduced (by Scheffer?) to Viardots Viardot circle now included: Berlioz, Saint-Saens, Franck, Rossini, Delacroix, Corot, Scheffer, Dore, Ponsard, Renan, Henri Martin, Emile Augier, Jules Simon, hornist Vivier; Chorley, Lord Leighton, Adelaide Sartoris, Liszt, Herzen, Anton and Nicolas Rubinstein

1856 Aug	Turgenev to western Europe; happy autumn at Courtavenel
Nov	Break with Turgenev.
1857, 20 Jul	Birth of fourth child, Paul Louis Joachim, at Courtavenel
1857–1858	Extensive tour of northern Europe (Warsaw, Berlin, Leipzig); May, London, Drury Lane
1858	Close friend Ary Scheffer died; developed close friendship with Julius Rietz
1858, Dec	Weimar, sang *Norma, Il barbiere di Siviglia*, Liszt's review and essay in *Neue Zeitschrift für Musik*
1859	Voice deteriorating; no operas in Paris, London; toured England, Ireland (Dublin), Lady Macbeth in Dublin
	Paris, Berlioz's new production Gluck's *Orphée*, close relationship with Berlioz due to *Orphée* and Berlioz's opera *Les Troyens*
1859–1861	*Orphée* great success; c.150 performances at Théâtre lyrique; Offenbach's *Orphée aux enfers* also playing
1861	Gluck's *Alceste*; also success, but clear that voice was near end
	Retired from stage; move to Baden-Baden, pleasant life, pupils, friends, began composing operettas, texts by Turgenev (restored to Viardot family circle): *Trop de femmes, L'Ogre, Le dernier sorcier*
1869, Apr	*Le dernier sorcier.* performed at Weimar
1870, spring	Weimar, 2 performances *Orphée*
1870, 3 Mar	Premiere Brahms's *Alto Rhapsody*, Jena
1870, fall	Left Baden-Baden for England, due to Franco-Prussian War, money tied up in France and in Baden-Baden; concertized in provinces, taught (Manuel Garcia Jr. in London since 1848)
1871	Paris, Turgenev now lived with Viardot family; Courtavenel gone; found villa, Les Frênes, in Bougival; Turgenev built dacha for himself in garden
1875–1883	Winters in Paris (Turgenev had top floor); summers in Bougival
1883, 5 May	Louis Viardot died; with Turgenev to Bougival
1883, 31 Oct	Turgenev died
1883–1910	Lived in Paris; taught until 1901; Saint-Saëns remained close friend; dedicated *Samson et Delila,* begun 1868, to her (role originally written for her but never performed in public); opera staged 1877 in Weimar (thanks to Liszt), in Paris not until 1890
1901	Légion d'honneur
1910, 18 May	Pauline Garcia Viardot died, Paris, almost 89

Bibliography

The standard biography in English of Viardot remains that by April FitzLyon, published in 1964, *The Price of Genius: A Life of Pauline Viardot*. FitzLyon draws wherever possible on contemporary sources, but many Russian sources were at that time unavailable. She calls attention to new materials appearing already at that time, and of course today in 2004 much more material is becoming accessible in the former Soviet Union. Clearly, there is opportunity here for a musical scholar with the appropriate linguistic skills to provide a new biography that would take into account the many Russian sources now available. This is particularly important since so much of Viardot's career was involved with Russian music and she played a significant role in introducing it to western Europe.

Works about Viardot
In addition to the works listed below, biographies and letters of the composers Viardot worked with—Berlioz, Chopin, Gounod, Liszt, Meyerbeer—and of such close friends as Sand, Turgenev, Scheffer, et al., are very informative.

Barry, Nicole. *Pauline Viardot: L'Égerie de Sand et de Tourgueniev*. Paris: Flammarion, 1990.
   This study is rich, packed with information, and has a solid bibliography but lacks note documentation. The author worked with Jacques-Paul Viardot (grandson of Pauline and Louis Viardot) and his wife Pierrette. The novelistic approach, however, offers reconstructed conversations, such as "Bientôt, pense Pauline, la *Sapho* de Gounod révélera au monde un nouveau genie. Avec lui, elle fera triompher l'idéal de Consuelo: instruire et élever l'humanité au moyen de l'art" (221), or a dialogue between Ivan and Pauline in which he informs her that her death is near: "Est-ce l'heure pour moi? demande-t-elle tout bas. Ivan acquiesce de la tête" (408).
Desternes, Suzanne, and Henriette Chandet, with the collaboration of Alice Viardot. *La Malibran et Pauline Viardot*. Paris: Librairie Artheme Fayard, 1969.
   This book written with the collaboration of the singer's granddaughter Alice Viardot, is often helpful, and valuable for the descriptions by Alice Viardot of her grandmother's teaching.
FitzLyon, April. *The Price of Genius: A Life of Pauline Viardot*. New York: Appleton-Century, 1964.
   As stated above, this book remains the single most useful source for information about Viardot.
Franz Liszt, "Pauline Viardot-Garcia," *Neue Zeitschrift für Musik* 5 (28 January 1859): 49–54.
Pope, Rebecca A. "The Diva Doesn't Die: George Eliot's *Armgart*." In *Embodied Voices: Representing Female Vocality in Western Culture*. Edited by Leslie C. Dunn and Nancy A. Jones. Cambridge: Cambridge University Press, 1994.

This is an interesting and provocative study of *Armgart,* Gluck's *Orphée,* and Viardot's role as model for Eliot's protagonist.

Shuster, Carolyn. "Six Mazurkas de Frédéric Chopin transcrites pour chant et piano par Pauline Viardot." *Revue de musicologie* 75/2 (1989): 265–83.

Shuster presents useful excerpts from Viardot's arrangements of Chopin's mazurkas and also from Viardot's manual for singers, *Une heure d'étude: Exercices pour voix de femme* (1880; reprint, New York: Belwin Mills, Kalmus Vocal Series, no. 9190). Although Shuster's goal is to demonstrate what can be learned about interpretation of Chopin's music from Viardot's transcription, the essay is very informative about the circumstances of the transcriptions and provides very useful discussions of the vocal formulations.

Waddington, Patrick. "Henry Chorley, Pauline Viardot, and Turgenev: A Musical and Literary Friendship. "*Musical Quarterly* 67 (1981): 165–92.

Informative article about the relations among these three personages and about Viardot's relations with other contemporaries. Provides material from letters and essays.

General Reference Works

Berlioz, Hector. *Memoirs of Hector Berlioz from 1803 to 1865 Comprising His Travels in Germany, Italy, Russia, and England.* Translated by Rachel Holmes and Eleanor Holmes, annotated, translated, and revised by Ernest Newman. 1932. Reprint, New York: Dover Publications, Inc., 1966.

Chopin, Frederic. Arthur Hedley, trans. and ed., *Selected Correspondence of Fryderyk Chopin* (New York: McGraw Hill Book Company, Inc., 1963), 322.

Chorley, Henry Fothergill. *Modern German Music.* 1854. Reprint, New York: Da Capo Press, 1973.

_____. *Thirty Years' Musical Recollections.* 1862. Reprint, edited with an introduction by. Ernest Newman. New York: Vienna House, 1972.

Ferris, George. *Great Singers—Faustina Bordoni to Henriette Sontag.* New York: D. Appleton and Co., 1895.

Klein, Herman. *Great Women Singers of My Time.* London: G. Routledge & Co., 1931.

_____. *Thirty Years of Musical Life in London.* London and New York: The Century Co., 1903.

Krehbiel, Henry Edward. *Chapters of Opera.* New York: Henry Holt & Co., 1908.

Pleasants, Henry. *The Great Singers from the Dawn of Opera to Our Own Time.* New York: Simon and Schuster, 1966.

Chapter 13

Lillian Nordica
(12 December 1857 – 10 May 1914)

"To choose one, only one, to represent all American singers, [I] would accord the honor to Lillian Nordica, as the noblest, the most profoundly moving, the least concerned with mere effect—whether effect of vocalization or effect of conscious histrionics; the singer who in the fundamental appeal of the fully matured voice was the most richly endowed of all the great American operatic artists." With these words American critic Oscar Thompson explained his choice of Nordica as the outstanding American soprano of all those he had heard— Emma Eames, Minnie Hauk, Emma Albani, Geraldine Farrar, Olive Fremstad.[1]

She was indeed the quintessential American singer. Born Lillian Norton in Farmington, Maine, educated at Boston's just opened New England Conservatory of Music, gifted not only with a stunning voice but with equal energy and persistence, she enjoyed for nearly forty years a career unmatched so far by any of her compatriots—a career that included being the first American to create a role (Elsa in *Lohengrin*) at Bayreuth, that temple to Richard Wagner. She died in Java 10 May 1914 in the midst of an ambitious, strenuous tour at the age of 57. Her last concert appearance in America was in Reno, Nevada.

* * * * *

The characteristics of Lillian Nordica's voice praised early in her career—purity of tone, freshness, power, and an extensive range—continued to be extolled throughout her life. Even in her last years of singing, when she was in her fifties, these qualities were noted. Her first venture to Europe, in fact her first real job, was with a brass band—a partnership that required a powerful voice. An English reviewer wrote that she sang "with great effect the national air, 'The Star Spangled

Banner'" and added that Miss Norton (as she was then) had "a soprano voice of bright and sympathetic quality and extensive compass."[2]

Less than a year later, April 1879, Miss Norton had moved into the world of opera: her first paid role in Italy (in Europe in fact) was Violetta in Verdi's *La traviata,* at the opera house in Brescia. A Professor Robinson of New York was present and described her sound for the American newspapers:

Miss Norton's voice is a soprano of great range, power, volubility, and of a richness of quality probably not surpassed and scarcely equaled by that of any voice in Europe. It is simply indescribably magnificent. Her acting is good, graceful and natural, and she throws her soul into her singing and acting so thoroughly as at once to captivate every listener. She also dresses richly and in excellent taste.

Miss Norton is a dawning star of the first magnitude. Her few weeks' singing here have given her such fame in Italy that numbers of offers of engagements have already been made her from some of the largest cities. Miss Norton gives the credit for her vocal culture solely to Mr. O'Neill of the New England Conservatory of Music, from whom alone she has received vocal lessons.[3]

These are the qualities that remained with her: power, great range, richness of quality, volubility. Typical is the acknowledgement by Norton of her debt to Mr. O'Neill for the strict and thorough vocal training she had received at his hands. (The reference to her dress reflects the fact that singers generally provided their own costumes, a singular expense for a young singer just beginning a career.) The *Boston Herald* in December 1883, while bemoaning her lack of dramatic force, nonetheless praised her voice for the "beauty and purity of its tone [which] was noticeable in all her numbers." The Boston *Globe* reviewing the same performance noted the "brilliancy and purity" of her singing but mourned her lack of expression.[4]

French reviewers in 1882 noted "an exotic flavor by no means disagreeable" (M. H. Moreno) and a "fresh, true voice managed with taste" (the critic for *Le Menestrel*). Was the exotic flavor the result of an accent? (But Moreno specified that her "foreign accent is barely perceptible.")[5] In 1886, when Nordica was 29, the critic for the *San Francisco Daily Examiner* described her voice as "simply brimming over with youth, magnetism and effervescent sweetness, Mme. Nordica is singularly gifted . . . It is very unusual to find in the same voice lower and middle registers of such power and purity, and high notes that can be attacked with such accuracy and sustained with such ease."[6]

Cosima Wagner, high priestess of the Bayreuth Wagner shrine, wrote in 1894 to a confidant that in Miss Nordica she "recognized a very gifted, talented and seriously zealous woman . . . Her voice, intelligence, capacity for expression are extraordinary"; she chose Madame Nordica to create the role of Elsa for Bayreuth.[7] Cosima's son Siegfried concurred with his mother's view: "With an artist of her talent and of her reputation it is really touching to watch with what indefatigable zeal she dedicates herself to the perfection of her role. We are all highly enchanted to have found for [Elsa], which vocally is one of the most exacting, an artist of the most eminent ability."[8]

The Wagners were right; Otto Floersheim, editor of *The Musical Courier* wrote of the performance:

No German Elsa I ever saw could . . . be compared to Nordica as far as the dramatic conception . . . of this most essentially German character is concerned. The pronunciation of a language not her own was absolutely flawless and each syllable was clearly comprehensible. The beauty and sweetness of her vocal organ stood her in good stead; her intonation was always as pure and flawless as that of a fine flute, her technique is superb and her musical phrasing delightful and artistic to a degree.[9]

Of perhaps greatest significance are the descriptions by Engelbert Humperdinck, composer and Wagner disciple:

Her singing and her acting were both masterly. Having enjoyed a perfect Italian training, her voice is . . . clear and euphonic, displaying a uniformly developed beauty and an almost classic art. Her *piano* is particularly charming and effective and yet entirely without the tremolo with which many singers hope to hide the want of soulful warmth.[10]

The testimony of her fellow singer, Ernestine Schumann-Heink, is equally evocative: "In the days of Nordica's singing of Italian and coloratura roles, her velvety tones were better than those of any singer among them. What a wonderful voice it was! When will there be such another? Her high C in Verdi's Requiem, spun out like a thread of golden light, will linger in my memory eternally."[11]

Even as late as 1913, when Nordica was fifty-six, had been singing professionally for nearly four decades, and had a cold, the critic for the Boston *Transcript* having noted problems of pitch, breath, and weariness, wrote "Yet, now and then, for an instant, her voice summons and unites the three qualities that made it in its prime a great voice in opera house and concert hall—its large, rich beauty, its warmth of power, and its bright and glowing resonance."[12] In Australia, in July 1913, reviewing one of her very last concerts, the critic of the Sydney *Sun* wrote "The voice still remains fresh and vibrant, powerful, and of wide compass. One of the most remarkable things about the technique of the singer is her marvelous breath control and power of sostenuto which enables her to take double phrases without apparent effort. Then she has a glorious shake, the most perfect in its closeness and purity of intonation that has ever come under the notice of the writer."[13] These are the very qualities mentioned in the earliest reviews: "bright and sympathetic quality and extensive compass" (London, 1878), "great range, power, volubility, and of a richness of quality" (Professor Robinson, in Brescia, 1879), and it was these qualities that remained the hallmark of her voice.

Without doubt the long life of her voice was the result of her technical training in her youth. Even reviewers who disparaged her acting or her expressive powers were obligated to give credit for her technical abilities. Bernard Shaw, for example, who was not pleased by her Elsa—dramatically or vocally—noted, nevertheless her technique: "Miss Nordica turned Elsa of Brabant into Elsa of Bond Street, by appearing in a corset. She produces her voice so skillfully that its want of color, and her inability to fill up with expressive action the long periods left by Wagner for that purpose, were the more to be regretted."[14] Again and again, reviewers, colleagues, admirers refer to her marvelous technique; this too, like the power and wide range of her voice, was noted from early in her career. She herself explained that she had had an extremely thorough and solid foundation in her studies with John O'Neill at the New England Conservatory; he exercised a combination of solid technical training and discipline with respect to repertoire—no student was ever allowed to take on music above their present capabilities. Her preparation was so thorough that her subsequent studies in Paris (1878) and then in Milan (1878–1879) were primarily coachings in languages and dramatic skills. When she approached Antonio Sangiovanni (of the Milan Conservatory) for lessons, he declared she was nearly ready for the opera stage; she needed a "few weeks' practice in Italian methods, that's all" and he added that she had "nothing to unlearn"[15]—a real paean of praise for the teaching of Professor O'Neill. Sangiovanni put her to work on such repertoire as *Lucia, Rigoletto, Faust, Norma,* and then the heavier *Aïda.* It was surely this combination of sound technical training, native power and resonance of tone, plus work in these light but extremely virtuosic roles that permitted Nordica to sing an extraordinarily wide range of roles. There was little she could not sing, and she seldom refused any opportunity. Stories abound of her willingness to step in at the last moment for an indisposed (or unhappy) colleague: for example, in 1899 she sang the role of Aïda and, turning away from the audience, also that of the Priestess (that singer having suddenly become ill). In 1900, on 15 February she sang *Götterdämmerung* in Philadelphia, she was called the morning of the 17th and asked to replace that evening the indisposed Marcella Sembrich in *La traviata* (an opera she had not sung for six years) at New York's Metropolitan Opera, and on the19th she was back on stage as Valentine in *Les Huguenots.*[16]

To her excellent technique and rich sound, she added determination, energy, and a willingness to work far beyond the mere acquisition of vocal technique. These qualities also remained with her, with the result that throughout her career she grew steadily as a musician. This was recognized by the New York critics after her 27 November 1895 *Tristan* at the Metropolitan Opera, with Jean de Reszke under the baton of Anton Seidl. Irving Kolodin called it "the most important event in the decade's history of musical performance,"[17] and the critic of the *New York Herald* wrote:

So splendidly was it sung, so passionately enacted . . . surely such things as the finale of the first act, the love duet in the second and the long Tristan scene [the composer] never heard, not even in his mind's ear . . .

The greatest surprise of the evening was undoubtedly Nordica's Isolde . . . Not only did she sing with the charm and beauty of tone, the impeccable intonation, and the clarity of phrasing, which made her famous, but besides she carried through the character, possibly the most arduous in operatic literature, with a splendor of tone, a freedom of posture and gesture, and an authority that amazed the onlookers.

Let no one speak of Mme. Nordica as merely a beautiful singer hereafter. Her Isolde stamps her as one of the greatest lyric artists of the day. Note ye American prima donnas, what high ideals and incessant application will lead to.[18]

W. J. Henderson wrote in the *New York Times*,

Mme. Nordica simply amazed those who thought they had measured the full limit of her powers. She has placed herself beside the first dramatic sopranos of her time. Her declamation was broad and forcible, and . . . she sang absolutely in tune all the evening . . . Nothing more beautiful than the close of the "Sink hernieder" passage in the duo between her and Mr. de Reszke has been heard here, and certainly it has never been better sung anywhere.[19]

The accolades for her Wagner roles were extended also to other operas, in particular for her Aïda sung in 1893 at the Metropolitan Opera:

[A]s a dramatic singer Mme. Nordica in many roles is altogether without parallel at the present day . . . in my opinion no other singer of dramatic music combines such chasteness of style, or what is ordinarily called purity of method, with such volume and again such delicacy of tone.

As Aida her triumph . . . was overwhelming . . . [she sang] the well known music of Aida with dazzling beauty and splendor of tone and with amazing authority . . . into her acting she threw such intensity and such a variety of accent as to make you wonder at the woman's marvelous artistic strides.[20]

Nordica spent long hours of study and practice on the Wagnerian roles—Elsa, Elisabeth, Kundry, Isolde (in Italian, German, and finally French), all three Brünnhildes—which she added to an enormous repertoire of lighter roles ranging from Violetta (*La traviata*) to Norma. Her study of the lighter roles and acquisition of the technique to handle florid roles gave her an agility in all parts of her range; her energy and persistence enabled her to master the linguistic and vocal demands of the heavy dramatic roles. She could—and did—sing just about anything.

* * * * *

She was not just purebred American, Lillian Norton was a true Downeaster.[21] Born 12 December 1857 in Farmington, Maine, she was the sixth daughter of Amanda Allen Norton and Edwin Norton; in 1864 the family moved to Boston where they eked out an existence, not in poverty, but certainly not in comfortable circumstances. Edwin had tried farming, then he tried to run a boarding house, and finally disastrously he experimented with photography: a lamp blew up and left his abilities permanently impaired. Amanda's job at Jordan Marsh kept the family afloat. Significantly music, and singing in particular, played a central role in Norton family life. The young Lillian, a pupil in a music class with Luther Mason,[22] was the only student to recognize the notes of the scale which he wrote on the board; solfeggio was part of daily life in the Norton household. It was not Lillian, however, but her older sister Wilhelmina who was the hope of the family—a hope that was dashed when having just begun a very promising career as a singer Wilhelmina died in 1869 of typhoid fever. Two years later mother Amanda, having suddenly really *heard* the fourteen-year-old Lillian's voice, took her off to sing for Wilhelmina's former teacher, Professor John O'Neill, at the recently (1867) founded New England Conservatory. Lillian's high C landed her squarely in O'Neill's studio where she spent the next five years (1871–1876). The New England Conservatory (NEC) occupied the upper floors of the old Boston Music Hall. At the top of a flight of stairs in this old building Lillian found a gate she could squeeze through into the Music Hall and thus enjoy a great variety of concerts, by such musicians as pianist Anton Rubinstein, or conductor Hans von Bülow. Such musical treats must have been welcome; they also bear witness to her enterprising nature and her lifelong interest in music—not just her own sphere, but the entire world of music.

O'Neill was a severe taskmaster, long on work and short on praise. Nordica told once of taking an aria to O'Neill and being laughed out of the room at her audacity for attempting something so far beyond her abilities. She moralized: "Many cannot stand four years of fault-finding . . . They spend their money for the privilege of weeping rather than that of gaining knowledge."[23] The determination that stood her in good stead throughout her career was already apparent in those early days. Lillian Norton gained knowledge—knowledge of all kinds of music—and an absolutely solid vocal technique that remained the foundation of her art throughout her career. Throughout her career, also, she gave credit to Professor O'Neill for having set the foundation of her art so solidly that when she made up her mind to move into the arena of opera she lacked only the dramatic techniques and experience with stagecraft needed for the theatre; her vocal technique was entirely adequate. Even in her last years this technique was still extolled: violinist Albert Spalding performed with her in 1908 and remembered that even though the piano was tuned lower than usual to ease the production of high Bs and Cs, "Her immense technical equipment and long experience were great strategical allies." He also noted her imposing entrances: "No majesty born to the purple could have competed with her royal entrances and exits. The audience was spellbound before she sang a single note."[24]

In June 1876 Lillian graduated from the New England Conservatory, having spent five years in thorough preparation with relatively little public performance. On 27 June she sang at the Conservatory exhibition performance Handel's "Let the Bright Seraphim" for the first time in public. With her mother she then moved to New York; the family split in various directions: the sisters were now married, and Edwin Norton went to live with Annie. This was the end of family life for the Nortons, and the beginning of Lillian Norton's professional years. After a few insignificant appearances in New York, she auditioned for P. S. Gilmore[25] to sing with "Gilmore's Band." She got the job on the basis of her renditions of "Care campagne" (Bellini's *La sonnambula*) and "Let the Bright Seraphim," and, to the disgust of Professor O'Neill, set out with the Band on a tour of the western United States. Her fee climbed to $50 per concert as she toured with Gilmore in the west and in the east. After a New England Conservatory reunion concert on 6 April 1878, in which she shared honors with the young American pianist Amy Fay, she sailed on 4 May with the Band (and her mother) for Europe. Gilmore's Band and its stunning soprano performed sixty-five concerts in six weeks; they captivated audiences in Liverpool, Dublin, London (the Crystal Palace), Manchester, Amsterdam, Brussels, ending in July in Paris (where the agent not only failed to publicize the concert but absconded with all of Gilmore's funds). Norton, having been paid regularly along the way, lent Gilmore the money to continue his tour; he repaid it twice over at the end of the Paris engagements. Norton and Gilmore now parted ways, and she spent the following year preparing herself to enter the world of European opera.

Now 21 years old, Lillian had a plan. She spent the rest of that summer of 1878 in Paris studying voice and drama and opera roles with François Delsarte, and being coached by a Spanish tenor, Emilio Belari (a leading tenor at Les Italiens). Her days were filled with work: acting lessons, work with a pianist to learn opera roles and practice, two hours of French each day, music study, a lesson with Delsarte, and three lessons per week with Belari. Her brother-in-law, William Baldwin, helped financially, Lillian gave lessons, and they lived from her savings from the Gilmore tours. She planned to spend six months in Paris and then move on to Milan to finish herself, but the Paris sojourn was brought to an abrupt end by Delsarte's severe heart attack in early November. A few days later the Nortons departed for Milan to work with Antonio Sangiovanni at the Milan Conservatory. He took her on *gratis,* recommended just "a few weeks' practice in Italian methods," and set her to learning lighter repertoire but with the goal of moving on to weightier roles: her ten operas were *Lucia, Rigoletto, Linda di Chamonix, La traviata, I puritani, Faust, Il trovatore, Les Huguenots, Norma,* and last the more heavily dramatic *Aïda.* Sangiovanni planned that she make her debut in the fall of 1879, and he recommended that she now take the name of "Giglio Nordica." Although Giglio soon disappeared, she remained Nordica for the rest of her life.

On 10 March 1879 "Giglio" made her *prova* (i.e., trial, and therefore unpaid) at the Manzoni Theatre in Milan, singing Elvira in Mozart's *Don Giovanni.* The papers praised her voice, her method, her musical style, and her stage presence. The call came, from Brescia, and on 26 April 1879 she sang her first paid performance in Italy, probably her first paid performance in an opera, as Violetta in Verdi's *Traviata.* She had to repeat the great aria "Ah fors'è lui" at the end of Act I; pandemonium ensued, plus nine curtain calls. Lillian Norton, a.k.a. Giglio Nordica, was on her way. Lillian wrote to her father in May 1879:

I have had a grand success and no mistake. Such yelling and shouting you never heard. The theatre is packed. I put right into the acting, and you would not know me. It makes me laugh to see men and women cry and wipe their noses in the last act [of *Traviata*].[26]

The summer of 1879 marked the beginning of her real Italian career and of lively participation in European social life. Her French and Italian were now both excellent; during 1879–1880 she sang secondary and leading roles in Genoa, Nice, Monaco, Aquila, and continued to work with Sangiovanni. Mother Amanda wrote home in January 1880:

I wish you could all have the privilege of seeing and hearing La Nordica once, not that she is the greatest—or yet a finished artist, but because she is destined to rank with the greatest . . . It takes the most extraordinary exertion, energy, self-denial, patience, perseverance, courage, and a certain intellectual acumen and will, that brooks no obstacles—and tears, and finally as the Italians say, a certain musical discretion, and disposition inborn, which comes from no known teaching. [27]

In September 1880 after an appearance in Venice Norton/Nordica travelled to Russia and the St. Petersburg opera, where she was contracted to sing two or three nights each week. Costumes were provided by the house; the company included Sofia Scalchi, Marcella Sembrich, and the baritone Antonio Cotogni. Her first appearance was as Filina in *Mignon,* in which she was received with great success; her second role was Marguerite de Valois in *Les Huguenots* which was equally successful. Amanda described the scene:

[The] whole theatre is lighted with *electric lights* and the instrumentation of the *imperial orchestra* is grand beyond imagination and poor little *Lilly Norton* rides onto the scene with as much dignity and coolness as ever did the original—and the papers said she sang as probably *no* Queen could sing.[28]

But the success of this first season was saddened by the death on 24 December 1880 of Edwin Norton in Boston; Amanda read the news during Lillian's performance and waited to tell her until the opera had ended.

Although this was a time of some unrest in Russia (Alexander II was assassinated on 13 March 1881, at the end of Nordica's first season), opera flourished, and Nordica was engaged for a second season, 1881–1882. During the summer of 1881 she appeared in Königsberg and Milan and then went on to Paris where she worked with Jean-Baptiste Sbriglia. She probably also established some good contacts in Paris, for the following year she turned down the offer of a third season in St. Petersburg to accept a contract with the Paris Opéra. Her debut (22 July 1882) as Marguerite in *Faust* was received not effusively but well—applause "saluted and accompanied the new American debutante throughout the evening"[29] wrote M. H.

Moreno. Ironically, her most severe criticism came from her fellow Americans: an attack in August in the Boston papers (*Herald* and *Music and Drama*) plus subsequent attacks and ill-advised defenses provoked Amanda finally to write a sharp rebuttal which was published 21 October 1882 in the *Boston Home Journal*. She reviewed her daughter's achievements and abilities and asserted that the American reporters were sour because they had not been bought off; the attacks ceased.[30]

Thus, we see Lillian Norton, Giglio Nordica, now firmly Lillian Nordica at the age of twenty-four, established in Paris with a three-year contract with the Opéra reported to pay $12,000 per year which included a clause requiring a $10,000 forfeit if she left before the end of the contracted period. And now she made the first serious error in her career (she would make two more similar errors): she fell in love with and married her cousin Frederick Allen Gower. Attractive, extremely wealthy (at the time of their marriage), Gower swept her off her feet. (He apparently came up with the $10,000 forfeit for the Paris Opéra.) The rather condensed honeymoon with her new husband was followed by an only partially successful American tour with the impresario Colonel James Henry Mapleson and his opera company (titled grandly "Her Majesty's Opera Company") after which Nordica, her husband, and her mother settled unhappily in London. Now it became clear that Gower expected Nordica to give up her career and be a stay-at-home wife, since in his view she no longer needed to support her family. Horror stories soon circulated about Gower's refusal to permit his wife to sing even at home, his willful destruction of her scores—scores she had studied with their creators, Gounod, Ambroise Thomas, even perhaps Verdi. The bubble burst completely in August 1884 and Mrs. Gower returned to a life shared with mother and occasional sister. On 18 July 1885 Fred Gower obligingly went on a balloon ride by himself and disappeared somewhere over the English Channel. His balloon showed up in late afternoon without him; he was never found, and the mystery was never explained. His disappearance, however, led to the discovery that in real life his financial situation was not at all good; it was in fact close to disastrous. Lillian who surely had every right to financial security after the miseries of her short-lived marriage, found that Gower's millions had vanished.[31] The love for which she had given up her European and American careers had been very costly. Time to go back to work.

She began in January 1886 with Colonel Mapleson and the return of "Her Majesty's Opera Company" to the United States. After a fairly successful and very exciting, sometimes calamitous, tour, the Company, which included the redoubtable American soprano Minnie Hauk (with her husband Baron von Wartegg) and an Italian tenor, Luigi Ravelli, sailed with Mapleson for Europe. In March 1887 Nordica appeared for the first time in opera in London: at Covent Garden in *La traviata* with a tenor who seems to have been drafted from the chorus (according to Bernard Shaw who explained that the real Alfredo had refused to sing because Mapleson owed him so much money). Nordica remembered her sinking feeling as she met her Alfredo for *truly* the first time at the ball in Act I: "Of course my ensemble numbers were ruined, but I had a chance in my arias, and how hard I tried in them! The next day I was known in London."[32] The *Musical Times* reported that the performance introduced a "competent soprano . . . qualified by nature for her work, having a good presence, a capital voice, and some measure, but not enough of dramatic feeling." Of her second appearance, as Gilda in *Rigoletto,* the critic noted in the same review that "her 'Caro Nome' took the taste of the house immensely, not without adequate reason."[33]

And now opportunity presented itself and Nordica grasped it firmly. Augustus Harris, an impresario with big ideas, was determined to bring a season of Italian opera to the Drury Lane Theatre which he had leased since 1879. He announced a company that included Jean and Edouard de Reszke and a number of other stars. Lillian secured a meeting with Harris and offered her services. He turned her down; she persisted; the conductor Luigi Mancinelli may have argued her case, because Harris finally agreed to put her on his list and pay her £40 per performance in the very doubtful case that they would need her. The contracted famous soprano showed up with a vibrato as wide as her figure; one rehearsal showed the impossibility of using her, and Miss Nordica was summoned. Her *Traviata* on the second night of the season met resounding applause. (Unlike other Violettas of the time who wore the latest Paris fashions, she appeared in period costume as did the rest of the cast; she may well have been the first to do so.)

Nordica was back on track. She sang Elvira in *Don Giovanni* (with Victor Maurel as Giovanni and Minnie Hauk as Zerlina), Marguerite in *Faust* with the de Reszkes and Maurel, and finally *Aïda.* Harris inquired if she could sing the role. She had never done it but she knew it and sang it at Drury Lane without a rehearsal. Her final triumph that summer came on 6 July 1887 when she sang Valentine with the de Reszke brothers in Meyerbeer's *Les Huguenots*; she had learned the role in one week. The performance was a huge success; Nordica remembered having been so excited that she sang faster and faster, especially in her grand duet with Jean de Reszke. Whenever she was close to Jean he whispered "Pas si vite," and Edouard stood in the wings hissing at her: "Non sì allegro."[34] The critic for the *Sunday Times* Herman Klein wrote years later: "No words of praise are too strong for the acting and singing of Miss Nordica and Mr. Jean de Reszke in the great duet. They rose fully to the occasion and evoked a storm of applause."[35] Nordica had been singing publicly for eleven years. She was now truly on her way after the disastrous interlude of her marriage.

An important aspect of English musical life was—and is—oratorio. Nordica now made her way into this field, with early and great success. She replaced Emma Albani in Sullivan's cantata *The Golden Legend,* to the enthusiastic praise of the *Musical Times*: "Mme. Nordica's embodiment of Elsie is a remarkably artistic creation, carefully considered and extremely sympathetic; no more satisfactory exponent of the part has yet appeared."[36] So sympathetic indeed that the composer, who had spurned her request to meet with him to go through the part, came to her Hampstead home to thank her in person. She sang at a State banquet in Buckingham

Palace and the following day sang "Let the Bright Seraphim" in Westminster Abbey. She was established, thanks to her persistence 'in seeking to sing with Augustus Harris's Drury Lane Theatre and thanks to her willingness and readiness to take on whatever opportunity arose, e.g., the role of Aïda or Valentine. In addition, she never stopped reaching for the next highest level. She told Herman Klein, who had now become a friend, "I feel I must work harder than ever now. I would like to settle in London and go on studying as many new roles as I can master. I know my voice is not yet under entire control. A singer should never be satisfied, but go on working, working all the time."[37] Professor O'Neill had done a thorough job in his training of the young Lillian Norton—not just in supervising the development of a solid vocal technique but in instilling in her the sense of need for growth as a musician.

In the summer of 1888 Nordica sang at Kroll's Theatre in Berlin with great success; the operas included *La traviata, Faust, Rigoletto, Il trovatore, Les Huguenots, Robert le Diable,* and *L'Africana.* At the end of the season she and her mother vacationed in Ems where they met the de Reszke brothers and Herman Klein who had just seen *Die Meistersinger von Nürnberg* in Bayreuth. He came to Ems specifically to persuade the de Reszkes to visit the Wagner shrine. In the event the de Reszkes, Nordica (with her mother), and the tenor Jean Lassalle all went to Bayreuth, saw *Meistersinger* and another opera, and were overwhelmed by the unique structure of the theatre (with orchestra underneath the stage and invisible to singers and audience alike), the quality of the performances, and the music. Nordica seems to have felt immediately a deep affinity for the music of Wagner. In 1889 she sang a new role—Elsa in *Lohengrin*—at Covent Garden; Bernard Shaw was not favorably impressed, "Miss Nordica turned Elsa of Brabant into Elsa of Bond Street by appearing in a corset" (see above, page 190), but it should be remembered that Shaw was an ardent Wagnerite.[38] The role of Elsa— sung in Italian, the usual language for German operas in London—was to take on immense significance for Nordica.

In the spring of 1891 Nordica settled with her mother in London, where that year she took part in the spring concerts of conductor Hans Richter who had close ties to the Bayreuth musical scene. She also met at a charity concert arranged by the Australian soprano Nellie Melba the next unfortunate love of her life, Zoltan Döme. Her life had by now settled into regular appearances singing opera and oratorio in England intermixed with tours of the United States. The American tour of 1889 was typical: under the aegis of Henry E. Abbey and Maurice Grau and featuring Adelina Patti and Emma Albani in addition to Nordica, it included performances in Chicago, Mexico City, San Francisco, Denver, Omaha, Chicago, Boston, and finally New York where the company performed at the Metropolitan Opera House. Curiously, in light of the success of this tour, when in 1891 Abbey and Grau decided to do a season of French and Italian opera at the Metropolitan, Nordica was not invited to join the company. She, however, canny as ever, signed on for a four-month tour of the United States, which included appearances at the

Worcester Music Festival, with the Boston Symphony under Arthur Nikisch, and with the Philharmonic Society in New York under Anton Seidl. Thus she was close at hand when on 18 December Emma Albani was unable to sing the role of Valentine in *Les Huguenots*; Nordica stepped in on two days' notice and saved the night to great applause: her death scene and duo with Jean de Reszke were "sung with warmth and superbly acted" wrote the critic for the *Musical Trade Review.*[39] This, just after Amanda Norton had died in London on 28 November.

The twelve years from 1891 to 1903 were Nordica's prime. Her life had fallen into a regular routine of operas, oratorios, and tours in England and the United States. In Chicago she sang with Theodore Thomas (whose goal in life seems to have been to outplay whatever soloist was working with him), and she met Susan B. Anthony and became enthusiastically caught up in the suffragette movement. In 1893 she became a regular member of the Metropolitan Opera in New York, singing with Emma Calvé, Nellie Melba, Pol Plançon, the de Reszkes, Emma Eames, Jean Lasselle, and the contralto Sofia Scalchi. On 9 March 1894 she sang Elsa (in Italian) with the Metropolitan company in Boston. On the return to New York she sang Aïda (18 April 1894) to rapturous reviews. The critic for the *New York Herald* wrote: "[the] revival of *Aida* plainly proved . . . that as a dramatic singer Mme. Nordica in many roles is altogether without parallel at the present day" and he marvelled at "the woman's marvelous artistic strides"[40] (see above, page 191).

"Artistic strides" well describes Nordica's career. She never stopped working, never stopped growing, never failed to accept any challenge. But the greatest stretch was about to come. Hans Richter had recommended Nordica to Cosima Wagner to create the role of Elsa in the first production at Bayreuth of *Lohengrin.* After some deliberation (and further consultation), Cosima made the leap and invited the young American (she was 36) to take on the role. So on 22 May 1894 Nordica arrived in Bayreuth to begin the most intense labor of her life. She had of course already sung Elsa, but only in Italian. Now she set out, with Frau Wagner, to create the role in its original, pure Wagner, form. The schedule was formidable:

9–11 a.m.	Study text of the opera with Cosima Wagner
11–1 p.m.	Piano rehearsal with Herr Kniese, the répétiteur
1–3	Free time
3–5 or 6 p.m.	Study the role.

Even the Wagners were impressed by Nordica's dedication. Siegfried wrote to his friend, Otto Floersheim of her "indefatigable zeal," her dedication, her tireless work at the "perfection of her role."[41] In July the rehearsals began; there were twenty-six before the first performance.

And Nordica's German Elsa fulfilled every expectation. Floersheim, editor of *The Musical Courier,* wrote "No German Elsa I ever saw could . . . be compared to Nordica as far as the dramatic conception . . . of this most essentially German character is concerned."[42] Cosima sent her an exquisite lace fan with "Elsa" woven into the fabric "as a small token for a grand performance." Nordica herself wrote in a letter to her aunt "Well, when *the* day arrived, the opera fitted like an old glove and I was not at all nervous, but I kept my mind on my business, I can tell you, as it was almost impossible to keep the Italian words from preceding the German which were new in the race—I felt that the eye of the musical world was upon me and that the stars and stripes were in my keeping and must be brought forth in victory."[43]

A tour of Germany followed in which she sang Elsa many times; she was hailed as "the American nightingale." In Leipzig she sang Elsa in German, then followed it with Violetta in Italian. Professor Bernard Vogel wrote of her singing at the Gewandhaus concert in Leipzig: "She has conquered this audience and has most victoriously asserted her position as one of the greatest of living singers."[44]

Nordica was now at the pinnacle of fame: she had conquered the musical worlds of Europe and the United States and even the sacred halls of the Wagner temple at Bayreuth. It is sad to report that, once again, love had reared its treacherous head, and her infatuation with Zoltan Döme had turned into love on her part and a determination to get married on his. She held him off until 1896: when he showed up at the Indianapolis Festival in May of that year she capitulated. This marriage, which endured until 1904, was marked by his infidelities and exploitation of her fame. She had learned from her first experience, so she was at least not financially damaged, but it was nonetheless a painful eight years as she became disillusioned about Döme's musical ability as well as his marital behavior. In spite of discord at home, the years were marked by continued and brilliant successes as well as a number of sensational battles over promised roles, anti-American bias in casting, even suffragism.

In the summer of 1895 she again worked with Cosima Wagner, this time in Lucerne on the role of Isolde primarily, but also on the *Siegfried* Brünnhilde. During that fall she sang Isolde at the Metropolitan Opera (27 November) with Jean de Reszke under the baton of Anton Seidl. Her success was complete. Reviewers spoke of the passion, beauty, feeling, purity of enunciation, "impeccable intonation, and the clarity of phrasing," and called on American singers to note what could be achieved by "high ideals and incessant application"[45] (see above, pages 190–91).

On 15 April 1896, after the bridal scene in *Lohengrin* which was part of the Abbey-Grau Company's two-week season at the Metropolitan opera house, Nordica was presented with a basket of roses, under which was concealed a casket containing a tiara of diamonds. She was now the Wagnerian soprano of her day. Not only had she created the Elsa for Bayreuth, but she had sung Isolde, Elsa, and Venus (*Tannhäuser*) with other companies and she was completing the study of all three Brünnhildes, with plans to sing them in New York during the next (1896–1897) season.

But New York that fall, as one newspaper headline screamed, was doomed to "Opera without Nordica." The *Siegfried* Brünnhilde, Nordica's by all rights, had been given by Maurice Grau to Nellie Melba, supposedly at the suggestion of

Nordica's frequent partner Jean de Reszke; and the *Walküre* production had been cancelled. A war of letters, some private, some public, ensued, with Nordica by no means the loser though she did not sing in New York. Again, always canny when it came to her career, she embarked on a large-scale tour of the United States, returning to New York with a profit estimated at $46,000, a very tidy sum in those pre-income-tax days. The *Herald* described her as the "brainiest prima donna America ever produced."[46] On 26 December 1896, Nellie Melba appeared at the Metropolitan Opera with Jean de Reszke in *Siegfried*; it was a disaster. Melba's voice was totally unsuited to Wagner, and the critics stated this quite plainly. She herself said "I have been a fool. I will never do it again,"[47] and in January she sailed for Paris (home of her teacher Madame Marchesi) presumably to work off the damage done to her Wagner-strained vocal cords.

Nordica did sing her Brünnhildes: in January 1898 she sang the *Götterdämmerung* Brünnhilde in Philadelphia (with the Walter Damrosch company); in February 1898 she sang the *Walküre* Brünnhilde at the Met in New York; and in the spring at Covent Garden, after a peaceful reunion with Jean de Reszke in *Tristan und Isolde*, she sang the entire Ring Cycle with de Reszke. Sadly, success in her professional life was not echoed in her personal life; Döme's womanizing, coupled with what Nordica now recognized as musical failings, were creating problems as early as 1899, though they were not divorced until 1904 (due to his resistance, claiming illness, etc.). A loss occurred in her professional life when the warm relationship with Bayreuth ended: in the summer of 1901 Nordica opened the Prinzregenten Theater in Munich with *Tristan*; Cosima Wagner did not permit such competition, and Nordica was placed permanently on the Wagners' black list. When Nordica visited Bayreuth in 1904 to see *Parsifal* she was pointedly excluded from Mme Wagner's reception for "visiting artists"; Nordica left Bayreuth never to return.

Nordica's last decade, 1903–1913, was marked by physical failing: in 1897 she had suffered a coach accident followed by very serious pneumonia which may well have damaged her health. She suffered periodically from neuritis and from bronchitis (she smoked on occasion!), but she persisted stubbornly in carrying out extended concert tours and in performing long operas which must have been heroic feats of endurance. In December 1905 she was singing Brünnhilde in a Metropolitan Opera production of *Götterdämmerung,* when during the Immolation Scene oil from a torch spilled on the stage floor and burst into flame. Nordica, facing the pyre, had her back to the blaze, but glancing over her shoulder saw it and as everyone else on stage stood transfixed she turned, and with her own torch in her right hand, gathered her gown in her left, and stamped out the fire, without, as the cellist Jean Gérardy remarked afterwards, missing a single note.[48] She sang twenty performances that season at the Met and then did her customary cross-country tour. She had now conceived the idea of creating at her home, Villa Amanda in Ardsley-on-Hudson, an American Bayreuth, which would include a training center for singers, performance and rehearsal halls, and a theatre for production of plays, especially Shakespeare. The executive board would consist only of women (Nordica had become an ardent suffragette), but the advisory board would include men.

On tour with the San Carlo Opera Company in 1907 and 1908, she was greeted enthusiastically wherever she went, and it is clear from the reviews that the voice was still gloriously there. Thomas Nunan reported in the San Francisco *Examiner* on Nordica's singing in *Les Huguenots*: "Her high notes with the Nordica volume and the Nordica sureness were marvelous voice productions, as clear, as fresh and as youthful in tone as any I have ever heard. Nordica of yesterday afternoon [31 March 1908] was better than even the Nordica we had heard in previous years."[49] Another critic wrote after hearing her sing *La traviata* that same season: "After all these stressful and triumphant years she can return easily to the realm of the coloratura and show that brilliancy and vocal flexibility are still a prize in the esteem of the people."[50] Professor O'Neill's foundation was holding strong.

In the spring of 1908 she sang at Symphony Hall in Boston and was fêted at a reception at the New England Conservatory; a few days later (23 March 1908) the audience in New York's Carnegie Hall rose spontaneously at her entrance. In July of that same year she made her third and final mistake in the marital arena and married George Washington Young.

Although Nordica sang Isolde at the Metropolitan Opera under Arturo Toscanini in 1909 to an ovation unmatched since the final appearance of Marcella Sembrich, she was literally forced out of the Met by the manager Giulio Gatti-Casazza; and that Isolde proved to be her final performance at the Met. One of her last great performances was in that same role of Isolde, which she had sung first in Italian and then triumphantly in German; now she determined to sing once more in Paris and to sing that very role in French. On the advice of Jean de Reszke, restored to the status of trusted friend, she sought out an elderly French schoolmaster in the remote village of Brides-les-Bains and spent a number of weeks there working with him on the role, never letting him know who she was or what her motivation was. At one point he marveled at her voice and asked if she had ever sung in public; for him she sang at a mass in the village church. Her labors, as usual, paid off. On 19 October 1910, she sang Yseult at the Paris Opéra, and the Paris critics marveled: at the "dramatic power of her interpretation" and "her classic and noble style"; "She spoke the recitatives without artifice, but with a force, an intensity and a penetrating sentiment which were moving to a supreme degree"[51] Her final victory: she had indeed conquered Paris. She sent the schoolmaster the *Figaro* review and her portrait as Isolde with a letter explaining the need for her *incognita* and asking forgiveness for the deception.

During the winter of 1910 she sang *Faust* again in Boston, and this time her most severe critic Philip Hale bowed in recognition of a stunning interpretation:

Even the well seasoned opera goer must yesterday have experienced a new sensation. He saw an original interpretation of Marguerite . . . an impersonation that was spontaneous in the eye of the beholder, and not thoughtlessly, recklessly spontaneous, as though the actress, relying on her personality, was experimenting . . . The Marguerite of Madame Nordica was a woman who dreamed and loved and paid the cost . . . This Marguerite was the conception of Madame Nordica . . . her reverie while she sang of Thule's King, singing with thoughts on her own knight, will long haunt the memory by reason of the exquisite simplicity of true emotion.

Madame Nordica took the Jewel Song at an unusually slow pace . . . There was always the expression of wonder, "Who am I, that I should have these jewels?"

Her singing in the duet with Faust was the quiet ecstasy of love . . . And in the Church Scene there was agony without convulsions, the despair that by its numbed intensity is the more terrible.

There were many other features in this memorable performance, triumphs of dramatic instinct and dramatic intelligence, moments of vocally emotional beauty, phrases charged with longing, supreme happiness, terror, wild regret. There were moments when Madame Nordica showed herself a rounded artist by what she did not do and did not attempt.[52]

Nordica seldom relaxed. She stirred up a great furor in the United States by her outspoken remarks about American singers, American opera, opera in English. Extremely articulate, she never hesitated to make her feelings known. The planned American Bayreuth had been moved to her new home, with G. W. Young, in Deal Beach, New Jersey. The French Yseult was followed by a German Isolde at the Royal Opera in Berlin (May 1911; she was now 54). That same year she presided with President William Howard Taft over the groundbreaking for the Panama-Pacific Exposition in San Francisco. Young was by now showing signs of financial troubles; in spite of this and other marital problems and in spite of bouts with neuritis and rheumatism, Nordica continued her tours and benefits. Her last season at London's Covent Garden had been 1902; in 1912 she returned to sing twelve performances there, appeared also at the Crystal Palace, and sang for King Edward and Queen Alexandra On 5 July 1912, she sang for the last time in England, in a performance of Schubert's *An die Musik*. In early 1913, she made a strenuous tour of the American West Coast, then sang Isolde in Boston (26 March; her last appearance there), a concert on 23 April in New York's Carnegie Hall, and set out once again toward the West Coast. She sang with the Cavallo Symphony Orchestra in Lakeside, Colorado, on 6 June, and on 12 June sang for the last time in America at Reno, Nevada.

On 17 June 1913 she sailed, with "Mme. Nordica's Co." consisting of her pianist Romayne Simmons, a tenor Paul Dufault, a young violinist Franklin Holding, her companion Ada Baldwin, and a maid, for Honolulu. Two highly successful performances at the Opera House and a visit to former Queen Liliukalani, were followed by embarkation for Australia, where the party arrived on July 21st, in the middle of winter.

In spite of the vicissitudes of the journey, of the weather, of a smallpox scare in Sydney that caused the entire party to be vaccinated, Nordica was in good voice as the critic for the Sydney *Sun* reported:

The voice still remains fresh and vibrant, powerful, and of wide compass. One of the most remarkable things about the technique of the singer is her marvelous breath control and power of sostenuto which enables her to take double phrases without apparent effort. Then she has a glorious shake, the most perfect in its closeness and purity of intonation that has ever come under the notice of the writer. [53]

Five concerts in Sydney were followed by a visit to Melbourne, then four more Sydney concerts, all immensely successful. Nordica at the same time dealt with the end of her marriage: she recognized the impossibility of restoring "the sacred confidence and trust I reposed in him . . . I have been duped, betrayed, deceived and abused," and she admitted ruefully "I'm just a poor picker of husbands."[54]

The tour plan was to go to New Zealand, then to Java, Calcutta, Rangoon, Singapore, and Hong Kong, work in perhaps a tour of Persia, then continue to Odessa, Moscow, and St. Petersburg, ending even in Paris and London. But this was not to be.

Dufault defaulted; he left the company on its return to Melbourne. On 25 November 1913 Nordica, with Simmons and Holding and a local tenor Walter Kirby, presented a concert at the Melbourne Auditorium, in which they performed the Miserere scene from *Trovatore*, Brünnhilde's battle-cry, and "Ritorna vincitor" from *Aïda*. The critics loved it. As an encore Nordica sang "The Last Rose of Summer." Two days later she collapsed in what the papers called a "complete nervous breakdown" or a "severe indisposition."[55] But at the end of three weeks she was enough recovered to travel, and the company sailed from Sydney on 17 December on the Royal Dutch Mail Ship *Tasman*. By this point, Nordica had to be carried on board; her health was apparently still quite precarious. The ship would traverse one of the world's most dangerous passages, the Torres Strait; even though the sea was calm, the ship ran into a coral reef and suffered severe damage. Finally pulled off the reef two days later, the damaged ship then encountered stormy seas. By the time they reached Thursday Island, Nordica was dangerously ill with pneumonia and had to be carried from the ship. She remained on Thursday Island for three months, suffering from bronchial pneumonia exacerbated by the exposure on board the *Tasman* and nervous exhaustion. In spite of ghastly surroundings— heat, noise of complaining frogs, mosquitos—Nordica slowly improved, surely due in part to the faithful attendance of her pianist and her violinist. On 28 March she sailed with her "company," for Batavia in Java, a thirteen-day journey. In greater comfort at the Hotel des Indes in Batavia she continued to improve and began again to make plans for a sixty-concert tour in America. But then, her heart failed. At around 5:00 a.m. on 10 May 1914, Lilllian Nordica died.

* * * * *

Nordica's greatest significance may well lie in her career as a model for young singers. She herself said, rather over-modestly, that her talent was not great, but that she had always worked very hard and thus in the end achieved as much or more than others. Her life was indeed marked by hard work, from the very earliest days studying with the demanding John O'Neill at the New England Conservatory to the end, when on her deathbed in Batavia, she was nevertheless planning a sixty-concert tour of America. She never flinched at taking on a formidable task; she was always ready to face a challenge, whether it was creating the first Elsa for Bayreuth under the ruthless supervision of Cosima Wagner, learning the role of Valentine (*Les Huguenots*) in a week, or singing her own role of Aïda and that of the First Priestess at the Metropolitan Opera performance on 4 March 1899 when Mathilde Bauermeister, the Priestess, was suddenly indisposed.

Her life serves, too, as a new model in that she was educated musically almost exclusively in the United States, having entered the New England Conservatory in its second year. Professor O'Neill insured that she had a solid foundation of technique, refused to let her sing music unsuitable for her stage of development, trained her carefully in the *bel canto* literature, and saw to it that the quality of her voice was even over a very wide range. When, at the age of twenty-one she worked with Antonio Sangiovanni of the Milan Conservatory, he pronounced her ready technically to launch her career in opera. Indeed after six months of work with him, she made her Italian debut as Violetta and was in her words "a grand success." A grand testimony to the work of Professor O'Neill. This foundation stood her in good stead throughout her life; even in her last years, in her fifties, suffering from neuritis and bronchitis, she was able to draw on that formidable technique and remind her audiences of the grandeur of her voice.

The gamut of her roles is astounding—Donna Elvira, Marguerite, Violetta, Lucia, Valentine, Desdemona, Elsa (in Italian, 1889; in German at Bayreuth, 1894; in French at the Paris Opéra,1898), Isolde (also in Italian, German, and in French at the Paris Opéra in 1910), all three Brünnhildes, Gioconda, Donna Anna, Aïda— and documents eloquently the solid training she enjoyed as a young singer and her own intelligent management of roles and voice.

She was very successful as an American in Europe, beginning with her first seasons in St. Petersburg and the Paris Opéra, although the progress of her career was interrupted by her first disastrous marriage. She managed her return to the stage cannily, asserting her ability to perform at the Drury Lane Theatre and then being ready to make the leap when opportunity came and the soprano under contract turned out to be unsuitable. Nordica came to the rescue of many impresarios, substituting for ailing divas on notice as short as two days. She toured America extensively throughout her career, certainly making a good deal of money by doing so but also bringing music to all parts of the United States. She sang in snowstorms, she sang by the light of a single kerosene lamp, she sang at great festivals, and she was welcomed wherever she went. Appropriately enough, the last appearance in America of this great American singer was in Reno, Nevada, in June 1913. She managed her career herself and did so very intelligently; the *New York Herald*'s assessment of her as the "brainiest prima donna America ever produced" was right on the mark. The ultimate recognition in Europe of her ability and artistry was her selection by Cosima Wagner to create the role of Elsa at Bayreuth; she was the first American singer to be so honored.

Nordica was consistently supportive of other singers, generous with her praise and never displaying jealousy or demanding to be treated as the star. This singer was seemingly indefatigable; her energy was legendary, and combined with her discipline and intelligence made her a formidable artist. Throughout her life, too, she spoke out against injustice whether it was her own personal injury (as when Melba was given the role of Brünnhilde in 1896) or the cause of suffragism or more generally the shabby treatment accorded American singers in their own country. The *New York Sun* sent a reporter to interview Ms. Nordica shortly after she had been forced out of the Metropolitan Opera by Gatti-Casazza and just six days after Arturo Toscanini conducted the world première (10 December 1910) of Puccini's *La fanciulla del West* (Girl of the Golden West). Nordica was eloquent and managed to cover a number of fronts in the interview:

I feel that whatever Mr. Gatti-Casazza has done to me is slight in comparison with the insult put on the American artists of the company when Signor Puccini's *Girl of the Golden West* was produced here. American singers should have been allowed to have some share in the performance. No other opera house in the world would have allowed singers of its own nationality to be ignored on such an occasion. They have proved good enough for the other operas of Puccini. Miss Farrar has made a triumphant success in *Madama Butterfly* and *La Boheme* and Riccardo Martin has sung with her frequently in that opera. Mme. Eames sang in *Tosca* frequently. The Americans seem to have been good enough for everything excepting the one American opera that Puccini has written. Don't tell me that Geraldine Farrar and Riccardo Martin would not have been splendid in the work . . . I have been in the West myself and know what the life of the miners there is. That is the reason I know how good the Americans would have been in the opera and how untrue to the spirit of this country the music is.

There has been no detail of the surrender of the Metropolitan Opera House to the Italians so disheartening to an American and discreditable to the powers that are in control there as the insult put on the American singers in the company by refusing to allow them any share in the first opera ever written that pretended to be based on modern American life.[56]

She did little or no teaching, although this might have changed had she lived long enough to realize something of her "American Bayreuth" dream. She would certainly have been a very demanding teacher, in the tradition of Professor O'Neill but complemented by her own self-discipline and demands of herself. In 1906 she dictated to a young friend, H. Ernestine Ripley, a short article "How to Sing a Ballad," which was eventually published in the *Musical Digest* (March 1931) and is reprinted in the biography by Ira Glacken.[57] Earlier, in the summer of 1901, during a vacation in the Black Forest of Germany she created with her friend William Armstrong acting as secretary a little booklet, *Lillian Nordica's Hints to Singers,*

Transcribed by William Armstrong.[58] The concluding line of their creation sums her philosophy and her career:

Great discipline, from early years, is required of all who would become professional singers, but it is the loveliest life in the world.[59]

*   *   *   *   *

In 1927 some Farmington citizens formed the Nordica Memorial Association, with Ernestine Schumann-Heink an old colleague of Nordica's as honorary president. Nordica's birthplace was bought, renovated, and turned into a museum, The Nordica Homestead Museum. Here are collected miscellaneous materials having to do with her life and career; the Association has worked over the years to keep the memory of Nordica alive.[60]

In 1943, on 17 March at Portland, Maine, the USS *Lillian Nordica* was launched—the first Liberty Ship named after a musician. Margaret Chase Smith was "matron of honor," and Doris Doree of the Metropolitan Opera Association sang some Nordica favorites including "Let the Bright Seraphim." The ship came through World War II unscathed although on several occasions all the ships around her were bombed or torpedoed; her fortunate crew called her "the Lucky Lillian." Said her captain, Robert Bloxom, USMM, at the end of the war: "She has well served the country that built her, and honored the great lady whose name she bears."[61] A fitting epitaph for the hard-working American singer, who summed up her career often: "Plenty have voices equal to mine, plenty have talents equal to mine; but I have worked."[62] She once told her friend William Armstrong that at her funeral she wanted

a baritone to sing Wotan's Farewell and an orchestra to play the funeral march from *Götterdämmerung.* "For me that music has such dear memories. And then I want some great speaker to say," she hesitated, reflected, "to say . . . 'She did her damnedest.'"[63]

Timeline

1857, 12 Dec	Lillian Norton, born Farmington, Maine, 6th daughter Amanda Allen and Edwin Norton
1864	Moved to Boston; older sister Wilhelmina Kossuth Norton soprano studied with John O'Neill, New England Conservatory (NEC), founded 1867
1868	Parepa-Rosa Grand Opera Company, *Il Trovatore*, Boston Theatre; Lillian's first opera. Music class with Luther Mason
1869, 24 Nov	Sister,Wilhelmina, beginning career as singer, died typhoid fever
1871	Amanda <u>heard</u> Lillian sing, took her to Prof. O'Neill
1871–1875	Work with O'Neill at NEC
1874, 22 Oct	First professional engagement: sang Grande Valse by Venzano between performances by Warren Dramatic Association
1876, Apr	Sang for Therese Tietjens: Mad Scene (*Lucia*), met with her, Teresa Carreño (then a singer!), Mme Bertucca Maretzek (wife of impresario Max Maretzek) harpist in Tietjens's entourage.
1876, 24 Jun	Graduated NEC
27 Jun	Exhibition performance NEC, sang "Let the bright Seraphim" first time in public. With mother to New York and professional life; coached with Mme Maretzek; auditioned successfully for P. S. Gilmore of "Gilmore's Band"
3 Dec	Last New York concert with Gilmore, western tour with band (Prof. O'Neill disgusted)
1877	Handel and Haydn Society (Boston); short tour with Theodore Thomas's orchestra, $50/concert
1877, Nov	Gilmore's band, New York Academy of Music; second tour with Gilmore, in east
1878	Concerts around United States: Springfield, New York, St. Louis, Cleveland; reunion concert at NEC on 6 Apr: Norton and Amy Fay featured
1878, 4 May	Europe with Gilmore's brass band (and mother Amanda), triumph for Gilmore and Norton: Liverpool, Dublin, London's Crystal Palace, Manchester, Amsterdam, Rotterdam, The Hague, Brussels, Antwerp, Paris
1878, mid-Jul	End of Norton's singing with Gilmore; began preparations for operatic career: dramatic, vocal coaching and French lessons in Paris; then to Milan Conservatory to work with Antonio Sangiovanni, name change to "Giglio Nordica"
1879, 10 Mar	Manzoni theatre, Milan: *prova* as Elvira in *Don Giovanni*
1879, 26 Apr	First paid performance Italy: Violetta, Teatro Guillaume, Brescia; repeated "Ah, fors'è lui," 9 curtain calls, total success
1879, summer	Began real Italian career and European social life; sang Genoa,

	Nice, Monaco, Aguila; continued work with Sangiovanni
1880, Sep	St. Petersburg opera, 5 months, with Scalchi, Sembrich, Cotogni
1880, 24 Dec	Edwin Norton died, Boston
1881	Re-engaged for next season in St. Petersburg
13 Mar	Alexander II assassinated
	Königsberg, Milan, Paris; St. Petersburg for winter season.
1882	Turned down third season St. Petersburg for contract with Paris Opéra, sang for Verdi; Paris debut as Marguerite (*Faust*); success, Paris critics friendly; attacks in American newspapers
1883	Last performance Paris Opéra as Ophélie,broke contract to marry Frederick Gower, 22 Jan 1883
Sep	United States, Farmington, Boston, unfavorable reception, New York, with Mapleson, not well-received
1884, Jan	With Mapleson tour to Chicago, great notices; London with husband and mother; marriage going sour
1884, Aug	Left Gower
1885, Jul	Gower disappeared in balloon
1886, Jan	Boston with Col. Mapleson and "Her Majesty's Opera Company" (Minnie Hauk, Marie Engle, Felia Litvinoff Ravelli, conductor Arditi); no success New York (Academy of Music); tour: Boston *Rigoletto, Don Giovanni* (Elvira), *Traviata* full houses, Philadelphia, Baltimore, Washington, Pittsburgh, Chicago, St. Louis, Kansas City, Denver, Cheyenne, Salt Lake City, San Francisco
1892, winter	United States, concerts in Chicago; met Susan B. Anthony, also William Armstrong, critic from *Chicago Tribune,* who became close friend
1893, Nov	New York Metropolitan Opera reopened (after dark year), Nordica now regular member of company; sang with New York Philharmonic under Anton Seidl, conductor
1894	Bayreuth: Nordica created first Elsa; deeply involved with Zoltan Döme; German tour, many Elsas; "the American nightingale"
1894	New York,Met, Donna Anna (Mozart's *Don Giovanni*), Maurel as Don Giovanni
1895, summer	Lucerne worked on Isolde, *Siegfried,* Brünnhilde with Cosima Wagner
1895, 27 Nov	Sang Isolde with Reszke, under Anton Seidl; busy with three Brünnhildes (*Siegfried, Walküre, Götterdämmerung*)
1895–1896	Peak year: Isolde, Elsa, Venus
1896, 15 Apr	Presentation at Met after Bridal Scene in *Lohengrin,* of crown of diamonds. 233 diamonds, 1/8 to 1.5 carets, set in platinum
May	Married Zoltan Döme
10 Nov	New York headline: Opera without Nordica! Melba to sing

	Siegfried Brünnhilde, *Walküre* cancelled; battle in papers; Nordica on cross-country tour to San Francisco, profit of $46,000; *New York Herald*: "The brainiest prima donna America ever produced"
26 Dec	Melba sang Brünnhilde: disaster; Melba retreated to Paris
1897	Paris Opéra, *Lohengrin* in French; not particularly successful; peace with de Reszke, coach accident, serious illness (pneumonia)
1898, 11 Jan	Sang her first *Götterdämmerung* Brünnhilde, Philadelphia
4 Feb	*Walküre* Brünnhilde, first anywhere, with Walter Damrosch's opera company headed by Lilli Lehmann (old enemy from Bayreuth) at New York Metropolitan
1898, spring	Covent Garden *Tristan,* Nordica and de Reszke, Ring cycle, with Jean and Edouard de Reszke, Schumann-Heink
fall	Chicago: *Walküre,* New York, Venus (*Tannhäuser*), Leonora (*Trovatore*), and Isolde with Jean de Reszke (*Tristan*)
1899	Problems with Döme, newspaper stories, etc.
1901, summer	Munich: opened Prinzregenten Theater with *Tristan,* to fury of Cosima Wagner (end of relations); anonymous letters telling her to go home, but success with audience; with Armstrong to Bad Boll in Schwarzwald, dictated *Hints to Singers*
1901 fall, winter	Long tour, traveled in private railroad car "The Brünnhilde"
1902 summer	Last season at Covent Garden, 12 performances in heroic roles, sang at Crystal Palace, chorus of 3,000, orchestra of 500; sang privately for King Edward and Queen Alexandra; on verge of collapse—marital problems?
1903 June	"Venice in New York," an entertainment, for J. S. Duss, bandleader, in Madison Square Garden, with Edouard de Reszke; spectacle, soft drinks, main attractions were Nordica and Reszke! Big bucks; Nordica entered in gondola, sang "Inflammatus" and "Star Spangled Banner" dressed in gorgous gowns from Worth of Paris; Munich, Prinzregenten Theater, 2 *Tristans,* one Ring Cycle, all three Brünnhildes on 26, 27, and 28 Aug
1904, spring	Nordica singing with Damrosch and New York Symphony Orchestra; dreadful bronchitis, vocal problems; divorced Döme
1904, summer	Bayreuth to see *Parsifal,* which she would sing at Met in fall; snubbed by Cosima, left after last *Parsifal,* never returned
1905, 29 Dec	New York Met: *Götterdämmerung,* on-stage fire stamped out by singing Nordica
1906, Apr	Cross-country tour; plan for American Bayreuth, at Harmon, (New York), Institution of Music, Festival House, open-air theatre, Shakespeare, oratorios, symphonies; management by board of women directors, with "advisory" board of men

1907	Oscar Hammerstein and Manhattan Opera House
1908, Jan	San Carlo Opera Company of New Orleans: *La Gioconda, Huguenots*; tours with SCOC to Los Angeles, Baltimore, Washington, Chicago
spring	New England tour with Walter Damrosch; important concert at Symphony Hall, Boston, reception at New England Conservatory
23 Mar	Carnegie Hall New York, audience rose as she entered
29 May	London Queen's Hall, concerts, sang with Nikisch
29 Jul	Married mistake no. 3, George Washington Young
1909	Interest in suffragism
8 Nov	Met company, Boston, opened new Boston Opera House in *La Gioconda*
8 Dec	New York, Isolde under Toscanini
1909–1910	20 performances contracted with Met; forced out after 8, by manager Gatti-Casazza
1910, 19 Oct	Nordica's first *Tristan y Yseult* in French, Paris Opéra, (spent 1910 summer coaching with old schoolteacher in tiny village of Brides-les-Bains
1910	Press interview about American singers, American opera, opera in English, stirred up great furor; tours with San Carlo Opera Company, Boston, Canada, Kansas, Oklahoma
1911, 29 May	Isolde at Royal Opera Berlin; American Bayreuth plan transferred to Young's new mansion, "Oakwood Hall" in Deal Beach (New Jersey)
Sep	Short tour, Keokuk (Iowa), Lincoln, Mormon Tabernacle, Salt Lake City, 8000 people including President Taft; Reno, Berkeley (first to sing in Greek Theatre)
	Groundbreaking for Panama-Pacific Expo of 1915; Nordica with Taft in Presidential car; he lifted the golden spade as she sang the Star Spangled Banner
	San Francisco, 2 concerts, spoke (and sang) for woman suffrage; bill passed, women full voters in California
1912, spring	Health problems, neuritis, continued with San Carlo Opera Company, concert tour, suffrage speeches
May	London, sailed on Savoie with Mary Garden, tried in vain to convert her to suffragism
14 Jun	Queen's Hall, Immolation Scene with 12 recalls; orchestra conducted by young Leopold Stokowski
15 Jul	Recital, Schubert *An die Musik*; last performance in England
19 Dec	Chicago, Isolde (Schumann-Heink as Brangäne), suffering from severe rheumatism
1913, 31 Jan	West Coast tour: British Columbia, Portland, Pasadena, Phoenix
26 Mar	Boston, Isolde, final opera performance

20 Apr	Last appearance Boston: Symphony Hall; hard times: neuritis; domestic problems; loss of thousands to Young
23 Apr	Last New York concert, Carnegie Hall, in good voice; good reviews
Jun	Tour of western states
12 Jun	Last concert in America: Reno, Nevada
17 Jun	Sailed with her own company for Honolulu and Australian tour
24 Jul	Sydney, first concert; smallpox scare, all vaccinated; break with Young; tour continued to Melbourne, Sydney, New Zealand, Tasmania, back to Melbourne for second series of concerts
25 Nov	Nordica's last concert, Melbourne Auditorium
end Nov	Nordica ill: "severe indisposition" "complete nervous breakdown"
17 Dec	Sailed for Java; disasters, reef, storms, reached Thursday Island New Year's Day 1914; Nordica now had pneumonia. After three months recovered enough to sail on to Java, end of March; recovered partially, then her heart failed
10 May 1914	Lillian Nordica died, Batavia, c. 5:00 a.m., at 57

Bibliography

Ira Glacken's biography remains the only book about Nordica and her career. A number of other sources such as Herman Klein's *Great Women Singers of My Time,* Bernard Shaw's music criticism, Oscar Thompson's *The American Singer* include discussion of her career. The Nordica Memorial Association supports a museum (Norton's birthplace) in Farmington, Maine.

Works about Nordica

Glacken, Ira. *Yankee Diva: Lillian Nordica and the Golden Days of Opera.* New York: Coleridge Press, 191963.

Full, detailed account of Nordica's life and career. Great source for quotations from reviews, letters, and personal interviews. Chronology is sometimes difficult to follow, but the book is packed with information and primary sources. Glacken is an enthusiastic admirer of Nordica, which shows in his clear partisanship in accounts of her battles, but he is also objective enough to present different sides of various issues, and material is generally well documented. Includes her short article, "How to Sing a Ballad," and the booklet, *Lillian Nordica's Hints to Singers.* Includes a discography with an essay, "Recordings and Lillian Nordica," by William R. Moran.

General Reference Works

Eaton, Quaintance. *Opera Caravan: Adventures of the Metropolitan on Tour (1883–1956).* New York: Farrar, Straus & Cudahy, 1957.

Finck, Henry T. *Success in Music and How It Is Won.* New York: Charles Scribner's Sons, 1909.

Henderson, William James. *The Art of Singing.* New York: The Dial Press, 1938.

Klein, Herman. *Great Women Singers of My Time.* London: G. Routledge & Co., 1931.

Eyewitness reports by an excellent, knowledgeable musical critic.

_____. *Thirty Years of Musical Life in London.* London and New York: The Century Co., 1903.

Kolodin, Irving. *The Metropolitan Opera, 1883–1939.* New York: Oxford University Press, 1940.

Krehbiel, Henry Edward. *Chapters of Opera.* New York: Henry Holt & Co., 1908.

Eyewitness accounts of opera.

Lahee, Henry C. *Famous Singers of Today and Yesterday.* Boston: L. C. Page Co., 1898.

Useful descriptions of the work of a number of singers during the mid to late nineteenth century.

Mapleson, J. H. *The Mapleson Memoirs.* 2 vols. Chicago, San Francisco, and New York: Belford, Clarke & Co., 1888.

Pleasants, Henry. *The Great Singers from the Dawn of Opera to Our Own Time.*

New York: Simon and Schuster: 1966.

Rosenthal, Harold. *Two Centuries of Opera at Covent Garden*. London: G. Putnam, 1958.

Ryan, Thomas. *Recollections of an Old Musician*. New York: E. P. Dutton, 1899.

Shaw, Bernard. *London Music in 1888–89, as Heard by Corno di Bassetto (Later Known as Bernard Shaw)*. New York: Dodd, Mead & Co., 1937.

Ascerbic but honest and very telling accounts of music in London by an early Wagnerite.

_____. *Music in London, 1890–94*. London: Constable and Co., 1932.

Thompson, Oscar. *The American Singer.* New York: the Dial Press, Inc., 1937.

Solid, well-documented information about American singers and their world.

Wagnalls, Mabel. *Stars of the Opera*. New York and London: Funk & Wagnalls, 1907.

Fulsome accounts of Ms. Wagnalls's visits with a number of divas; does, however, quote Nordica directly and gives first-hand description of her visit with the singer.

Chapter 14

Nellie Melba
(19 May 1861 – 23 February 1931)

She was no actress. A friend is reported to have said that when Melba wished to express moderate emotion she raised an arm; for deep emotion she raised both arms. Reviewers agree almost unanimously that dramatic interpretation was not Melba's forte. But they also agree that the voice had an extraordinary power. W. J. Henderson addressed this aspect in the obituary for the *New York Sun* (28 February 1931):

[H]er interpretative power was superficial. She conquered rather by the sensuous spell of the voice, by the brilliancy and fluency of her ornamentation and the symmetrical lines of her delivery than by the awakening of feeling in her hearers.[1]

Max Harris assailed the limits of description when he wrote (in 1983) "a voice so wondrous that she ruled Covent Garden with all the subtlety of a bosomy Adolf Hitler from 1892 to 1926."[2] An extreme comparison, perhaps, but it makes two significant points: (1) the voice was truly astounding, and (2) the personality was as powerful as the voice.

*   *   *   *   *

Descriptions speak again and again of the "silvery" timbre of the voice; "pure," "boy-like," "natural," "ease" similarly occur and recur. Accuracy of intonation was praised by even that dragon of musical criticism, George Bernard Shaw (who worshipped at the shrine of Emma Calvé, Melba's archrival): "You never realize how wide the gap between the ordinary singer who simply avoids the fault of singing obviously out of tune and the singer who sings really and truly in tune, except when Melba is singing."[3] This perfection of intonation never left her, nor did her trill, the Melba hallmark. Henderson called it "ravishing," and recalled how on the evening of her Metropolitan Opera debut, "she sang in the cadenza of the mad scene [from *Lucia*] a prodigiously long crescendo trill which was not merely astonishing, but also beautiful."[4] Anton Seidl, who often conducted her performances, was more specific:

The trill in her case is of quite fabulous sostenuto; for instance, she has at her command a long powerful crescendo on the highest notes that is without parallel, and yet performed with a clearness and certainty which simply excite astonishment and are at the same time soft, clinging and cajoling.[5]

About that trill, Melba said simply: "I was born with a natural trill."[6]

The following description in Henderson's obituary is based on his hearing Melba in New York between 1893 and 1909:

One could have said . . . of Melba's [voice]: "It is the unique voice of the world." This writer never heard any other just like it. Its beauty, its power, its clarion quality differed from the fluty notes of Patti . . . it had splendor. The tones glowed with a starlike brilliance. They flamed with a white flame. And they possessed a remarkable force which the famous singer always used with continence.

The Melba attack was little short of marvelous . . . Melba indeed had no attack; she opened her mouth and a tone was in existence. It began without ictus, when she wished it to, and without betrayal of breathing. It simply was there. When she wished to make a bold attack, as in the trio of the last scene of *Faust,* she made it with the clear silvery stroke of a bell . . . Her staccati were as firm, as well placed, and as musical as if they had been played on a piano. Her cantilena was flawless in smoothness and purity. She phrased with elegance and sound musicianship as well as with consideration for the import of the text. In short, her technic was such as to bring out completely the whole beauty of her voice and to enhance her delivery with all the graces of vocal art.[7]

Writing about Melba's debut at the Paris Opéra (8 May 1889) in Goring Thomas's *Hamlet,* August Vitu wrote for *Le Figaro:*

[A] marvellous soprano voice, equal, pure, brilliant, and mellow, remarkably resonant in the middle register, and rising with a perfect *pastosita* up to the acute regions of that fairylike major third. That which ravished us was not alone the virtuosity, the exceptional quality of that sweetly timbred voice, the exceptional facility of executing at random diatonic and chromatic scales and trills of the nightingale, it was also that profound and touching simplicity and the justness of accent which caused a thrill to pass through the audience with those simple notes of the middle voice, "je suis Ophélie."[8]

What is perhaps most remarkable is that from beginning to end of her long career, she continued to sing with little loss of control, sang her most demanding roles until she was nearly 60, and still retained her vocal powers sufficiently to astound her students, her friends, and even the critics. John Brownlee, an Australian tenor, who made his Covent Garden debut on the occasion of Melba's farewell, 8 June 1926, wrote that everyone from the King and Queen on down came to pay last homage to Melba:

The atmosphere was charged almost beyond endurance. A lot of people . . . were afraid it would be a pathetic spectacle and wished it were over. Some were sorry for the old girl of over 67 [actually 65] and for what they thought would be Melba's ordeal.

It didn't turn out that way. Melba's ordeal became Melba's triumph. She confounded her staunchest admirers. She sang so beautifully that years seemed to recede as in a fairy tale, and there stood again the great prima donna of a quarter of a century ago. The voice had almost a youthful charm and freshness. The heavenly legato was still there, and the wonderful technique. It was a miracle. The people who had come out of a sense of duty were as in a trance. Then they went wild with excitement.[9]

Brownlee's description is confirmed by the portion of this evening which can be heard today on eleven twelve-inch sides recorded by The Gramophone Company.[10]

Melba had made her triumphant debut at the Théâtre de la Monnaie in Brussels almost thirty-nine years earlier. This voice remarkable for not only its sound, its timbre, but also for its impeccable intonation, its virtuosity, and that astounding trill, had been thrilling audiences for nearly four decades. Was this longevity due to the singular physiology of Nellie Melba? Surely, this was a factor. But equally important were the singer's technique and care of her voice throughout her career—technique and care that are attested by the reviews throughout her career. Adverse criticism never referred to technique or musicianship but had to do with what some critics found to be an unmoving quality of her performance. Neville Cardus heard her sing in her late forties; after admiring her perfect intonation, even at that Covent Garden farewell, he noted her "very serious limitation as an artist. Never once did her singing move me in an imaginative way; it was flawless vocalism pure and simple; . . . Whatever she was singing, it was always Melba, the incomparable vocalist."[11]

Melba's choice of repertoire reflects her careful use of the voice. With one disastrous exception, she limited herself strictly to singing only roles that fit the range and quality of her voice. That one exception was the role of Brünnhilde in *Siegfried,* and she knew as she stepped on stage that it was a terrible mistake (the New York critics were in complete agreement). Henderson warned her that it was "like seeing a piece of Dresden china attacked by a bull."[12] Henry Krehbiel found that "the music of the part does not lie well in her voice, and if she continues to sing it, it is much to be feared there will soon be an end to the charm which her voice discloses when employed in its legitimate sphere. The world can ill afford to lose a Melba, even if it should gain a Brünnhilde. But it will not gain a Brünnhilde."[13] Melba called herself a fool, relinquished the role immediately, and departed for

Paris to rest for the remainder of the season (and perhaps to seek the healing help of her former teacher Mathilde Marchesi). She never again made such a mistake.

Contemporary descriptions of Melba's singing repeat over and over the same words—silvery, pure, natural, smoothness, ease, elegance—and marvel at her technical prowess. The same words appear in Melba's lectures and writings about singing and are echoed in reports from her students. She set high value on naturalness, ease, and elegance; but she also stressed the work that lay behind acquisition of these qualities and the importance of understanding the physiological and mental processes involved. It may well be to the discipline of such studies and to her conscientious preservation of excellent health and physical condition that she owed the longevity of her career. For with little loss of control she continued to sing her most demanding roles until she was nearly sixty, and even after that her vocal powers continued to astound all who heard her. We have already noted the description by her tenor partner John Brownlee of her farewell performance at Covent Garden when she was sixty-five. The London *Telegraph* was somewhat more restrained but essentially in agreement:

It were stupid to say that time has not had an effect. It certainly has; but even so, if a little of its old mellowness is gone, no singer . . . is steadier in tone, or hits the notes, as it were, more precisely or accurately. For Dame Melba, the excessive *vibrato* and *tremolo* so commonly found today is not, and never was characteristic. The art is still there as shown in the extraordinarily touching singing of the *Salce!* and the *Ave Maria* from *Otello* . . . a colossal night of music and a glorious exhibition of the noble art of singing as singing should be.[14]

The weakest aspects of Melba's art in the early years (and indeed throughout her career) were undeniably her acting and her stage presence. It is entirely characteristic that she recognized these failings and made up her mind to correct them. She sought out Sarah Bernhardt who enthusiastically responded with suggestions extending from stance and movement to make-up. Following Bernhardt's counsel, Melba found a dancer with whom she studied movement and the art of make-up. Perhaps the most formative schooling for the singer, however, was gained from work with the tenor, Jean de Reszke who, with his baritone brother Edouard, dominated European opera. (The two brothers also sang often with Lillian Nordica; see Chapter 13.) Melba learned from de Reszke how to move on stage and, perhaps more significant, how not to move but to complement with her body language what her voice expressed. She responded to de Reszke's artistry with a new level of artistry in her own performance. This transformation was recognized by the famously hard-to-please Bernard Shaw in his review of an 1892 performance of Hermann Bemberg's *Elaine* in which both Melba and de Reszke sang. Whereas in spite of "the perfection of her merely musical faculty," he had earlier thought her "hard, shallow, self-sufficient, and altogether unsympathetic," he now marvels at the change:

I find Madame Melba transfigured, awakened, no longer to be identified by the old descriptions—in sum, with her heart, which before acted only on her circulation, now acting on her singing and giving it a charm which it never had before. The change has completely altered her position: from being merely a brilliant singer, she has become a dramatic soprano of whom the best class of work may be expected.[15]

Melba never lacked for self-confidence, but she never missed an opportunity to learn. Returning with Mary Garden from a command performance in the provinces, she spent the train ride querying Garden about performing Tosca (Melba never, however, sang the role).[16] She devoted six weeks with Puccini at his home in Lucca to studying the role of Mimi in *La bohème*—an opera that she introduced in London. In addition to Puccini, she worked with Delibes, Gounod, Massenet, Thomas, Verdi; thus she could, and did, claim to sing the music as the composer had indicated to her. Although she seldom won accolades for her acting, she conquered, as Henderson wrote, through her voice. Mary Garden's account of a performance at Covent Garden of *La bohème* tellingly summarizes the Melba experience:

Melba had the most phenomenal effect on me of any singer I ever heard . . . of course Melba didn't look any more like Mimi than Schumann-Heink did. I never saw such a fat Mimi in my life. Melba didn't impersonate the role at all—she never did that—but, my God, how she sang it! . . . the last note of the first act . . . is a high C, and Mimi sings it when she walks out of the door with Rodolfo . . . The way Melba sang that high C was the strangest and weirdest thing I have ever experienced in my life. The note came floating over the auditorium of Covent Garden: it left Melba's throat, it left Melba's body, it left everything, and came over like a star and passed us in our box, and went out into the infinite. I never heard anything like it in my life, not from any other singer, ever . . . My God how beautiful it was! . . . That note of Melba's was just like a ball of light. It wasn't attached to anything at all— it was *out* of everything.[17]

* * * * *

Nellie Melba was born Helen Porter Mitchell, 19 May 1861 in Richmond, Melbourne, in Australia.[18] Her parents, Isabella and David Mitchell, were both musical; amateur music-making formed an integral part of the family's life. As a child, Nellie was constantly humming; after her mother complained, she whistled instead. She recalled crawling under the piano to listen while her mother played and sitting happily on her father's lap as he played the harmonium. In 1875 she began attendance at the Presbyterian Ladies' College in Melbourne where she studied organ in addition to the usual curriculum. Here she came under the tutelage of Ellen Christian, an English contralto who had studied with Manuel Garcia Jr. (brother of sopranos Maria Garcia Malibran and Pauline Garcia Viardot; see Chapter 12). Around 1879 or 1880 she began to study singing in Melbourne with an Italian tenor, Pietro Cecchi. Cecchi, a graduate of the Academy of Music in Rome, had made a career for himself singing opera in Italy before coming to tour Australia in 1871 with the States Company opera troupe. Nellie worked with Cecchi over a period of six or seven years.

In October 1881 Nellie's mother died, followed a few months later by the death of her youngest sister, Vere, aged 4. The following year she accompanied her father on a visit to Queensland. Here she met Charles Armstrong, the youngest son of an Irish baronet, whom she married on 22 December 1882; their son George was born 16 October 1883. Two months later Nellie returned to Melbourne with her son.

The young Mrs. Armstrong now resumed her voice lessons with Cecchi and began performing with some regularity in Melbourne and its environs. In 1886 David Mitchell was appointed commissioner to the Indian and Colonial Exhibition. The entire Mitchell household, including Charles Armstrong, journeyed to London where they arrived in late April and set up house at 89 Sloane Street. Though Nellie profited from hearing the great voices of the day (Patti, Nilsson, Albani, Santley) as well as such instrumentalists as Sarasate, Hallé, and de Pachmann, she was unable to make any headway as a singer. The decision was made to go to Paris, where she hoped to study with Madame Mathilde Marchesi, who, like Ellen Christian, had been a student of Manuel Garcia Jr. Marchesi was now one of the most effective and powerful voice teachers of the time. With the help of a letter of introduction from a former student of Marchesi, Nellie had secured an audition. Taking the now four-year-old George, she set off for Paris and her future.

Marchesi, born Mathilde Graumann in Frankfurt am Main, had enjoyed a substantial career singing in concerts (but only one opera, *Il barbiere di Siviglia*) throughout Europe and England, appearing often with Salvatore Marchesi whom she married in 1852. She had studied with Otto Nicolai in Vienna before working with Garcia in Paris and London, and she had herself held posts as professor of singing at the Vienna Conservatory, in Cologne, then again in Vienna. She was experienced as a performer, as a teacher, and she knew everyone. In 1881 Marchesi and her husband returned to Paris where she established her own school of singing (for whatever reason, the Paris Conservatory would not hire her); her students included Emma Calvé, Emma Eames, Mary Garden, Sybil Sanderson, and in 1886 Helen Armstrong. Now she listened to Armstrong and rushed out of the room to proclaim to her husband: "Salvatore, j'ai enfin une étoile!"

When Nellie Armstrong came to Madame Marchesi she was twenty-five years old. She had, in addition to a remarkable natural ability to sing, the advantage of ten to twelve years of fairly regular study, first with Christian of the same Garcia method as Marchesi, and then with Cecchi of the old Italian school of singing (Cecchi had studied at the Rome Conservatory), so she had a good fundamental vocal technique. Melba remembered later with gratitude that Marchesi was willing to work with the voice as she found it and did not attempt to mould it into anything else. For some reason, Melba disliked acknowledging the value of her studies with Cecchi; Marchesi was the teacher she credited. But, even though throughout her career, she turned to Marchesi for advice and occasional help (surely after the

Brünnhilde disaster!), she actually studied with her little more than one year. This year was devoted to making some corrections—Melba writes[19] that she was, for example, carrying her chest notes too high—and to transforming the young Australian into an opera star, a process that included the study of dress, manners, and society, as well as the learning of operatic roles. Marchesi expertly assessed the capacity of the voice and was able to give her student an almost infallible ability to select roles that would suit her voice. The one mistake ever made by Melba was to sing that Brünnhilde in New York; she did not persist in her folly and was spared the dire consequences of lasting damage to her voice, but she spent most of the spring season that year resting.

At the end of a year with Marchesi, on 13 October 1887, Helen Armstrong, now Nellie Melba,[20] made a triumphant debut as Gilda at the Théâtre de la Monnaie in Brussels. But an engagement at Covent Garden the following May was not particularly successful—half-empty houses, few critics, and those not very responsive; when the impresario Augustus Harris offered Melba the part of the page in *Ballo in maschera,* she tells us her reply was to "pack my trunks and to go straight back to Brussels."[21] A year later (8 May 1889), Melba debuted at the Paris Opera as Ophélie in Thomas's *Hamlet* to ecstatic reviews from the critics who spoke of "supreme virtuosity," "sweetly timbred voice," "trills of the nightingale," "profound and touching simplicity," "justness of accent," and concluded that Madame Melba was "the most delicious Ophélie . . . since the days of Christine Nilsson and Fides Devries."[22] In response to pleas from an ardent English supporter, Lady Gladys de Grey (who became a lifelong friend), Melba returned to Covent Garden in June 1889 . . . and triumphed. This occasion marked the beginning of a reign at Covent Garden that endured for nearly thirty-seven years.

But the next two decades were filled with fresh triumphs as well. In the spring of 1891 she sang at the Imperial Theatre in St. Petersburg with the de Reszke brothers; in the spring of 1892 she sang for the first time in Italy, beginning with *La traviata* in Palermo before moving on to other cities. That same year she sang at Covent Garden Hermann Bemberg's *Elaine* dedicated to her and to Jean de Reszke in July and in the autumn she tried out *Aïda,* which however she soon abandoned as a role not well-suited to her voice or personality (she also detested the necessary make-up). The year 1893 was again momentous: in March she made her La Scala debut in *Lucia di Lammermoor* in the face of threats and anonymous letters warning her of poison in her food, stiletto attacks, etc., and telling her to give up La Scala and leave Milan immediately. Fortunately she persisted (with the firm support she tells us of her secretary Louie Mason) and, as she recalls, was greeted after her first recitative with "an immense 'Brava! Brava!' [that] echoed all over the theatre. The rest of the performance, though I say it myself, was a crescendo of triumph, and I am told that after the Mad Scene the applause went on for ten minutes."[23] In May she sang Covent Garden's first Nedda (*I Pagliacci*; she did not sing the actual premiere which took place in Milan in May 1892), and in the fall she debuted at New York's Metropolitan Opera in *Lucia.* After the Met season she toured across the United States, appearing in Boston, Chicago, Denver, St. Louis, Salt Lake City, Minneapolis, San Francisco. Melba was at the peak of her power and the peak of her success. In 1902 she returned to Australia for the first time since her departure in 1886; this was the first of many returns to present concerts in the major cities and even in 1909 to tour the great Outback.

Melba spent the years of World War I, 1914–1918, working energetically and successfully for the war effort (she is attributed with having raised over £100,000), giving benefit concerts in Australia, New Zealand, Canada, and the United States. At the end of the war she was named Dame Commander of the new Order of the British Empire. That year she returned to sing in Covent Garden and toured the English provinces as well.

Melba had always dreamed of bringing real opera to Australia. Already before the war in 1911, she had brought her own opera company with the tenor John McCormack. In 1924 (she was 63 and still singing) she came with a second company, and she returned in 1928 with a third company. It was with them that she made her farewell to the operatic stage in Sydney. She sang for the last time in Australia that November in Geelong.

Over the next three years Melba visited Europe, especially London and Paris, a number of times. She had experienced health problems at various times since 1921 when she had been forced to enter a nursing home for "something internal,"[24] and she had undergone intestinal surgery in 1923. She kept going, whether it was tours or teaching—she began teaching gratuitously at the Melbourne Conservatorium in 1914 and continued that till the end of her life (she left a legacy of £8,000 to the Conservatorium to fund the Melba Scholarship). In 1929, she was occupied with a proposed Melba Conservatorium in Paris (it was to be funded by private money but never came to fruition). She was returning by ship to Australia in early 1931 when she fell very ill. Taken to St. Vincent's Hospital in Sydney, she died on 23 February.

*   *   *   *   *

The student of Melba has the distinct advantage of finding specific instruction from Melba herself on her method. Throughout her career she spoke and wrote often about the care and training of the voice. Her first writing on the topic, "The Care of the Voice," appeared in 1895 as an interview with Anton Seidl;[25] the last, a sixty-three-page book, *The Melba Method,* appeared in 1926 and includes vocalises for high and low voices. Her method, which she lays out in that first publication, was based on maintenance of good health and intelligent, thoughtful study. It might in fact be defined by the very words critics used to describe her singing: natural (she points out that the singer need not gulp for air but may simply open the mouth and LET the lungs fill), easy and unforced (she speaks of the dangers of tension), consideration of the text (diction is of paramount importance as is understanding of the text). She urges singers to conserve their voice, telling us that she never learns a part by singing it: "you do not catch me simply memorizing on my voice what can be as well done on a mechanical instrument." Rather she sings the music only after it has been firmly established in her mind, and she sings it then *pianissimo* except at rehearsal: *pianissimo* in private, and the *forte* is sure to come all right in public." Melba was convinced that the long-preserved freshness of her voice was due to this combination of conservation of the voice coupled with maintenance of the other muscles of the body. She summarized her philosophy on the physiology of singing: "while I save none of my other muscles, but take much physical exercise, I use my voice for the public only."

She advises singers to "look after the posing of the voice," for if this were not done, the voice could be fatally injured, and recalls that "When I first went to Marchesi . . . I sang as well as I do to-day, but for one break in my voice. Marchesi corrected that at once, and placed the registers properly." She adds a warning about the importance of singing roles that suit the voice and points out that "one's nature may be one of passionate intensity, and one's voice of a quality unfit for the strain of expressing exalted sentiments, intense feeling, and profound emotion." (Ironically this appeared in 1895, just one year before Melba herself made the near-fatal error of attempting the role of Brünnhilde.)

She urges that singers study their anatomy: the functions of the larynx, the pharynx, the tongue, the hard and soft palates should be as familiar as the moving of a finger. She recommends visiting a throat specialist to gain information about the physiology of the throat and mouth. Her detailed instructions and breathing exercises leave no doubt as to her own very detailed knowledge about this area.

Finally, Melba emphasizes the need for good, sound musicianship, which must include the ability to learn music on an instrument and the ability to study it so thoroughly that the performer is in possession not just of the notes but of the significance of the notes and has the ability to make music of those notes. She could and did from time to time accompany herself at the piano in performances. For the lesson scene in *Il barbiere di Siviglia*, for example, there would appear magically a piano on which she played while she sang, which meant of course that she was not dependent on the conductor but could choose anything she wanted as her fancy directed: at a performance in San Francisco she selected the *Star-Spangled Banner*!

Melba was obviously blessed with a sturdy physique, but she understood how to preserve the good health that must have played a vital factor in the longevity of her career and she advises all singers to discover and follow whatever regimens will keep them in top physical shape. She recommends walking outdoors or when that is not feasible using dumb-bells indoors. She urges moderation in all matters of food and drink, eating lightly and drinking less (love affairs are less injurious in her view than overindulgence in alcohol). The 1895 article quotes her as saying: "It is not poetic, but it is plain truth that upon the condition of the stomach depends chiefly the condition of the voice . . . It requires a little self-denial, of course, to abstain from rich dishes and wines; but my fare is invariably of the simplest kind,"[26] by which she meant steaks and chops plus vegetables and fruits.

Throughout her life Melba was the subject of gossip; colorful rumors about her sexual adventures and lavish parties abounded. She did indeed enjoy giving and attending splendid parties, she enjoyed eating well, and at least one celebrated affair (with Louis-Philippe, Duc d'Orléans, nine years her junior) is well documented. This affair was serious enough that her husband attempted to fight a duel with the Duc and when that failed had his attorneys serve divorce papers on Melba and on the Duc as co-respondent.[27] Often circumstances afforded a false impression, and it must be added that especially in Australia people delighted in believing the worst. Tales of excessive drinking in particular dogged her tracks: John Norton, publisher of a newspaper named, ironically enough, *Truth,* persecuted her relentlessly with diatribes about "champagne capers," "outrages against good manners," and "insults to Australian citizens." Shortly after his first attack on Melba, Norton had to be forcibly hospitalized for alcoholism. But his work left a lasting smear, so that even today many Australians think of her as "a real boozer."[28] For the record, her closest acquaintances asserted that though she might indulge in an occasional glass of sherry or a sip of champagne, she believed that alcohol could damage her vocal cords, and thus she avoided excessive use. The amazing preservation of her vocal powers for so long is convincing evidence of her physical well-being—impossible if she had indulged herself in the fashion of which she was so often accused. Moreover, colleagues refer constantly to Melba's meticulous study of music and her extraordinary discipline, which seems to have extended to most areas of her life. She enjoyed life, and her life was indeed very enjoyable. But Melba was a hard-headed business woman and a realist, and she understood quite well the workings of her body and her voice. This statement from her autobiography rings true:

You cannot take liberties with your voice. You must always regard it as your most precious possession, a possession, moreover, of infinite delicacy, which the slightest false treatment may injure.[29]

Until the beginning of the twentieth century, singers' voices outlived them only in the memories of their audiences and in descriptions provided by contemporaries. Melba was among the first to complement these sources with recordings, which were made over a period of two decades, from 1904 to 1926. The remarkable qualities of the voice are apparent in spite of the quality of the recordings and attest to the accuracy of contemporary evidence. Since the recordings span two decades, from 1904 to 1926, they are of particular interest (revealing changes in the voice, as well as in recording techniques).[30] Melba's lectures and writings about singing reveal also much about her own singing, and, together with reports of her teaching at the Conservatorium, form a real contribution to vocal methodology. She represents the continuation of two important traditions—the old Italian school of Pietro Cecchi and the newer but still essentially Italian school of Manuel Garcia through both Christian and Marchesi—but these are complemented by her own analysis of technical training and her modern ideas about physical health. Her stress on musicianship and on mental (as opposed to physical) work in the study of singing represents a healthy departure from the "repetition makes perfect" school of learning.

Melba's emphasis as well on the importance of maintaining good health and a strong physique was a new element in the teaching of singing. Is this perhaps a byproduct of her youth in Australia where such activities as fishing, camping, wandering on foot or horseback were not seen as unusual or unnatural for a girl? The contrast between Nellie Mitchell's life in Australia and Marchesi's tenets is striking: Marchesi for example banned horseback riding because it would damage the vocal cords; she also forbade her singers to wash their hair and was horrified at the idea of a full body bath with the potential dangers of catching cold. Melba's teaching in Australia created a group of healthy young female singers, many of whom carried on her methods in satisfactory if not stellar careers as performers and/or teachers.

For Australia, Melba's triumphs were particularly significant: for the first time a native Australian (though of Scotch descent) was recognized as one of the world's greatest artists. Her successes were enthusiastically reported, frequently with chauvinistic hoopla, in Australian newspapers; when she returned at last to Australia after sixteen years in Europe she was given the equivalent of a ticker-tape parade. W. Arundel Orchard, director of the New South Wales Conservatorium, wrote in 1943: "Melba was more than a great singer, she was an institution and did more to bring Australia before the world in the early days of this century than anybody or anything else . . . her name will live for many a long day."[31] More important, however, than her burnishing of the Australian image in Europe were her contributions to cultural life in Australia—her frequent tours all over the country and her very real dedication to teaching at the Conservatorium. She was by no means the first to bring opera to Australia (her old teacher Pietro Cecchi had been part of a touring company there back in 1871), but the tours she led to almost every corner of this enormous land were enthusiastically welcomed and greatly enriched the cultural life. She often aided aspiring musicians (unless they were coloratura sopranos) by securing engagements for them or with money; for every story of her malice toward rivals, two appear of her generous, often covert assistance to young artists. (But she was careful to distinguish the deserving from the opportunistic suppliants—which fueled the rumors about her malicious behavior to other musicians.) She brought to the international world of opera a welcome freshness, but she also brought to Australia a knowledge of the principles and recognition of the merits of the older European traditions of singing. Thanks to her teaching, she effectively established in Australia a school in which the Italian and the Garcia approaches were preserved in the meld that was her own method.

Melba's career began slowly. Scattered performances in Australia were followed by only a few opportunities to sing in London. She made in fact no headway in London until after she had studied with Madame Marchesi and until after she had made triumphant debuts in both Brussels and Paris. Did Marchesi change Melba's voice? Not much, according to Melba. But Herman Klein heard her in 1886 and describes her voice then as having a "lovely natural quality" but "untrained"; he gives "full credit to Mme. Mathilde Marchesi for the improvement . . . two years later."[32] Was Melba's break-through due to Marchesi's having had the connections essential to producing a star (her étoile) from star material? Was Melba's 1889 triumph at Covent Garden the result of changes in her performance from the year before when she had been received quite coolly? Or was this triumph created by Melba's having secured in 1889 full support of the London social world—thanks to the admiration of Lady de Grey—and of the production forces at Covent Garden where Lady de Grey's husband was a member of the board? Such questions can receive only partial and hypothetical answers. Melba in 1886 was fresh from the provinces and was perhaps somewhat wanting in *savoir faire,* in "finish." Marchesi probably did not do much to the voice beyond correcting a few problems, but she surely was able to advise Melba as to appropriate roles and interpretations. Marchesi could provide the needed "finish" and could see to it that Melba came in contact with the right people. All the elements of success were in place, and Melba was ready.

Timeline

1861, 19 May	Helen Porter Mitchell born Richmond, Melbourne
c. 1880	Lessons with Pietro Cecchi in Melbourne
1881, Oct	Mother, Isabella Dow Mitchell, died
1882, Jan	Vere, youngest sister (4) died
1882	Queensland with father, gave two concerts, met Charles Nesbitt Frederick Armstrong
1882, 22 Dec	Married Armstrong
1883, 16 Oct	Birth of son, George Armstrong
c. 1883	Return to Melbourne, continued voice study, some concerts, minor success
1886	London with father (newly appointed commissioner to Indian and Colonial Exhibition in London), husband, son; few appearances, contacts, no success
1886	Paris to study with Madame Mathilde Marchesi
1887, 13 Oct	Debut, Théâtre de la Monnaie, Brussels, as Gilda
1888, 24 May	London, Covent Garden as Lucia—not a success
1888	Paris Opera, Ophélie (Thomas's *Hamlet*)
1889, 8 May	1890 Paris Opéra, Juliette, Marguerite
1889, 15 Jun	Covent Garden, Juliette with Jean de Reszke and Edouard de Reszke; triumph
1890–1914	Covent Garden (except 1906–1908)
1891, Feb	St. Petersburg, with de Reszkes
1892, spring	Palermo, *La traviata*
5 Jul	Covent Garden, Bemberg's *Elaine,* dedicated to Melba and Jean de Reszke
autumn	*Aïda,* soon dropped from repertoire
1893, Mar	La Scala, debut, *Lucia di Lammermoor*
19 May	First Nedda (*I Pagliacci*) for Covent Garden
fall	Metropolitan Opera, New York, first season (debut in *Lucia*)
1893	After Met season, toured, Boston, Chicago, Denver, Washington, St. Louis, Philadelphia, Salt Lake City, Minneapolis, San Francisco
1896, 30 Dec	Met, Brünnhilde (*Siegfried*), 1 disastrous performance
1902	Australia (September–March 1903), first return; frequent returns after this one
1904–26	Recordings
1906–1908	United States, Australia; no performances at Covent Garden
1907, Jan-Mar	Sang with Oscar Hammerstein's Manhattan Opera, New York City
1908–1909	Season with Hammerstein
1909	Returned to Covent Garden; tour of Australian Outback

1911, Sep	Australia with her own opera company (tenor John McCormack)
1913, 22 May	Celebrated 25 years at Covent Garden, *La bohème,* with McCormack
1914, early	Paris, with Boston Opera Company; tour of United States, Canada; closed opera season at Covent Garden
Aug	World War I; Melba to Australia; war work, Red Cross, relief concerts, tours in Australia, New Zealand, Canada, U.S.; raised more than £100,000 for war effort; began teaching at Melbourne Conservatorium
1918	Dame, Commander of new Order of the British Empire; Covent Garden, toured English provinces; concerts in Australia
1921 on	Occasional health problems
1924	With another opera company to Australia; still singing at 63
1925	Her last English tour; wrote autobiography, *Melodies and Memories*
1926, 8 Jun	Covent Garden farewell
7 Dec	Last performance at Old Vic, London
1928	With her third (and last) opera company to Australia
Aug	Sydney: farewell to operatic singing
Nov	Geelong: last Australian concert; returned to London
1931	Returning by ship from London to Australia
1931, 23 Feb	Died Sydney, St. Vincent's Hospital; buried Lilydale, Australia

Bibliography

Works about Melba

Melba, Nellie. *Melodies and Memories*. 1926. Reprint, Freeport NY: Books for Libraries Press, 1970.
> Written with the anonymous assistance of a young Englishman, Beverley Nichols, these memoirs are delightfully informative but data must be confirmed in other, more objective sources. Nichols later created in his purported fictional novel *Evensong* an unmistakable portrait of Melba that is both disparaging and patronizing.

Colson, Percy Colson. *Melba: An Unconventional Biography*. London: Grayson & Grayson, 1932.
> This is in fact all too conventional in its chatty, gossipy presentation of (undocumented) anecdotal material ("When I had lunch with the diva . . ."). Useful, but data must be confirmed in other sources.

Hetherington, John. *Melba: A Biography*. New York: Farrar, Straus and Giroux, Inc., 1968.
> Hetherington's work remains the best all-around biography, though he does not deal very much with the musical aspects of Melba's career. This and the compilation by William Moran give a relatively full view of the singer's personal and professional lives.

Moran, William R., compiler. *Nellie Melba: A Contemporary Review*. With notes and discography. Westport, CT: Greenwood Press, 1985.
> This is probably the single most useful work on Melba. The compilation includes essays on Melba's life and career; contemporary reviews; memories of her from friends, colleagues, students; a generous sampling of her writings about singing; and an excellent discography. Six articles by Melba that appeared in an Adelaide newspaper, *The Advertiser,* are included making them for the first time easily accessible. Moran provides also a good overview of writing about Melba from early days through 1984.

Murphy, Agnes. *Melba: A Biography*. 1909. Reprint, New York: AMS Press, 1974.
> This biography is in fact (as Moran points out) virtually an autobiography, since Murphy was at the time Melba's secretary and thus was writing what Melba wished to see printed.

Radic, Therese. *Melba: The Voice of Australia*. Melbourne: The Macmillan Company of Australia Pty Ltd, 1986.
> Radic's book provides much information about Australian attitudes toward Melba drawing upon primary sources such as reviews, letters, and newspaper stories, and includes many photographs.

Wechsberg, Joseph Wechsberg. *Red Plush and Black Velvet: The Story of Dame Nellie Melba and Her Times*. Boston: Little, Brown & Co., 1962.
> Wechsberg expounds on the topic of the diva, presents many anecdotes with no documentation, and does not hesitate to reconstruct conversations between Melba

and Marchesi, for example, or add undocumented details to accounts, as: "When Nellie stepped over the threshold she sang 'a trill of welcome'" (page 82). Even worse, the book is replete with errors.

General Reference Works

Finck, Henry T. *Success in Music and How It Is Won.* New York: Charles Scribner's Sons, 1909.

Henderson, William James. *The Art of Singing.* New York: The Dial Press, 1938.

Klein, Herman. *Great Women Singers of My Time.* London: G. Routledge & Co., 1931.

_____. *Thirty Years of Musical Life in London.* London and New York: The Century Co., 1903.

Both of Klein's books provide eyewitness reports by an excellent, knowledgeable musical critic.

Kolodin, Irving. *The Metropolitan Opera, 1883–1939.* New York: Oxford University Press, 1940.

Krehbiel, Henry Edward. *Chapters of Opera.* New York: Henry Holt & Co., 1908. Eyewitness accounts of opera.

Lahee, Henry C. *Famous Singers of Today and Yesterday.* Boston: L. C. Page Co., 1898.

Pleasants, Henry. *The Great Singers from the Dawn of Opera to Our Own Time.* New York: Simon and Schuster: 1966.

Rosenthal, Harold. *Two Centuries of Opera at Covent Garden.* London: G. Putnam, 1958.

Shaw, Bernard. *London Music in 1888–89, as Heard by Corno di Bassetto (Later Known as Bernard Shaw).* New York: Dodd, Mead & Co., 1937.

Ascerbic but honest and very telling accounts of music in London by an early Wagnerite.

_____. *Music in London, 1890–94.* London: Constable and Co., 1932.

Wagnalls, Mabel. *Stars of the Opera.* New York and London: Funk & Wagnalls, 1907.

Chapter 15

Jane Bathori
(14 June 1877 – 21 January 1970)

I was truly attracted to the modern musicians and for me it has always been the greatest joy to learn contemporary works: I feel that they are very close to my taste, to my understanding, and to my possibilities . . . I have always felt that one has not the right to ignore the works of one's time, literary as well as musical.[1]

These words spoken by Jane Bathori in a radio interview in 1953 effectively sum up her life and career. More than any other performer of her time, Bathori was associated with the new music produced all around her and she sought to further its cause in a multitude of ways—as performer, and as performer who was at once vocalist and pianist and often accompanied herself; as director of ensembles and of productions; as manager of a performance venue; as teacher in her early days in Brussels, in her later years in Argentina, and throughout her life in Paris. She found in the music of her contemporaries an art that suited her unique gifts, and her contemporaries found in her an enterprising, innovative partner who thrust their music into the public sphere.

*   *   *   *   *

Bathori's voice as described by Marc Pincherle, music critic and musicologist, was "a voice that opened to her any repertoire: a voice of average volume, but admirably sonorous, supple, and miraculously in tune."[2] In 1904 the critic Jean Marnold described her work for a review in *Le Mercure de France*: "Mme Bathori 'of the Monnaie' [an important opera theatre in Brussels] revealed an exceptionally gifted artistic talent. She sings the music of Debussy with much charm and a very accurate sentiment, and she sings accompanying herself with a marvelous ease, which is definitely exceptional in her case."[3] A concert on 23 January 1908 at the

Salle de la Société de Photographie of music by Emmanuel Chabrier included the *Ode à la musique* (1890) sung by Bathori as soloist with a chorus of her students under the direction of composer and conductor Reynaldo Hahn. The reviewer scarcely knew what to praise most: "her intelligence, her musicality, her vocal technique, or her pianistic talent. When Mme Bathori sings, accompanying herself, *L'Isle heureuse* (1890) or the Lied (1862) one has the sensation that it is the only way to interpret Chabrier—that is to say, with fire and simplicity."[4] The musicologist Léon Vallas wrote for a Lyon newspaper in 1914: "Jane Bathori . . . possesses a very secure vocal technique, which is not common. Next, no less rare, she is an accomplished musician, a brilliant and perfect singer, an artist full of intelligence and sensitivity."[5] We may note that while all remark on her technique, her musicianship, her intelligence, her pianistic skills, none comments on vocal beauty or range. This is revealing: the voice itself was not remarkable, but coupled with Bathori's extraordinary musicianship and her superb ear, it did indeed permit her to sing any repertoire. Even more unusual, and in fact a feat approached only by the violinist-pianist-singer Marcella Sembrich (1858–1935),[6] was her ability to accompany herself at the piano, with the same high level of technique and style that characterized her singing. Darius Milhaud in his letter-preface to Bathori's booklet *Sur l'Interprétation des mélodies de Claude Debussy* referred to the first time he heard her sing, accompanying herself at the piano:

What an admirable singer you were, who could while singing with such a pure style, such clear diction, such a discreet and interior charm, play with the subtle sonorities of the piano, and with such an aristocratic touch and such ease.[7]

Bathori's voice was not large or extensive in range but was handled with the utmost dexterity and intelligence, coupled with the truly extraordinary musicianship revealed in her vocal and pianistic skills and particularly in her astounding ability to combine the two. Moreover the aspects of her singing which are remarked upon repeatedly—purity, clarity of diction, intonation, technique, intelligence—are the very qualities essential to the performance of new music, perhaps especially the new music of France during the first half of the twentieth century. Jane Bathori enjoyed the happy fate of finding the world for which her gifts were precisely suited, and the even happier fate that these gifts were such that they remained viable throughout a professional life that spanned more than six decades.

*   *   *   *   *

Jane Bathori was born Jeanne-Marie Berthier in Paris, 14 June 1877.[8] Her father was a pawnbroker and her mother a seamstress. Her musical gifts were discovered early, when her mother was surprised by the child's ability to repeat and remember melodies. The acquisition of a piano when Jeanne-Marie was seven led to her study with Hortense Parent with a career as professional pianist in mind, but when she was eighteen or so, she decided that her tiny hands would not permit her to play a good deal of the solo repertoire and she turned to the development of her voice. Working with Mme Brunet-Lafleur (wife of the conductor Charles Lamoureux), she was able to build on a good natural voice and her innate musical talent as well as the years of training as a pianist. Another singer named Jeanne Berthier was prominent in Paris, so Jeanne-Marie Berthier chose Jane (pronounced as Jeanne) as her first name and then selected Bathori from the list of B's in the Larousse dictionary, undaunted by the fact that among the Bathoris[9] was a Transylvanian princess who liked to bathe in the blood of children.

In 1897, at the age of twenty, she made her Paris debut at La Bodinière with the pianist-composer Reynaldo Hahn in a concert of his music, a momentous occasion for her both professionally and personally. In the audience was Émile Engel, a fifty-year-old tenor from Luxembourg known for his interest in new music and especially for his performance of Chabrier. Engel became her coach, promoter, and soon her husband. The two performed contemporary music together, organized soirées known as "Une Heure de musique" which they presented in Brussels and in Paris, and founded together a small conservatory. In spite of their obvious rapport with respect to music, their political views were very different, especially about the notorious Dreyfus affair, and they parted ways (Engel finding comfort in the arms of a young student), finally divorcing in 1921.

During the decade from 1897 to 1907 Bathori performed as singer, as pianist, and as singer-pianist in Brussels and Paris. She sang for a season at the Théâtre de la Monnaie in Brussels; with Engel and others she performed contemporary music extensively at the Libre esthétique, a society devoted specifically to avant-garde work by composers, artists, writers. Here for example Bathori presented the Belgian première of Debussy's *Chansons de Bilitis* singing and accompanying herself, and she accompanied Engel in the Belgian première of Ravel's "Asie" (from *Shéhérazade*). In 1904 she stepped in with no rehearsal for the indisposed Jane Hatto to sing "Asie" with the composer at the piano at the Bouffes-Parisien in Paris. Following this amazing performance she sang seven additional premières of Ravel's works, including on 12 January 1907 the *Histoires naturelles*—the work in which Ravel for the first time omitted setting the nearly unheard final "e" of many French words. The audience was outraged. Bathori remembered: "If they didn't throw their footstools at me it was because they had none! I knew that the row came from a group of musicians from the Schola, pupils of Vincent d'Indy, totally lacking in comprehension. You know, those people with blinders . . ."[10] But by 1914 when she sang the equally controversial *Trois Poèmes de Stéphane Mallarmé,* at the Société musicale indépendante with Désiré-Emile Inghelbrecht conducting there was no rioting, only enthusiasm.

By 1912 Bathori had made herself known as an operatic singer of such roles as Micaëla in *Carmen,* as a piano accompanist and a first-class sightreader, and as an excellent interpreter of new music. She had been engaged by Arturo Toscanini to sing Alberto Franchetti's *Germania* with Enrico Caruso at La Scala in 1902, two years after making her opera debut in Nantes; in 1912 she sang for the Nantes opera the premiere of Léon Moreau's *Myrialde*. Hahn praised her dramatic ability in his review: "those who have heard her only in concert or in intimate settings . . . can only imagine how interesting and arresting she is [in the theatre], how communicative her emotion is, and how profoundly the simplicity of her acting, joined with the perfect style and variety of her singing, moves the spectator."[11]

Now, however, in spite of having established a solid reputation as an operatic singer, she withdrew from opera to concentrate on the concert and recital format and increasingly on contemporary music. By 1914 she had performed publicly the music of such contemporary French composers as Chabrier (1841–1894), Debussy (1862–1918), Fauré (1845–1924), Charles Koechlin (1867–1951), Albert Roussel (1869–1937), and Reynaldo Hahn (1874–1947); she was close friends with most of the younger composers and had sung premières of their music, often with them at the keyboard. She played with Hahn the première of his two-piano composition *Le Ruban dénoué*. It may well be that a future of singing Micaëla and other similar roles night after night held less charm for her than a career filled with singing new compositions, meeting new challenges, and enjoying new work. However that may be, during this decade she was departing from the traditional path of development and moving into a world that she would make her own—the world of modern French song.

But it was not as a singer alone that she would make her mark in this world. The decade from 1904 to 1914 was, as Linda Cuneo-Laurent points out, Bathori's period as singer and performer; during the following decade she emerged as Bathori the impresario. Since early in the century Bathori and Engel had been presenting new music in their "heures de musique." In 1912 they had done a series "La Musique à travers les Poètes et les Ages" in Paris, and they had begun a series of Sunday musicales at their home which had become a regular meeting place for young musicians. These soon included the young French composers dubbed by critic Henri Collet "Les Six"—Georges Auric (1899–1983), Louis Durey (1888–1979), Arthur Honegger (1892–1955), Darius Milhaud (1892–1974), Francis Poulenc (1899–1963), and Germaine Tailleferre (1892–1983)—and their close friend Erik Satie (1866–1925). By 1914 Bathori had sung at his request a number of Milhaud's songs. She met Satie at a conference on his music at which Honegger and Durey were also present; the Spanish pianist Ricardo Viñes introduced Bathori to his student Poulenc. Thus she was very much in the center of French musical life when, in 1917, she took over the direction of the Théâtre du Vieux-Colombier during the absence of its owner and director Jacques Copeau (who went with his troupe to New York for two years). Here, from 1917 to 1919, Bathori put on a series of productions that ranged from small theatrical musical events to concerts sometimes with small orchestras, sometimes with two pianos. The Théâtre du Vieux-Colombier became the home of new music in Paris. Music by Les Six, by André Caplet, by Satie was performed. During the first season events included both old and new chamber music, premières of avant-garde works, music from abroad, lectures with musical illustrations; the old was performed alongside the new, so works by Milhaud, Poulenc, Satie were heard along with music of Rameau, Lully, Bach, Mozart.

It was an adventurous period, historically as well as musically. Certainly the doings at the Théâtre du Vieux-Colombier must have provided relief from the grim spectacle of Paris in the last year of World War I—the hardships of war meant that rehearsals were often interrupted by alarms, musicians went home walking great distances along the tracks of the subway, a number of the musicians came in from the military camp at Versailles. In light of this the revivals and premières, produced during those two years seem nothing short of miraculous: Adam de la Halle's thirteenth-century musical play *Le Jeu de Robin et Marion, La jeune Fille à la fenêtre* by Eugène Samuel, Debussy's *La Demoiselle élue,* Chabrier's *Une Education manquée* and excerpts from *Le Roi malgré lui,* parts of Pierre de Bréville's *Eros vainqueur,* of Louis Aubert's *Le Forêt bleu,* Hahn's *Pastorale de Noël, Noctem quietam, Etudes latines, Le Ruban dénoué,* André Caplet's *Inscriptions champêtres,* Koechlin's *Trois Poèmes* and *Cinq Chansons de Bilitis,* Honegger's *Le Dit des jeux du monde* (which, Bathori recalled much later, was greeted with "applause, whistles, all sorts of interjections. It was the sweetest folly"[12]), Poulenc's *Rapsodie nègre* (for the eighteen-year-old Poulenc his first important public performance). The performers included professional musicians plus any composer capable of performing. All hands were called on to perform all things: in addition to composing Fernand Ochsé made costumes, designed sets, and did lighting for productions. Louis Durey wrote: "Jane Bathori, the great singer who premiered or interpreted so to speak all the contemporary vocal music, without expecting anything in return, put her immense talent at the service of youth. She opened to us the doors of the Théâtre du Vieux-Colombier which she had rented to make music there. All our first works were born there."[13] The Théâtre's success was legendary:

Hall full to bursting always. They say it is one of the rare places in Paris to hear good music at the moment. It is presented simply, intimately. Usually chamber music. I think they will be doing [Ravel's] *L'Heure espagnole* in an unpolished state, nicely, without a fuss, presenting it to the public in a more lively way than that of the ordinary concert, without pretensions, without innovation, practically without décor, with discretion, a simplicity of good conscience.

. . . their orchestra, small but select, is excellent.

The group as a whole gives the impression of enlightened amateurs who receive pleasure and give pleasure to their friends. That gives you an idea.[14]

André Mangeot writing in *Le Monde musical* summed it all up:

While theaters with all the means for doing something new and beautiful merely mark time, a theater with a stage as large as a pocket handkerchief which has nothing—no financial backing, no subscription audience, no resident company—offers premieres or revivals, in the space of one month, of four major productions.

It is Jane Bathori who accomplishes this miracle. What a diligent and perfect artist. She is heard in the afternoon at the Société nationale singing, to her accompaniment, the *mélodies* of our young composers—even the most obscure and hard to grasp—and, several hours later, in costume, she comes on stage, always self-possessed, in complete control of her voice. And during intermission she prepares the projects for the following day. This activity, this feverish work, could produce hastily prepared interpretations. But go hear *L'Education manquée* and tell me in what theatre you have heard such a perfect performance.[15]

It could not, of course, continue. Bathori had to shut down in March 1918, in part because Paris was under bombardment, in part because of everyday difficulties such as lack of communication (no more mail), lack of transportation (no more subway), and lack of funds. Nevertheless, she managed to run a second season, a bit reduced, from December 1918 through the spring of 1919. Copeau returned in the fall and took over the theatre,[16] ending the great days of the Théâtre du Vieux-Colombier as a locus of experimental, innovative music-making. But the value of the undertaking and the unusual work of its director had made their mark. Émile Vuillermoz wrote in January 1919:

Performances continue on the small stage of Jacques Copeau which maintains, under the intelligent musical direction of Jane Bathori, the sympathetic character of a laboratory of experiments worthy of the esteem of all artists. While our large musical factories are dozing, mechanically producing the usual products, this little atelier looks for and finds interesting innovations. If musicians are not ungrateful . . . they will mount a guard of honor around this valiant house which, in the face of theatrical and musical decadence, carries out such beautiful artistic work.[17]

Bathori went on with her concert career with performances abroad in Amsterdam, London, Brussels, Milan, Algiers, Barcelona, Prague, and other cities, but at the same time maintained an active role in the contemporary music life of Paris. Recognized now as one of the foremost interpreters of modern music, she performed the music of Les Six, of Satie, and of Satie's new "group," the *École d'Arcueil* (Henri Cliquet-Pleyel, Roger Désormière, Maxime Jacob, Henri Sauguet). Valentine Hugo described a reading at Bathori's home of Satie's new *Socrate* for an invited audience which included the poet Jean Cocteau and the writer-painter Max Jacob: "Satie accompanied her at the piano. It was unforgettable . . . the beautiful, moving voice of the singer [Bathori], the overpowering beauty of this unusual work . . . We were all in tears."[18]

She performed with Milhaud and others as singer and pianist in France as well as elsewhere. On 29 May 1920 Milhaud and Bathori were in Chelsea, England, playing Poulenc's *Sonata for Four Hands*, Satie's *Morceaux en forme de poire,* along with music by Milhaud, Durey, Honegger, Auric; on 22 December of the same year Bathori alone sang and played Poulenc's *Bestiaire,* Durey's *Quatre Épigrammes de Théocrite,* and played, with André Salomon, Tailleferre's *Jeux de plein air.* She continued to work with Les Six but as these composers became more independent of each other and more famous she moved to work with newer, younger composers. For example, a program on 17 May 1926 consisted entirely of first performances and included Henri Sauguet's *Le jeune Homme sur les bords du ruisseau,* Henri Cliquet-Pleyel's *Le Beau de Tripoli de Damas,* Maxime Jacob's *Trois Poésies d'Alfred de Musset.*[19] Her curiosity never left her: in her last years, seen at a concert of music by Pierre Boulez, she reportedly said "One must hear everything!"[20]

In 1926 she traveled with Georges Jean-Aubry to Buenos Aires; her assignment was to provide illustrations during a series of conferences on French music given by him. This was a journey laden with consequence. For the next seven years, until 1933, she spent half of each year in Argentina teaching and performing new French music. In 1933 she sang the role of Concepción in the first Argentina performance of Ravel's *L'Heure espagnole,* at the Teatro Colón. She spent most of World War II (1940 to 1945) in Argentina, where at first she served as professor at the conservatory of Mendoza. In 1942 with the cultural attaché Robert Weibel-Richard, the writer Roger Caillois, and the philosopher Paul Benichou, she founded in Buenos Aires the Institut français d'études supérieures, where she taught voice, directed a choir, and produced over the next several years (1942–45) a number of major works including *La Pastorale de noël* (Hahn), *Dido and Aeneas* (Purcell), *L'Incoronazione di Poppea* (Monteverdi), *Robin et Marion* (de la Halle), and *Les Malheurs d'Orphée* (Milhaud). The influence was not a one-way street; when she returned to Paris in 1946 she brought with her contemporary Argentinian music which she presented in various formats, completing the cross-fertilization that had begun with her journey twenty years earlier to provide examples of French music.

Bathori began working with singers at the French radio in the 1930s. In 1947 she began a series of broadcasts that continued until 1966 titled *Les Musiciens que j'ai connus, Expositions de mélodies inédites,* and *Musique retrouvée.* The five interviews taped in 1953 for Radio-Lausanne, with Stéphane Audel, are invaluable sources of information about her work and the music of the time.[21] Her only vocal recording, made in 1929, of *mélodies* (Columbia Records) was complemented in 1948 by her recording as pianist for singer Irène Joachim of Debussy compositions, which won the Grand Prix du Disque.

Although as Bathori grew older she no longer sang in public, she never ceased to find ways to perform or have performed the music that was so important to her—the new music created by young musicians. In 1947 her Ensemble Bathori sang the French premiere of Britten's *Ceremony of Carols.* She continued to teach— at the Conservatoire International, at the École normale de musique, at the Schola Cantorum. In 1951, at the age of 74, she organized concerts of contemporary music at La Maison de la pensée française. Ten years later, in 1961, she presented the Mayer lectures, "Les Musiciens que j'ai connus," at the Institute of Recorded Sound in London. She had much earlier, in 1932, published a booklet, *Conseils sur le chant*. In 1953 at the urging of Milhaud she published *Sur l'Interprétation des mélodies de Claude Debussy* and followed it in 1957 with a recording—*Cours d'interprétation: De Chabrier à Satie*.

She just never stopped. When she could no longer sing, she continued to direct ensembles and work as a pianist. When she could no longer make music in these ways she increased her lecturing activities. According to Claire Bergrunn, Bathori's student in Argentina and Paris, this indefatigable woman was in a train returning from a lecture to her home in Paris when she died on the 21st of January 1970.[22]

*   *   *   *   *

Jane Bathori is probably the first singer in modern history to dedicate her life and her talents to the avant-garde music of her time. At her debut in 1897 she sang the songs of the composer-pianist who accompanied her; even during a brief period (about ten years) of dalliance with traditional operatic roles, she was steadfast in her devotion to contemporary art. Her innate gifts were uniquely suited to this music and she reinforced these with her solid musicianship and sparkling intelligence; add to this that she clearly relished performing music that presented a challenge, and we have the recipe for the ultimate performer of the avant-garde whether in the sixteenth or the twentieth century. That she was an excellent pianist as well as singer made it possible for her career to span more than six decades; her work as accompanist in her sixties and seventies provided a channel of communication between the composers she had worked with in her youth and the singers she was accompanying and coaching in her late years. Her lectures provide invaluable, intimate information about the musical world of Paris during one of the most exciting eras of music and art.

She was a composer's ideal in that she aspired to transmitting the composer's work, without stamping her own identity upon it. She was not just unselfish in her dedication to her art but truly self-*less*. A number of works were conceived for her, for example Ravel's *Histoires naturelles* and *Noël des jouets*. Léon Vallas goes so far as to suggest that a number of works might *not* have come into existence but for her.[23]

Her work as entrepreneur, as director, as producer, was scarcely less important than her work as performer. During the brief time at the Théâtre du Vieux-Colombier she brought to the public a stunning and varied array of music, old and new, including a number of premières. She also brought to the public a new sense of what music could do, of how music could speak to the issues and aesthetics of the contemporary world, and how music too could depart from the language of the past and take on a contemporary vocabulary. Her enterprising energy carried over to her radio broadcasts, organization of concert series, productions of musical theatre pieces, and the communication established between the musical worlds of France and Argentina.

Bathori taught over the years both privately and in various schools. Her teaching and coaching activities were complemented by the booklets she published in 1932 and 1953 and by the *Cours d'interprétation: De Chabrier à Satie* recorded in 1957. Like her performing, her work as teacher was unique in providing a direct channel of communication with composers of the late nineteenth and early twentieth centuries.

Bathori represents a twentieth-century model of a new type of singer—the singer who, as did many in the far past, works with the composer in the creation of their living art. Bathori's descendants include such artists as Cathy Berberian and Jan de Gaetani, to whom the words of Léon Vallas apply as they did to Bathori: "devoted with complete selflessness (désintéressement) to modern music . . . for more than ten years there has not been a young [French] composer who is not indebted to her for the first performance of one of his works."[24]

Of all the praises that came her way, however, the epitaph that surely would have pleased Bathori most would have been Georges Jean-Aubry's words from a 1913 Belgian review: "I hear her sing the lament of *Mélisande* or the youthful fresh joy of *La bonne chanson* and I feel that in her voice it is our French heart that speaks . . . She is modern French song incarnate."[25]

Timeline

1877, 14 Jun	Jeanne-Marie Berthier born in Paris, father pawnbroker, mother seamstress
1884	Studied piano with Hortense Parent; tiny hands dissuaded her from pursuit of career as concert pianist
c. 1895	Studied voice with Mme. Brunet-Lafleur (wife of conductor Charles Lamoureux)
1898	Paris debut at La Bodinière with pianist-composer Reynaldo Hahn; heard by Émile Engel, 50-year-old tenor from Luxembourg who became her coach, promoter, and in 1897 or 1898 her husband
1897–1907	Sang with Engel, emphasis on contemporary music, "Une heure de musique" (Paris and Brussels), founded small conservatory together; seriously different political views, especially over Dreyfus affair; (Engel left her for a younger student, they divorced 1921); first Belgian performance of the *Chansons de Bilitis* (Debussy/Louÿs, 1897) singing and accompanying herself, and of Ravel's "Asie," Bathori at piano, Engel singing.
1902	Engaged by Toscanini to sing Franchetti's *Germania* with Caruso
1904	Performing in Brussels at Théâtre de la Monnaie 1904 and at Society Libre-Esthétique (contemporary music); premiered many new works by Chausson, Duparc, Koechlin, Bréville, et al.
1904, Nov	Stepped in for indisposed Jane Hatto to sing Ravel's "Asie," at Bouffes-Parisien in piano/vocal version with composer at keyboard
1905–1907	Performed premieres of seven of Ravel's works
1909	First performances of Debussy works: *Trois Chansons de Charles d'Orléans,* 11 March
1911, 4 Jan	*Le Promenoir des deux amants,* by Bathori and Debussy at Société nationale
c. 1912	Bathori known as opera singer (such roles as Micaëla, Bruneau's *Le Rêve,* Massenet's *Cendrillon*), as piano accompanist, first-class sightreader, excellent interpreter of modern music; retired from opera and devoted herself to modern music
1914, 14 Jan	Société musicale indépendante, Inghelbrecht conducting, *Trois Poèmes de Stéphane Mallarmé,* no riot, only enthusiasm; again in London, 18 March 1915, under Sir Thomas Beecham.
1916	Conference on Satie held by composer Roland-Manuel; present were Honegger, Durey, Bathori (Bathori's first meeting with Satie).
1917	Viñes introduced Poulenc to her; Honegger introduced by Fernand Ochsé (the artist); Poulenc and Honegger met at her home

1917–1919	Took over direction of Théâtre du Vieux-Colombier; put on a wide variety of productions ranging from small theatrical musical events to concerts, sometimes with small orchestra, with two pianos. TdVC became main place for music, especially new music, in Paris during these very difficult two years; music by Les Six, André Caplet, Satie, stage works.
1918–1919	Emergence of Les Six: Auric, Durey, Honegger, Milhaud, Poulenc, Tailleferre; spokesperson, Jean Cocteau, manifesto, *Le Coq et l'Arlequin* (1918); new style, bare-bones, *dépouillé,* Cocteau called for "la musique sur laquelle on marche,"
1919, Feb	Short tour in Italy with Alfredo Casella
1919	Recognized widely for her work in cause of contemporary music, articles in *La Française, L'Éclair, Brétagne* (cites 50 concerts in 4 months, describes her as "a superlative, internationally renowned artist, a 'godsend' ('bonne aubaine')"
1919-1926	Performing music of Les Six, of Satie, and of Satie's new "group" the *École d'Arcueil* (Henri Cliquet-Pleyel, Roger Désormière, Maxime Jacob, Henri Sauguet), concerts in Paris, also Amsterdam, London, Brussels, Milan, Algiers, Barcelona, Prague;
1920, 14 Feb	Bathori sang public premiere of Satie's *Socrate* at concert of Société nationale, with Suzanne Balguerie and André Salomon; performances with Milhaud and others as singer and pianist; works dedicated to her, works performed by her with composers
1926	First journey to Buenos Aires, with Georges Jean-Aubry to provide illustrations during series of conferences on French music given by him
1926–1933	Half of each year in Argentina, teaching, performing new music of France; other half in Paris
1929	Recorded number of *mélodies* for Columbia records
1930s	Paris: concerts featuring especially Satie, Sauguet, Les Six
1932	Published booklet, *Conseils sur le chant*
1933	Sang at Teatro Colón Concepción in first Argentina performance of Ravel's *L'Heure espagnole*
1934	Set up weekly concerts at l'Académie de la Coupole, sang in many other concerts, with Inghelbrecht worked with singers at radio
1940	Return to Argentina, professor at Conservatory of Mendoza
1942	Founded Institut Français d'Etudes Supérieures with cultural attaché Robert Weibel-Richard, writer Roger Caillois, philosopher Paul Benichou; taught voice, directed choir, produced old and new works (by Hahn, Purcell, Monteverdi, Fauré, Milhaud, de la Halle)

1946	Return to Paris, bringing with her new music of Argentina
1947-1966	Broadcasts on French radio
	1947–1948, *Les Musiciens que j'ai connus*
	1948–1949, *Cycle de la mélodie*
	1950–1963, *Expositions de melodies inédites*
	1963–1966, *Musique retrouvée*
1947	Ensemble Bathori sang French premiere of Britten's *Ceremony of Carols;* masterclasses on interpretation of Fauré, Debussy, Ravel
1948	As pianist, recorded music of Debussy with Iréne Joachim, Grand Prix du Disque; concerts with Joachim
1949	Taught at Conservatoire International
1951	Course on interpretation at École normale de musique, first of similar series at Schola Cantorum. Began to organize concerts of contemporary music at La Maison de la pensée française
1953	Published *Sur l'Interprétation des mélodies de Claude Debussy,* Taped 5 interviews for Radio-Lausanne, with Stéphane Audel
1957	Made professor at Schola Cantorum
	Recorded *Cours d'interprétation: De Chabrier à Satie*
	To Moscow, member of jury of vocal competition
1961	Invited to London to present 3 lectures on *Les Musiciens que j'ai connus* (published in translation in *Journal of the British Institute of Recorded Sound*)
1963	Similar lecture given at Phonothèque nationale, *Quelques Souvenirs de ma carrière depuis 1900*
1964	Early recordings re-released, Pathé-Marconi's *Voix illustres* series
1964–1967	Frequent lectures
1970, 21 Jan	Died, Paris (or in train returning to Paris)

Bibliography

Jane Bathori's writings about music are extremely informative about her views as musician, performer, teacher. Although mostly available only in French, reading of them repays the effort. Much of the material is given in translation in the publications noted below by Linda Cuneo-Laurent and Carol Kimball.

Works by Bathori

Bathori, Jane. *Conseils sur le chant.* Paris: Schola Cantorum, 1932.

_____. "Souvenir" in *Hommage à Maurice Ravel*: Numéro special de *La Revue musicale* (December 1938): 179–81.

_____. "Debussy exige une interprétation scrupuleuse." *Arts* (March 1948): n.p.

_____. *Sur l'Interprétation des mélodies de Claude Debussy.* Paris: Les Editions ouvrières, 1953. See below, English translation with introduction by Laurent.

_____. "Entretiens avec Jane Bathori." Interviews by Stéphane Audel. Radio Lausanne, 1953. Bibliothèque Nationale, Paris. Photocopy.

_____. "Au sujet de l'interprétation des mélodies de Debussy." *Musique et Radio: Revue technique et professionelle de musique* No. 512 (January, 1954): 1, 3.

_____. "Les Musiciens que j'ai connus." The Mayer Lectures. Translated by Felix Aprahamian in *Journal of the British Institute of Recorded Sound* 5 (1961/ 1962): 144–51; 6 (1962): 174–80; 15 (1964): 238–45.

_____. "Le *Socrate* d'Erik Satie." *Musica* No. 191 (April 1970): 15.

_____. *On the Interpretation of the Mélodies of Claude Debussy.* Preface by Darius Milhaud. Translation and Introduction by Linda Laurent. Stuyvesant, NY: Pendragon Press, 1998.

This translation by Professor Laurent makes available to the English reader Bathori's invaluable essay on interpreting the *mélodies* of Debussy. Laurent's introduction is a useful supplement to her unpublished disseration of 1982.

Works about Bathori

Cuneo-Laurent, Linda. "The Performer as Catalyst: The Role of the Singer Jane Bathori (1877–1970) in the Careers of Debussy, Ravel, "Les Six," and Their Contemporaries in Paris 1904–1926." Ph.D. diss., New York University, 1982.

Cuneo-Laurent's dissertation remains the most informative source about Bathori and her work. She gives generous quotations from such primary sources as letters, newspaper and journal articles and reviews, interviews, etc. Her bibliography includes information about the primary sources—Bathori's own publications, recordings, and scripts of radio broadcasts, plus recorded interviews with her—and about secondary sources from the very general (Norma Evenson's *Paris: A Century of Change 1878–1978,* [Berkeley: University of California Press, 1979]) to the very specific (Henri Sauguet, "Mes Rencontres avec Maurice

Ravel," *La Revue musicale* [January-February, 1939]: 11–12). Cuneo-Laurent based her work on intimate knowledge of the personal archives of Jane Bathori and also conducted numerous interviews with composers, performers, former students, and others who worked with Bathori. The dissertation includes a list of *mélodies* first performed by Bathori and of *mélodies* dedicated to her. Although the author concentrates on the period from 1904 to 1926, she surveys the early years as well as Bathori's life from 1926 to her death in 1970 (Appendix A provides an overview of the years 1926–1970).

Kimball, Carol. "Jane Bathori's Interpretive Legacy." *Journal of Singing* 57, no. 3 (January/February 2001): 17–45.

A very useful discussion of Bathori's interpretive abilities and procedures and her legacy as seen in recordings by other singers.

_____. Review of *Jane Bathori: Musicienne extraordinaire. The Complete Solo Recordings* (Marston, 51009-2, 1999) and *Dawn Upshaw: Hommage à Jane Bathori* (Erato, 27329-2). *The Opera Quarterly* 17, No. 1 (Winter 2001): 118–24. Informative review of the very important set of Bathori's recordings, coupled with critical analysis of Upshaw's recent recital in Paris of *mélodies* first performed (and in some cases also recorded) by Bathori. The recording was made live at Upshaw's Paris recital.

Chapter 16

Marian Anderson
(27 February 1897 – 8 April 1993)

Throughout her life Marian Anderson, as an American black woman, faced and overcame barriers that had little or nothing to do with her voice. That she surmounted these hurdles magnificently is eloquent tribute to her courage, endurance, and determination. Everything came late for her: she graduated from high school at the age of twenty-four, she debuted at the Metropolitan Opera at the age of fifty-eight, she achieved only minor successes until her Berlin debut in October 1930 and the subsequent (November) breakthrough tour of Scandinavia when she was thirty-three.

* * * * *

Unlike the other singers in this book, Marian Anderson left a significant legacy of recordings that give a good sense of her voice. (Other singers made recordings, notably Jane Bathori and Lillian Nordica, but all who heard them sing live mourned the infidelity of the recorded image.) On the other hand, recordings of Anderson in early years do not display the glories of her voice any more than do the recordings made during this same period of Amelita Galli-Curci (1882–1963, retired 1936) or the very popular Alma Gluck (1884–1938). Thus descriptions of Anderson's voice during those years are important complements to the recordings.

Even in her earliest appearances, the unusual quality of Anderson's voice drew attention. Her 1916 performance in Handel's *Messiah* (with Roland Hayes) elicited from the journal *Crisis* a reference to her "dark, sweet, full-blossomed contralto."[1] The following year she sang in Savannah where the critic tried to explain her voice: "A contralto, its range is amazing and the upper notes as perfect and full as the lower, with a lovely middle register . . . unusual in its quality . . . more like an exquisite wind instrument than like the human voice, the tones ringing out like a clarionet."[2] (The program included "Deep River," "Go Down Moses," "Danny Boy.") Another Savannah critic found her voice to be "exquisitely rich and full and mellow" with marvelous control, "the music just seeming to come without any effort from the singer."[3] In April 1924 the *New York Sun* reviewer wrote of her debut at Town Hall: "Miss Anderson possesses one of the best contralto voices heard in this town in many moons. It is pure contralto, of even quality, imposing in its freely produced and resonant lower register, which is without the forced opacity often heard in contraltos, and velvety in the medium."[4] A London newspaper clipping mentioned the "peculiar timbre common to colored vocalists."[5] (Was this a reference to the "thick vibrato" noted by a Swedish reviewer in 1930? who continued, however: "But what does it mean in this case! . . . The delighted audience once again filled the hall to capacity.")[6] Herbert Peyser in the *New York Telegram,* reviewing her Carnegie Hall recital of 2 March 1930, waxed eloquent about her voice: "[one of the] rarest voices of the time—a noble contralto, spontaneous in utterance, amazingly rich in timbre and, except for some hard and faultily produced high notes, smooth as satin in texture . . . welcome absence of coarse or exaggerated chest tones, ample and remarkably even scale. It lends itself most beautifully to sustained, long-breathed cantilena."[7] Reviews of the Berlin recital in 1930 noted "a dark, blue-black dark voice . . . In sound [it] sounds somewhat unusual to our ears, exotic: but we readily take a fancy to its appeal."[8] Taken altogether, we have a portrait of a true contralto, dark, warm, yes a vibrato, amazingly full, rich, velvety, and even in quality throughout its large range; in addition reviewers agree that the singing is natural, unforced, produced without effort.

After the first few years of admiration for the phenomenal voice, however, reviewers coupled eloquent praise of the sound with suggestions that she needed to grow musically, that her interpretations were sadly lacking in understanding, that in short without the appropriate studies and discipline she would remain merely the possessor of a beautiful sound without ever achieving the status of an artist. For example, of her concert in May 1922 at Witherspoon Hall in Philadelphia, after mentioning the "exceptional resonance and richness in [her] lower register," the reviewer continued "what the youthful artist most needs is to develop enlivening passion, and an emotional accent of warmth and color in her remarkable voice."[9] The critic of the *New York Age* wrote that same year: "As it is now, this young girl stands and sings with a voice of power and purity, charming and entrancing her audience by the sheer beauty of her tonal production. But when she 'wakes up,' injecting life's passion into her vocal outpourings, she will indeed have become a great singer."[10] The review of her debut on 23 December 1923 with the Philharmonic Society in Philadelphia noted her "superb contralto," but specified that she had much to learn "in the intellectual and dramatic values of singing."[11] In spite of minor successes—a concert at the Renaissance Casino in Harlem (New York City) in 1924, winner of the Lewisohn Stadium contest in 1925—critics, while noting the beauties of the sound, referred frequently and consistently to a lack of artistic development, lack of ability to sing European music, lack of interpretative acumen.

The *New York Sun* reviewer of her 1924 Town Hall debut praised "one of the best contralto voices heard in this town in many moons" but continued "till she broadens her imagination and acquires a knowledge of the art of color she will probably not realize all her ambitions" and, specifically with respect to the German lieder, "Miss Anderson betrayed a sad want of understanding of the deeper meanings of her lyrics and of lied interpretation."[12]

Anderson was devastated, and the success of her Lewisohn Stadium performance, "the voice in a thousand—or shall we try ten thousand or a hundred thousand?"[13] did little to assuage the wounds, particularly since reviewers continued to note a lack of artistic maturity and of interpretative abilities. Olin Downs writing about the Lewisohn Stadium concert for the *New York Times* was enthusiastic—"The beauty and expressive capacities of her voice and the native interpretive ability of the artist made an immediate and excellent impression"—but concluded by saying that it was "a voice and a talent of unusual possibilities."[14] Anderson was twenty-eight and critics were still referring to her "possibilities."

It became clear to her that she needed to work with teachers who could direct her studies toward correcting these deficiencies. Like Lillian Nordica, Anderson's vocal technique and vocal gifts were undisputed. Unlike Nordica, she had not had the musical education she could have found in a music school. Like Nordica, again, at this point Anderson felt the need to work with European teachers. As with Nordica also, Anderson's European mentors found it mainly unnecessary to alter her vocal technique. Both Nordica and Anderson needed language skills—German, French, Italian—and Anderson desperately needed tutoring and coaching in repertoire. While Nordica was determined to conquer the world of opera, Anderson's arena was art song. It took Anderson several years longer, but she too achieved the pinnacle of success in her world. She spent three lengthy periods of study in Europe—in London (November 1927 to September 1928) and in Berlin (summers of 1930 and 1931). At the end of her first summer in Berlin, just after her debut in the Bachsaal, Anderson was engaged for a tour of Scandinavian cities. The review of her concert in Helsinki reveals succinctly and eloquently the immensity of her achievement:

[A] singer of both magnificent voice and an interpreter of high artistry. Anderson sings with such self-confidence as far as the stylistic side of the performance goes that one cannot talk about a more cultivated art of singing. But there is, in addition, the singer's sincere and ardent inner relationship to what she is performing, such a genuine dedication that one cannot really tell if she actually expects any applause for herself.[15]

Although over the next few years her success and reputation grew immensely, this breakthrough in the fall of 1930 seems to have radically influenced her performance. She wrote in *My Lord, What a Morning*: "it is possible that I sang with a freedom I had not had before. I know I felt that this acceptance provided the basis for daring to pour out reserves of feeling I had not called upon."[16]

Anderson had realized, at the age of thirty-three, the potential not only of her remarkable voice but of her powers for interpretation and projecting that interpretation, something she had been able to do very early with the music of her childhood—i.e., church, spiritual, black folksong—but had struggled to achieve with the repertoire of classical music, especially non-English materials. As her voice deteriorated, and it did inexorably as she aged, her interpretative powers continued to grow, while her determination and willingness to work at musical communication never lessened.[17] When she sang in Israel in 1955, for example, she delighted her audience by performing the *Alto Rhapsody* of Brahms in Hebrew.

*   *   *   *   *

Marian Anderson was born 27 February 1897 to John Berkley Anderson and Anna Delilah Rucker in South Philadelphia. Their neighborhood was racially mixed as were the schools (which had, however, exclusively white teachers). Her first musical experiences were in her family church; very early her unusual gift was noticed and exploited—Anderson remembered finding on the street a handbill with her picture on it: "Come and hear the baby contralto, ten years old."[18] She sang in choirs, often doing small solos and duets, and her Aunt Mary took her from church to church where she performed for at first very small sums—a quarter or a half-dollar—but soon for as much as $5.00. It all went home to be shared with family. In 1909 her father suffered an accident at work (the Reading Terminal) and after lying ill for several weeks died of heart failure just after Christmas 1910. After John Anderson's death the family fell on hard times, and eventually moved in with his parents, Isabella and Benjamin Anderson. Anna Anderson worked at a tobacco factory and took in laundry (later she scrubbed floors at Wanamaker's); the young girls did all they could to help, delivering laundry, etc., but it was a difficult life. In addition to dealing with real poverty, they were living in a small three-story row house with their grandparents, their aunt, two other cousins, and boarders. Benjamin Anderson, a gentle soft-spoken man, was a devout member of a congregation of black Jews who called themselves Hebrews or Israelites. Marian seems to have been drawn particularly to him, but he died one year after John Anderson. It was her father's sister, Mary, who most energetically nourished Marian's musical abilities, and who now frequently took on the task of fund-raising for various causes including help for the young singer.

When in 1912 Marian graduated from the Staunton Grammar School, she was fifteen, and Isabella Anderson was adamant that she go to work to help support the family. High school, though free, would nevertheless involve purchase of materials, of clothing, and perhaps most important would deprive the family of Marian's earnings as a singer—a small but significant income derived from singing with various church and community groups and for other social activities within the black community. The People's Chorus, with which Marian had sung since she was ten or eleven, put on a concert (26 March 1914) featuring music by black musicians; Marian's voice was singled out by the critic of the *Philadelphia Tribune* as a "singularly rare contralto."[19] Singing in public put her in contact with a number of other performers and with community leaders, several of whom were interested in encouraging young talent. Perturbed by the plight of this amazingly talented young woman who could neither attend high school nor study with a voice teacher, the Union Baptist Church took up a collection for Marian and raised $17.02, which was given to her to be used where most needed. In addition the Church promised to pay for voice lessons, but the difficulty now was to find an appropriate teacher— which meant a white teacher, with professional training as well as professional contacts. This was difficult: in segregated Philadelphia it was rare to find any white teacher who would take black students, for to do so usually meant losing all their white students. Marian went from teacher to teacher in vain. One sad day she attempted to enroll at a music school in her neighborhood; the cute young receptionist told her flatly "We don't take colored." Remembering the incident later she said "I was as sick as if she'd hit me with her fist right in the middle of my stomach, and I mean really, physically sick."[20] Finally, and purely by chance, Marian found a teacher. The family had become friends with John Thomas Butler, a dramatic reader and elocutionist of color, whose job on a mail car took him regularly past the Anderson home. When one day he heard Marian sing, he asked Isabella Anderson's permission to take her to sing for a friend of his, Mary Saunders Patterson, an extremely energetic black voice teacher who also directed many vocal and choral activities in the black community. Patterson immediately accepted Marian as a student and flatly refused to be paid for lessons, saying that she could be repaid when the young singer had made her way. Marian Anderson was eighteen, and she had just taken her first step toward a career as a professional singer. She had at this point no knowledge of foreign languages; her repertoire consisted of church or school music and a few songs by Stephen Foster and Ethelbert Nevin. Patterson worked with her mainly on repertoire and on what Anderson called the controlling and channeling of the voice—i.e., placement and projection.

In June 1915 the People's Chorus gave a benefit concert with the explicit goal of raising money for Marian's education; with the help of G. Grant Williams, editor of the *Tribune* and a tireless promoter of cultural events in the black community, $250 was raised, a committee was formed, and it was decided that Marian should study now with Agnes Reifsnyder, a contralto, still performing, and one of the very few white teachers who dared to take students "of color" (though Agnes Pitt, a talented black contralto, had to enter through the backdoor so that she would be thought a servant and Reifsnyder's other students would not leave her).[21] They worked on "medium and low tones" and on expanding her repertoire. The continued support of the People's Chorus made it possible for Marian to enter William Penn High School that fall.

Anderson remained at this business-oriented institution for three unhappy years, trying to learn bookkeeping and stenography, skills that all the Andersons including Marian thought would provide financial security for her. But these nonmusical subjects were difficult for her, and her slow progress was made even slower by frequent, unexcused absences to fulfill singing commitments. One of the bright spots of this difficult period was the joy she experienced as well as the good critical reception from singing Handel's *Messiah* with Roland Hayes. Hayes, already a noted black singer in America, was much admired by Anderson, and he served in many ways as a mentor. He himself after striving to build a career in the United States went to Europe where he was much better received. In 1917 Anderson herself experienced the racism of the deep south, when she went with her mother to perform a concert in Savannah, Georgia. Consigned on the train to the "Jim Crow" car, she said she only felt safe when the car blinds were completely lowered.[22] The hospitality and her reception in Savannah compensated, but it was the first of many similar, indeed worse, experiences.

The principal of William Penn invited a "Mr. Rohrer" to hear Marian sing. This prescient gentleman, whose first name remains unknown, urged her to abandon thoughts of a business career and to study as much music as possible. In the fall of 1918, Marian now twenty-one transferred from William Penn to the South Philadelphia High School for Girls; she entered as a sophomore, so little had she accomplished in the three uncomfortable years at William Penn. The new school, in which students moved at their own rate of progress (modeled after the Dalton school), was entirely different. Although Marian was apparently the only black student in her class, she was not ostracized; rather the class delighted in her presence and her abilities. Her teachers excused her absences to fulfill singing commitments; indeed they helped her make up the work. She graduated three years later, at the age of twenty-four. Of the many addresses presented at the graduation ceremonies on 20 June 1921, one was entitled "We Have Music and Marian Anderson."

After working briefly in the summer of 1919 with Oscar Saenger, she began vocal studies with Giuseppe Boghetti (born Joe Bogash in Philadelphia in 1896— an American, just one year older than Anderson). Boghetti was experienced, knew the repertoire, and was able to help Anderson in many ways. She continued to work with him through the few successes and many disappointments that marked the next decade. Between 1921 and 1928 Anderson did a good deal of touring with a very light-skinned black pianist Billy King; much of the concertizing was in the south where they had to deal with problems of racism (exacerbated by their different skin colors?). In 1924 she made her first recordings, for the Victor Talking Machine Company, of spirituals in Burleigh arrangements; these were in fact the first recordings by a black singer for a major American recording company.[23] Anderson's Philadelphia debut with the Philharmonic Society at the Academy of Music on 23 December 1923 was followed in February 1924 by a well-received performance at the Renaissance Casino in New York City's Harlem. But her program in April at New York's Town Hall—officially her New York debut—was a disaster. The concert started late, the hall was at best half filled, and the reviews were devastating, remarking on the exceptional beauty of her voice but pointing out her lack of interpretative ability, with respect both to the use of vocal color and understanding of the lieder she sang (see above, pages 246–47).

The brightest point of this period, and it was indeed bright, was her winning in 1925 a contest sponsored by the National Music Council and New York City's Lewisohn Stadium. The prize was a performance in August 1925 with the New York Philharmonic at Lewisohn; many of the critics present at the concert had reviewed the Town Hall debacle of spring 1924 and could scarcely believe they were hearing the same singer. But Anderson was wise enough to realize that, in spite of the warm praise for her singing of one aria and three spirituals at the Stadium, the earlier reviews of the Town Hall concert were still accurate. She had a beautiful, remarkable voice; her vocal technique was solid. But the intellectual and spiritual maturity to make her an artist was wanting. Anderson determined now that she must find teachers who could help her address these failings; it was clear to her that she could find such teachers only in Europe. She devoted the next two years to touring, saving every penny, spending nothing on herself. When Anna Anderson fell ill, however, and was unable to go to work at Wanamaker's where she was still scrubbing floors, Marian did not hesitate to use her savings. She called the Wanamaker supervisor and said coolly: "I just wanted to tell you that Mother will not be returning to work." Anderson said later "I felt, I must say, a glowing satisfaction."[24]

In October 1927 with all her savings she sailed for England and the future. In London she worked with the composer Roger Quilter and she studied French and German; she rented a room in Steyning in Sussex in order to work there with the very elderly Raimund von Zur Mühlen. Zur Mühlen, one of the truly great interpreters of lieder, had sung for Brahms and had also studied with Clara Schumann the lieder of Robert Schumann and Schubert. His accompanist remembered hearing him say "A voice of gold!"after Anderson sang Gluck's "O del mio dolce ardor." Anderson herself was deeply embarrassed that she did not know the meaning of each word in the song—remedying this failing was an essential part of her growth as interpretive artist. Unfortunately just before Christmas Zur Mühlen collapsed and was unable to continue teaching. Anderson returned to London, where she lived with the singer John Payne and his wife. They were joined in January 1928 by another black singer, Alberta Hunter. Hunter, one of the twentieth century's great blues singers (still singing at the Cookery in New York in the 1980s, she died in 1984), was extremely uninhibited and frank—the very opposite of Anderson; the two nonetheless became friends. John Payne's house was a center for young black students and professionals in London, including such singers as Paul Robeson, Amanda Ira Aldrich whose father had been a famous black actor and who had studied at the Royal College of Music with Jenny Lind (Lind taught at the RCM from 1883 until1886), Mark Raphael (a close friend of Roger Quilter and well-known interpreter of his music), and Louis Drysdale with whom Anderson studied during the first part of 1928. Drysdale, a perpetuator of the *bel canto* style, had studied at the Royal College with Gustave Garcia, son of

Manuel Garcia Jr., the best-known vocal teacher of the nineteenth century (it was to him Jenny Lind had turned when she had vocal difficulties early in her career; see Chapter 11, pages 154–55). Manuel Garcia's father, Manuel Sr., was a well-known opera singer and voice teacher, and his sisters Maria Malibran and Pauline Viardot were two of the greatest singers of their time (see Chapter 12). Just as Zur Mühlen had provided a direct link with the lieder tradition, Drysdale was a direct connection with the technique, the style, and the repertoire of western European music—precisely what Anderson needed. In spite of all the musical contacts made during her stay in England, it was Drysdale whose method she cited repeatedly.

In June 1928 Anderson sang in Wigmore Hall, her London debut. Wigmore, one of the finest recital halls in the world, near-perfect acoustically, which seats 550, was well-suited to such a recital.[25] She sang Schubert and Schumann lieder, Quilter songs, arias from Purcell's *Dido and Aeneas,* Debussy's *L'Enfant prodigue,* and a group of spirituals. The English critics were reserved, noting the beauty of her voice, its peculiar "timbre common to colored vocalists,"[26] and remarking that while the voice was "of an undeniably beautiful quality . . . Her attack is often loose. She has a good command of languages, but her English needs tidying."[27] The *Times* noted her warm, rich tone, and another reviewer described "a certain naïve appeal in her readings that compensated for occasional lack of subtlety."[28]

Her Proms concert on 16 August was received with greater enthusiasm: critics noted as usual her "voice of fine quality through its entire range," but, which must have pleased her immensely, also found that "she delivered the big phrases [of Verdi's 'O don fatale'] with an *understanding of their style*" (emphasis added).[29] The *Daily Mail* also liked "O don fatale," and remarked that "the singer had been well trained, every note was musical, and her Italian was good."[30] The *Daily Chronicle* was even more enthusiastic, and informative: "Miss Anderson has a contralto voice of exceptionally fine quality and big compass. Her first solo was the famous Verdi aria, 'O don fatale' ('Don Carlo'), which on account of its unusual range, usually is transposed for most contraltos. But Miss Anderson sang it in the original key, with fine beauty of tone and *dignity of style*."[31] Six months of hard work—and loneliness—had paid off. But there was still need for work, as the critics in her native land were only too willing to tell her.

Anderson returned to the United States in September 1928. She was now under contract with the concert manager Arthur Judson. A combination of Judson's inability and perhaps discomfort in promoting a black artist and the real difficulties created by the economic depression of the time resulted in fewer engagements for the singer than might have been expected; Judson relied too on the contacts already made by Anderson and her pianist Billy King. That first season Judson managed to arrange just sixteen concerts. In June 1929, however, she was invited to sing in Seattle with the American Philharmonic Orchestra, for the opening concerts of the University of Washington summer music festival, where her success was enormous. Audience and critics alike were delighted; she sang both with orchestra and in her encores with just piano accompaniment. The following season, she was booked for twenty-one concerts. Among the first was a recital in November 1929 in the Chicago Orchestra Hall. The audience was large and enthusiastic, and the critics were also pleased: in her performance of Donaudy's "O del mio amato ben" she approached "perfection in every requirement of vocal art—the tone was of superb timbre, the phrasing of utmost refinement, the style pure, discreet, musicianly." But she also sang a Brahms lied and the Mozart "Alleluia," and though praising her coloratura—unusual for a contralto—in the "Alleluia," the critic experienced "a letdown, and we took away the impression of a talent still unripe . . . This is perhaps Miss Anderson's greatest lack—temperamental abandon and swing."[32] ("Swing" is a curious word to use in the context of a concert of classical music; would it have been applied to a white singer?) Herbert Peyser reviewing her recital at Carnegie Hall in the spring of 1930 included the now usual references to the beauty of her "noble contralto," but continued to find "a want of ingrained emotional temperament behind her singing" and thought the German songs still lay "considerably beyond Miss Anderson's imaginative and emotional scope."[33]

Anderson had been under the management of Arthur Judson since fall 1929; both the terms of her contract with him and his lack of ability to find her appropriate opportunities were quite unsatisfactory. She worked again with Boghetti, studied theory and piano with a private teacher (throughout her life she was conscious of her lack of basic music education), and saved her money. The Chicago concert in November 1929 led to her being invited to apply for a Rosenwald fellowship. This fellowship to support study abroad had been established by a Chicago financier, Julius Rosenwald, specifically for blacks who showed promise in leadership or in the arts; its receipt in the spring of 1930 enabled her to return to study in Europe, this time in Berlin.

She spent the summer of 1930 studying German, working over the words of lieder and poetry with the family she lived with, and coaching with Kurt Johnen, a well-known teacher in Berlin. Johnen, trained as musicologist and pianist, had worked extensively with the psychology of music, particularly with relation of rhythm and phrasing to the performer's physiology—breathing, pulse, etc. This program of study was well-calculated to address Anderson's needs—language, understanding, physical communication (enhancing her innate ability to communicate what she understood, e.g., spirituals). On 10 October 1930 she sang for the first time in Berlin, in the Bachsaal, and she was ready. Michael Raucheisen, one of the best accompanists in Europe, was at the piano. Artur and Karl Ulrich Schnabel were in the audience, as was also the contralto Mme Charles Cahier who would become a close friend and musical coach. Reviews of the Berlin recital mark a turning point for Anderson's career: "tremendous success yesterday in the Bachsaal . . . a dark, blue-black dark voice, which she handles with artistic accomplishment and taste . . . Marian Anderson is very musical, and she gives, without any posing, strong and genuine expression and is a mistress of the styles of performance . . . The ballad "The Three Gypsies" by Franz Liszt is one of her showpieces: she can sing it twice without tiring the attention of her enthusiastic listeners . . . She is successful with gradations and nuances [of tone], acquired from brilliant perceptions which enthrall [the listener] spontaneously."[34] Reviews continued to appear for several weeks; each must have been increasingly gratifying for Anderson: "Her command of our language and of our world of feeling was amazing" (*Berliner Tageblatt*);[35] "But this remarkable woman even sings German songs with a natural superiority in her mastery of style, her diction is skillfully accentuated and her musicality is impressive" (*Morgenpost*);[36] "All these German songs, especially those by Beethoven, she sings with profound understanding, inspired and thoroughly musical as one does not hear them but quite rarely" (*Deutsche Allgemeine Zeitung*).[37] These reviews must have gone far toward assuaging the wounds of earlier years; they also mark just how far the intensity and passion of Anderson's dedication had brought her. She had taken up the challenge of German lieder, and the victory was sweetly and conclusively hers. To this repertoire she could now bring the depth of understanding of music, text, and style, and the ability to communicate that understanding which had marked her singing of spirituals.

The Berlin reception was, however, but a harbinger of even greater success. The Scandinavian tour that followed provided another real breakthrough for Anderson. The first black singer to perform in Scandinavia, she was received so warmly, so enthusiastically, that as she wrote later it seemed to give her a freedom never before enjoyed to "pour out reserves of feeling I had not called upon."[38] She began the tour with pianist Sverre Jordan and finished it with Kosti Vehaven who would work with her for many years. They gave a dozen or so concerts in the course of three weeks; it was hectic and disorganized, since concerts were added to their schedule in response to demand, but it was an important change of attitude for Anderson to experience. She returned to America and another year of management by Judson who provided fewer concerts than desired and also provided little service, leaving a great deal of administrative details (travel, etc.) for Anderson and her accompanist Billy King to handle.

The following summer (1931) Anderson was again in Berlin, studying again with Johnen, using the second half of her Rosenwald grant. When in August she sang the *Vier ernste Gesänge* of Brahms, the eminent musicologist Max Friedländer who had been a close friend of the composer proclaimed her interpretation as "the very greatest miracle which I ever heard in the long years of my life."[39] His praise was equaled by reviewers: "Remarkable how the singer succeeded in a rendering both musical and artistic, remarkable the extent to which she accommodated herself to the characteristic emotional outlook of this typical North German world of feeling."[40] A second Scandinavian tour was just as successful as the first; during its course she visited Jan Sibelius and with Vehanen sang for him four of his songs to the composer's complete delight. When a few days later she sang a folksong in Finnish as an encore, Vehanen at the piano was so moved "I felt big tears rolling down my cheeks and could scarcely see the music."[41] For her very last concert in Finland, at the Helsinki Conservatory, she sang two of the Sibelius songs (though in German translation) and repeated her folksong in Finnish. It had been an exhilarating if exhausting six weeks during which she performed twenty-two concerts.

Back in the United States that fall, still under the management of Judson, times were bad. She sang twenty concerts over a period of five months. It was the depression, but it was also a case of inadequate management. Anderson was thirty-five; in spite of her growing success in Europe, she seemed to make little progress in her own country. When she was offered a contract to do twenty concerts in Scandinavia during October and November 1933 she accepted at once. This was the most successful tour of all. She wound up doing one hundred sixteen concerts over the next seven months, and at the end of it she was the darling of Scandinavia, second perhaps only to Jenny Lind. She went from Scandinavia to Paris where she gave two concerts. The first on 2 May for which she programmed Schubert lieder, Rachmaninoff songs, and Chaminade's "L'Èté" was called by *Le jour* "a dazzling victory," and the critic praised the "astonishing expertness of diction that brings her interpretations intensely to life . . . this strange charm and this succession of fascinations that are radiated by her extraordinary personality."[42] She sang in London on 9 May to a quite cool reception although some mention was made of "admirable" breath control and "excellent" phrasing.[43] The English composer Constant Lambert was the single exception: he termed her singing of Sibelius's "Die Libelle" one of the two "most outstanding pieces of singing" he had heard in recent years.[44] On 30 May she sang again in Paris, at the Salle Gaveau, and repeated her earlier triumph. But this time the energetic and enterprising impresario Sol Hurok was in the audience; he asked Anderson and Vehanen to meet with him the following day and he offered them a contract. Anderson had to negotiate withdrawal from her contract with Judson; in fact Judson made no difficulties, and by the end of the summer Anderson was prepared to sign with Hurok. This was for her the beginning of a new career in the United States.

Her third Paris recital, in the Salle Gaveau on 14 June was a glorious affirmation of the success of the first two. One of the most vivid accounts of her work came from the American music historian Gilbert Chase, Paris correspondent for the *London Daily Mail*:

[T]he beautiful quality of the voice, with its uniquely moving timbre in the lower register, the perfect steadiness and control of the tone . . . extraordinary range of dynamic shading, the absolute homogeneous nature of the voice . . . the consummate artistry of the phrasing . . . [and] the intangible spiritual factors which make Marian Anderson's singing so utterly satisfying . . . [she] triumphed through sheer artistry . . . this young coloured singer [gives] such wonderfully convincing and intensely artistic expression to the sublimest lyrical thoughts of such composers as Beethoven, Schumann and Schubert.[45]

That summer Anderson explored expansion of her repertoire to include operatic roles (in particular, Amneris in Verdi's *Aïda*) and to this end studied briefly with

Tullio Voghera at the Stockholm Opera; in the course of a life devoted entirely to opera he had worked with many singers, including Enrico Caruso and Jussi Björling. She also spent a few weeks with her friend Mme Charles Cahier in Germany, working on Mahler's *Rückert Lieder, Knaben Wunderhorn,* and *Kindertotenlieder.* (Mme Cahier, a well-known contralto, was in the Bachsaal on the occasion of Anderson's Berlin debut in 1930, and the singers had become good friends; Anderson's long-time pianist Kosti Vehanen had served for five years as Mme Cahier's accompanist.) Then the season began and she was off to Scandinavia for September and October, Holland and Paris in November followed by more concerts in Holland, France, Switzerland, and Belgium. She was working now with conductors and orchestras, which was not nearly as comfortable for her as was singing with her own pianist. Kosti Vehanen wrote that Anderson found it difficult to work with someone new because

she is hesitant about explaining to others how she wants to interpret a song and is reluctant to insist that a song shall be interpreted in her way. Often in singing with orchestras, Miss Anderson has found that the conductor's idea of the interpretation differs considerably from hers. Because of the short time available for rehearsals, it has not always been easy for her to make clear to him her conception, and for that reason she has not always been satisfied with the results.[46]

In January she set out with Vehanen for a tour of the Soviet Union, where she was received with wild enthusiasm. Anderson remembered later that the people from the back half of the house would rush to the front and stand there pounding on the stage boards with their fists and roaring "Deep River" and "Heaven, Heaven."[47] Shostakovich came backstage to meet her, Ippolitov-Ivanov invited Anderson and Vehanen to a banquet in his home, the soprano Antonina Nezhdanova came to all her recitals, Stanislavsky invited her to tea and offered to coach her in the role of Carmen. (Anderson expressed regret later that she had not accepted his offer, even at the cost of giving up the remainder of the tour.) February saw concerts in Warsaw, Vienna, Prague, Budapest, Monte Carlo with the conductor Dmitri Mitropoulos who became a staunch supporter. She continued to Italy for concerts in Turin, Rome, Trieste, Venice, Milan, before returning to the USSR in May for five concerts in Leningrad (now St. Petersburg) and six in Moscow. After performing in Ukraine, Georgia, and Azerbaijan, Anderson and Vehanen traveled to Kharkov and Odessa and then on to Baku for the final concert of the tour. An extraordinarily arduous journey brought them to the spa town of Kislovodsk where they rested for two weeks. Here, Anderson enjoyed a brief relationship with a Russian Jewish actor and reciter, Emanuel Kaminka. Their parting was final; although Anderson kept the letters written almost daily by Kaminka, she apparently never answered any of them.[48]

Having heard Anderson sing in Vienna, the Archbishop of Salzburg suggested that she sing a charity concert in the Salzburg Cathedral as part of the 1935 summer festival. Such an invitation at that time seems either naïve or provocative on the part of the Archbishop; he must have known that an American black singer would be anathema in Salzburg already a center of Nazi fascist activity. Anderson's European manager Helmar Enwall requested a date for the concert, but the authorities replied that "earlier experiences speak against it." When news of the ban appeared in New York papers the festival authorities explained that the program was already entirely in place and there was nothing to be done. Much negative publicity persuaded festival authorities to yield; Anderson's concert could take place in the Mozarteum, but not as an official part of the festival. When finally on 28 August Anderson sang her recital, Bruno Walter was conducting *Don Giovanni* at the Festspielhaus. Word of an amazing voice spread during the opera's intermission, with the result that some of the Festspielhaus audience made the short walk to the Mozarteum. Reviews were disappointing: the critics spoke mostly of the color—shade and hue—of Anderson's skin. But when Anderson was presented a few days later at a private recital in the ballroom of the Hôtel de l'Europe, the audience included many of the artists present in Salzburg that summer; after the concert Bruno Walter and Arturo Toscanini came back to congratulate the artist. It was on this occasion that Vehanen and Mme Cahier heard Toscanini make his famous statement: "What I heard today one is privileged to hear only once in a hundred years." (Vehanen's version is slightly different from that of Mme Cahier: "Yours is a voice such as one hears only once in a hundred years.")[49]

In the fall of 1935 Anderson returned to the United States. She and Hurok had decided that her accompanist would be Kosti Vehanen with whom she had now been working for some three years, instead of Billy King her accompanist from the early days of her career. King was devastated and did not hesitate to plead his case on grounds of his need and of their history together: "My Mother is heart sick to think that you would turn so against me, when she knows our financial plight and how dependent we both were on this coming American tour."[50] But Anderson recognized her need for an accompanist of Vehanen's calibre—in terms of experience, technique, and repertoire—though the decision cost her a good deal of soul-searching. She even consulted her friend Harry Burleigh (the very successful black baritone and composer) who told her forthrightly that King was simply not up to her present level: he "lacked poetry and imagination and technique too . . . he would be quite impossible."[51]

All was in place. Anderson's years of struggle had yielded a consummate artist—the magnificent voice was coupled now with a surety of style and interpretation based on her study of languages, texts, and method of developing an interpretation. The final piece was the contract with Hurok: she had now a brilliant and forceful agent who was from both an artistic and a business viewpoint vitally interested in her career. Unlike Judson, Hurok had no compunction whatsoever about using whatever was necessary to secure engagements for his artists. He would promise Anderson's presence on a concert tour only if other artists or companies were included in the package; vice versa, any demurs about hiring a black singer were met with threats of canceling other artists. Success followed success. On 30 December 1935 Anderson sang again in Town Hall. This time the house was full, and the critics were delighted with no reservations. Howard Taubman reviewed it for the *New York Times*: "Marian Anderson has returned to her native land one of the great singers of our time . . . possessor of an excelling voice and art. Her singing enchanted an audience that included singers . . . she was mistress of all she surveyed."[52] Her program included Handel arias, Schubert lieder, Finnish songs, her old warhorse "O don fatale," and spirituals. Her triumph was complete. She had indeed won entry to the world she sought; she had even achieved this victory with an added physical disability: a few weeks earlier she had fallen down a flight of stairs on the Île de France and broken her ankle. She sang with a full cast on her leg, but managed to keep this from her audience by going on stage with the curtain down, arranging herself by the piano, and being so discovered when the curtain rose.[53]

The next few years were filled with triumphs: she sang at the Philadelphia Academy of Music and at Carnegie Hall in January 1936; she sang at the White House for Eleanor and Franklin Roosevelt in 1936 and again for the visit of King George VI and Queen Mary in 1939. She sang at the prestigious Ann Arbor May Music Festival in May 1937, in the company of Lauritz Melchior, Kirsten Flagstad, and with conductor Eugene Ormandy. And on Easter Sunday 1939 Anderson sang for a crowd of seventy-five thousand at the Lincoln Memorial in Washington. The outdoor setting was brought about by the refusal of the Daughters of the American Revolution (DAR) to permit her to sing in Constitution Hall, which they controlled. Their most prominent member, Eleanor Roosevelt responded by resigning from the organization on 26 February 1939; the following day she explained her decision in her nationally syndicated column "My Day." The uproar that resulted brought unwelcome attention to the DAR and to similar acts of discrimination (which shamefully continued albeit less overtly). The publicity also made Anderson, rather to her discomfort, a powerful symbol of racial discrimination. In spite of the clamor, it is sad to note that Anderson was unable to find a suitable hotel room in Washington: she stayed in the home of Gifford Pinchot, a former governor of Pennsylvania. She sang "America," "O mio Fernando," Schubert's "Ave Maria," and after a brief intermission a group of spirituals including "Gospel Train," "Trampin'," "My Soul's Been Anchored in de Lord," and as an encore "Nobody Knows the Trouble I've Seen."[54]

Honors accrued: a doctorate from Howard University in 1938; in 1939 the Spingarn Medal, an award given annually by the President of the NAACP (National Association for the Advancement of Colored People) for the "highest or noblest achievement by an American Negro during the preceding year or years" which had been given to only two other musicians: Roland Hayes and Harry T. Burleigh. The medal was presented on 2 July 1939 by Eleanor Roosevelt at the annual conference of the NAACP, which took place appropriately in the former capital of the Confederacy, Richmond, Virginia.

Through it all Anderson toured regularly in the United States and Europe. Hurok in fact accepted so many engagements for her that she finally had to protest and insist on her need to rest after travel and between performances. In 1937 she sang forty-four concerts around the United States, in 1938 the number was sixty, and during the season of 1938–1939 she sang eighty concerts. Her fee rose from $400 the first season to as much as $2,000 by 1939. In 1940 her new contract with Hurok gave her two-thirds of the gross, his usual terms for his top artists.

Racial discrimination remained a problem in southern states. Texas, rather surprisingly, was the state most accessible to Anderson: her first season with Hurok she sang only in Houston but after that she appeared in Dallas, Fort Worth, and San Antonio as well. She sang frequently on radio programs such as the General Motors Hour, the Ford Hour, etc., which brought her voice and name into the homes of America. Still, although the prominent conductors Dmitri Mitropoulos, Pierre Monteux, and Eugene Ormandy were stalwart in their support of her she had far fewer engagements with orchestras than did other singers of comparable stature; it is unclear whether this was due to racial discrimination, but for whatever reasons it changed for the better after World War II.

The years from 1939 to 1943 brought problems: Europe was shut off by the onset of World War II. Kosti Vehanen, her faithful and deeply sympathetic accompanist, got himself involved in some kind of sexual indiscretion and on the advice of Hurok quietly returned to Scandinavia, so Anderson was forced to find a new pianist. In the summer of 1940 she selected an Austrian Franz Rupp, a fine musician who had worked with such instrumentalists as violinist Fritz Kreisler, cellist Emanuel Feuermann, and violist William Primrose, and whose wife had been an opera singer in Austria. Her repertoire shifted away from the Scandinavian she had worked on with Vehanen toward the German, especially the music of Brahms and Handel.

In the summer of 1943, Anderson married Orpheus Fisher (known in family circles as King, not be confused with her former accompanist Billy King), an old acquaintance who had for a number of years urged her to marry him and settle into a home. She was reluctant, recognizing the implicit demand that she give up her career; marriage on 17 July relieved but did not resolve the conflict of career versus home, which continued throughout most of her professional life. Marriage brought with it the problem of purchasing a home: ironically this would not have been a problem for Fisher who was light-skinned and passed easily back and forth (as did Billy King) between black and white worlds, but in spite of Anderson's stature as an internationally recognized artist, when she was known as the purchaser houses were suddenly no longer for sale. (They were seeking a property in the northeast, i.e., near New York.) In the end, as Anderson told the writer Emily Kimbrough in an interview, they were forced to buy one hundred acres, twice as much land as they needed "so we wouldn't contaminate the neighborhood."[55] Even then, according to Fisher, the original owner tried to stop the sale but it was too late.[56]

Further honors came to Anderson: in 1940 she was awarded a membership medal from the NAACP; that same year she was given an honorary doctorate by Temple University, and in 1941 she received the Bok Award, given "to a Philadelphian who had done some service that redounds to the credit of the city." With the $10,000 award Anderson put in place the Marian Anderson Scholarship Fund; on the basis of a competition this Fund awarded grants of a few hundred to a thousand dollars to vocalists between the ages of sixteen and thirty (it continued to give grants until 1973). In 1942 Anderson was invited by the DAR to sing in Constitution Hall, in support of the war effort. Anderson requested unsegregated seating; to both her and Hurok's surprise the request was honored, and she sang there on 7 January 1943. Touring continued during the war years, with the addition now of frequent performances for soldiers, in hospitals and at military camps. The singer was now regularly accompanied by a Hurok representative, Isaac Jofe, who made all arrangements and undoubtedly shielded Anderson from many uncomfortable confrontations with hotel staff, hall managers, in restaurants (she carried with her, in addition to iron, ironing board, and sewing machine, a hotplate and some dishes so that she could if necessary make a meal in her room).

In 1944, Anderson began to suffer vocal problems. She had earlier been susceptible to problems brought on by fatigue, and had wisely insisted that she not be subjected to overwork. Now, however, critics began to note specific problems— flatness of pitch on occasion or unevenness over her range. She found eventually an excellent coach, Edyth Walker who was able to help her considerably, but early in January 1946 a cyst was discovered on her esophagus. Throughout 1947 and the spring of 1948 she continued to perform; finally in June of 1948 she was forced to have surgery. The thought of removing a cyst so close to her vocal cords was dreadful; the surgery was, however, entirely successful and by the end of August she was once again working, very carefully, with Franz Rupp. By the spring of 1949 she was ready to sing, and sailed with Rupp for her first European tour since World War II. They performed in Paris, London, Scandinavia (Kosti Vehanen played for her in Stockholm, a grand reunion), Switzerland, Belgium, the Netherlands. She was presented with the Order of the White Rose, Finland's highest civilian award, for her work in furthering the music of Sibelius and of Yrjö Kilpinen. But she noticed, as did others, that fatigue was affecting her voice. Critics in Stockholm noted that her singing took more work, her *forte* was less free, flatness of pitch was remarked upon. In Brussels, the review was harsh: "this [singer] would be merely her double and a mere reflection of her, I would say to you that the real, the great Marian Anderson survives in our memories."[57] In Liège the critic wrote that "only in the Negro spirituals" did she have the same old power.[58] Style and interpretation, those qualities that had eluded her for so long, became now the focus of praise. For example, the critic for the *Neue Zeitung* wrote of her concert in Munich: "the astonishing empathy and adaptability with which Anderson made the specifically German emotional world of the Schubert lied her own . . . in critical places one is surprised by a wonderfully accomplished phrase or even a single tone in which her soul seems to open. From such moments the whole song achieves a new illumination. Her natural expressiveness imparts to songs like 'Der Erlkönig' and 'Der Tod und das Mädchen' a deeply moving dramatic power, while in others, like 'Liebesbotschaft,' the charm of her delivery is spellbinding."[59]

In spite of such mixed reviews (and surely also her own reservations about her singing) and in the face of marital problems deriving from Fisher's desire for a stay-at-home wife, she continued to perform throughout the next decade. A pattern was established: a tour of the United States during the fall and winter, central America in the spring, followed by Europe and then South America in the summer. In 1953 she toured as far as Japan, where she sang at the Japanese court for the empress Nagako, and Korea, where she sang for the soldiers both in the field and in hospitals. Vocal problems continued to be noted in reviews, but her artistry was consistently praised.

The final musical bastion of the United States fell when in January 1955 Marian Anderson sang for the first time at the Metropolitan Opera in New York City. The Met's general director, Rudolf Bing, who strongly advocated hiring without heed of race or any other non-musical attribute, asked Sol Hurok at a party if Anderson might be interested in singing there. It should be noted that as early as 1944 the New York City Opera, founded by László Halász, had hired black singers; Hurok felt, however, that Anderson should sing opera in New York at the Metropolitan or not at all. One month short of her fifty-eighth birthday, Anderson sang two performances as Ulrica in Verdi's *Un ballo maschera*. It may well have been the most difficult feat of her career, but everyone from directors to coaches was eager to help her. Olin Downes wrote for the *New York Times* that in spite of problems in Ulrica's first appearance in the opera, soon "her voice took on its normal resonance and emotional appeal . . . There was no moment in which Miss Anderson's interpretation was commonplace or repetitive in effect. In Ulrica's one-half act, by her native sensibility, intelligence, and vocal art, Miss Anderson stamped herself in the memory and the lasting esteem of those who listened."[60] Other critics were not so gentle and referred to vocal problems, regretting with much justice that the debut came so late in Anderson's career.

There was no question that Anderson's voice was deteriorating, even as her interpretative abilities grew. The magazine, *Jet,* published in April 1954 a collection of reviews of Anderson's present work: the harshest was by the *Chicago Tribune*'s Claudia Cassidy (known for her extreme views), saying that Anderson was "in the pitiful dusk of a glorious career" and that her voice was now "a ravaged ghost, rusted, unsteady, often (painfully) out of tune."[61] But in January of the same year the critic for the *New York Times* had written "She brings such sincerity, such imaginative insight, and such comprehending musicianship to everything she does that she always makes a deep impression. Each of her selections, too, emerges as a small, self-contained drama, which is freshly conceived and tellingly projected."[62] Similar pairs of reviews prevailed throughout this last part of Anderson's career. Reception of her 1955 tour of Israel in 1955 is typical. The critics noted problems with technical resources, but were united in praising her artistry and style, referring to her "uniquely warm-hearted talent for expressing Schubert songs, their melodic line, and . . . the appropriate tonal color to them . . . achieving unsurpassed vocal perfection in songs like 'Wohin,' 'Tod und das Mädchen,' and 'Erlkönig.'"[63] In Jerusalem she sang Brahms's *Alto Rhapsody* in Hebrew. The critics marveled at this feat, but they also fervently praised the interpretation: "Recovered from her indisposition she had not only perfect control in all registers of her wonderful voice, but the deepest penetration into the spirit of this masterpiece. One could scarcely imagine a more moving rendition."[64] Her 1959 Carnegie Hall concert demonstrated once again her stature as an artist and her loss of vocal resources. Ross Parmenter wrote in the *New York Times* that "as an interpreter, as a mistress of dramatic projection and as a compassionate human being of moving sincerity, the contralto was as impressive as ever." He had to add, however, that "the years have taken the toll of her vocal resources. For all the early part of her program last night, her voice was thin, reedy and shaky. And later, when she was able to summon up more volume, it was not always under the surest control."[65] She was sixty-two.

Still she did not quit. In 1957 she was elected Woman of the Year by the American Association of University Women. In 1959, the same year that her tour in January garnered very poor reviews, she was appointed a member of the thirteenth United States delegation to the United Nations. In 1961 she sang the Star-Spangled Banner at the inauguration of John F. Kennedy as President of the United States; in May of that year she attended a conference in the Soviet Union and the Casals Festival in San Juan, Puerto Rico; and in October she undertook another European tour, singing in London, Paris, and Scandinavia. To this she added Australia and New Zealand, and sang a special broadcast from Berlin on Christmas Day. In 1963 she took part in an integrated tour of Texas in February, a real milestone in race relations in the United States, and she participated in the NAACP March on Washington in August. In July of that year President Kennedy awarded her the Presidential Medal of Freedom, which was presented her on 6 December by Lyndon B. Johnson, President now after the assassination on 22 November of President Kennedy. Finally, at the end of 1963, she announced that her retirement would take place after one final world tour. That final tour began in October 1964 in the DAR's Constitution Hall in Washington and ended on 18 April 1965 in Carnegie Hall. Although she did make a few more singing appearances and several as narrator—in Copland's *Lincoln Portrait* for example—her career was at an end. The very last appearance, nicely, was with her nephew James DePreist conducting the Chicago Symphony Orchestra on 10 July 1966; she narrated Copland's *Preamble for a Solemn Occasion* and sang a group of spirituals at the end of the program.[66]

Anderson's mother Anna had died 10 January 1964; her husband King died 26 March 1986; on 1 February 1990 her sister Ethel DePreist died. In 1991 Anderson underwent a routine physical examination which detected early bowel cancer. She refused any kind of intervention, but continued to lead a life as normal as possible. In July 1992 she flew to Portland, Oregon, to live with her nephew Jimmy DePreist and his wife Ginette. She died there on 8 April 1993.

* * * * *

Marian Anderson, the destroyer of racial hurdles, is of course the first image that comes to mind. Although she herself did not like this image, it would be unrealistic not to recognize the immensity of her achievement in opening doors for black singers. It would also be unrealistic not to acknowledge the immensity of the challenges she faced—from the difficulty of getting a high school education or of finding a voice teacher to the problems of conducting a singing career in a country where she often was not permitted to stay in hotels.[67] That she, unlike several of her contemporaries, e.g., Roland Hayes, Paul Robeson, chose to pursue her career in the United States instead of the much more liberal (at least with respect to race) countries in Europe, provokes wonder. Credit must be given appropriately to such supporters as Sol Hurok and Eleanor Roosevelt and to Anderson's own determination to work in her native land.

Marian Anderson's achievements in Europe are also significant, however, in a very different way. Although she had not enjoyed the solid basic training in music that Lillian Nordica could boast, she like Nordica was an American, and in addition to her blackness carried the mantle of her country on her shoulders. She like Nordica recognized her need for training in the repertoire of western Europe, and again like Nordica absolutely astounded her contemporaries with her determination and her willingness to work. In Europe Anderson was not just a black singer; she was also an American singer. When Dean Dixon was appointed conductor of the Frankfurt Radio-Orchestra, the German citizenry shook their heads, not because he was black but because he was American. Marian Anderson demonstrated, as had Nordica and such other singers as Emma Nevada, Minnie Hauk, Olive Fremstad, that American singers, in addition to displaying formidable technique, *could* achieve an understanding of and the ability to communicate the depth of European music.

Finally, an overview of Anderson's development from being merely the owner of a remarkable voice to being a consummate artist is instructive for all singers but especially for those who have experienced forms of discrimination that prevented them from growing into their inherent gifts. If racism coupled with poverty prevented her rapid growth, her intelligence, persistence, and determination brought her, however slowly, to full realization of her artistic power.

In looking back over her life, it seems tragic that so many of her achievements were accomplished so late. Early in her career, critics admired the beauty of her voice and deplored her lack of artistic maturity; in her final years as a singer her vocal faults were remarked while her artistry was praised. The period of about twenty years, 1931–1953, when voice and musicianship were equally matched seems woefully brief. But surely there has rarely been anyone who accepted challenges with such fortitude and the glories of success with such modesty as this black singer who truly laid open new paths for her artistic descendants.

Timeline

1897, 27 Feb	Marian Anderson born South Philadelphia, to John Berkley Anderson and Annie Delilah Rucker
1907	Early concert, printed handbills with Anderson's picture and "Come and hear the baby contralto, ten years old"
1910	Father died Dec; moved to his parents Isabella and Benjamin (died 1911)
1912	Graduated from grade school; no high school
1914-1921	Struggles for education; 1914 People's Chorus concert; rejection by music school; first teacher: M. S. Patterson, black contralto
1915, 23 Jun	People's Chorus benefit for Marian's education raised $250 New teacher Agnes Reifsnyder, white contralto
1915	Return to high school, William Penn, business-oriented
1916, Easter	Sang alto solos in *Messiah* with Roland Hayes
1917, May	First experience singing in the deep south
1918, fall	Transferred to South Philadelphia High School for Girls
1919, summer	Studied 6 weeks with Oscar Saenger, Chicago; heard by NAACP
1919, late fall, or 1920	Began vocal study with Giuseppe Boghetti
1921, 20 June	Graduated from high school
1921-1928	Tours with Billy King; first recordings for RCA Victor (spirituals)
1923, 23 Dec	Debut with Philharmonic Society, at Academy of Music; first black artist to appear with the Society
1924, 18 Feb	Renaissance Casino in Harlem (New York City): well-received
1924, 10 Apr	Town Hall, New York, disaster, half-full hall, poor reviews
1925	Won Lewisohn Stadium contest; 26 Aug concert
1925-1926	Tours mainly in south, audiences segregated and unsegregated; travel always difficult, humiliations, frustrations
1927, fall	London, worked with Roger Quilter, Raimund von Zur Mühlen, Louis Drysdale; studied German, French; contacts with Amanda Ira Aldrich (pupil of Lind), Mark Raphael, Alberta Hunter (blues singer), Elena Gerhardt; problems of black musicians in London
1928, 15 Jun	Wigmore Hall, European debut
1928, 16 Aug	London Proms
1928, 28 Sep	Return to United States
1929-1930	Contract Judson management, disappointing
1929, June	Success in Seattle with American Philharmonic Orchestra
1929, Nov	Chicago, Orchestra Hall concert, led to Rosenwald fellowship
1929, 30 Dec	Carnegie Hall, spirituals praised, German lieder beyond her
1930, summer	Berlin, studied with Kurt Johnen.
1930, 10 Oct	Berlin debut Bachsaal; Nazi threat growing
1930, fall	Tours in Scandinavia, hectic, stunning successes, first black

	singer to perform in Scandinavia; United States tours expanded; Judson management still disappointing; return to Berlin to study with Johnen
1931, fall	Second Scandinavian tour; visit to Jan Sibelius, Nov
1932	Back in United States, still with Judson, 20 concerts over 5 months; work with Hall Johnson; studies with Frank La Forge; economic depression, unemployment, few concerts; accepted offer of concerts in Scandinavia, Oct and Nov
1933, fall	Scandinavian tour: great success, tour extended to 20 concerts in Jan, Feb 1934, extended to another 30+, with a raise of fee
1934, 2 May	Paris debut, Salle Gaveau; triumph
1934–1935	Tours in Scandinavia, Soviet Union, recitals in Paris and London; enthusiastic reviews; met Shostakovich, Ippolitov-Ivanov, Stanslavsky; sang in Nazi Salzburg; Arturo Toscanini: "What I heard today one is privileged to hear only once in a hundred years"; end of contract with Judson, return to US as Hurok artist
1935, 30 Dec	Town Hall, New York, with broken ankle; triumph at home
1936 16 Jan	Philadelphia Academy of Music, huge success.
1936 20 Jan	Carnegie Hall New York, packed, Anderson famous
1936	Tour of United States, sang at White House for Roosevelts
1936, Apr	Europe, tour in Spain, 2 concerts Salzburg summer (not part of Festival)
1937 Jan	Tour across United States: 44 concerts
1937 May	Sang at Ann Arbor May Music Festival, Ormandy conductor
1937–1938	60 concerts; according to Hurok, Anderson earned $238,000
1938–1939	80 concerts; requested Hurok limit her engagements; Anderson now significant part of American musical scene in spite of racial problems that banned her performing or prohibited black people from attending her concerts; sang in Houston, San Antonio, Fort Worth, Dallas; radio important venue; fee usually $2,000 Honors: Howard University doctorate,
1939	Ban by DAR on Anderson's concert in Constitution Hall; involvement of NAACP, Eleanor Roosevelt, Harold Ickes, Washington School Board and Washington chapter of American Federation of Teachers, formation of Marian Anderson Citizens' Committee, Roosevelt's resignation from DAR 26 Feb 1939 and "My Day" column 27 Feb Washington, Lincoln Memorial Concert Easter Sunday, 75,000 people
1939, 8 Jun	Sang at White House for King George VI and Queen Elizabeth
1939, 2 Jul	Spingarn Medal for "highest or noblest achievement by an American Negro during the preceding year or years" presented by Eleanor Roosevelt

1940, summer	Kosti Vehanen forced to return to Scandinavia; new pianist, Franz Rupp; shift in repertoire from Scandinavian toward German; recordings with Rupp; new contract with Hurok: no more than 50/60 concerts in US per year, Anderson to get 2/3 of gross (usual Hurok practice for his top artists)
1940	NAACP membership medal; Temple University honorary doctorate
1941	Bok Award, $10,000, used to set up Marian Anderson Scholarship Fund; recording ended (ban on record production except for war effort and use in home until Dec 1944); continued radio work
1942, Sep	Invited by DAR to sing in Constitution Hall on Anderson's terms
1943, 6 Jan	Dedication of mural commemorating Lincoln Memorial Concert, Harold Ickes spoke again
1943, 7 Jan	DAR-sponsored concert in Constitution Hall; proceeds given by Anderson to United China Relief, instead of Army Emergency Relief Fund
1943, 17 Jul	Married Orpheus Fisher, ages given as 38 and 43, actually 46 and 42
1944, Dec.	Returned to recording with Rupp; vocal problems; found help with Edyth Walker during late 1940s
1946, Jan	Discovered cyst on esophagus, put off surgery
1946, end	Subject of cover story in *Time*
1947, spring	Health poor; continued singing, forced to quit early summer 1948
1948, 29 Jun	Surgery successful: removed cyst without touching vocal cords; new contract with Hurok, 70 per cent of gross
1949, spring	European tour: Paris, London, Scandinavia, Switzerland, Belgium, Netherlands. Paul Robeson stirring up political furor Order of the White Rose, Finnish government, for her championing music of Sibelius and Kilpinen; fatigue affecting performances and voice; marital conflicts: Anderson's continued performing versus Fisher's desire for stay-at-home wife
1949-50	15th annual American tour; European tour in summer, followed by South American tour; pattern for decade: United States tour in fall, winter, central America in spring, Europe, South America in summer
1950s	Criticized for refusal to take stand against segregation; Richmond (Virginia) concert picketed, tickets returned, blacks did not attend
1952 Jan	Sang for first unsegregated audiences in Florida (Jacksonville, Miami)
1952 Apr	Sang at Lincoln Memorial during memorial service for Harold Ickes
1953, 14 Mar	Sang to unsegregated audience in DAR's Constitution Hall
1953, spring	Japan tour; sang at Japanese court for empress Nagako; Korea,

concerts, sang for troops in field and in hospitals; new home with Fisher; marital problems less severe; vocal problems, noted in reviews but with praise of growth as interpreter; *Litteris et Artibus*, from Swedish government, presented by King Gustav; Dickinson University, honorary doctorate; established Marian Anderson Recreation Center, South Philadelphia

1954, Sep	Hurok asked informally by Rudolf Bing if Anderson would sing at Metropolitan Opera
1955, Jan	Hired for 3 performances (did 2) to sing Ulrica in *Un ballo in maschera*; at Met; first performance 7 Jan; vocal problems persisted; worked with Marion Freschl
1955, spring	Concerts in Israel, sang Alto Rhapsody of Brahms in Hebrew
1957	Asian tour, for ANTA (American National Theater and Academy) AAUW Woman of the Year
1959	Selected as member of the 13th United States delegation to the United Nations; Jan tour, poor reviews
1961	Sang Star-Spangled Banner at presidential inauguration of John F. Kennedy
1961, spring	Soviet Union conference; Casals Festival, San Juan (Puerto Rico)
1961, fall	European tour, London, Paris, Scandinavia, Australia, New Zealand; Dec, Berlin, sang special broadcast for Christmas Day.
1962	King ill, hospitalized; Australia, New Zealand tour, critics disappointed (Anderson now 65)
1963, Feb	Integrated tour of Texas, milestone in race relations; Austin stayed in Driskill Hotel's Jim Hogg suite
1963, 28 Aug	March on Washington by NAACP, with Anderson, Camilla Williams, Mahalia Jackson
1963, Jul	Awarded Presidential Medal of Freedom by Kennedy, presented 6 Dec by now-President Lyndon B. Johnson (after Kennedy's assassination)
1963, 12 Dec	Announced retirement after world tour
1964, 10 Jan	Anna Anderson died
1965, 3 Jul	Narrated Copland, *A Lincoln Portrait*; continued to do narrations after retirement as singer
1966, 9,10 Jul	Last public appearances, Chicago Symphony, under nephew James DePreist
1975, Jan	Fisher had serious stroke, recovered enough to go home
1977, 27 Feb	Carnegie Hall, 75th birthday celebration (she really 80!)
1977	United Nations Peace Prize
1978, Aug	Congressional Medal
1986, 26 Mar	Fisher died
1990, 1 Feb	Ethel DePreist (sister; mother of James) died
1991, summer	Routine exam showed early bowel cancer; refused surgery or

	other intervention
1992, 9 July	Moved to Portland, Oregon, to live with Ginette and James DePreist
1993, 27 Feb	Anderson 96; Mar, suffered epileptic seizure
1993, 8 Apr	Died, 4:30 a.m., in Portland

Bibliography

Many books have been written about Marian Anderson. They range from stories for children to slightly mawkish tales for adults. The works listed below are the most important for learning about Anderson's life and career. Of these, the biography that appeared in 2000 by Allan Keiler stands in the forefront.

Works about Anderson
Anderson, Marian. *My Lord, What a Morning: An Autobiography by Marian Anderson*. New York: The Viking Press, 1956.
> Written with Howard Taubman (music critic for *The New York Times*). A moving, fairly accurate account of her life and work.
Keiler, Allan. *Marian Anderson:A Singer's Journey*. New York, London: Scribner, 2000.
> Well-written, thorough, objective, everything impeccably documented, excellent bibliography and discography, this book <u>must</u> be a starting point for anyone wishing to learn about Marian Anderson. Keiler has worked extensively with the archives of unpublished materials in various collections, including the Eleanor Roosevelt Papers, the Library of Congress NAACP Papers, the Women's History Archive at Smith College, and the Marian Anderson Papers at the University of Pennsylvania. He also interviewed Miss Anderson in the last year of her life and worked with the full cooperation of her nephew James DePreist.
Sims, Janet L. *Marian Anderson: An Annotated Bibliography and Discography*. Westport, CT: Greenwood Press, 1981.
> An excellent and thorough compilation of information about research sources and Anderson's recordings.
Vehanen, Kosti. *Marian Anderson: A Portrait*. New York and London: McGraw Hill Book Company, Inc., 1941.
> This book by Anderson's long-time accompanist gives many insights into her way of working, of studying repertoire, and her attitude toward performing.

General Reference Works
Bing, Sir Rudolf. *5000 Nights at the Opera*. Mattituck, N.Y.: Ameron House, 1972.
Goodwin, Doris Kearns. *No Ordinary Time. Franklin and Eleanor Roosevelt: The Home Front in World War II*. New York: Simon & Schuster, 1994.
Hurok, Sol, with Ruthe Goode. *Impresario: A Memoir*. New York: Random House, 1946.
Kessler, Harry, Graf. *In the Twenties: The Diaries of Harry Kessler*. Trnaslated by Charles Kessler. New York: Holt, Rinehart and Winston, 1971.
Kirby, John B. *Black Americans in the Roosevelt Era: Liberalism and Race*. Knoxville: University of Tennessee Press, 1980.
Lash, Joseph P. *Eleanor and Franklin: The Story of Their Relationship Based on Eleanor Roosevelt's Private Papers*. New York: W. W. Norton and Company, 1971.

Noble, Jeanne L. *Beautiful, Also, Are the Souls of My Black Sisters: A History of the Black Woman in America.* Englewood Cliffs, N.J.: Prentice-Hall, 1978.

Southern, Eileen. *Biographical Dictionary of Afro-American and African Musicians.* Westport, Conn.: Greenwood Press, 1982.

Steane, J. B. *The Grand Tradition: Seventy Years of Singing on Record.* London: Duckworth, 1974.

Watkins, T. H. *The Great Depression: America in the 1930s.* Boston: Little, Brown and Company, 1993.

Notes

All references to the print edition of the *New Grove Dictionary of Music & Musicians*, ed. Stanley Sadie (London: Macmillan Publishers Limited, 1980) are to the first edition published in 1980 and are cited simply as *New Grove*. All references to *Grove Music Online*, ed. L. Macy (http://www.grovemusic.com) are cited as *Grove Music Online*, with the date of access.

Chapter 1

1. Anthony Newcomb, *The Madrigal at Ferrara, 1579–1597,* 2 vols. (Princeton: Princeton University Press, 1980), 1:7–11.

2. See Baldessare Castaglione, *The Book of the Courtier*, The Singleton Translation, An Authoritative Text Criticism, ed. Daniel Javitch (New York and London: W. W. Norton & Company, 2002), Book II, especially item 12, p. 76.

3. Newcomb, *The Madrigal,* 1:99. See pages 1:90–103 for discussion of the *concerti delle donne* in Florence, Rome, and Mantua. Alfred Einstein's *The Italian Madrigal,* 3 vols. (Princeton: Princeton University Press, 1949), 2:825–35, also offers descriptions of the *concerto delle donne* at the Ferrara court; see especially 2:826–27 for lively descriptions by visitors of a musical evening during which Peverara sang and for accounts of the festivities celebrating her marriage. Iain Fenlon provides an excellent study of music at the Mantuan court in *Music and Patronage in Sixteenth-Century Mantua,* 2 vols. (Cambridge: Cambridge University Press, 1980).

4. *Vincenzo Giustiniani: Discorso sopra la musica,* trans. Carol MacClintock, *Musicological Studies and Documents* (n.c.: American Institute of Musicology, 1962), 9, 69.

5. Luzzaschi's 1601 publication, *Madrigali per cantare et sonare, A uno e doi, e tre Soprani, fatti per la Musica del già Ser^mo Duca Alfonso d'Este* includes three pieces that well represent the repertoire of the Ferrara court: "Aura soave di segreti accenti," "O primavera gioventù dell'anno," and "Ch'io non t'ami."

6. Newcomb, *The Madrigal,* 1:App. I, 183–84. D'Arco died 20 June 1611.

7. Giustiniani, *Discorso,* 70–71.

8. Striggio to Duke Francesco de' Medici, 29 July 1584, quoted in Newcomb, *The Madrigal,* 1:55.

9. Caccini to Grand Duke Ferdinand de' Medici, 11 October 1592, quoted in Newcomb, *The Madrigal,* 1:58.

10. Urbani, the Florentine ambassador in Ferrara, reporting to the Florence court, March 1580, quoted in Newcomb, *The Madrigal,* 1:11.

11. Brancaccio's assignment was to "take part now and then in a *musica secreta,* which is being prepared by some ladies of the court." See Anthony Newcomb, "Courtesans, Muses, or Musicians" in *Women Making Music,* ed. Jane Bowers and Judith Tick (Urbana and Chicago: University of Illinois Press, 1987), 95–96. Considering himself a nobleman rather than a musician required to sing when requested, Brancaccio refused to sing on the occasion of a visit in 1583 by the Duke de Joyeuse; he was summarily dismissed from the Ferrara court (Newcomb, *The Madrigal,* 1:App. I, 186).

12. Cavalier Giacomo Grana to ?, 8 September 1582, quoted in Newcomb, *The Madrigal,* 1:67.

13. Leonardo Conosciutti to ?, 28 July 1584, quoted in Newcomb, *The Madrigal,* 1:68.

14. Claudio Monteverdi, *Canti amorosi* in *Madrigali guerrieri, et amorosi,* 1638 (rev. ed., Vienna: Universal Edition, 1967), 246–58. Newcomb (*The Madrigal,* 1:27–28, 28 n) believes this passage may be a description of the ladies' singing.

15. Monteverdi's avant-garde writing in his madrigals came in for severe criticism from Giovanni Maria Artusi (c.1540–1613) in his theoretical treatise, *L'Artusi, overo delle imperfettioni della moderna musica ragionamenti dui* (Venice, 1600). Monteverdi's brother, Giulio Cesare, responded to these criticisms in the *Foreword* to *Il quinto libro de'madrigali* [1605] (printed at the end of Monteverdi's *Scherzi musicali,* Venice, 1607) with what has become the standard definition of the new music, the *seconda prattica,* of the seventeenth century: "By Second Practice . . . he understands the one that turns on the perfection of the 'melody,' that is, the one that considers harmony commanded, not commanding and makes the words the mistress of the harmony." "Claudio and Giulio Cesare Monteverdi," *Source Readings in Music History,* rev. ed., ed. Leo Treitler (New York and London: W. W. Norton & Company, 1998), 540.

16. Charles Peter Brand, *Torquato Tasso: A Study of the Poet and of His Contribution to English Literature* (Cambridge: At the University Press, 1965), 11, 143–44. Since Tasso could surely not have loved Peverara before she attained

the mature age of 10 or 11, this means that she would have been born c. 1553 and thus in 1580 she would have been at least twenty-seven—not exactly young by sixteenth-century standards, even though reports in 1580 refer to "a young lady." It also means that she was still singing and amazing her listeners when she was thirty-nine, in 1592. Newcomb puts her birth earlier at c. 1545 which would make her thirty-five at the time of her employment by the Ferrarese court and forty-seven in 1592.

17. Urbani, Dispatch of 22 February 1583, quoted in Newcomb, *The Madrigal,* 1:39 and App. V, no. 46 (1:267).

18. See Newcomb, *The Madrigal,* App. I, 1:187–90, for general information about Peverara. See above, note 16, for discussion of Peverara's birth date.

19. Castiglione, Book 3, item 9, 154–55.

20. Newcomb, "Courtesans," 96.

21. See Newcomb, *The Madrigal,* App. I, for biographical information about d'Arco, Guarini, and Molza. Anna Guarini was murdered on 2 May 1598 by her jealous husband, Ercole Trotti.

22. Ibid., 153. Alfonso died without an heir and the realm was handed over by the Pope Clement VIII to his nephew Pietro Aldobrandini in late 1598.

23. Einstein, *The Italian Madrigal,* 827, says 5 January.

24. Newcomb, "Courtesans," especially 93–94.

25. Jacopo Peri, "To My Readers," preface to *L'Euridice: An Opera in One Act, Five Scenes,* ed. Howard Mayer Brown in Recent Researches in the Music of the Baroque Era, vols. 36–37 (Madison: A-R Editions, Inc., 1981).

26. "con la nuova maniera de pasaggi, e raddoppiate inuentati da mei quail hora ado pera cantando l'opere mie già molto tempo, Vittoria Archillei [*sic*], cantatrice di quala eccellenza, che mostra il grido della sua fama." Giulio Caccini, preface to *L'Euridice: Composta in musica in stile rappresentativo* (Firenze: Edizioni Musicali Otos, 1980). Caccini's *L'Euridice* was completed and printed in December 1600 but was not performed until 5 December 1602; Peri's *Euridice* was performed on 6 October 1600 (Peri's earlier work, the pastoral *Dafne,* was first performed in 1598).

27. Sigismondo d'India, preface to *Il primo libro di musiche da cantar solo,* ed. Federico Mompellio, Instituta et Monumenta, Serie I: Monumenta No. 4 (Cremona: Athenaeum Cremonense, 1970), 24.

28. Giustiniani, *Discorso,* 70.

29. Quoted in Tim Carter, "Finding a Voice: Vittoria Archilei and the Florentine 'New Music,'" in *Feminism and Renaissance Studies,* ed. Lorna Hutson (Oxford: Oxford University Press, 1999),450–67, where the entire sonnet—the original Italian and English translation—is given. See also Carter, "A Florentine Wedding of 1608," *Acta musicologica* 55 (1983): 89–107.

30. Lucia Caccini was the first wife of Giulio; after her death sometime after 1590, he married her sister Margherita (Newcomb, *The Madrigal,* 1:91 n. 6).

31. Simone Cavallino da Viterbo, quoted in Iain Fenlon, *Music and Patronage*

in Sixteenth-Century Mantua (2 vols. Cambridge: Cambridge University Press, 1980), 1:131. Fenlon provides a thorough and fascinating account of the celebrations, 1:129–31.

32. Newcomb, *The Madrigal,* 1:93–95.

33. See Carter, "Vittoria Archilei," 452–56, for review of the biographical data concerning Archilei's personal and professional life.

34. See Pietro de' Bardi, "Letter to Giovanni Battista Doni, 1634" in *Source Readings in Music History,* rev. ed., 523–25, for the traditional account of the doings of the Florentine *Camerata.*

35. Luca Marenzio, "Cedan l'antiche tue chiare vittorie," *Il secondo libro de madrigali a sei voci* (Venice: Gardano, 1584).

36.   Tal forse intenerir col dolce canto
       Suol la bella Adriana i duri affetti
       E con la voce e con la vista intanto
       Gir per due strade a saettare i petti;
       (E in tal guisa Florinda udisti, o Manto,
       Là ne' teatri de' tuoi regi tetti,
       D'Arianna spiegar gli aspri martiri
       E trar da mille cor mille sospiri.
       Adone, 7.88.

Text and translation may be found in Ellen Rosand, *Opera in Seventeenth-Century Venice: The Creation of a Genre* (Berkeley: University of California Press, 1991), 384.

37. Ibid.

38. Colin Timms, "Monteverdi, Claudio," *New Grove.*

39. Prunières, *Monteverdi,* 78. Prunières adds that the commander-in-chief of the Mantuan army, Carlo Rossi, was unable to maintain order.

40. Timms, "Monteverdi," 524.

41. Newcomb, "Courtesans," 102–03.

42. Eric A. Nicholson, "The Theater," in *A History of Women in the West,* vol. 3: Renaissance and Enlightenment Paradoxes, ed. Natalie Zemon Davis and Arlette Farge (Cambridge, Mass.: Harvard University Press, 1993), 295–314.

43. Timms, "Andreini, Giovanni [Giovan] Battista,'" *New Grove.* Significantly *New Grove* has no entry for Giovanni Battista's mother, Isabella Andreini, who was well-known as performer, possibly composer, and particularly as a poet. Newcomb, ("Courtesans," 102–03) calls her "the most famous woman of the Italian stage from her debut in the late 1570s until her death in 1604." A one-line entry under Ramponi dismisses Virginia Ramponi Andreini as "Italian musician, wife of Giovanni Battista Andreini."

44. Tim Carter with Anne MacNeil, "Andreini [née Ramponi], Virginia ['La Florinda']," *Grove Music Online,* accessed 24 May 2004.

45. Ibid.

46. Both *La ferinda* and *La centaura* are discussed by Timms in his *New Grove*

entry for Andreini.
47. Rosand, *Opera,* 384.
48. Ibid.
49. Argia Bertini, "Basile, Adriana," *New Grove.*
50. ma à Mantua la Sig.ra Adriana benissimo cantare, benissimo sonare et benissimo parlare ho udito, sino quando tace et acorda, ha parte da essere mirate et lodate degnamente fui forzato assicurar la quanto. Monteverdi to Cardinal Ferdinando Gonzaga, 28 December 1610, *The Letters of Claudio Monteverdi,* rev. ed., trans. and ed. Denis Stevens (Oxford: Clarendon Press, 1995), 72.
51. Grillo to Monteverdi, 28 March 1610, Alfred Einstein, "Abbot Angelo Grillo's Letters as Source Material for Music History," in *Essays on Music* (New York: W. W. Norton & Company, Inc., 1962), 170–71.
52. Monteverdi to Cardinal Ferdinando Gonzaga, 22 June 1611, Denis Arnold and Nigel Fortune, eds., *The Monteverdi Companion* (New York: W. W. Norton & Company, Inc., 1968), 35.
53. André Maugars, "Response to an Inquisitive Person on the Italian Feeling about Music," in Carol MacClintock, comp., trans., ed., *Readings in the History of Music in Performance* (Bloomington and London: Indiana University Press, 1979), 122–23.

Chapter 2

1. *Il primo libro delle musiche á una e due voci,* which was published in Florence in 1618, has recently appeared in a handsome in a new edition: Francesca Caccini *Il primo libro delle musiche (1618):* A Modern Critical Edition, ed. Dragan Karolic (Kassel: Furore Verlag, 2003). A few songs are included in the anthology by A. Bonaventura, *Arie di Francesca Caccini e Barbara Strozzi* (Rome, 1930), and in Carolyn Raney, "Francesca Caccini, Musician to the Medici, and her *Primo Libro (1618)"* (Ph.D. diss., New York University, 1971). *La liberazione di Ruggiero dall'isola d'Alcina,* published in 1625, was recorded for the first time by Nannerl Records (NR-ARS 003) in 1993.
2. Claudio Monteverdi to Cardinal Ferdinando Gonzaga, 28 December 1610, *Letters of Monteverdi,* 72.
3. Doris Silbert, "Francesca Caccini, Called La Cecchina," *Musical Quarterly* 32 (1946): 51.
4. Carolyn Raney, "Francesca Caccini's 'Primo Libro,'" *Music and Letters* 48 (1967): 351.
5. Silbert, "Caccini," 53; see also Raney, "Caccini. (2) Francesca Caccini [Francesca Signorini; Francesca Signorini-Malaspina; Francesca Raffaelli; 'La Cecchina']," *Grove Music Online,* accessed 16 May 2004.
6. Raney, "Francesca Caccini's 'Primo Libro,'" 353.
7. Raney, "Francesca Caccini," *Grove Music Online,* accessed 16 May 2004.

8. See for example, "Ardo infelice, e palesar non tento," in Caccini *Il primo libro delle musiche (1618): A Modern Critical Edition,* 15–27.

9. Silbert, "Caccini," 50

10. Ibid., 61.

11. Ibid., 59.

12. Raney, "Francesca Caccini's 'Primo Libro,'" 357.

13. Karin Pendle, "Lost Voices," *Opera News* (1992): 18.

14. Francesca Caccini, *La liberazione di Ruggiero dall'isola d'Alcina.* Nannerl Records, NR-ARS 003.

15. Raney, "Caccini. (2) Francesca Caccini" *New Grove.*

16. See Caccini, "Dov' io credea le mie speranze vere," in *Il primo libro delle musiche (1618): A Modern Critical Edition,* 11–14.

17. Paolo Fabbri, *Monteverdi,* trans. Tim Carter (Cambridge: Cambridge University Press, 1994 (originally published in Italian as *Monteverdi,* Turin: E.D.T. Edizioni di Torino, 1985), 215–16.

18. See Pietro de' Bardi, "Letter to Giovanni Battista Doni, 1634" in *Source Readings in Music History,* 523–25 for the traditional account of the doings of the Florentine *Camerata.*

19. According to H. Wiley Hitchcock in his *New Grove* entry for Giulio Caccini, Caccini was so extremely jealous of Peri's success with first *Dafne* of 1598 and then *L'Euridice* that he forbade his own singers to sing Peri's music in *L'Euridice* insisting they sing music he composed for them, and he then rushed his own *L'Euridice* into print by December of 1600 (although it was not performed until 1602). Hitchcock's entry is very informative about Caccini's life and music.

20. Raney, "Francesca Caccini's 'Primo Libro,'" 351; Silbert, "Caccini," 52; also Raney, "Francesca Caccini," *Grove Music Online,* accessed 16 May 2004.

21. Emil Vogel,"Marco da Gagliano: Zur Geschichte des florentiner Musiklebens von 1570–1650," *Vierteljahrsschrift für Musikwissenschft,* 5 (1889): 422–23; Edmond Strainchamps, "New Light on the *Accademia degli Elevati* of Florence," *Musical Quarterly* 62 (1976): 507–35, 509–10.

22. Raney, "Francesca Caccini," *Grove Music Online,* accessed 16 May 2004.

23. Silbert, "Caccini," 52.

24. Raney, "Francesca Caccini's 'Primo Libro,'" 357.

Chapter 3

1. Ellen Rosand, "Barbara Strozzi, *virtuosissima cantatrice*: The Composer's Voice," *Journal of the American Musicological Society* 31 (1978): 241–81, 242 and n. 7. Sir John Hawkins, *A General History of the Science and Practice of Music* (1776; reprint of 1853 edition, New York: Dover Publications, Inc., 1963), 594.

2. Rosand, "Barbara Strozzi," 252–53.

3. Ibid., 253.

4. *Le glorie degli Incogniti overo gli huomini illustri dell'accademia de' Signori Incogniti* (Venice: Valvasense, 1647), quoted in Rosand, "Barbara Strozzi," 243. The book contains biographies of the illustrious members of the *Accademia degli Incogniti.*

5. François-Joseph Fétis, *Biographie universelle des musicians et bibliographie générale de la musique,* 8 vols. (Paris: Firmin Didot Frères, 1864) listed Opus 4 as *Cantate a voce sola.* Rosand ("Barbara Strozzi," 261 n. 73) points out that since Opus 3 was published in 1654 and Opus 5 in 1655, it may be that Opus 5 was simply misnumbered, and thus there never was an Opus 4. On the other hand there are very few examples of the other volumes, so Opus 4 may indeed have simply disappeared. The title given to Opus 4 by Fétis is different from the titles of Opus 3, *Cantate ariete a una, due e tre voci* and Opus 5, *Sacri musicali affetti*; it is similar, however, to the title of Opus 6: *Ariette a voce sola.*

6. Rosand, "Barbara Strozzi," 266–77. See especially the lengthy example presented in Rosand's article and her perceptive discussion of its stylistic implications.

7. Ibid., 242.

8. See Ellen Rosand, *Opera,* 230–32, for discussion and brief excerpts from *Le glorie* (published by the Incognito Press). A handsome portrait of Anna Renzi is provided on page 229.

9. Rosand, "Barbara Strozzi," 245.

10. This thorough education in musical arts and skills is not unprecedented: undoubtedly Laura Peverara, Tarquinia Molza, Livia d'Arco composed some of the music they sang; certainly their documented improvisations show their abilities in this area. Adriana Basile in a letter of 26 June 1620 to Isabelle of Savoy, refers to her own compositions (cited in Rosand, "Barbara Strozzi," 254), and Monteverdi suggests that Basile and her sisters write their own music for a wedding piece: "as regards the sirens, the three sisters (that is, Signora Adriana and the others [her sisters Margherita and Tolla]) would be able to sing them and also compose the music," Monteverdi to Alessandra Striggio, letter of 9 December 1616; *The New Monteverdi Companion,* ed. Denis Arnold and Nigel Fortune (London, Boston: Faber and Faber, 1985), 35.

11. Rosand, "Barbara Strozzi," 244–45.

12. Ibid., 256–57. Marcesso's collection was published in Venice by Magni, 1656; Tonalli's in Venice by Vincenti, 1656. See 260 n. 73 for detailed information about works by Strozzi in other anthologies.

13. Ibid. Rosand lists the dedicatees (259 n. 70) and prints of Strozzi's work (260 n. 73).

14. Beth Glixon, "New Light on the Life and Career of Barbara Strozzi," *Musical Quarterly* 81 (1997): 311–35; and "More on the Life and Death of Barbara Strozzi," *Musical Quarterly* 83 (1999): 134–41. The information about Strozzi's financial dealings, her children, and her relationship with Vidman is drawn entirely

from these two very important articles.

15. Rosand, "Barbara Strozzi," especially 249–52.

16. Ibid., 251.

17. Maurice Rowdon, *The Silver Age of Venice* (New York, Washington: Praeger Publishers, 1970), Chapter 8, "La Zentildonna," 92–113.

18. Carolyn Raney, "Strozzi, Barbara," *New Grove.*

19. Rosand, "Barbara Strozzi," 252.

20. Ellen Rosand and David Rosand, "Barbara di Santa Sofia and Il Prete Genovese: On the Identity of a Portrait by Bernardo Strozzi," *Art Bulletin* 63 (1981): 249–58. The portrait is now in the Gemäldegalerie in Dresden. Bernardo Strozzi is apparently entirely unrelated to Barbara; he also painted a portrait of Giulio Strozzi and the portrait of Claudio Monteverdi which is currently in the Tiroler Landesmuseum Ferdinandeum, Innsbruck.

21. The portrait of Strozzi is reproduced in the article by the Rosands; the portrait of Renzi appears in *New Grove* as well as in Ellen Rosand's *Opera in Seventeenth-Century Venice,* 229.

22. Rowdon, *Venice,* 94.

Chapter 4

1. Poi cominciasti afflitta
   Tue querele Canore
   Con tua voce divina,
   Disprezzata Regina,
   E seguendo il lamento
   Facevi di dolore
   Stillar in pianto, e sospirar Amore.
   Sò ben'io, che se vero
   Fosse stato il cordoglio,
   E l'historia funesta,
   Alla tua voce mesta,
   Alle dolci parole, ai cari detti.
   Si come i nostri petti
   Colmaro di pietade, ah sò ben'io,
   Neron s'havrebbe fatto humile, e pio.

This anonymous description is given in Ellen Rosand, *Opera,* 385.

2. Rosand, *Opera,* 232.

3. Ibid.

4. Ibid.

5. Ibid., 232–33.

6. See Rosand's discussion of operatic mad scenes in *Opera,* 121–22.

7. Ibid., 121–22; see also Gary Tomlinson, "Twice Bitten, Thrice Shy:

Monteverdi's 'finta' *Finta pazza*," *Journal of the American Musicological Society* 36 (1983): 303–11.

8. See Rosand, *Opera,* especially pp. 234–35, for discussion of Renzi's roles and her persona as a prima donna in seventeenth-century Venice.

9. John Evelyn, *The Diary of John Evelyn,* ed. William Bray (New York and London: M. Walter Dunne, Publisher, 1901), I; 202,

10. Ibid., I, 213.

11. Beth L. Glixon and Jonathan E. Glixon, "Marco Faustini and Venetian Opera Production in the 1650s: Recent Archival Discoveries," *The Journal of Musicology* 10, no. 1 (1992): 65.

12. Beth L. Glixon, "Private Lives of Public Women: Prima Donnas in Mid-Seventeenth-Century Venice," *Music & Letters* 76, no. 4 (1995): 518.

13. Ibid., 515–16. Glixon provides the complete text of the contract and discusses the implications of its terms.

14. Thomas Walker, "Renzi [Rentia, Renzini], Anna," *New Grove.*

15. Beth Glixon, "Private Lives," 519.

16. Strozzi, *Le glorie della signora Anna Renzi,* quoted in Rosand, *Opera,* 232.

17. See the discussion by Rosand of this link in "Barbara Strozzi," 249–53.

18. See Rosand, *Opera,* 119–24, for an informative discussion of opera devices and scene types.

Chapter 5

1. Evrard Titon du Tillet, "From the First Supplement to *The Parnassus of France*" (1743), in *Source Readings in Music History,* rev. ed., 572–73. Titon was first steward in the household of the Duchess of Burgundy married to the heir to the French throne, the grandson of Louis XIV. Titon proposed to erect an immense sculpture in honor of the great poets and musicians of the time of Louis XIV. He was unable to secure funding for the sculpture but published in 1727 a description with biographical information of all the figures to be included, with Lully at the highest point. He published several editions, each containing more great figures: the 1732 edition has 259 entries, and the supplement to the 1743 edition, "The Famous Actors and Actresses of the Comedy and Opera, Whom Death Has Taken or Who Have Left the Theater," opens with an essay on Marie Le Rochois.

2. Ibid., 572.

3. James R. Anthony, *French Baroque Music from Beaujoyeulx to Rameau,* rev. ed. (New York: W. W. Norton & Company, 1978), 116. See also pp. 20–21 and 57–58. Remnants of Lully's stranglehold on French music were still being felt in the nineteenth century, when for example Jacques Offenbach was long kept in his place by restrictions on the number and type of singers and instrumentalists allowed for his stage productions. Anthony also offers thorough

and well presented information about the complex history of the development of French music drama from the *cour de ballet* to the *tragédie lyrique*. See also his excellent entry for Lully in *New Grove*. Jean-Laurent le Cerf de la Viéville (1674–1707), French poet and musical amateur, was author of *Comparaison de la musique italienne et de la musique françoise* (3 vols., Brussels, 1704–1706), which is a veritable treasure house of information and informed opinion about French musical life of the late seventeenth century.

4. Titon, *Source Readings,* rev. ed., 572.

5. Quoted in Anthony, "Le Rochois, Marthe," in *New Grove*.

6. Titon, in *Source Readings*, rev. ed., 573.

7. The entire scene is reproduced in the *Norton Anthology of Western Music,* 4th ed., ed. Claude V. Palisca (New York, London: W. W. Norton & Company, 2001), 405–12.

8. De Blainville, quoted in Anthony, *French Baroque Music,* 80.

9. See Edward R. Reilly, "Quantz on National Styles in Music," *Musical Quarterly* 49 (1963):173.

10. *Memoires,* III, 1787, 38; quoted in Anthony, *French Baroque Music,* 84.

11. See Anthony, *French Baroque Music,* 84–87, for discussion of the various types of French air.

12. François Raguenet, "Parallèle des italiens et des français," in *Source Readings in Music History,* ed. Oliver Strunk (New York: W. W. Norton, Inc., 1950), 485.

13. Ibid., 485 n. 8. The essay is given in the anonymous English translation of 1709. According to Sir John Hawkins, the translator was J. E. Galliard (*Source Readings in Music History,* 473 n. 1). See also *Source Readings in Music History,* rev. ed., 670–78.

14. Julie Anne Vertrees [Sadie], "Antier, Marie," *New Grove*. English and French views of dramatic presentations continued to war over the centuries: see the radically opposed critiques of Giuditta Pasta's work cited in Chapter 9, especially pages 115–20.

15. The most helpful sources of information about Le Rochois are Titon's *Parnassus,* in *Source Readings in Music History,* rev. ed., 571–74; and James R. Anthony, "Le Rochois, Marie," *Grove Music Online,* accessed 26 June 2004.

16. Julie Anne Sadie, comp. and ed., *Companion to Baroque Music* (London: J. M. Dent & Sons Ltd., 1990), 127.

17. James Anthony, "Le Rochois, Marie," *Grove Music Online,* accessed 26 June 2004.

18. Julie Anne Sadie, "Antier, Marie," *Grove Music Online,* accessed 26 June 2004.

19. C'était, dit-on, une actrice excellente, et l'on vante la manière dont elle jouait les rôles de magicienne dans les opéras de Lulli. Fétis, "Antier, Marie," *Biographie universelle.*

Chapter 6

1. Fétis, *Biographie universelle,* states that Handel brought Faustina to London specifically to avenge himself on Cuzzoni with whom he had had frequent and violent battles. See Fétis, "Sandoni, (Francesca Cuzzoni)."

2. Olga Termini, "From Ariodante to Ariodante: 'Ariodante' by Pollarolo (Venice, 1718)," introduction to Carlo Francesco Pollarolo and Antonio Salvi, *Ariodante: Partitura dell'opera in facsimile* (Venice: Istituto Italiano Antonio Vivaldi della fondazione Giorgio cini Venezia, Dipartimento di storia e critica delle arti della università di Venezia, Drammaturgia musicale Veneta 13 (Milan: G. Ricordi & C. s.p.a., 1986), xxxiv; xlix-l.

3. Pietro Francesco Tosi, *Observations on the Florid Song (Opinioni de' cantori antichi e moderni o sieno osservazioni sopra il canto figurato),* trans. Johann Ernst Galliard, 2nd ed. (London: J. Wilcox, 1743), 171.

4. Ibid.

5. Giambattista Mancini, *Practical Reflections on Figured Singing (Pensieri e riflessioni pratiche sopra il canto figurato),* editions of 1774 and 1777 compared, trans. and ed. Edward Foreman (Champaign, Ill.: Pro Musica Press, 1967), 11 n. S, 94–95. Mancini was a student in Naples in 1728 and in Bologna in 1730; he was active as a singer from 1736 ("Mancini," *New Grove Online,* accessed 26 June 2003) in Italy and Germany. Since Cuzzoni's career was floundering by 1748, he could only have heard her sing some thirty years before he wrote the *Pensieri* in 1774.

6. Charles Burney, *A General History of Music: From the Earliest Ages to the Present Period (1789)* (1776–1789; reprint of 1783 edition with critical and historical notes by Frank Mercer, New York: Dover Publications, Inc., 1957), 2:737.

7. Winton Dean and Carlo Vitali, "Cuzzoni, Francesca," *Grove Music Online,* accessed 6 June 2004.

8. Johann Joachim Quantz, "The Life of Herr Johann Joachim Quantz, as Sketched by Himself," in *Forgotten Musicians,* ed. Paul Nettl (New York: Greenwood Press, Publishers, 1969), 312.

9. Ibid.

10. C. Steven Larue, *Handel and His Singers: The Creation of the Royal Academy Operas, 1720–1728* (Oxford: Clarendon Press, 1995) See especially the chapter (144–81) devoted to Cuzzoni and Bordoni.

11. Ibid. See especially138–39 for an excellent discussion of these aspects of Cuzzoni's art.

12. Anne Schnoebelen, "Sandoni, Pietro Giuseppe," *Grove Music Online* accessed 16 June 2004.

13. John Mainwaring, *Memoirs of the Life of the Late George Frederic Handel* (1760, with a foreword by J. Merrill Knapp, New York: Da Capo Press, 1980, 110–11, note.

14. Burney, *History,* 2:737.

15. Hawkins, *History,* 874.

16. Burney, *History,* 2:737.

17. Dean and Vitali (*Grove Music Online,* accessed 21 June 2003) name Cuzzoni as the "first female high soprano to distinguish herself in prime roles." I concur, but would have Bordoni share the title.

18. Larue, *Handel and His Singers,* 144–81.

19. Hawkins, *History,* 874; Burney, *History,* 2:737.

20. Mancini, *Reflections,* 10.

21. Quantz, "Life," quoted in Burney, *History,* 2:745–46.

22. Ibid., 746.

23. See the discussion by Stephen Larue in *Handel and His Singers,* 144–81, of Handel's composing to the voices of his two sopranos.

24. Burney, *History,* 2:743 n; the editor Frank Mercer points out that this remark was in fact made at the first performance of *Ottone,* 12 January 1723.

25. Ibid., 2:745 n. j.

26. Kees Vlaardingerbroek, "Faustina Bordoni Applauds Jan Alensoon: A Dutch Music-Lover in Italy and France in 1723–4," *Music & Letters,* 72 (1991): 547.

27. George J. Buelow, "A Lesson in Operatic Performance Practice by Madame Faustina Bordoni" in *A Musical Offering: Essays in Honor of Martin Bernstein,* ed. Edward H. Clinkscale and Claire Brook (New York: Pendragon Press, 1977).

28. Ibid., 92.

29. See Termini, 1.

30. Micrander [Johann Gottlob Kittel], "A Pleasant Brook [Bach]," in *The New Bach Reader: A Life of Johann Sebastian Bach in Letters and Documents,* ed. Hans T. David and Arthur Mendel, rev. and exp. Christoph Wolff (New York, London: W. W. Norton & Company, 1998), no. 307, p. 311. See also Robert L. Marshall, "Bach the Progressive: Observations on His Later Works," *The Musical Quarterly* 62 (1976): 313–57, for a fascinating examination of the significance of music in Dresden for J. S. Bach in his later years.

31. A[rnold?] Niggli "Faustina Bordoni-Hasse," in *Sammlung musikalischer Vorträge,* ed. Paul Graf Waldersee (Leipzig: Breitkopf und Härtel, 1880), 300–01.

32. Gloria Eive, "From the Cloister to the Concert Hall: Faustina B. Hasse and Maddalena L. Sirmen," paper presented at national meeting of American Society for Eighteenth-Century Studies, New Orleans, 18–22 April 2001, and further personal communication. My warm thanks to Dr. Eive for her information about the sources of this finding.

33. Niggli, "Faustina," 317.

34. Tosi, *Observations,* 52.

35. Mancini, *Reflections,* 10.

36. "The trill described by me is upon one note only . . . [the rule is] to begin with the first crotchet and to beat every note with the throat upon the vowel 'a' unto the last breve." Giulio Caccini, *Le nuove musiche,* 1602, in *Source Readings*

in Music History, 384.

37. *London Journal,* 27 October 1722, quoted in Otto Erich Deutsch, *Handel: A Documentary Biography* (1925; reprint, New York: Da Capo Press, Inc., 1974), 136.

38. *London Journal,* 4 September 1725, quoted in Deutsch, *Handel,* 185.

39. Quantz, "Life," 313–14. The performance had to have taken place before 1 June when Quantz left England.

40. Hawkins, *History,* 873 n.

41. Dean and Vitali, "Cuzzoni."

42. Tosi, *Observations,* 170–72.

Chapter 7

1. Die Natur hatte mich mit allem was zu einer vollkommnen [*sic*] Sängerin nöthig ist, begünstigt, Gesundheit, Kraft, brillante Stimme, grossen Umfang, reine Intonation, geläufigen Hals, einen lebhaften, leidenschaftlichen, gefühlvollen Charakter. "Eine Selbstbiographie der Sängerin Gertrud Elisabeth Mara" (referred to henceforth as Autobiography), contributed by O. von Riesemann, *Allgemeine musikalische Zeitung* (*AmZ*) 10, no. 32 (18 August 1875): col. 531.

2. Hier war es nun, wo ich ... die göttlichen Gesange dieser liebenswürdigen Sängerin hinter meinem Ripienbasse belauschte, und durch sie, an jedem Conzerttage, meine Freude und Vergnügen an meiner Lieblingskunst erhöhet fand. Ernst Ludwig Gerber, *Historisch-biographisches Lexicon der Tonkünstler* (Leipzig: J. G. I. Breitkopf, 1790–1792), col. 858 (referred to henceforth as *Lexicon*).

3. Ich sah [die Bravour-Arie *mi parenti, il figlio indegno,* aus *Britannicus* von Graun] durch, nahm das Tempo (nach meiner Art) noch halbmahl so geschwind, als es meine Vorgängerin die *Astroa* gesungen hatte. Die Astroa war zu der Zeit berühmt, weil sie vielleicht die erste war, die schwere Passagen sang, hauptsächlich arpeggien, sie passirte also für ein *non plus ultra.* Da mir aber schon dergleichen Passagen vorgefallen waren und ich überhaupt meine Kehle auf allerley Art geübet hatte, so sang ich diese Arie ... noch halbmahl so geschwind, sodass das Orchester, welches ein solches Tempo nicht gewohnt war, Mühe hatte nach zu kommen, welches dann machte, dass man mich für eine Art von Hexe hielt. Der König schien meine Fertigkeit zu bewundern. Die Arie war auch eine würkliche Aufgabe von Schwierigkeiten, lauter Arpeggios von Anfang bis zu Ende; sie war gewiss schuld, dass nachher alle Componisten, welche für mich zu schreiben hatten, das unsinnigste Zeug zusammen setzten was sie nur erdenken konnten. Ich kann deshalb nicht begreifen, warum man so viel Wunder aus der Catalani ihrem geläufigen Hals gemacht hat? Denn ich bin völlig überzeugt, dass ich die Passagen weit schneller als sie gemacht habe, und zwar mit Ausdruck, Schatten und Licht; davon weiss sie nichts. Autobiography, *AmZ* 10, no. 34 (25 August 1875): col. 534.

4. Ihre Stimme ist glänzend, voll und tönend, und bey einer bewundernswurdigen Leichtigkeit, so stark, dass ich sie mehrmals in Leipzig durch Chöre mit Pauken und Trompeten, welche mit nahe an funfzig Sängern und spielern besetzt waren, ohne dass sie sich im geringsten Gewalt anthat, deutlich vorgehöret habe. Ihr erstaunender Unfang, erstreckt sich vom ungestrichenen g bis dreygestrichenem e, vollkommen egal und gleich stark. Sie bringet durch ihren hellen Gesang alle Fibern der Zuhörer in Bewegung und setzt jedermann durch die Schnelligkeit, durch die Vollkommenheit und Runde ihrer Passagien in Entzücken und Erstaunen. Die von Bewunderung erfüllte Seele des Zuhörers erlaubt ihm nicht sie auszuhören; ein allgemeiner lauter Beyfall unterbricht gewöhnlich ihren Gesang. Und die grössten, die gewagtesten Schwierigkeiten verschwinden durch die Leichtigkeit, mit der sie sie vorträgt. Ihre eigenthümliche Manier ist zwar die Bravourarie. Aber vermöge ihres göttlichen Talents und ihrer vortreflichen Einsichten, singt sie auch Rondos und Adagios mit grosser Annehmlichkeit und Empfindung. Und es ist merkwürdig, dass sie im Conzert spiytuel zu Paris, die grosse Erwartung, die die Franzosen von ihr hatten, durch ein ausdruckvolles Rondo von Naumann, Tu m'intendi, vollkommen befriedigte. Sie singt ubrigens Deutsch, Italienisch, Französisch und Englisch, jede dieser Sprachen mit vollkommener Deutlichkeit und dem vortreflichsten Accente.

Sie ist nicht gross von Person, auch keine Schönheit, aber deswegen von keiner unangenehmen Bildung. Vielmehr leuchtet aus jedem ihrer Züge ihr vortrefl. Herz hervor, welches macht, dass man auf dem ersten Blick von ihr eingenommen ist. Gerber, *Lexicon,* cols. 856–65.

5. *Musical Reminiscences of the Earl of Mount Edgcumbe: Containing an Account of the Italian Opera in England from 1773 to 1834,* 4th ed., 1834 (reprint, New York: Da Capo Press, 1973), 52–53.

6. Ian Woodfield, *Opera and Drama in Eighteenth-Century London: The King's Theatre, Garrick and the Business of Performance* (Cambridge: Cambridge University Press, 2001), 148–52.

7. Ibid., 151.

8. George Hogarth, *Memoirs of the Musical Drama* (London: Richard Bentley, 1838), 216.

9. Burney, quoted in Hogarth, *Memoirs,* 219–20.

10. Burney, *History,* 2:893.

11. Ibid., 2:897.

12. Hogarth, *Memoirs,* 447–48.

13. Mount Edgcumbe, *Reminiscences,* 75.

14. die Mara hat gar nicht das glück gehabt mir zu gefallen—sie macht zu wenig um einer Bastardina gleich zu kommen—(denn, dies ist ihr fach;—) und macht zu viel—um das herz zu rühren wie eine Weber—oder, eine vernünftige Sängerin—. Letter to Leopold Mozart, Munich, 13 November 1780, in *Mozart: Briefe und Aufzeichnungen* (Kassel, London, New York: Bärenreiter, 1962), Vol. III, 18. La Bastardina, Lucrezia Agujari (1743–1783), illegitimate daughter of a

nobleman, listed in playbills as La Bastardina or La Bastardella, was known for the extremely wide range of her voice.

15. Zelter to Johann Wolfgang von Goethe, no date, quoted in Henry Fothergill Chorley, *Modern German Music* (1854; reprint, New York: Da Capo Press, 1973), 172.

16. Ibid., 173–74.

17. Mount Edgcumbe, *Reminiscences,* 115–16.

18. The biographical sketch draws mainly on two sources: Mara's Autobiography and the biography by Georg Christoph Grosheim: *Das Leben der Künstlerin Mara* (Cassel: Luckhardt'schen Hofbuchhandlung, 1823).

19. Zitter, wenn sie mit Drahtsaiten bezogen ist, welches damals als Mode-Instrument war und von allen Damen gespielt wurde. Ein deutscher Instrumentenmacher hatte eben eine mit einem tiefern Boden als gewöhnlich verfertigt, sie mit stärkern Saiten bezogen, wodurch sie einen schönen Ton bekam; mein Vater keufte sie mir. Autobiography, *AmZ* 10, no. 33 (18 August 1875): col. 514.

20. Grosheim, *Mara,* 20. According to *New Grove* (Christopher Hogwood and Charles Cudworth), Paradisi would have been Pietro Domenico Paradies, 1707–1791, a composer, harpsichord master, and especially singing teacher who worked in London from 1746 until near the end of his life.

21. einige englische Damen es nicht kleidend für ein Mädchen fanden. Autobiography, *AmZ* 10, no. 33 (18 August 1875): col. 515.

22. Art zu singen änderte sich, nachdem ich dem Casselschen und Braunschweigschen Theater fleissig und aufmerksam beygewohnt hatte. Autobiography, *AmZ* 10, no. 34 (25 August 1875): col. 530.

23. Pier Francesco Tosi (c. 1653–1752), an Italian castrato, was a proponent not only of the Italian school of singing but of the old, i.e., late seventeenth-, early eighteenth-century school of singing, ornamentation, etc. His treatise, *Opinioni de' cantori antichi e moderni* (1723), which was translated into Dutch (1731), English (1742), and German (1757), is an extremely important source of information about singers (e.g., Francesca Cuzzoni and Faustina Bordoni) and performance practice. See Tosi, *Observations,* 171.

24. Der Dienst war sehr commode. Der Carnaval dauerte ungefähr 6 Wochen; zwey Opern wurden einstudirt, jede 5 mal gegeben. Das Personal bestand in 8 Personen, *Porporino,* ein Contra-Alt und vortrefflicher Adagio-Sänger, war ein Mann von 60 Jahren *Concialini,* ein Sopran und angenehmer Cantabile-Sänger, mochte wohl 36 Jahr zählen . . . *Grassi,* ein mittelmässiger Tenorist, noch drey mittelmässige sopranisten. eine *Seconda Donna* Nahmens *Casparini* von 60 Jahren . . . und ich . . . Das Entrée zu der Opera war frey . . . Da das Opern-Haus sehr gross ist, so liess der König von einem jeden Regiment eine Compagnie ins Parterre gehen, um es zu erwärmen. Er selbst stand mit seinen Generals gleich hinter dem Orchester, und lorgnirte uns, sagte auch öfters Bravo. Autobiography, *AmZ* 10, no. 35 (1 September 1875): col. 545.

25. eine Cantate vor, welche durch seine leidenschaftliche Declamation, trotz

seiner rauhen Stimme, einen heftigen Eindruck auf mich machte. Autobiography, *AmZ* 10, no. 37 (15 September 1875): col. 579.

26. man sieht ihnen den stolz, grobheit, und wahre Effronterie im gesichte an. Letter to Leopold Mozart, Munich, 24 November 1780 in *Mozart: Briefe und Aufzeichnungen,* 3:31.

27. Grosheim, *Mara,* 45–47; also A. von Sternberg, *Berühmte deutschen Frauen des 18. Jahrhunderts* (Leipzig: F. A. Brockhaus, 1848), 279.

28. Grosheim confirms von Sternberg's account and adds the detail about the lifetime income, 47. Mara seems rather surprisingly not to have been bitter toward her ex-husband in spite of the toll he exacted on her life and career. Zelter reported that she once replied to his expression of wonder at her generosity toward her ne'er-do-well husband "But you must at least allow that he was the handsomest man ever seen!" Zelter to Goethe, quoted in Chorley, *Modern German Music,* I, 175.

29. Michael Kelly, *Reminiscences,* ed. with introduction by Roger Fiske (London: Oxford University Press, 1975), 153.

30. Ibid., 162. Punto was one of the great horn virtuosos of the time, much admired by Mozart ("Punto blast magnifique" [Punto blows magnificently] he wrote his father in 1778) and by Beethoven who created the horn sonata op. 17 for him.

31. Hogarth, *Memoirs,* 448.

32. Ibid.

33. grösste und herrlichste itzt lebende Sängerin in Deutschland, Italien, Frankreich und England, d.i. in der Welt. Gerber, *Lexicon,* col. 856.

34. Ich rahte einem jeden, welcher Sänger oder Sängerinnen bilden will, darauf zu sehen, dass sie die Violine oder Violoncell spielen lernen (wenn es auch nur die Scala ist), denn wie will man es sonst begreiflich machen, was ein paar comma zu hoch oder zu niedrig ist als bey Rückung der Finger? Autobiography, *AmZ* 10, no. 33 (18 August 1875): col. 515.

35. Richard Mackenzie Bacon, *Elements of Vocal Science: Being a Philosophical Enquiry into Some Principles of Singing* (London, c.1824), quoted in Hogarth, 216–17

36. freylich mochte wohl die Methode nicht die beste, und der Geschmack nicht der feinste seyn; allein, eine brillante Stimme, reine Intonation, geläufige Kehle ersetzten den Mangel der Kunst und Geschmacks. Autobiography, *AmZ* 10, no. 33 (18 August 1875): col. 516.

37. Da mag er aber wohl recht gehabt haben, denn wo hatte ich bis dahin Gelegenheit, eine italienische Methode (welche die einzige wahre ist, welcher alle Nationen, alle Sänger und alle Instrumentalisten nachzuahmen trachten) wo hatte ich Gelegenheit solche zu bekommen? Autobiography, *AmZ* 10, no. 33 (18 August 1875): col. 517 n. 8.

38. Beharrlickeit und Fleiss mussten mich also zur wahren Künstlerin machen, denn es war mir nicht genug, bloss Sängerin zu heissen. Autobiography, *AmZ* 10, no. 34 (25 August 1875): col. 531.

39. Daines Barrington, "Account of a Very Remarkable Young Musician," letter to Dr. Mathew Maty, Secretary of the London Royal Society, 28 November 1769; published in the *Philosophical Transactions of the London Royal Society*, vol. 60 (1771), 54–64; in *Mozart: Die Dokumente seines Lebens*, coll. and ed. Otto Erich Deutsch (Cassel: Bärenreiter, 1961), 86–92.

40. Bisher war sie nur grosse Conzertsängerin gewesen, indem sie jede Passagie, die selbst Violinisten Mühe machten, mit einer Leichtigkeit und Präcision herausgebracht, die jedermann in Erstaunen setzte. Aber nun bildete sie sich auch an der Seite des Concialini und des Porporino, zu einer empfindungsvollen Adagiosängerin und grossen Aktrize. Gerber, *Lexicon*, col. 860. I have unable to find any biographical information about Concialini. Porporino, an alto castrato, was born Anton Hubert (Antonio Uberti) in Verona, 1719, and enjoyed a career in Italy before settling in 1740 at the Berlin court. He died in Berlin in 1783. He was known as Il Porporino because of his status as a favorite of the well-known singer and teacher Nicola Antonio Porpora. See entry in K. J. Kutsch and Leo Riemens, *Große Sängerlexikon* (3rd exp. ed., Bern & Munich: K. G. Saur, 1997).

41.   Der Demoiselle Schmeling nach Aufführung der Hasseschen
      Santa Elena al Calvario, Leipzig, 1771
      Klarster Stimme, froh an Sinn
      Reinste Jugendgabe,—
      Zogst Du mit der Kaiserin
      Nach dem heil'gen Grabe.
      Dort, wo alles wohl gelang,
      Unter die Beglückten
      Riß Dein herrschender Gesang
      Mich den Hochentzückten.

      An Madame Mara zum frohen Jahresfest, Weimar 1831
         Sangreich war Dein Ehrentag,
      Jede Brust erweiternd;
      Sang auch ich auf Pfad und Steg,
      Müh' und Schritt' erheiternd.
      Nah dem Ziele, denk' ich heut
      Jener Zeit, der süßen;
      Fühle mit, wie mich's erfreut,
      Segnend Dich zu grüßen.

Johann Wolfgang von Goethe, Leipzig, 1771; Weimar, 1831; quoted in A[rnold?] Niggli, "Gertrud Elisabeth Mara: Eine deutsche Künstlerin des achtzehnten Jahrhunderts," in *Sammlung musikalischer Vorträge*, ed. Paul Graf Waldersee (Leipzig: Breitkopf & Härtel, 1881), 3:207.

Chapter 8

1. Anonymous description in *Candid and Impartial Strictures on the Performers in the Leading Theatres* (1795), quoted in Geoffrey Brace, *Anna . . . Susanna: Anna Storace, Mozart's First Susanna: Her Life, Times, and Family* (London: Thames Publishing, 1991), 14.

2. muss man bekennen dass sie sehr gut singt. Pezzl, *Viennese Sketches*, 1783, quoted in Brace, *Anna . . . Susanna*, 12.

3. —als wen man in einem quartetto nicht viel mehr redden als singen sollte— . . . aber was terzetten und Quartetten anbelangt muß man dem Compositeur seinen freyen Willen lassen—. Mozart to Leopold Mozart, Munich, 27 December 1780, in *Mozart: Briefe und Aufzeichnungen*, 3:72–73.

4. Wolfgang Amadeus Mozart, "Ch'io mi scordi di te?" "Non temer, amato bene," K.505, in *Neue Ausgabe sämtlicher Werke* (Kassel: Bärenreiter, 1971), ser. II, 7, 3, 175–200.

5. *The Times* (London), 26 April 1787, quoted in Brace, *Anna . . . Susanna*, 66.

6. *The Morning Chronicle* (London), 27? April 1787, quoted in Brace, *Anna . . . Susanna*, 67.

7. Este, *The Times* (London), 26 November 1792, quoted in Theodore Fenner, *Opera in London: Views of the Press, 1785–1830* (Carbondale and Edwardsville: Southern Illinois University Press, 1994), 545–46.

8. *Daily Advertiser* (London), 17 December 1789 [*sic*; 1787], quoted in Brace, *Anna . . . Susanna*, 70.

9. See Brace, *Anna . . . Susanna*, 68.

10. *The Times* (London), 26 November 1792, quoted in Fenner, *Opera*, 546. She sang Fabulina in Stephen Storace's opera *The Pirates*.

11. DuBois, *Monthly Mirror* (London), quoted in Fenner, *Opera*, 547.

12. See Brace, *Anna . . . Susanna*, 23, for the full example and discussion of the music which gives a good idea of her capabilities at that age—and of her teacher's expectations.

13. *A Secret History of the Green Room*, quoted in Brace, *Anna . . . Susanna*, 12.

14. Emperor Joseph II to Count Rosenberg, 14 August 1783, quoted in Brace, *Anna . . . Susanna*, 40.

15. Emperor Joseph II to Count Rosenberg, October? 1784, quoted in Brace, *Anna . . . Susanna*, 45.

16. Count Johann Karl Chr. H. Zinzendorf, *Diary: Tagebuch des Grafen Johann Karl Chr. H. Zinzendorf*, entry in 1783, quoted in Brace, *Anna . . . Susanna*, 38.

17. Emperor Joseph II to Comte de Mercy-Argenteau, Austrian ambassador to Paris, February? 1787, quoted in Brace, *Anna . . . Susanna*, 63.

18. *Journal* (Salisbury). 1 October 1787, quoted in Brace, *Anna . . . Susanna*, 70.

19. *Herald* (London), quoted in Fenner, *Opera*, 546.

20. *Chronicle* (London), 29? April 1787, quoted in Brace, *Anna . . . Susanna,* 67.

21. John Adolphus, Esq., *Memoirs of John Bannister, Comedian,* 2 vols. (London: Richard Bentley, 1839), 1:234.

22. Zinzendorf, *Diary,* entry for 7 January 1787, quoted in Brace, *Anna . . . Susanna,* 56.

23. Mount Edgcumbe, *Reminiscences,* 58–59.

24. Except where otherwise noted, biographical information is drawn from Geoffrey Brace's biography of Storace.

25. Brace, *Anna . . . Susanna,* 114.

26. The obituary in *Gentleman's Magazine* describes Storace's liaison with Braham as "a long intercourse in which a kind of curious acknowledgment of marriage was sustained"; see Brace, *Anna . . . Susanna,* 137, note to page 107. Sir John's house is today a museum (13 Lincoln's Inn Fields) in London, filled with his collections, which include an impressive number of Hogarth's works.

27. *Post, Times, Monthly Mirror, Morning Chronicle, Monthly Mirror* (1808), *Examiner,* 1808, quoted in Fenner, *Opera,* 546–47.

28. *No Song, No Supper* is the only extant opera by Stephen Storace. Adolphus (*Memoirs*) claims Nancy Storace's last performance was in *The Cabinet.*

29. See Brace, *Anna . . . Susanna,* 122.

30. These uncatalogued letters are in the collection of Sir John Soane's Museum in London. I am grateful to the Museum archivist Susan Palmer for allowing me complete access to the letters.

31. Obituary, *Gentleman's Magazine,* September 1817, quoted in Brace, *Anna . . . Susanna,* 122.

32. Roger Fiske, *English Theatre Music in the Eighteenth Century,* 2nd ed. (Oxford and New York: Oxford University Press, 1986), 272–73.

33. Roger Fiske, "Storace: Stephen (John Seymour) Storace," *New Grove.*

34. James Boaden, quoted in Fiske, *English Theatre Music,* 273.

35. H. Sutherland Edwards, *History of the Opera from Monteverdi to Donizetti,* 2 vols., 2nd ed. (1862; reprint, New York: Da Capo Press, 1977), II, 4.

36. Adolphus, *John Bannister,* I, 231.

37. James Boaden, *Memoirs of John Philip Kemble* (2 vols. (London: n.p., 1825), 2:14; quoted in Fenner, 547.

38. Haydn to John Bland, 12 April 1790, quoted in H. C. Robbins Landon and David Wyn Jones, *Haydn: His Life and Music* (Bloomington: Indiana University Press, 1988), 178. Robbins Landon and Jones suggest the possibility that this cantata might be "Miseri noi, misera patria," two manuscript copies of which are in the Library of Congress, Washington, D. C.

39. Mount Edgcumbe, *Reminiscences,* 58–59.

Chapter 9

1. Stendahl [Henri Beyle], *Life of Rossini by Stendhal,* 2 vols., new rev. ed., trans. and annotated Richard N. Coe (Seattle: University of Washington Press, 1970). Chapter 35 is titled "Madame Pasta."
2. Ibid., 372.
3. Ibid., 374.
4. Ibid., 376–77.
5. Ibid., 377.
6. Ibid., 374. Recently Anne Midgette wrote in the *New York Times* of a modern contralto, Ewa Podles, with "three distinct registers, from a deep, almost masculine low through a warm middle voice with a whiskyish burr to firm if slightly slender top notes." Midgette explains that this tradition "extends back through Maria Callas to a time when it was considered part of a solid vocal technique." Midgette, "A Contralto Breaks the rules, Vocal and Histrionic," *New York Times,* 31 January 2004.
7. Ibid., 375, 380.
8. Ibid., 378, 372.
9. Sa voix était un peu voilée, dans le premier morceau qu'elle a chanté; elle est, en general beaucoup plus agreeable dans les tons bas que dans les notes d'en haut . . . *Annales Politiques, Morales et Littéraires* (Paris), 23 June 1816; quoted in Kenneth A. Stern, "A Documentary Study of Giuditta Pasta on the Opera Stage" (Ph.D. diss., City University of New York, 1983), 11.
10. *Journal des Débats* (Paris), 5 September 1816, quoted in Stern, "Pasta," 4.
11. *Morning Post* (London), 13 January 1817, quoted in Stern, "Pasta," 16.
12. Leigh Hunt, *The Examiner* (London), 19 January 1817,; quoted in Stern, "Pasta," 16.
13. agile omogenea ed estesa voce and una osservabilissima ed animatissima espressione di canto e di azione, ed una non commune perizia nell'arte sua; laonde tutte queste doti, realmente da lei possedute, non mancano per ora che d'un più deciso sviluppo, per classificarla nella prima categoria delle nostre più distinte virtuose. *Gazzetta Privilegiata di Venezia,* 7 Sept 1818, quoted in Stern, "Pasta," 28.
14. quella vera eloquenza di canto che penetra le vie del cuore; azione giusta ed espressiva. *Corriere delle Dame* (Padua), 24 Oct 1818, quoted in Stern, "Pasta," 30.
15. La sua voce è agile, estesa ed esercitata; il suo canto dolce, ed ornato sobriamente . . . Questa giovane virtuosa è molto applaudita; e gli applausi non son di favore ma di giustizia. *Gazzetta di Milano,* 9 August 1819, quoted in Stern, "Pasta," 42.
16. tanta grazia e precisione di canto si può ben sentire, ma non così facilmente descrivere. *Il Nuovo Osservatore Veneziano,* 13 February 1821, quoted in Stern, "Pasta," 63–64.
17. Mme Pasta joint à tous les dons extérieurs une voix fort belle et d'une expression vraiment dramatique and sa voix de soprano attaque avec la plus grande

facilité les notes les plus aiguë. *Journal des Débats* (Paris), 6 June 1821, and *Courrier des spectacles*; 7 June 1821, both quoted in Stern, "Pasta," 70.

18. très-belle dans les cordes bas et dans le *medium,* tend un peu à baisser dans les cordes hautes. Une pareille voix, très difficile par se nature à maîtriser, se refuse ordinairement aux agrémens du chant; cependant Mme Pasta, sans être prodigue d'agrémens, ce qui n'est pas un mal, nous en fait entendre d'une exécution parfaite et d'un gout irreproachable. Elle a chanté tout son role avec âme. *Courrier des spectacles* (Paris), 14 June 1821, quoted in Stern, "Pasta," 72.

19. La voix de Mme Pasta, pleine, égale et bien timbrée, dans le medium et dans les cordes hautes, paraît un peu voilée dans les tons graves; ses sons, dans cette region de la voix, rappellent souvent ceux de Mme Grassini [who had been court singer to Napoleon from 1806 to the end of his reign and was therefore well-known in Paris], qui avait le même défaut, bien racheté par l'expression attendrissante qu'il donne quelquefois aux accens de la cantatrice. *Le Drapeau blanc* (Paris), 11 June 1821, quoted in Stern, "Pasta," 72.

20. La voix de cette cantatrice est forte et étendue; mais les sons graves en sont voiles et ne répondent point à l'éclat de la quinte haut. *Journal des Débats* (Paris), 8 June 1821, quoted in Stern, "Pasta," 73.

Il est impossible de mieux dire le récitatif et de donner au chant plus d'âme et d'expression; un organe encore un peu rebelle, qu'elle doit avoir eu beaucoup de peine à former, se refuse quelquefois à ses efforts, mais il faut une oreille excercée pour s'en apercevoir, on n'est généralement frappé que de sa force et de son étendue. *La Quotidienne* (Paris), 18 June 1821, quoted in Stern, "Pasta," 73.

enlevé victorieusement tous les suffrages. Elle a passé ce qu'on attendoit de son âme et de son talent; elle a été sublime. On l'a applaudie avec fureur . . . sa voix, un peu voilée, est éminemment dramatique, sa manière noble et pure; sa chaleur entraînante. Castil-Blaze, *Journal des Débats* (Paris), 25 April 1822, quoted in Stern, "Pasta," 91.

21. *The Times* (London), 26 April 1824, quoted in Stern, "Pasta," 111; *The Examiner* (London), 2 May 1824, ibid., 111–12; *Morning Chronicle* (London), 26 April 1824, ibid., 112.

22. *Morning Herald* (London), 11 May 1825, quoted in Stern, "Pasta," 120; *The Examiner* 15 May 1825, ibid., 120; *Quarterly Musical Magazine and Review* (London), 1825, p. 278, ibid., 120–21.

23. *Quarterly Musical Magazine and Review* (London), 1825, p. 278, quoted in Stern, "Pasta,", 121.

24. *The Atlas* (London), 23 July 1826, quoted in Stern, "Pasta," 163.

25. On s'attendait bien que le role de Tancrède serait chanté par Mme Pasta d'une manière supérieure; mais personne n'eût pu croire qu'une jeune et jolie femme représentat, avec cette noblesse imposante, avec un intérêt si touchant et si vrai, le chavlier Syracusain; son front, son maintien, ses accens respirent la devise que Voltaire a donnée au héros: *l'Amour et l'Honneur!* elle chante la pièce italienne, et joue la pièce française. *La Quotidienne* (Paris), 28 April 1822, quoted

in Stern, "Pasta," 90.

26. Francois Couperin, *Les gouts-réunis,* Paris, 1724.

27. *Le Reveil* (Paris), 14 August 1822, quoted in Stern, "Pasta," 92.

28. *Le Reveil,* 31 August 1822, quoted in Stern, "Pasta," 92.

29. *Morning Herald* (London), 21 May 1825, quoted in Stern, "Pasta," 122; *Quarterly Musical Magazine and Review* (London), 193, ibid., 123–24.

30. *The Examiner* (London), 2 May 1824, quoted in Stern, "Pasta," 112.

31. *Morning Post* (London), 26 Jan 1817, quoted in Stern, "Pasta," 17.

32. *Morning Chronicle* (London), 3 February 1817, quoted in Stern, "Pasta," 18.

33. *The Examiner* (London), 7 July 1817, quoted in Stern, "Pasta," 22.

34. C'est n'est pas seulement le chant et le jeu de la même actrice, embellis, perfectionnés, portés à un plus haut degré d'expression; c'est une autre actrice et une autre cantatrice supérieure à la première; c'est en un mot une nouvelle creation du rôle de Desdémone. *La Quotidienne* (Paris), 18 Dec 1825, quoted in Stern, "Pasta," 144; Mme Pasta a joué et chanté d'une manière miraculeuse, Stendahl, *Journal de Paris,* 17 Dec 1825, ibid.

35. Come cantante la Pasta ha la risorsa d'una voce amabile, estesa ed esclusivamente limpida e forte nelle bellissime sue corde alte. La sua agilità nei gorgheggi, nei trilli, nelle scalate, è sorprendente . . . ed i fiori che vi sparge sono sempre variati, graziosi, e giudiziosamente innestati. *Foglio di Verona,* 28 Dec 1829, quoted in Stern, "Pasta," 201.

36. See Stern, 219, for a thorough discussion of Pasta's voice as revealed by this opera.

37. See Vincenzo Bellini, *Norma: Tragedia lirica in due atti,* Felice Romani, librettist (Milan and New York: G. Ricordi, 1870, 1945).

38. Fétis, *Biographie universelle.* See Stern, "Pasta," 1–2, for discussion of this issue. Fétis also believed that Pasta was a student at the Conservatory of Milan; Stern finds no evidence for that. Except where otherwise indicated biographical information is drawn from Stern's very thorough and detailed dissertation.

39. See Stern, "Pasta," 26.

40. Elle est petite, bien faite et jolie; mais elle a besoin d'étudier . . . puisqu'elle est à Paris, elle est à bonne école, pour prendre facilement de l'aisance dans sa demarche et dans ses gestes. *Annales politiques, morales et littéraire* (Paris), 23 June 1816, quoted in Stern, "Pasta," 11.

41. elle met beaucoup d'intelligence dans sa manière de jouer. Mais au Théâtre Italien il faut de la voix et de la méthode, et al voix de Mme Pasta, quoiqu'assez agréable, n'a ni force ni étendue, et sa méthode est nulle. *Journal des Débats* (Paris), 16 August 1816, quoted in Stern, "Pasta," 13.

42. Mme Pasta a étonné par quelques inspirations heureuses et des moments de force auxquels elle n'a pas jusqu'ici accoutumé le public. *Journal des Débats* (Paris), 5 September 1816, quoted in Stern, "Pasta," 14.

43. noble, fière, tendre et touchant. *Journal des Théâtres,* 30 August 1821,

quoted in Stern, "Pasta," 75.

44. Mount Edgcumbe, *Reminiscences,* 13. See Stern, "Pasta," 41–44, 52–53, for thorough discussion of the possible influences on Pasta by Grassini and Pacchierotti.

45. Stendahl, *Rossini,* 386.

46. voce, metodo, anima, portamento e grazie tutte sue proprie. *Gazzetta Piemontese,* 3 Oct 1820, quoted in Stern, "Pasta," 58.

47. Rachele Negri to Antonio Zanatta, 12 March 1821: "acordato ciò che ha domandato," quoted in Stern, "Pasta," 64.

48. toute la difference qui existe entre une écolière et une virtuose. *L'Étoile* (Paris), 17 June 1821, quoted in Stern, "Pasta," 71.

49. Puisse-t-elle trouver en Angleterre . . . un public qui sache l'écouter et l'entendre! *La Pandore* (Paris), 5 January 1824, quoted in Stern, "Pasta," 107.

50. non pas pour le chant, il y a long-temps que Mme Pasta est arrivée à la perfection, mais pour le jeu. *Journal de Paris,* 29 Sept 1824, quoted in Stern, "Pasta," 118.

51. See Stern, "Pasta," 156–57.

52. Letter of 12 December 1831, from Paris to Titus Woyciechowski at Poturzyn, *Selected Correspondence of Fryderyk Chopin,* trans. and ed. with additional material and commentary by Arthur Hedley. (1963; reprint, New York: Da Capo Press, 1979), 100.

53. Cette transition sublime, préparée avec beaucoup d'art et exécutée avec une force de sentiment, une vérité effrayante dans les accens et le geste, a frappé de terreur toute l'assemblée et lui a arraché un cri d'admiration. Je parle d'abord de cette scène, attendu qu'elle est la plus remarquable de la pièce. Mme Pasta a joué tout le reste de son rôle avec profondeur, noblesse, sentiment; elle s'est surpassée: c'est le plus bel éloge qu'on puisse lui addresser. Nous avons vu successivement cette actrice charmante sous le costume brillant de l'épouse d'Otello; l'armure de chevalier lui sied à ravir, le turban Moabite la rend séduisante. A tous ces riches ajustemens, magicienne Médée. *Journal des Débats* (Paris), 16 January 1823, quoted in Stern, "Pasta," 99–100.

54. Einen schönen Triller, mit solch fein schattirten Abstufungen, und einer an's Unglaubliche gränzenden Ausdauer. *Allgemeine musikalische Zeitung* (Leipzig), 1829, 233, quoted in Stern, "Pasta," 193.

55. come attrice ella è un modella d'arte a niuna seconda . . . come cantante la Pasta può esser vinta nella purezza dei suoni e nella forza della voce— nell'espressione difficilmente avrà chi la pareggi non che la vinca. *Gazzetta di Milano,* 28 April 1829, quoted in Stern, "Pasta," 194.

56. certo la Pasta fu ravvisata allora la soma maestra del canto drammatico *I Teatri* (Milan), 1828, 44–5, quoted in Stern, "Pasta," 194.

57. come cantante e come attrice, lasciò a desiderare alcune cose *Censore universale dei teatri* (Milan), 5 January 1831, quoted in Stern, "Pasta," 206.

58. *The Court Journal* (London), 14 May 1831, quoted in Stern, "Pasta," 210.

59. bien plus flexible; elle execute maintenant la gamme chromatique descendante et le trille avec beaucoup d'agilité. *Journal des Débats* (Paris), 5 Sept. 1831, quoted in Stern, "Pasta," 213.

60. sa voix, toujours légèrement voilée, se prêtre mieux que jamais à l'expression dramatique des situations fortes; c'est une voix de tragédienne: elle a surtout été admirable dans la dernière scène; cette transition de l'ivresse de la folie à la raison, à la terreur, ces cris d'une pauvre femme qui voit la mort devant elle, elle a rendu tout cela avec une pathétique et une vérité inimitables. *La France nouvelle* (Paris), 8 Sept. 1831, quoted in Stern, "Pasta," 213–14.

61. *Morning Post* (London), 3 May 1833; *Morning Herald* (London), 3 May 1833, quoted in Stern, "Pasta," 234.

62. *The Times* (London), 1 July 1833, quoted in Stern, "Pasta," 236.

63. *Morning Post* (London), 18 May 1837, quoted in Stern, "Pasta," 245.

64. *Morning Herald* (London), 18 May 1837, quoted in Stern, "Pasta," 246.

65. Chorley, *Thirty Years' Musical Recollections* (London: Alfred A. Knopf, 1926), 92–93.

66. *The Times* (London), 9 July 1850, quoted in Stern, "Pasta," 254–55.

67. *Morning Chronicle* (London), 12 July 1850, quoted in Stern, "Pasta," 255.

68. Ibid.

69. Chorley, *Recollections,* 92–93.

70. *Lettres à une inconnue,* (Paris: Michel Lévy frères, 1874), 2:20, quoted in Stern, "Pasta," 257–58.

71. John Ebers, *Seven Years of the King's Theatre* (London: William Harrison Ainsworth, 1818), 219–20. During his years as director/manager at the King's Theatre Ebers put on a number of Rossini operas and brought Pasta to London as his main star; his account of the period is lively and extremely informative though with an understandable bias.

72. Stern, "The Theatre of *Bel Canto,*" *Opera News* 40 (1975/76): 12–14. Talma, one of the foremost actors of his day, bemoaned the contemporary reliance on studied (and traditional) gesture and posture, exclaiming that he had to "be content with putting [truth] into the costumes," since it was impossible to obtain in the plays. A close friend of the novelist and playwright Victor Hugo, Talma finally found his perfect drama in Hugo's *Cromwell,* the play that as Stern points out turned out to be "the first blast of the Romantic revolt"; it was written for Talma in spite of his advanced years and not for a younger actor as might seem more appropriate. (See Stern, "Pasta," 14.)

Chapter 10

1.   Guter Adler, nicht ins Weite
      Mit der Leier, nicht nach oben!

Unsre Sängerin begleite,
Daß wir Euch zusammen loben. Johann Wolfgang von Goethe, for Wilhelmine Schröder-Devrient, quoted in Julius Bab, *Die Devrients: Geschichte einer deutschen Theaterfamilie* (Berlin: Georg Stilke, 1932), 88.

2. *Thayer's Life of Beethoven,* rev. and ed. Elliot Forbes (Princeton: Princeton University Press, 1967, 812.

3. Julius Bab, *Die Devrients,* 74. This book is about the entire Devrient family but gives a great of information about Wilhelmine Schröder after she married Karl Devrient. Unfortunately, Bab seldom documents his material; this quotation, however, is in complete agreement with other remarks by Weber.

4. Chorley, *Modern German Music,* 1:347.

5. Mount Edgcumbe, *Reminiscences,* 211.

6. Zu einer brillanten Coloratursängerin hätte sie es nie gebracht; theils widerstrebte ihre hohe Anschauung vom edlen Gesang dieser Virtuosität, die die Menge immer anstaunen wird, theils war ihr Kehlkopf zu schwerfällig. Was sie zu einer Partie wie die Norma an verziertem Gesang brauchte, hatte sie gelernt und führte die Passagen sauber aus, wenn sie dieselben auch nicht raketenmäßig in die Luft schleuderte. Eduard Genast, *Aus dem Tagebuche eines alten Schauspielers* (Leipzig: Voigt & Günther, 1862), 142–43.

7. Als declamatorische Sängerin stand Wilhelmine schon in der Mitte der zwanziger Jahre über vielen ihrer deutschen und italienischen Genossinnen, jetzt hatte ihr unermüdlicher Fleiß sich auch eine Volubilität des Kehlkopfs angeeignet, die hinreichte, eine Partie wie die Norma in gesanglicher Hinsicht künstlerisch auszuführen. Genast, *Tagebuch,* 152.

8. Chorley, *Modern German Music,* 347–48.

9. Ibid., 343–44.

10. Ibid., 345–47.

11. Mount Edgcumbe, *Reminiscences,* 213.

12. Ignaz Moscheles, *Recent Music and Musicians: As Described in the Diaries and Correspondence of Ignatz Moscheles*, edited by his wife, adapted from the original German by A. D. Coleridge (1873; reprint, New York: Da Capo Press, 1970), 241.

13. Chorley, *Modern German Music*, 344–45.

14. See Ludwig van Beethoven, *Fidelio,* libretto by Joseph Ferdinand Sonnleithner, Stephan von Breuning, et al. (New York: G. Schirmer, 1935), no. 9, Recitative and Aria, "Abscheulicher/Komm Hoffnung."

15. Weber, diary, quoted in John Warrack, *Carl Maria von Weber* (New York: The Macmillan Company, 1968), 263.

16. Frederic Chopin to Titus Woyciechowski, Paris, 12 December 1831, *Selected Correspondence,* 100. Chopin adds in the same letter: "Schröder-Devrient is here—but she's not such a sensation as in Germany. La Malibran played Othello and she was Desdemona. Malibran is small while the German lady is huge—it

looked as if *she* would stifle Othello!"

17. Die Pasta ist bei weitem nicht so groß als ihr Ruf, aber die Malibran tausendmal größer. Das ist eine Künstlerin, vor der man niederknieen muß. Quoted in Genast, *Tagebuch*, 283.

18. so ergriff ihn der hochdramatische Vortrag der unvergleichlichen Wilhelmine so gewaltig, daß er ihr Haupt in beide Hände nahm und sie mit den Worten: "Haben Sie tausend Dank für diese großartige, künstlerische Leistung!" auf die Stirn küßte; dann fuhr er fort: "Ich habe diese Composition früher einmal gehört, wo sie mir gar nicht zusagen wollte, aber so vorgetragen gestaltet sich das Ganze zu einem sichtbaren Bild." Genast, *Tagebuch*, 281–82.

19. Sie singt nicht wie andere Künstler singen, sie spricht nicht, wie wir es gewohnt sind. Ihr Spiel ist den Regeln der Kunst durchaus nicht konform, *es ist, als wüßte sie gar nicht, daß sie auf einer Bühne steht.* Sie singt mit der Seele noch mehr als mit der Stimme; ihre Töne entquellen mehr dem Herzen als der Kehle. sie vergißt das Publikum, sie vergißt sich selbst, um ganz in dem Wesen, das sie darstellt, aufzugehen. Bab, *Die Devrients,* 88; no source cited for quotation.

20. ihre tadelfreie Aussprache selbst in den schwierigsten Tonfolgen, die absolute Reinheit der Intonation und nicht zuletzt die große Kunst der Tonbeseelung. Carl Hagemann, *Wilhelmine Schröder Devrient* (Wiesbaden: Verlag der Greif, 1947), 28–29.

21. Ihr Recitativ, die größte Schwierigkeit, die ein dramatischer Sänger überwinden muß, stand nun auf der höchsten Stufe der Vollendung, und ich habe nie, weder von den berühmtesten italienischen noch deutschen Sängerinnen, solce musikalisch-charakteristische Declamation gehört. Genast, 145–46. Genast does not give a composer for *Montecchi und Capuleti.* It is probably Bellini's *I Capuleti e i Montecchi,* and in light of the *"und,"* was probably sung in German. Romeo was a role often sung by Pasta.

22. Chorley, *Modern German Music,* 345.

23. *Memoirs of Hector Berlioz from 1803 to 1865 Comprising His Travels in Germany, Italy, Russia, and England,* transl. Rachel Holmes and Eleanor Holmes, annotated, transl., rev. Ernest Newman (1932; reprint, New York: Dover Publications, Inc., 1966), 318; see discussion of Schröder-Devrient's work, 315–18.

24. Das Sinken ihres künstlerischen Gestirns in dieser spätern Periode wurde hauptsächlich durch das Zuviel in der Anwendung mancher Mittel bemerkbar, eben dieses Sinken zu verbergen. Sie verfiel in den Fehler, die Lichter zu scharf aufzusetzen, die Schatten zu verdunkelt daneben zu stellen; die *Contraste* sollten erreichen, was sonst die milde, anmuthvolle Verschmelzung, der leichtgeführte Zügel des Masses ihr gewann, selbst da, wo sie mit den vollsten stürmenden Schwingen die glänzendsten Ziele der Wirkung erstrebte. Ludwig Rellstab, quoted in Bab, *Die Devrients,* 94.

25. Dieser Moment der plastischen Darstellung mochte das Gefühl erregen, als habe ein schönstes Kunstwerk des Phidias plötzlich Leben gewonnen und

bewege sich vor uns mit dem Adel griechischer Götterbildung, indem ebenso der tiefste Schmerz einen leisen aber unvergänglichen Hauch der Anmut bewahrt, wie sich in dem Lächeln der Freude doch niemals die höhere Bedeutsamkeit göttlichen Ernstes, göttlicher Trauer verliert. Rellstab, ibid., 91.

26. Mount Edgcumbe, *Reminiscences,* 211–13.

27. Robert Gutman, *Richard Wagner: The Man, His Mind, and His Music* (New York: Harcourt Brace Jovanovich, Inc., 1968), 18–19. Gutman gives a good account of the young Wagner's reaction to his first acquaintance with both *Fidelio* and Schröder-Devrient.

28. Die entfernteste Berührung mit dieser außerordentlichen Frau traf mich elektrisch: noch lange Zeit, selbst bis auf den heutigen Tag, hörte und fühlte ich sie, wenn mich der Drang zu künstlerischem Gestalten belebte. Richard Wagner, "An seine Freunde," 1851; quoted in Hagemann, *Wilhelmine Schröder Devrient,* 59.

29. Except where otherwise noted, biographical information is based on the biography by Hagemann.

30. Diese Vorzüge, verbunden mit einem Schauspielertalent, wie noch wenige große Sängerinnen bewiesen haben, gewährten einen eigenen Zauber und entzückten die überraschten Zuhörer so sehr, daß das Haus vom Beifall widerhallte. Quoted in Bab, *Die Devrients,* 73. No source given, other than that the quote comes from "eine wohl ausgebildete, einfache, von allen Schnörkeleien entfernte Stimmführung" (a person who is probably well-educated, simple, removed from all stupid flattery).

31. Eduard Genast was present at the visit, which he had arranged, to the aged Goethe. He tells of the meeting and of Schröder-Devrient's singing of "Erlkönig" in his *Tagebuch,* 280–82. According to John Warrack ("Schröder-Devrient [née Schröder], Wilhelmine," *Grove Music Online,* accessed 21 June 2004), Genast's wife accompanied Schröder-Devrient's "Erlkönig."

32. Warrack, "Schröder-Devrient, Wilhelmine."

33. Ibid. Because of this weeping she was known as the "Queen of Tears."

34. Nichts darf ihr Geschlecht verraten, soll die ganze Situation nicht lächerlich werden. Sie muß gehen, stehen, hinknien wie ein Mann, sie muß den Degen ziehen und sich zum Kampf anstellen wie ein guter Fechter, und vor allen Dingen muß alles Weibische aus ihrem Kostüm verbannt sein. Keine zierlichen Locken, kein eingezwängter Fuß, keine schöne Taille. Das Hutaufsetzen und -abnehmen, das Handschuhaus- und -anziehen ist nicht minder wichtig. Quoted in Bab, *Die Devrients,* 91.

35. Schumann's dedication is a magnificent response to his recognition of her nature. The poem by Heinrich Heine is quintessential Romanticism with its imagery of light and darkness, snakes, diamonds, and the constant refrain "Ich grolle nicht."

Ich grolle nicht,	I don't complain
und wenn das Herz auch bricht,	even though my heart is breaking
ewig verlor'nes Lieb,	forever lost love.

Ich grolle nicht,	I don't complain,
und wenn das Herz auch bricht,	even though my heart is breaking,
Ewig verlor'nes Lieb!	Eternally lost love!
Ich grolle nicht.	I don't complain.
Wie du auch strahlst	Though you radiate the
in Diamantenpracht,	splendor of diamonds,
Es fällt kein Strahl in	No glimmer penetrates
deines Herzens Nacht,	the night of your heart,
Das weiss ich längst.	That I've long known.
Ich grolle nicht,	I don't complain,
und wenn das Herz auch bricht.	even though my heart is breaking.
Ich sah dich ja im Traume,	I saw you in my dream,
Und sah die Nacht in	And saw the night that
deines Herzens Raume,	fills your heart,
Und sah die Schlang',	And saw the snake
die dir am Herzen frisst,	that gnaws at your heart,
Ich sah, mein Lieb,	I saw, my love,
wie sehr du elend bist.	just how wretched you are.
Ich grolle nicht, ich grolle nicht.	I don't complain, I don't complain.

36. Warrack, "Schröder-Devrient, Wilhelmine."

37. Euryanthe ist ein rein dramatischer Versuch, seine Wirkung nur <u>von dem vereinigten Zusammenwirken aller Schwesterkünste hoffend,</u> sicher wirkungslos, ihrer Hülfe beraubt. Weber, Address to the Akademischen Musikverein zu Breslau, 20 December 1824, quoted in Peter Raabe, *Wege zu Weber* (Regensburg: Gustav Bosse, 1942), 123.

38. Several critics, Henry Chorley in particular, found her insistence on German methods highly objectionable, referring to the "obstinacy of national antipathy, which . . . made it penal to sing with grace, taste, and vocal self-command;" see above, page 139.

39. Die Schröder-Devrient war weder in der Kunst noch im Leben eine Erscheinung jenes Virtuosentums, das nur durch vollständige Vereinzelung gedeiht und in ihr allein zu glänzen vermag: sie war hier wie dort durchaus Dramatikerin, im vollen Sinne des Wortes, sie war auf die Berührung, auf die Verschmelzung mit dem Ganzen hingedrängt, und dies Ganze war eben in Leben und Kunst unser soziales Leben und unsere theatralische Kunst." Wagner, "An seine Freunde," quoted in Hagemann, *Wilhelmine Schröder Devrient,* 54.

Chapter 11

1. William Makepeace Thackeray, Richard Wagner, quoted in Edward Wagenknecht, *Jenny Lind* (Boston and New York: Houghton Mifflin Company, 1931), 38–39; Frederic Chopin to Wojciech Grzymala, Paris, 4 [May 1848], in

Selected Correspondence, 314–15.

2. Cori Ellison, "What the Three Tenors Learned from a Soprano," *New York Times,* 23 January 2000.

3. *Scribner's Magazine* 47, 429–30, quoted in Wagenknecht, *Jenny Lind,* 47.

4. Henri Appy, "Characteristics of Jenny Lind," *Century Magazine* 32 (1897): 554–58, quoted in Wagenknecht, *Jenny Lind,* 47.

5. Mrs. Raymond [Jenny] Maude, *The Life of Jenny Lind Briefly Told by Her Daughter"* (London: Cassell and Company, Ltd, 1926), 133.

6. Horatio F. Brown, *John Addington Symonds: A Biography* (New York: Charles Scribner's Sons, 1895), I, 198.

7. Maude, *Life,* 129.

8. Mozley, quoted in Wagenknecht, *Jenny Lind,* 24.

9. Carlyle, quoted in Wagenknecht, *Jenny Lind,* 38.

10. Samuel Longfellow, *Life of Henry Wadsworth Longfellow* (Boston: Houghton Mifflin Company [1886]); II, 179.

11. Letter to King of the Belgians, II, 144, Benson and Esher, *Letters of Queen Victoria;* quoted in Wagenknecht, *Jenny Lind,* 37.

12. Maude, *Life,* 128–29; see 128–30 for further discussion by Mrs. Maude of her mother's singing.

13. Ibid.

14. "Jenny Lind's Singing Method," Lind to Professor Bystrom, [Stockholm], 2 June 1868, transl. V. M. Holmstrom, *Musical Quarterly* 3 (1917): 548–51. Professor Bystrom is never given a first name, by Lind or by any of the references to this letter. I would suggest that it might be Oscar (Fredrik Bernadotte) Byström (1821–1909), who became inspector of the Swedish Royal Academy of Music in 1866, and in 1872 a professor. Although he followed a military career, he was well known in Stockholm in the 1840s as a song composer, a pianist, and a teacher. In the late 1870s he turned to church music, and in 1886 he dedicated himself to studying liturgical music in London, Paris, Solesmes, Milan, and Rome. Upon his return to Stockholm he hosted "motet evenings" featuring the music of Lassus and Palestrina. In 1899 he published *Sequenser, antifoner och hymnen.* (See Robert Layton and Lennart Rabes, "Byström, Oscar (Fredrik Bernadotte)," *Grove Music Online,* accessed 24 June 2004.) Byström's interest in vocal music and then particularly in church music would certainly have endeared him to Lind, although she would probably have been horrified by the interest in Catholic music and religion indicated by his visits to Paris, Solesmes, and especially Rome.

15. M. Sterling-Mackinlay, *Garcia the Centenarian and His Times* (New York: D. Appleton, 1908), 148, 288; quoted in Wagenknecht, *Jenny Lind,* 50.

16. Rumer Godden, *Hans Christian Andersen: A Great Life in Brief* (New York: Alfred A. Knopf, 1956), 171–74.

17. Chopin to Wojciech Grzymala, Paris, 4 [May 1848], *Selected Correspondence,* 314–15.

18. William Ashton Ellis, ed. *Richard to Minna Wagner: Letters to His First*

Wife (London: H. Grevel and Company, 1909), 40.

19. Except where otherwise indicated, biographical information relies on the most recent biography: Joan Bulman, *Jenny Lind: A Biography* (London: James Barrie, 1956).

20. *Dagligt Allehanda,* November 1830, quoted in Bulman, *Jenny Lind,* 16.

21. Ibid.

22. Lind to Marie Ruckman, n.d. [after 1 July 1841], quoted in Bulman, *Jenny Lind,* 42.

23. Ibid., 52.

24. Quoted in William Porter Ware and Thaddeus C. Lockard, Jr., *P. T. Barnum Presents Jenny Lind: The American Tour of the Swedish Nightingale* (Baton Rouge and London: Louisiana State University Press, 1980), 24–25.

25. Quoted in Charles G. Rosenberg, *Jenny Lind in America* (New York: Stringer and Townsend, 1851), 53.

26. Nashville *Daily American,* 1 April 1851, quoted in Ware and Lockard, *P. T. Barnum,* 81–82.

27. This song is in the William B. Bradbury Collection in the Music Division of the Library of Congress, Washington, D. C. The reference to Goldsmith/Goldschmidt dates the text as at least after her marriage in February 1852.

28. See Ware and Lockard, *P. T. Barnum,* Appendix III: Contract between Jenny Lind and P. T. Barnum and Appendix IV: Financial Account of the Jenny Lind Tour.

29. Mackinlay, *Garcia,* 148, 288, quoted in Wagenknecht, *Jenny Lind,* 50.

30. Lind to Marie Ruckman, n.d. [after 1 July 1841], quoted in Bulman, *Jenny Lind,* 42.

31. Holland and Rockstro, *Memoir of Madame Jenny Lind-Goldschmidt;* I, 115–16, quoted in Wagenknecht, *Jenny Lind,* 52.

32. Bulman, *Jenny Lind,* 315–16.

33. "Jenny Lind's Singing Method," 548–50, *passim.*

34. Ellison, "Three Tenors."

Chapter 12

1. April FitzLyon, *The Price of Genius: A Life of Pauline Viardot* (New York: Appleton-Century, 1964), 354–55. A somewhat different version is related by Patrick Waddington in "Henry Chorley, Pauline Viardot, and Turgenev: A Musical and Literary Friendship," *Musical Quarterly* 67 (1981): 181–82. Dickens, together with Chorley and Sullivan, was spotted by Turgenev, Louis Viardot, and the director of the theatre Léon Carvalho; the three of them took the Englishmen backstage, where Carvalho proclaimed: "Madame, je vous présente une fontaine."

2. J'ai voulu tout chanter et j'ai gâté ma voix, quoted in Suzanne Desternes and Henriette Chandet, with the collaboration of Alice Viardot, *La Malibran et*

Pauline Viardot (Paris: Librairie Artheme Fayard, 1969), 251.

3. Henry Chorley, quoted in FitzLyon, *Viardot,* 39.

4. Alfred de Musset, *Revue des deux mondes,* 1 January 1839; quoted in FitzLyon, *Viardot,* 51–52.

5. FitzLyon, *Viardot,* 77–78.

6. Ibid., 43.

7. Carolyn Shuster, "Six Mazurkas de Frederic Chopin transcrites pour chant et piano par Pauline Viardot" (*Revue de musicologie* 75/2 [1989]): 265–83. See page 271 for an account of the publications of Viardot's transcriptions.

8. a eu la gracieuseté de chanter mes mazourkas au concert de son théâtre—sans que je le lui ai demandé. Chopin to Mlle de Rozières, 30 June 1848, *Selected Correspondence,* 322.

9. Chorley, *Recollections,* 237–38.

10. Rebecca A. Pope, "The Diva Doesn't Die: George Eliot's *Armgart*" in Leslie C. Dunn and Nancy A. Jones, eds., *Embodied Voices: Representing Female Vocality in Western Culture* (Cambridge: Cambridge University Press, 1994), 139–51.

11. Berlioz, *Journal des Débats* 19(?) November 1859, quoted in FitzLyon, *Viardot,* 353.

12. Chorley, *Recollections,* 237.

13. Berlioz, quoted in FitzLyon, *Viardot,* 361.

14. FitzLyon, *Viardot,* 460.

15. Except where otherwise noted, the source of biographical information is April FitzLyon's *The Price of Genius: A Life of Pauline Viardot,* the only English language biography of Viardot.

16. FitzLyon, *Viardot,* 35.

17. Malibran's London debut took place in 1825 and was quite successful but was followed quickly by the Garcia family's departure for America. Her real fame began in 1828 with her stupendous debut in Paris.

18. Meysenberg is probably Charles Meysenberg (1785-c. 1828), son of a Paris piano builder. In 1799 he was a student at the Paris Conservatory where he won first prize in 1805; he also studied composition with Étienne-Nicolas Méhul. His compositions include three sonatas for piano, a sonata for piano and violin, a concerto for piano and orchestra, and *12 Morceaux faciles et brillant.* As he died c. 1828, Pauline's studies with him would have been brief, at the very end of his life.

19. FitzLyon, *Viardot,* 27.

20. Maria Malibran had parted from Eugène in 1828 but was unable to get an annulment of their marriage until 1835.

21. FitzLyon, *Viardot,* 37.

22. *Twelve Poems of Pushkin, Fet and Turgenev, Set to Music by Pauline Viardot-Garcia* (1864) and *Five Poems of Lermontov and Turgenev, Set to Music by Pauline Viardot-Garcia* (1869). See FitzLyon, *Viardot,* 383–84. The songs are so far unavailable in print, and I have been unable to locate them.

23. Desternes and Chandet, *Malibran et Viardot,* 223–24.

24. Meyerbeer, La Viardot, comme chanteuse et comme actrice, va à une hauteur tragique que je n'avais encore jamais vue au theater, quoted in Desternes and Chandet, *Malibran et Viardot,* 224. See also FitzLyon, *Viardot,* 243–45, for an account of the opera's reception.

25. Le success de Mme Viardot a été immense. Dans le role de Fidès, elle a déployê un talent dramatique dont on ne la croyait pas (en France) douée si éminemment. Toutes ses attitudes, ses gestes, sa physionomie, son costume même sont étudiés avec un art profound. Quant à la perfection de son chant, à l'extrême habileté de sa vocalization, à son assurance musicale, ce sont choses connues . . . C'est une des plus grandes artistes que l'on puisse citer dans l'histoire passée et contemporaine de la musique . . . C'est l'art pur et complet. Berlioz, quoted in Desternes and Chandet, *Malibran et Viardot,* 224.

26. C'est Malibran et Mlle Rachel réunie; sublime de vérité, d'expression, de grace et de sentiment. *L'Illustration* and *La Gazette de France,* quoted in Desternes and Chandet, *Malibran et Viardot,* 224.

27. Qui, jamais, s'est demandé si Mme Viardot était jolie, si même elle avait de la voix? Il y a dans son chant tant d'expression, tant de drame, de passion, de furia, qu'on l'écoute sans la voir, qu'on est ravi, transporté, sans songer à discuter la qualité ou l'étendue de sa voix. Charles de Boigne, Desternes and Chandet, *Malibran et Viardot,* 224.

28. FitzLyon, *Viardot,* 360–61.

29. See Waddington, "Chorley, Viardot, and Turgenev," 185, for Turgenev's letter to Chorley describing the planned production and inviting him to attend.

30. Chorley, *Recollections,* 232.

31. See the thorough and interesting discussion of Viardot and Eliot's *Armgart* by Pope, "The Diva Doesn't Die," 139–51.

32. Letter to Nadezhda von Meck, quoted in FitzLyon, *Viardot,* 456–57.

33. FitzLyon, *Viardot,* 340 n. According to FitzLyon, she gave the autograph in 1892 to Ambroise Thomas, Director of the Paris Conservatoire, specifying that it never leave the library of the Conservatoire even as a loan for exhibitions. The entry for *Don Giovanni, K.* 527, in the Köchel Catalog of Mozart's works states, however, that it was left to the Bibliothèque du Conservatoire du Musique and received in 1910 at Viardot's death.

34. Letter to Nadezhda von Meck, quoted in FitzLyon, *Viardot,* 457.

35. Ibid., 459.

36. The entire passage, which is paraphrased here, reads: "Bei Frau Viardot dient, wie bei allen großen Vortragenden, bei denen das heilige Feuer der Poesie nicht mangelt, die Virtuosität nur zum ausdruck von Idee, Gedanken, Charakter eines Werkes oder einer Rolle. Die Virtuosität ist nur dazu da, daß der Künstler im Stande sei, Alles zu können, was er will." Franz Liszt, "Pauline Viardot-Garcia," *Neue Zeitschrift für Musik* 5 (28 January 1859): 52.

37. Sie wird für alle Zukunft eine der Ersten in der vornehmen Gruppe der

Pasta, Malibran, Schröder-Devrient, Ristori, Rachel, Seebach u.a. bleiben, und noch immer durch die Mannichfaltigkeit von Begabungen, mit denen sie die Vorzüge der italienischen, französischen und deutschen Kunst verbindet, durch hervorragende geistige Bildung, durch die bevorzugte anlage ihrer Versönlichkeit, durch Noblesse des Charakters, durch die edle Haltung in ihrem Privatleben eine ganz besondere Stellung einnehmen. Ibid., 49.

38. Dennoch übertrifft sie in der Gesangkunst des zweiten Actes sich selber, wenn sie den unerschöpflichen Reichthum ihrer Coloratur und ihres seelischen Ausdrucks in den spanischen Liedern und in Chopin's berühmter Mazurka entfaltet. Wie sie da mit dem Goldstift ihrer Stimme die kühnsten Regenbogen in die Luft zeichnet, und dann mit Schwalbenraschheit aus der Tiefe in die Höhe sich schwingt, und auf dem Triller wie auf einem Zweige ruht und dessen Thautropften in perlenden kecken Cadenzen herunterschüttelt! Auch mit Gaben ihres Clavierspiels erfreute sie hier das Publicum, wenn sie präludirend oder phantasirend reizende Einfälle erhascht. Ibid., 53.

Chapter 13

1. Oscar Thompson, *The American Singer* (New York: The Dial Press, Inc., 1937), 394–95. Thompson (1887–1945) served as music critic for a number of American newspapers, including the *New York Times* and the New York *Sun.* Author of the well-known and well-used *Cyclopedia,* he also taught at the Curtis Institute in Philadelphia, Columbia University, and the New York College of Music.

2. *Daily News* (London), May 1878; quoted in Ira Glacken, *Yankee Diva: Lillian Nordica and the Golden Days of Opera* (New York: Coleridge Press, 1963), 38.

3. Unidentified clipping in Nordica Homestead Collection, quoted in Glacken, *Nordica,* 58.

4. *Boston Herald,* 20 December 1883, quoted in Glacken, *Nordica,* 116; *Boston Globe,* 20 December 1883, quoted in Glacken, *Nordica,* 116–17.

5. M. H. Moreno and the critic for *Le Menestrel* (Paris), quoted in Glacken, *Nordica ,* 90 (no further information given).

6. Quoted in Glacken, *Nordica,* 131.

7. Letter, Cosima Liszt Wagner to Count Fritz Hohenlohe-Langenburg, June 1894, quoted in Glacken, *Nordica,* 167–68.

8. Letter, Siegfried Wagner to Otto Floersheim, quoted in Glacken, *Nordica,* 169.

9. Floersheim, quoted in Glacken, *Nordica,* 171.

10. Engelbert Humperdinck, *Zeitung* (Frankfurt/Main), quoted in Glacken, *Nordica,* 177.

11. Remark to Nordica's close friend William Armstrong, quoted in Glacken, *Nordica,* 205.

12. *Boston Transcript,* review of concert in Boston's Symphony Hall, 20 April

1913, quoted in Glacken, *Nordica,* 260–61.

13. *Sun* (Sydney), July 1913, ibid., 263.

14. Bernard Shaw, *London Music in 1888–89,* as heard by Corno di Bassetto (later known as Bernard Shaw) with some further autobiographical particulars (New York: Constable and Co., 1937), 227.

15. Glacken, *Nordica,* 49.

16. Ibid., 209.

17. Irving Kolodin, *The Metropolitan Opera 1883–1935: A Candid History* (New York, Oxford University Press, 1936), 45.

18. *New York Herald,* November 1895, quoted in Glacken, *Nordica,* 181–82.

19. William J. Henderson, *New York Times,* November 1895, quoted in Glacken, *Nordica,* 182.

20. *New York Herald,* April, 1893, quoted in Glacken, *Nordica,* 164–65.

21. Except where otherwise indicated, biographical information is based on Glacken's thorough and painstaking work.

22. Luther Mason, at this time quite elderly, was an important pioneer in the area of music education in the public schools. Born 1818 in Maine, he was a pupil of Lowell Mason at the Boston Academy of Music. He may have been a distant relative of the Boston Mason family, which included a number of musicians: Lowell's son Daniel Gregory, a music publisher; William, a fine pianist who studied with Liszt; and in the next generation composer Daniel Gregory Mason. Luther Mason worked in Louisville (1853), Cincinnati (1856), and arrived in Boston in 1864 where he put in place a plan for teaching singing in primary schools using general classroom teachers. He also produced a series of school music textbooks, charts, and guides for a National Music Course; the 1st, 2nd, and 3rd *Music Readers*; and *Mason's Hymn and Tune Book. The Mason School Music Course* was published in 1898, two years after his death in Buchfield, Maine, in 1896.

23. Glacken, *Nordica,* 22–23.

24. Ibid., 242.

25. Patrick Sarsfield Gilmore (1829–1892) was an Irish-American bandmaster with big ideas. Among other feats, he organized around 1859 Gilmore's Grand Boston Band; he and his musicians joined the Union army in 1861; and he organized the National Peace Jubilee in Boston in 1869.

26. Lillian Norton to Edwin Norton, letter of 3 May 1879, quoted in Glacken, *Nordica,* 56.

27. Amanda Norton to Norton family, late January 1880, quoted in Glacken, *Nordica,* 64.

28. Amanda Norton to Norton family, October[?] 1880, quoted in Glacken, *Nordica,* 72.

29. Review by M. H. Moreno, quoted in Glacken, *Nordica,* 90.

30. Henry Haynie, "Lillian Norton: Sharp Comments upon her Paris Debut," *Boston Herald,* 14 August 1882; *Boston Music and Drama*; Amanda Norton, "Letter from Paris," *Boston Home Journal,* 21 October 1882, quoted in Glacken,

Nordica, 93–96.

31. See Glacken, *Nordica,* 95, 101–11, 121–28, for description of Gower's activities and their marriage including Gower's last balloon ride.

32. Ibid., 137.

33. *The Musical Times* (London), 1 April 1887, quoted in Glacken, *Nordica,* 135.

34. See Glacken, *Nordica,* 138.

35. Herman Klein, *Thirty Years of Musical Life in London* (London and New York: The Century Co., 1903).

36. *The Musical Times* (London), quoted in Glacken, *Nordica,* 140.

37. See Glacken, *Nordica,* 140.

38. Shaw, *London Music in 1888–89,* 227.

39. *New York Musical Trade Review,* quoted in Glacken, *Nordica,* 156.

40. *New York Herald,* April 1894, quoted in Glacken, *Nordica,* 164–65.

41. Siegfried Wagner, letter to Otto Floersheim, quoted in Glacken, *Nordica,* 169.

42. Floersheim, quoted in Glacken, *Nordica,* 171 (see above, page 189, for text of Floersheim's appraisal).

43. Nordica, letter to Aunt Lina, quoted in Glacken, *Nordica,* 170.

44. Bernard Vogel, "Madame Lillian Nordica. Her German tour. The Story of her Marvelous Successes as Told by the German Critics," quoted in Glacken, *Nordica,* 175.

45. *New York Herald,* November 1895, quoted in Glacken, *Nordica,* 181–82.

46. *New York Herald,* quoted in Glacken, *Nordica,* 191.

47. See Glacken, *Nordica,* 191. See above, Chapter 14, especially pages 217–18 for Melba's view of this episode. See also William Moran, "Aïda? Brünnhilde? How Big Was the Melba Voice?" in *Nellie Melba: A Contemporary Review* (Westport, Conn.: Greenwood Press, 1985), 74–75.

48. Glacken, *Nordica,* 225–26.

49. Thomas Nunan, *San Francisco Examiner,* quoted in Glacken, *Nordica,* 230.

50. Quoted in Glacken, *Nordica,* 235.

51. *Le Gaulois* (Paris), October 1910, quoted in Glacken, *Nordica,* 244.

52. Ibid., 249–50.

53. *Sun* (Sydney), July 1913, quoted in Glacken, *Nordica,* 263.

54. Glacken, *Nordica,* 265.

55. Ibid., 267.

56. Lillian Nordica, interview, *New York Sun,* 16? December 1910, quoted in Glacken, *Nordica,* 246–47. The premiere of *La fanciulla del West* was sung in Italian by Italian tenor Enrico Caruso, Italian baritone Pasquale Amato, and Czech soprano Emmy Destinn, under the direction of Italian conductor Arturo Toscanini.

57. Glacken, *Nordica,* 301–05.

58. *Lillian Nordica's Hints to Singers, Transcribed and with an Introduction by William Armstrong* (New York: E. P. Dutton Company, 1923); printed in

Glacken, *Nordica,* 309–53.

    59. Glacken, *Nordica,* 353.

    60. The Nordica Home Museum, 120 Nordica Lane, Farmington, Maine 04938, is open from 1 June to Labor Day.

    61. Glacken, *Nordica,* 274.

    62. Ibid., 160.

    63. Ibid., 259.

Chapter 14

    1. William James Henderson, obituary of Nellie Melba, *New York Sun,* 28 February 1931.

    2. Max Harris, *The Unknown Great Australian and Other Psychobiographical Portraits* (Melbourne, 1983), 27–28.

    3. Shaw, quoted in Thérèse Radic, *Melba: The Voice of Australia* (Melbourne: The Macmillan Company of Australia Pty Ltd, 1986), 186, margin.

    4. Henderson, obituary.

    5. Agnes G. Murphy, *Melba: A Biography,* (London: Chatto & Windus, 1909), quoted in William Moran, compiler, *Nellie Melba: A Contemporary Review* (Westport, CT: Greenwood Press, 1985), 12.

    6. *New York Herald Tribune Magazine,* 28 May 1961.

    7. Henderson, obituary.

    8. Quoted in Nellie Melba (with the anonymous assistance of Beverley Nichols), *Melodies and Memories* (1926; reprint, Freeport, NY: Books for Libraries Press, 1970), 63.

    9. William Moran, "Melba's Farewell at Covent Garden," in Moran, *Nellie Melba,* 278.

    10. See William Moran, "Discography: The Melba Recordings," in Moran, *Nellie Melba,* 463, for complete information about the numbers that were recorded during the farewell concert.

    11. Neville Cardus, *Music for Pleasure* (Sydney: Angus and Robertson, 1942), 69–71.

    12. Nellie Melba, "Where Is Happiness? Is It in Fame?" reprint of article in *The Herald* (Melbourne), 10 September 1927, in Moran, *Nellie Melba,* 238.

    13. Moran, "Aïda? Brünnhilde? How Big Was the Melba Voice?" in Moran, *Nellie Melba,* 74. See Ira Glacken's account of the *Siegfried* episode in *Yankee Diva: Lillian Nordica and the Golden Days of Opera,* 185–95.

    14. *London Telegraph,* quoted in Radic, 179.

    15. "Words from Bernard Shaw," in Moran, *Nellie Melba,* 68.

    16. Moran tells the story in his essay, "*La Calunnia,*" in Moran, *Nellie Melba,* 93.

    17. Ibid.

18. Except where otherwise noted, the source for biographical information is John Hetherington, *Melba: A Biography* (London: Faber & Faber, 1968).

19. Melba, *Melodies and Memories*, 36. Melba states that Marchesi "showed me how inferior all my other teachers had been."

20. Mrs. Armstrong was no name for an opera singer, declared Marchesi, and settled on "Melba" derived from Melbourne.

21. Melba, *Melodies and Memories*, 57–60.

22. See Radic, *Melba*, 56, for various critiques of the performance.

23. Melba, *Melodies and Memories*, 117.

24. Letter to Tommy Cochran, 10 October 1921, quoted in Radic, *Melba*, 181.

25. Nellie Melba, "The Care of the Voice," in Moran, *Nellie Melba*, 371, originally published in *The Music of the Modern World*, Anton Seidl, ed. All of the following recommendations by Melba are drawn from this interview.

26. Ibid., 370.

27. See Radic, *Melba*, 65–71, for an account of the affair, also Maie Casey, "Post-Mortem," in Moran, *Nellie Melba*, 360–61. Radic indicates that Melba's great fear was to lose guardianship of her son; in the event the divorce suit, which had begun to get nasty with accusations and counter-accusations by husband and wife, was dropped mysteriously—the result of political influence? Young George spent a number of years in America with a cousin, in Texas, Oregon, California, but returned to his mother when he was twenty-one.

28. See William Moran, *"La Calunnia,"* in Moran, *Nellie Melba*, 81–90, for discussion of this issue.

29. Melba, *Melodies and Memories*, 322.

30. See William Moran, "Discography," in Moran, *Nellie Melba*, 447–72, for an excellent and complete discography.

31. W. Arundel Orchard, "At the N. S. W. Conservatorium of Music," in Moran, *Nellie Melba*, 295. Originally published in Orchard, *The Distant View*, 1943.

32. Herman Klein, "Nellie Melba," in *Great Women Singers of My Time* (1931; reprint, Freeport, NY: Books for Libraries Press, Inc., 1968), 141.

Chapter 15

Except where otherwise indicated, translations are those of Linda Cuneo-Laurent.

1. j'étais vraiment attirée par les musiciens modernes et c'est toujours pour moi la plus grande joie de connaître les oeuvres des contemporains: je les sens tellement plus proches de mon goût, de ma compréhension et de mes possibilités . . . J'ai toujours pensé qu'on n'avait pas le droit d'ignorer les oeuvres de son temps, aussi bien littéraires que musicales. Stéphane Audel, *Entretiens avec Jane Bathori* (Interviews with Jane Bathori), Radio-Lausanne, 1953.

2. une voix qui lui ouvrait n'importe quel répertoire, une voix d'un volume moyen, mais admirablement timbrée, souple et juste à miracle. Marc Pincherle,

"La musique: Jane Bathori," *Les nouvelles litteraires,* 8 July 1954, unpaginated, quoted in Linda Cuneo-Laurent, "The Performer as Catalyst: The Role of the Singer Jane Bathori (1877–1970) in the Careers of Debussy, Ravel, "Les Six," and Their Contemporaries in Paris 1904–1926" (Ph.D. diss., New York University, 1982), 13.

3. Mme Jane Bathori, "de la Monnaie," y révéla une nature d'artiste exceptionnellement douée. Elle chante la musique de Debussy avec beaucoup de charme et un sentiment très juste, et elle la chante en s'accompagnant soi-même avec une aisance merveilleuse, ce qui n'est assurément pas banal en l'espèce. Jean Marnold, *Le Mercure de France,* July 1904, VII, 241–242, quoted in Cuneo-Laurent, *Performer as Catalyst,* 31–32.

4. de son intelligence, de son sens musical, de sa science accomplie de cantatrice ou de son charmant talent de pianiste. Quand Mme. Bathori chante en s'accompagnant ainsi et non autrement que doit être interprété Chabrier, c'est-à-dire avec entrain et simplicité. René Martineau, *Emmanuel Chabrier,* Paris: Dorbon Aîné, 1910, n.p., quoted in Cuneo-Laurent, *Performer as Catalyst,* 49–50.

5. Jane Bathori . . . possède une très sure technique vocale, ce qui n'est pas frequent. Ensuite—ce qui n'est pas moins rare—elle est une musicienne accomplie, aussi brillante que parfaite cantatrice, une artiste pleine d'intelligence et de sensibilité. Léon Valas, "Jane Bathori," *Tout Lyon,* 11 January 1914, quoted in Cuneo-Laurent, *Performer as Catalyst,* 64–65. Vallas trained in medicine but then turned to musicology and history. In 1908 he began teaching at the University of Lyons, taught at the Sorbonne in the 1920s, and from 1937 to 1943 served as president of the Société Française de Musicologie. He founded the music journal, *Revue musicale de Lyons,* known from 1912–1914 as *Revue de musique française,* and from 1920 to 1925 as *La nouvelle revue musicale.*

6. Sembrich was trained as both violinist and pianist. Her career was however based solidly on her extraordinary gifts as a singer. In one of her late concerts she performed as violinist and pianist and then accompanied herself at the piano as she sang an aria. See H. Goddard Owen, *A Recollection of Marcella Sembrich* (Bolton, Lake George: The Marcella Sembrich Memorial Association, 1950), 43–45, for accounts by the music reviewers W. J. Henderson, Henry Krehbiel, and James Huneker of Sembrich's multi-media performances.

7. Quelle admirable cantatrice tu étais qui pouvais, tout en chantant avec un style si pur, une diction si claire, un charme si discret et tellement intérieur, te jouer des sonorities subtiles, si aristocratiques et avec tant d'aisance, du piano. Darius Milhaud, Preface to *Sur l'Interprétation des mélodies de Claude Debussy,* no page number.

8. Biographical information comes except where otherwise noted from the dissertation by Linda Cuneo-Laurent, *Performer as Catalyst.* Cuneo-Laurent and Carol Kimball provide the only information available in English about the life and work of Bathori; both also include many reviews and assessments by her contemporaries of Bathori's work. Cuneo-Laurent's dissertation is the only full

study of Bathori to date.

   9. Linda Laurent, "Introduction to Jane Bathori," in *On the Interpretation of the Mélodies of Claude Debussy* (Stuyvesant, NY: Pendragon Press, 1998), 9.

   10. Si on ne m'envoya pas de petits bancs, c'est parce qu'il n'y en avait pas. J'ai su que le tapage était parti d'un groupe de musicians de la Schola, élèves de Vincent d'Indy, manquant totalement de compréhension. Vous savez, les gens qui ont des visières. Audel, *Entretiens,* III, 20, quoted in Cuneo-Laurent, *Performer as Catalyst,* 19.

   11. ceux qui ne l'ont entendue qu'au concert ou dans les milieux intimes . . . ne peuvent se figurer combien elle est, au théâtre, intéressante et attachante, combien son emotion est communicative et combien la simplicité de son jeu, jointe au style parfait et à la variété de son chant, agit profondément sur le spectateur. Reynaldo Hahn, review, *Le Journal,* 19 September 1912, quoted in Cuneo-Laurent, *Performer as Catalyst,* 11.

   12. des applaudissements, des sifflets, des interjections de toutes sortes. C'était la douce folie. Bathori, Minet broadcast, RTF, 1957, quoted in Cuneo-Laurent, *Performer as Catalyst,* 112.

   13. Jane Bathori, la grande cantatrice qui créa ou interpréta pour ainsi dire toute la musique vocale contemporaine et qui mettait sans compter son immense talent au service des jeunes, nous ouvrit toutes grandes les portes du théâtre du Vieux-Colombier qu'elle avait loué pour y faire de la musique. Toutes nos premières oeuvres y virent le jour. Frédéric Robert, *Louis Durey: L'aîné des Six* (Paris: Les Editeurs Français Réunis, 1968), quoted in Cuneo-Laurent, *Performer as Catalyst,* 82–83. Cuneo-Laurent points out that Bathori did not rent the theatre; Jacques Copeau lent it to her.

   14. Salle archi-pleine, toujours. On dit: "C'est un des très rares endroits de Paris où l'on entende de bonne musique en ce moment." C'est présenté très simplement, intimement. Genre musique de chambre. Je crois qu'ils joueront *L'Heure espagnole* sans mise au point, gentiment, sans en faire un plat, pour la présenter au public d'une façon plus vivante que le concert ordinaire, mais sans aucune prétention, sans trouvaille, presque sans mise en scène, avec une discretion, une simplicité de bonne conscience.

   . . . leur orchestre, peu nombreux mais choisi, est excellent.

   L'ensemble donne l'impression d'amateurs éclairs, qui se font plaisir et font plaisir à des amis. Voilà le ton. Jacques Copeau, Roger Martin du Gard, *Correspondance,* with annotated text by Claude Sicard, 2 vois. (Paris: Editions Gallimard, 1972), 268, quoted in Cuneo-Laurent, *Performer as Catalyst,* 89–90.

   15. Tandis que piétinent et marquent le pas les théâtres qui ont tout ce qu'il faut pour faire du neuf et du beau, une scène grande comme un mouchoir de poche, qui n'a rien—ni subvention, ni clientèle, ni troupe,—crée ou refait vivre coup sur coup, dans l'espace d'un mois, quatre ouvrages . . .

   Ce miracle, c'est Mme Jane Bathori qui l'accomplit. Quelle artiste diligente et parfaite! On l'entend, l'après-midi, à la Société Nationale, chanter, comme en se jouant, les poèmes de nos jeunes compositeurs—fuissent-ils les plus imprécis et les moins saisissables—et, quelques heures après, costumée, elle entre en scène, toujours aussi sûie, d'elle même, aussi maîtresse de sa voix, préparant, pendant l'entr'acte, ses projets du lendemain. Cette activité, cette fièvre de travail pourraient donner lieu à des interpretations improvisées. Allez donc entendre l'Education manqué [*sic*], et dites-moi en quell théâtre du monde vous avez entendu une exécution aussi parfaite? A. Mangeot, "Théâtre du Vieux-Colombier," *Le Monde musical* (Paris), 1918, 11, quoted in Cuneo-Laurent, *Performer as Catalyst*, 106.

16. Copeau was not very happy with Bathori because of structural changes that had been made in the house. The rift was eventually healed, but it seems to have been serious at the time. For more information, see Cuneo-Laurent, *Performer as Catalyst*, 124.

17. On continue à travailler courageusement sur la petite scène de Jacques Copeau qui conserve, sous l'intelligente direction musicale de Jane Bathori, ce caractère sympathique de laboratoire d'expériences qui lui avait valu l'estime de tous les artistes. Pendant que nos grandes usines de musique s'endorment dans leur fabrication mécanique d'articles courants, ce petit atelier cherche et trouve d'intéressantes innovations. Si les musicians ne sont pas des ingrates—malheureusement, ils le sont, en général, plus que tous les autres bipèdes de la création—ils monteront une garde d'honneur autour de cette vaillante maison qui, en pleine decadence théâtrale et musicale, réalise un si bel effort d'art. Emile Vuillermoz, "La Musique," *Éclair*, 7 January 1919, quoted in Cuneo-Laurent, *Performer as Catalyst*, 125–26.

18. Satie l'accompagnait au piano. Ce fut inoubliable . . . la belle voix émouvante de la chanteuse, la beauté bouleversante de cette oeuvre unique . . . Nous étions tous en larmes. Valentine Hugo, "Le Socrate que j'ai connu," *La revue musicale* (Paris), no. 214 (June 1952): 143, quoted in Cuneo-Laurent, *Performer as Catalyst*, 133.

19. Cuneo-Laurent, *Performer as Catalyst*, 164.

20. Il faut tout entendre! Reported by the singer Irène Joachim. Ibid., 177.

21. I am deeply indebted to Dr. Carol Kimball for giving me copies of these interviews in French, which are in the archives of the Bibliothèque Nationale, Paris.

22. Claire Bergrunn, telephone interviews by Carol Kimball, 24 January and 5 March 2001. Bergrunn studied with Bathori in Argentina and in Paris. I am grateful to Dr. Kimball for sharing this information with me.

23. "It is even possible to believe that, without Mme. Bathori, certain works might never have been written." (Il est même permis de croire que, sans Mme. Bathori, certains ouvrages n'auraient jamais été écrits.) Léon Vallas, "Jane Bathori," *Tout Lyon*, 11 January 1914, quoted in Cuneo-Laurent, *Performer as Catalyst*, 64–65.

24. dévouée avec un complet désintéressement à la musique moderne . . . depuis

plus de dix ans il n'est pas un jeune compositeur [français] qui ne lui soit redevable de la 'creation' de qualqu'un de ses ouvrages. Vallas, "Jane Bathori," quoted in Cuneo-Laurent, *Performer as Catalyst,* 64–65. Cuneo-Laurent uses the word "disinterest" to translate "désintéressement"; I believe "selflessness" indicating Bathori's lack of self-interest is a better interpretation in this passage.

25. Je l'écoute chanter la plainte de Mélisande ou la juvenile et fraîche joie de la *Bonne Chanson* et je sens bien que dans sa voix, c'est notre coeur qui parle . . . . Elle incarne la mélodie française moderne. Georges Jean-Aubry, *L'Art moderne,* (11 May 1913; reprinted in his book *La musique française d'aujourd'hui);* quoted in Cuneo-Laurent, *Performer as Catalyst,* 63–64.

Chapter 16

1. *Crisis,* May (1916); quoted in Allan Keiler, *Marian Anderson: A Singer's Journey* (New York: Scribner, 2000), 36–37.

2. *Savannah Morning News,* 29 December 1917, quoted in Keiler, *Anderson,*38.

3. *Savannah Press,* 29 December 1917, quoted in Keiler, *Anderson,* 394 n. 27.

4. *New York Sun,* 26 April 1924, quoted in Keiler, *Anderson,* 60–61.

5. Unidentified London newspaper clipping in Anderson's papers, quoted in Keiler, *Anderson,* 79–80.

6. *Suomenmaa* (Helsinki), 27 November 1930, quoted in Keiler, *Anderson,* 105.

7. *New York Telegram,* 3 March 1930, quoted in Keiler, *Anderson,* 91.

8. *Vossische Zeitung* (Berlin), 11 October 1930, quoted in Keiler, *Anderson,* 98.

9. *Philadelphia Public Ledger,* 19 May 1922, quoted in Keiler, *Anderson,* 54.

10. *New York Age,* 3 June 1922, quoted in Keiler, *Anderson,* 54–55.

11. *Philadelphia Public Ledger,* 24? December 1923, quoted in Keiler, *Anderson,* 57.

12. *New York Sun,* 26 April 1924, quoted in Keiler, *Anderson,* 60–61; see also 396 n. 23.

13. F. D. Perkins for the *New York Herald Tribune,* 27 August 1925, quoted in Keiler, *Anderson,* 63.

14. *New York Times,* 26 August 1925, quoted in Keiler, *Anderson,* 397 n. 31.

15. *Suomenma* (Helsinki), 27 November 1930, quoted in Keiler, *Anderson,* 105.

16. *My Lord, What a Morning: An Autobiography by Marian Anderson* (New York: The Viking Press, 1956), 145.

17. Keiler (*Anderson,* 276, 315–16) suggests that Anderson, though constantly working at repertoire and interpretation was nonetheless a bit lazy when it came

to the daily toil of keeping the voice in first-rate physical condition and that without a demanding coach she was apt to slacken a bit in vocal exercise.

18. Keiler, *Anderson,* 15. Except where otherwise indicated biographical information is based on Keiler's thorough and painstaking work.

19. *Philadelphia Tribune,* 4 April 1914, quoted in Keiler, *Anderson,* 28.

20. Keiler, *Anderson,* 30.

21. Ibid., 29.

22. Ibid., 38.

23. Ibid., 55–56.

24. Ibid., 66.

25. Wigmore, originally Bechstein Hall, opened in 1901; Zur Mühlen was one of the participants in the two inaugural concerts (others were Busoni, Ysaÿe, Pachman).

26. Unidentified London newspaper in Anderson's papers, quoted in Keiler, *Anderson,* 80.

27. *Observer* (London), 17 June 1928, quoted in Keiler, *Anderson,* 399 n. 28.

28. Unidentified London newspaper clipping in Anderson's papers, quoted in Keiler, *Anderson,* 79–80.

29. *Times* (London), 17 August 1928, quoted in Keiler, *Anderson,* 399 n. 30. Keiler quotes a number of reviews in this note.

30. *The Daily Mail* (London), 17 August 1928, quoted in Keiler, *Anderson,* 399–400 n. 30.

31. *Daily Chronicle* (London), 17 August 1928, quoted in Keiler, *Anderson,* 399–400 n. 30.

32. *Chicago Evening American,* 19 November 1929, quoted in Keiler, *Anderson,* 90.

33. Keiler, *Anderson,* 90.

34. *Vossische Zeitung* (Berlin), 11 October 1930, quoted in Keiler, *Anderson,* 98.

35. *Berliner Tageblatt,* 4 November 1930, quoted in Keiler, *Anderson,* 99.

36. *Morgenpost* (Berlin), 12 October 1930, quoted in Keiler, *Anderson,* 402 n. 18.

37. *Deutsche Allgemeine Zeitung* (Berlin), 17 October 1930, quoted in Keiler, *Anderson,* 402 n. 18.

38. *My Lord,* 145.

39. Keiler, *Anderson,* 109.

40. *Deutsche Allgemeine Zeitung* (Berlin), 7 August 1931, quoted in Keiler, *Anderson,* 109.

41. Keiler, *Anderson,* 112–13.

42. *Le jour* (Paris), 4 May 1934, quoted in Keiler, *Anderson,* 133–34.

43. *The Morning Post* (London), 10 May 1934, quoted in Keiler, *Anderson,* 134.

44. *Sunday Referee* (London), 13 May 1934, quoted in Keiler, *Anderson,* 134.

45. *The Daily Mail* (London), 19 June 1934, quoted in Keiler, *Anderson,* 137.

46. Kosti Vehanen, *Marian Anderson: A Portrait* (New York and London: Whittlesey House, 1941), 65–66.

47. *My Lord,* 176.

48. See Keiler, *Anderson,* 152–54, for discussion of the relationship and Anderson's attitude.

49. Vehanen, *Marian Anderson,* 130; Keiler, *Anderson,* 156, gives Vehanen's version but includes Mme Cahier's in a note, 407 n. 61.

50. Billy King to Anderson, 23 August 1935, in Marian Anderson Papers, Rare Book and Manuscript Library, University of Pennsylvania, quoted in Keiler, *Anderson,* 157.

51. Harry T. Burleigh to Anderson, 16 October 1935, Marian Anderson Papers, quoted in Keiler, *Anderson,* 158.

52. *New York Times,* 31 December 1935, quoted in Keiler, *Anderson,* 161.

53. Keiler, *Anderson,* 161.

54. See Keiler, *Anderson,* 181–217, for a thorough, objective, and thoughtful review of the events leading up to and surrounding the Easter Sunday performance.

55. Emily Kimbrough, "My Life in a White World," *Ladies' Home Journal* 77 (1960): 176, quoted in Keiler, *Anderson,* 223.

56. Keiler, *Anderson,* 223.

57. *La Lanterne* (Brussels), 17 June 1949, quoted in Keiler, *Anderson,* 252.

58. *Le Soir* (Liège), 19 June 1949, quoted in Keiler, *Anderson,* 252.

59. *Neue Zeitung* (Munich), 7 June 1949, quoted in Keiler, *Anderson,* 254.

60. *New York Times,* 8 January 1955, quoted in Keiler, *Anderson,* 274–75. Anderson was contracted to sing three performances in January 1955 but because of her busy concert schedule sang only two (the first was in New York, the second in Philadelphia). She was engaged to sing again the following season, four performances in New York, one in Cleveland, and one in Boston.

61. *Jet,* 22 April, 1954, quoted in Keiler, *Anderson,* 267.

62. *New York Times,* 25 January 1954, quoted in Keiler, *Anderson,* 267.

63. *Ha Arez,* 22 April 1955, quoted in Keiler, *Anderson,* 278.

64. *Jerusalem Post,* 20 April 1955, quoted in Keiler, *Anderson,* 278.

65. *New York Times,* 30 March 1959, quoted in Keiler, *Anderson,* 294–95.

66. James DePreist has enjoyed a long and distinguished career as a conductor. He is now Director of Conducting and Orchestral Studies at the Juilliard School, Laureate Music Director of the Oregon Symphony, and Principal Artistic Advisor for the Phoenix Symphony.

66. Until 1947 black entertainers such as Eartha Kitt and Lena Horne did indeed sleep, eat, and gamble in the Las Vegas casinos in which they performed. From 1947, however, until the middle 1950s, black artists were forced to find quarters on the city's predominantly black West side. In 1955 the Moulin Rouge, an integrated casino, opened. That same year the Sands hotel and casino, responding to protests by such stars as Horne and Nat King Cole, became the first resort again to give shelter to its black entertainers. See Eugene Moehring, "Civil Rights in a Resort City" in *Resort City in the Sunbelt: Las Vegas, 1930–1970* (Reno and Las Vegas: University of Nevada Press, 1989), 182.

General Bibliography

Although encyclopedias are not usually included in bibliographies, the New Grove dictionaries are invaluable resources, especially for singers from 1500 to 1800, and are therefore included here:

The New Grove Dictionary of Music & Musicians. Edited by Stanley Sadie. London: Macmillan Publishers Limited, 1980.

Grove Music Online. Edited by L. Macy. http://www.grovemusic.com.

Adolphus, John. *Memoirs of John Bannister, Comedian.* 2 vols. London: Richard Bentley, 1839.

Anthony, James R. *French Baroque Music from Beaujoyeulx to Rameau.* Revised edition. New York: W. W. Norton & Company, 1978.

Berlioz, Hector. *Memoirs of Hector Berlioz from 1803 to 1865 Comprising His Travels in Germany, Italy, Russia, and England.* Translated by Rachel Holmes and Eleanor Holmes; annotated, translated, revised by Ernest Newman. 1932. Reprint, New York: Dover Publications, Inc., 1966.

Bianconi, Lorenzo. *Music in the Seventeenth Century.* Translated by David Bryant. Cambridge: Cambridge University Press, 1987. (Originally published as *Il seicento,* Turin: Edizioni di Torino, 1982.)
Excellent general history of seventeenth-century music, especially Italian, but including France and England, and providing several important primary documents, e.g., descriptions of a musical banquet in Florence in 1608, a court ballet in Turin in 1620, etc.

Biba, Otto, and David Wyn Jones. *Studies in Music History Presented to H. C. Robbins Landon on His Seventieth Birthday.* London: Thames and Hudson Ltd., 1996.

Bing, Sir Rudolf. *5000 Nights at the Opera.* Mattituck, N.Y.: Ameron House, 1972.

Bingley, William. *Musical Biography: Memoirs of the Lives and Writings of the Most Eminent Musical Composers and Writers Who Have Flourished in the Different Countries of Europe during the Last Three Centuries.* 1834. Reprint, New York: Da Capo Press, 1971.

Bowers, Jane, and Judith Tick, eds. *Women Making Music: The Western Art Tradition, 1150–1950.* Urbana and Chicago: University of Illinois Press, 1987.

Brown, Howard Mayer, and Stanley Sadie, eds. *Performance Practice: Music after 1600.* New York: W. W. Norton & Company, 1989.

_____. *Performance Practice: Music before 1600.* New York: W. W. Norton & Company, 1989.

Burney, Charles. *A General History of Music: From the Earliest Ages to the Present Period (1789).* 1776–1789. Reprint with critical and historical notes by Frank Mercer: New York: Dover Publications, Inc., 1957.

Burney's *History* and the *History* of Hawkins also published in 1776 are the earliest histories of music in English. Both works include many references to contemporary composers and performers. Burney's writings are characterized by a sharp ear and candid expression of his views on music and musicianship.

Carter, Tim. *Music in Late Renaissance & Early Baroque Italy.* London: Batsford, 1992.

Chopin, Fryderyk. *Selected Correspondence of Fryderyk Chopin.* Translated and edited by Arthur Hedley. 1963. Reprint, New York: Da Capo Press, 1979.

Chorley, Henry Fothergill. *Modern German Music.* 1854. Reprint, New York: Da Capo Press, 1973.

_____. *Thirty Years' Musical Recollections.* New York: Alfred A. Knopf, 1926.

Clayton, Ellen Creathorne. *Queens of Song: Being Memoirs of Some of the Most Celebrated Female Vocalists who have performed on the lyric stage from the earliest days of opera to the present time.* Freeport, N.Y.: Books for Libraries Press, 1972.

Cook, Susan C., and Judy S. Tsou. *Cecilia Reclaimed: Feminist Perspectives on Gender and Music.* Urbana and Chicago: University of Illinois Press, 1994.

Eaton, Quaintance. *Opera Caravan: Adventures of the Metropolitan on Tour (1883–1956).* New York: Farrar, Straus & Cudahy, 1957.

Edwards, H. Sutherland. *The Prima Donna, Seventeenth to Nineteenth Century.* 2 vols. London: Remington and co., 1888.

Einstein, Alfred. "Abbot Angelo Grillo's Letters as Source Material for Music History." In *Essays on Music.* New York: W. W. Norton & Company, Inc., 1962.

_____. *The Italian Madrigal.* 3 vols. Translated by Alexander H. Krappe, Roger H. Sessions, and Oliver Strunk. Princeton: Princeton University Press, 1949.

Evelyn, John. *The Diary of John Evelyn.* Edited from the original mss. by William Bray. 2 vols. New York and London: M. Walter Dunne, Publisher, 1901.

Evelyn's account of his travels through Europe is very informative about the political, social, and cultural scene.

Fabbri, Paolo. *Monteverdi.* Translated by Tim Carter. Cambridge: Cambridge

University Press, 1994. (Orig. published in Italian as *Monteverdi*, Turin: E.D.T. Edizioni di Torino, 1985.)

Fenlon, Iain. *Music and Patronage in Sixteenth-Century Mantua*. 2 vols. Cambridge: Cambridge University Press, 1980.

First-rate study of the Mantuan court and its music in the sixteenth century. It deals extensively with spectacle and large undertakings (e.g., Chapter 3, "Guglielmo Gonzaga and the Santa Barbara Project"). Especially useful for information about women singers in Chapter 4, "Vincenzo Gonzaga and the New Arts of Spectacle" (pp.119–62). Volume 2 provides musical examples. Excellent, extensive bibliography.

Fenner, Theodore. *Opera in London: Views of the Press, 1785–1830*. Carbondale and Edwardsville: Southern Illinois University Press, 1994.

Reviews by London papers of performances, with commentary by Fenner.

Ferris, George. *Great Singers—Faustina Bordoni to Henriette Sontag*. New York: D. Appleton and Co., 1895.

Fétis, François-Joseph. *Biographie universelle des musicians et bibliographie générale de la musique*. 8 vols. Paris: Firmin Didot Frères, 1864.

Finck, Henry T. *Success in Music and How It Is Won*. New York: Charles Scribner's Sons, 1909.

Fiske, Roger. *English Theatre Music in the Eighteenth Century*. Oxford, New York: Oxford University Press, 1986.

Gerber, Ernst Ludwig. *Historisch-biographisches Lexicon der Tonkünstler*. Leipzig: J. G. I. Breitkopf, 1790–1792.

Very useful lexicon in German of composers and performers.

Girdham, Jane. *English Opera in Late-Eighteenth-Century London: Stephen Storace at Drury Lane*. Oxford: Clarendon Press, 1997.

Giustiniani, Vincenzo. *Discorso sopra la musica*, 1628. Translated by Carol MacClintock. Musicological Studies and Documents. No city: American Institute of Musicology, 1962.

Gutman, Robert. *Richard Wagner: The Man, His Mind, and His Music*. New York: Harcourt Brace Jovanovich, Inc., 1968.

Hammond, Frederick. "Musicians at the Medici Court in the Mid-Seventeenth Century," *Analecta Musicologica* No. 14 (1974): 151–69.

Useful for lists of musicians at the courts of the Grand Dukes of Tuscany from 1590 to 1669.

Hawkins, Sir John. *A General History of the Science and Practice of Music*. [First published 1776.] Reprint of 1853 edition with new introduction by Charles Cudworth: New York: Dover Publications, Inc., 1963.

Hawkins's *History* and that of Charles Burney also published in 1776 are the earliest histories of music in English. Both works include many references to contemporary composers and performers.

Henderson, William James. *The Art of Singing*. New York: The Dial Press, 1938.

Highfill, Philip H. Jr., Kalman a. Burnim, and Edward a. Langhans. *A Biographical*

Dictionary of Actors, Actresses, Musicians, Dancers, Managers, and Other Stage Personnel in London 1660–1800. Carbondale, Ill.: Southern Illinois University Press, 1973.

Hogarth, George. *Memoirs of the Musical Drama*. London: Richard Bentley, 1838.

Hurok, Sol, with Ruthe Goode. *Impresario: A Memoir.* New York: Random House, 1946.

Hutson, Lorna, ed. *Feminism and Renaissance Studies*. Oxford: Oxford University Press, 1999.

Kelly, Michael. *Reminiscences of Michael Kelly, of the King's Theatre, and Theatre Royal, Drury Lane.* 1826.Edited with an introduction by Roger Fiske. London: Oxford University Press, 1975.

Kelly's colorful *Reminiscences* present much useful information; his occasional lapses are corrected in the careful explanatory notes provided by the editor.

Kessler, Harry, Graf. *In the Twenties: The Diaries of Harry Kessler.* Translated by Charles Kessler. New York: Holt, Rinehart and Winston, 1971.

Kirkendale, Warren. *The Court Musicians in Florence during the Principate of the Medici, with a Reconstruction of the Artistic Establishment.* Florence: Olschki, 1993.

Klein, Herman. *Great Women Singers of My Time.* London: G. Routledge & Co., 1931.

————. *Thirty Years of Musical Life in London.* London and New York: The Century Co., 1903.

Kolodin, Irving. *The Metropolitan Opera, 1883–1939.* New York: Oxford University Press, 1940.

Krehbiel, Henry Edward. *Chapters of Opera.* New York: Henry Holt & Co., 1908.

Lahee, Henry C. *Famous Singers of Today and Yesterday.* Boston: L. C. Page Co., 1898.

Larue, C. Steven. *Handel and His Singers: The Creation of the Royal Academy Operas, 1720–1728.* Oxford: Clarendon Press, 1995.

First-rate study of Handel's operas for the singers he worked with during the years of the Royal Academy, 1720–1728.

Lumley, Benjamin. *Reminiscences of the Opera.* London: Hurst and Blackett, Publishers, 1864.

Director for twenty years of Her Majesty's Theatre, Lumley brings great expertise and practical knowledge to his accounts of the mid-nineteenth-century London operatic world.

MacClintock, Carol. *Readings in the History of Music in Performance.* Selected, translated, edited by Carol MacClintock. Bloomington and London: Indiana University Press, 1979.

Includes Baldassare Castiglione, excerpt from *The Book of the Courtier* (22–27), and Vincenzo Giustiniani, excerpt from *Discorso sopra la musica,* (27–29). Very short excerpts, but included in a readily accessible reference work.

Mancini, Giambattista. *Practical Reflections on Figured Singing,* (*Pensieri e*

riflessioni pratiche sopra il canto figurato), editions of 1774 and 1777 compared, translated, and edited by Edward Foreman. Masterworks on Singing, Vol. VII. Champaign, Ill.: Pro Musica Press, 1967.
Very helpful, technical descriptions of vocal practice during early and middle of eighteenth century.

Mapleson, J. H. *The Mapleson Memoirs.* 2 vols. Chicago, San Francisco, and New York: Belford, Clarke & Co., 1888.

Marshall, Kimberly, ed. *Rediscovering the Muses: Women's Musical Traditions.* Boston: Northeastern University Press, 1993.

McVeigh, Simon. *Concert Life in London from Mozart to Haydn.* Cambridge: Cambridge University Press, 1993.

Milhous, Judith, Gabriella Dideriksen, and Robert D. Hume. *The Pantheon Opera and Its Aftermath: 1789–1795.* Vol. 2 of *Italian Opera in Late Eighteenth-Century London.* Oxford: Clarendon Press, 2001.

Monteverdi, Claudio. *The Letters of Claudio Monteverdi.* Revised edition, translated and introduced by Denis Stevens. Oxford: Clarendon Press, 1995.

Moscheles, Ignatz. *Recent Music and Musicians: As Described in the Diaries and Correspondence of Ignatz Moscheles.* Edited by his wife, adapted from the original German by a. d. Coleridge. 1873. Reprint. New York: Da Capo Press, 1970.

Mount Edgcumbe, Richard. *Musical Reminiscences of the Earl of Mount Edgcumbe: Containing an Account of the Italian Opera in England from 1773 to 1834.* 4th ed., 1834. Reprint, New York: Da Capo Press, 1973.
Thorough descriptions of concert and operatic performances by a well educated and sensitive connoisseur of theatrical and concert music, who writes with the authority of knowledge of the London scene and the personal experience of having attended the musical events he describes.

Mozart, Wolfgang Amadeus. *Mozart: Briefe und Aufzeichnungen, Gesamtausgabe.* Collected and annotated by Wilhelm a. Bauer and Otto Erich Deutsch. 6 vols. Kassel: Bärenreiter, 1962–1975.

_____. *The Letters of Mozart and His Family.* 3rd ed. Chronologically arranged, edited, and translated by Emily Anderson. 3rd ed. New York and London: W. W. Norton & Company, 1966.
Miss Anderson's overall excellent translations of Mozart's letters make them easily accessible to non-German readers. Anderson was the first to produce an unexpurgated edition of the letters.

_____. *Mozart's Letters, Mozart's Life: Selected Letters.* Translated by Robert Spaethling. New York: W. W. Norton, 2000.
Spaethling's lively translations are vivid and very true to Mozart's language.

Neuls-Bates, Carol, ed. *Women in Music: An Anthology of Source Readings from the Middle Ages to the Present.* Rev. ed. Boston: Northeastern University Press, 1996.

Newcomb, Anthony. "Courtesans, Muses, or Musicians." In *Women Making Music:*

The Western Art Tradition, 1150–1950. Edited by Jane Bowers and Judith Tick. Urbana and Chicago: University of Illinois Press, 1986.
Thoughtful essay on the female musicians of the late sixteenth century. Excellent in every respect, this essay is particularly helpful with details about the connections—familial, political, artistic—among the courts of Ferrara, Florence, Mantua, Rome.
_____. *The Madrigal at Ferrara, 1579–1597.* 2 vols. Princeton: Princeton University Press, 1980.
Excellent, thorough study of the Ferrara court, its music, its musical personnel, and the historical context. *The Madrigal at Ferrara* provides much more coverage both geographically and musically than the title implies; see especially Chapter V: "Imitations of the Ferrarese *'Concerto delle Donn*e' 1584–1589."
Petty, Frederick Curtis. *Italian Opera in London: 1760–1800.* Ann Arbor: UMI Research Press, 1972.
Very informative about the opera scene of this period. Provides useful data about performances, personnel, etc. Complements more recent studies, such as those by Milhous, Diderikson, Hume and Price, Milhous, Hume in the 2-volume *Italian Opera in Late Eighteenth-Century London,* and Fenner's *Opera in London.*
Thorough, well-documented comprehensive work. Invaluable source for general and more specialized information about performers and theatres during this period.
Pirrotta, Nino. "*Commedia dell'Arte* and Opera." *Musical Quarterly* 41 (1955): 305–24.
Pleasants, Henry. *The Great Singers from the Dawn to Opera to Our Own Time.* New York: Simon and Schuster: 1966.
Price, Curtis, Judith Milhous, and Robert D. Hume. *The King's Theatre, Haymarket: 1778–1791.* Vol. 1 of *Italian Opera in Late Eighteenth-Century London.* Oxford: Clarendon Press, 1995.
Thorough, well-documented comprehensive work. Invaluable source for general and more specialized information about performers and theatres during this period.
Quantz, Johann Joachim. "The Life of Herr Johann Joachim Quantz, as Sketched by Himself." In *Forgotten Musicians,* ed. Paul Nettl. New York: Greenwood Press, 1969.
Reilly, Edward R. "Quantz on National Styles in Music," *Musical Quarterly* 49 (1963): 163–87.
Rosand, Ellen. "Barbara Strozzi: *virtuosissima cantatrice*: The Composer's Voice." *Journal of the American Musicological Society* 31 (1978): 241–81.
This essay deals specifically with the career of Strozzi, but includes much useful data about the musical world of Venice in the seventeenth century.
_____. *Opera in Seventeenth Venice: The Creation of a Genre.* Berkeley: University of California Press, 1991. The most important source of information about Venetian opera in the seventeenth century; includes an excellent

bibliography and copious musical examples.

Rosenthal, Harold. *Two Centuries of Opera at Covent Garden.* London: g. Putnam, 1958.

Rosselli, John. "From Princely Service to the Open Market: Singers of Italian Opera and their Patrons, 1600–1850." *Cambridge Opera Journal* 1 (1989): 1–32.

Ryan, Thomas. *Recollections of an Old Musician.* New York: E. P. Dutton, 1899.

Sadie, Julie Anne. *Companion to Baroque Music.* Compiled and edited by Sadie. London: J. M. Dent & Sons Ltd., 1990.

A very useful general compendium of information about performers and composers during the Baroque age. The first and most extensive section, "Places and People," is organized by country or region; a second section addresses "Forces and Forms; and the third is devoted to issues of performance practice.

Shaw, Bernard. *London Music in 1888–89, as Heard by Corno di Bassetto (Later Known as Bernard Shaw).* New York: Dodd, Mead & Co., 1937.

_____. *Music in London, 1890–94.* London: Constable and Co., 1932.

Solie, Ruth A., ed. *Musicology and Difference: Gender and Sexuality in Musical Scholarship.* Berkeley, Los Angeles and London: University of California Press, 1993.

Southern, Eileen. *Biographical Dictionary of Afro-American and African Musicians.* Westport, Conn.: Greenwood Press, 1982.

Steane, J. B. *The Grand Tradition: Seventy Years of Singing on Record.* London: Duckworth, 1974.

Strainchamps, Edmond. "New Light on the *Accademia degli Elevati* of Florence." *Musical Quarterly* 62 (1976): 507–35.

Strunk, Oliver, ed. *Source Readings in Music History.* New York: W. W. Norton & Company, Inc., 1950.

Thompson, Oscar. *The American Singer.* New York: The Dial Press, Inc., 1937.

Solid, well-documented, information about American singers and their world.

Tomlinson, Gary. "Twice Bitten, Thrice Shy: Monteverdi's 'finta' *Finta pazza.*" *Journal of the American Musicological Society* 36 (1983): 303–11.

Tosi, Pietro Francesco. *Observations on the Florid Song (Opinioni de' cantori antichi e moderni o sieno osservazioni sopra il canto figurato).* Translated by Johann Ernst Galliard. 2d ed. London: J. Wilcox, 1743.

Perhaps the most important single source of information about early eighteenth-century vocal practice. Tosi (1646–1732) was known to be conservative and thus speaks with disdain of "modern" degeneration of the art, but also speaks with the expertise of a trained singer and renowned performer and teacher.

Treitler, Leo, ed. *Source Readings in Music History.* Rev. ed. New York, London: W. W. Norton & Company, 1998.

Vogel, Emil. "Marco da Gagliano: Zur Geschichte des florentiner Musiklebens von 1570–1650." *Vierteljahrsschrift.*

Wagnalls, Mabel. *Stars of the Opera.* New York and London: Funk & Wagnalls, 1907.

Wagner, Richard. *Mein Leben.* 2d ed. Leipzig: Breitkopf & Härtel, 1914.

_____. "Über Schauspieler und Sänger." *Gesammelte Schriften,* ix. Leipzig, 1873; English translation, v, 1896.

Weiss, Piero. *Opera: A History in Documents.* New York and Oxford: Oxford University Press, 2002.

Woodfield, Ian. *Opera and Drama in Eighteenth-Century London: The King's Theatre, Garrick and the Business of Performance.* Cambridge: Cambridge University Press, 2001.

Zinzendorf, Count Johann Karl. *Diary. Tagebuch des Grafen Johann Karl Chr. H. Zinzendorf.* Manuscript in French, in Kabinettsarchiv, Haus-, Hof-, und Staatsarchiv, Vienna.

One of the best sources of information about musical and theatre life in Vienna during the late eighteenth century. An ardent devotee of opera and theatre, Zinzendorf confided to his *Diary* candidly and knowledgeably his views on performances and performers. Translations of his comments appear in standard biographies of Mozart, Haydn, books about Vienna, etc.

Index

About the Author

ISABELLE EMERSON is Professor of Music, Department of Music, University of Nevada, Las Vegas.